Mythos and Cosmos

Mythos and Cosmos

Mind and Meaning in the Oral Age

John Knight Lundwall PhD

C&L Press
Academic Publishing

DEDICATION

Unto Sean and Craig, Dan and Susan,
Fellow explorers who would not yield;
Who sailed past deltas towards Starry Nile,
Beyond shallows and deeps and storm-swept fields;
Finding foot and fortune at the Blessed Isles,
Where fount of Milky Ocean is revealed.

Happy the man whom the gods love, and whose secrets he knows---
Their rubrics---his life is designed for sacred dances and joy:
In the mountains the wild delight of Bacchus in his soul.
His ritual he undergoes: Cybele's orgies, great Mother's.
He shakes the thyrsus on high.
With ivy he crowns his brow for great Dionysus.
---Euripides, *The Bacchae*

CONTENTS

ACKNOWLEDGMENTS

Writing this book has been a labor of love and patience. I am grateful to all the individuals who helped me during the process. My friends in academia were always supportive, and there were many librarians who helped me sort through books and papers with efficiency. There were several people who read my early manuscripts and offered much needed notes and advice. Particularly, Susan Paidhrin showed great interest in my work, and her thorough comments were very helpful. The playwright Matthew Bennet also took particular interest in the work, and gave me pages of notes from an "outsider's" perspective.

I would like to offer a special thanks to Lynde Mott, who did all the illustrations for this book. Her time and friendship have been priceless during this process. Finally, I would like to offer great appreciation to my editor, Genelle Wells, who passed away while working on this project. Not only did she tighten up my writing, but she was a wellspring of encouragement. She is dearly missed.

None of this would have been possible without the full support of my wife, Stephanie, or my children, Madison, Jacob, and Max. They sacrificed much while I spent many days and nights working on this book. I am truly humbled by their love and support.

LIST OF ABBREVIATIONS

BD   Faulkner, Raymond, trans. *The Egyptian Book of the Dead, The Book of Going Forth by Day*. San Francisco: Chronicle, 1994.

CH   Eliade, Mircea. *Cosmos and History: The Myth of the Eternal Return*. New York: Harper Torchbooks, 1959.

EG   Foster, Benjamin R. trans. "The Epic of Gilgamesh." *The Epic of Gilgamesh: A Norton Critical Edition*. New York: W. W. Norton & Co., 2001, pp. 1-95.

EGHA   Foster, Benjamin R. trans. "Gilgamesh and Huwawa A." *The Epic of Gilgamesh: A Norton Critical Edition*. New York: W. W. Norton & Co., 2001, pp. 104-15.

HM   De Santillana, Giorgio and Hertha Von Dechend. *Hamlet's Mill: An Essay Investigating the Origins of Human Knowledge and Its Transmission through Myth*. Boston: David R. Godine, 1977.

MJSP   Nibley, Hugh. *The Message of the Joseph Smith Papyri: An Egyptian Endowment*. Salt Lake City, UT: Deseret Book, 2005.

PT   Faulkner, Raymond, trans. *The Ancient Egyptian Pyramid Texts*. Oxford: Clarendon, 1910.

TC   Nibley, Hugh. *Temple and Cosmos*. Salt Lake City, UT: Deseret Book, 1992.

TK   De Lubicz, R. A. Schwaller. *The Temples of Karnak*. Rochester, VT: Inner Traditions, 1982.

LIST OF FIGURES

INTRODUCTION

From childhood I was always fascinated with ancient stories. I grew up on Bible stories, and dutiful parents instructed me on their historical truth and moral pronouncements. Over time, however, I wondered how literally one could take a talking snake? Surely the greatest miracle of the Flood was not that Noah survived it, but that he found some way to stuff two of every animal, bird, and creeping thing, with a hoard of food and reservoir of fresh water, not to mention the fields of hay required for the toiletries, in a three-story boat slightly larger than a football field? I have been told that it is easy for small children to believe in such things, but I remember as a small child raising my hand and asking my Sunday School teacher if Noah had used a shrink-ray? How else could he fit everything in?

As I grew a little older I was introduced to Greek and Norse mythology. I came to love these tales as much as the Bible stories but noticed that determining the logistics of the plot was no longer the point. What of the talking serpent? Did not Herakles encounter such a creature as he sought the golden apples at the great Tree of the Hesperides? Did not the serpent bruise Orion's heel, and in turn was crushed under foot as Orion strode to the stars? What of the Great Flood? Was not the great deep traversed by Bergelmer, the Norse giant who survived the deluge in his ark? Or by Utnapishtim, who gained immortality by surviving the flood and entering the domain of the gods? Is not a greater apocalypse foretold in the far-off days of Ragnarok? Do not all these stories transcend, in total, the literal human experience?

By the time I arrived at college, unbeknownst to me I was already on a life long journey centered around the world of ancient myth. I have no idea why this work called to me. I did not want it to. I tried a semester in pre-med only to find my personal health on the decline. I sought out business and law, thinking only of money and career, but I never could seem to fold myself into the furrows of technique and calculation. While attending a forum for world economics of the 21st century, I found myself ignoring the speakers while reading passages out of the Vedas. This did not bode well for a business career. Meanwhile, my dalliance at the school of law only made me yearn for the far off days of Ragnarok.

Eventually, I completed a doctorate in comparative myth studies. Many people ask me what kind of degree that is? I tell them it is the study of ancient myth and religions. This satisfies most people. The study of ancient myth for me, however, has always been about the historicity of the eternal present. This sounds like a contradiction, or perhaps a clever introduction to the ideas of Carl Jung. It is neither. After reading hundreds of books and articles on the theories of ancient myth I have come to the conclusion that most of these theories are projections of the present self onto the past. Perhaps Jung has something to contribute after all, for it appears that our conception of history is often the product of the ego.

There are many serious and sobering questions that the past is always asking us. While greater scholars than I have tackled many points in history, for the most part the questions posed from the past by myth-making societies—societies that represent ninety-nine percent of human history—remain unanswered. This means that we human beings living in the modern age have yet to discover a great many things, not only about our ancestors but also about ourselves. It turns out some of these nagging questions would not leave me alone, and I have spent several years considering only a few of them.

History is a funny thing. We all walk out of it without ever seeing its full complexity. A newborn chick never sees its own egg but only its broken shell. Humanity and history have the same relationship; it is impossible to see a thing if it is big enough! While recent history is far more recognizable, the truth is every event has a near infinite number of relationships that help create it. By the time an event unfolds, all the constituents that helped form that event are already fading into fragments. This is why two opposing lawyers in a courtroom can credibly argue the same set of historic facts from completely different points of view. This does not mean they are both right, but only that numerous arguments can be made about the same set of facts. What is needed is a sure knowledge of the event, the motive and behavior of its participants, and, as much as possible, objective honesty about that knowledge. How this process fares in the courtroom is about the same as it fares in our history books. Listening to professors argue over the complexities of past events, motives, and movements is very much like listening to a courtroom drama, with the huge exception that in a professor's classroom there is rarely an opposing point of view.

Ancient history is made up of vast amounts of mostly irrecoverable data. As one historian puts it, "our awesome lack of knowledge about the ancient world imprisons us within a discourse of plausibilities, not probabilities" (Berlinerblau 73). Another historian sums up this situation simply, "It seems a depressing reality unless one simply chooses to ignore it" (cited in Berlinerblau 73). This statement is a shocking confession that should be printed on the cover page of every book about ancient history. Meanwhile, humankind's pre-history, the time before writing, is simply a vast, empty canvas bespeckled with only a few ink blots. Our interpretations of pre-history tend to be a measure of our own, present, psychological state of mind; not unlike giving a Rorschach's test to a new-born chick staring at its shattered shell—results may vary.

The study of ancient myth turns out to be an excellent Rorschach's test for the modern mind considering its own history. What do these sparse and broken narratives mean? There are so many different interpretations of the data that coming to some form of final conclusion is impossible. What interests me is not the final conclusion of it all, but rather the *a priori* assumptions that inform the differing conclusions.

Over the years I have lectured to students and the public in classrooms and at conferences and have discussed my materials with scholars and interested inquisitors. Through these interactions I have become keenly aware of three underlying assumptions many people have about the ancient past. These assumptions color all their interpretations of the past and mold the kind of questions they put to history. While there are more positions than these three, they tend to be the most common, and I have categorized them into three groups.

The first group I call the Howlers. This name sounds like a pejorative, but it is not; rather, it is a historical point of view. In 1965 an astronomy professor at Boston University named Gerald Hawkins published a book entitled *Stonehenge Decoded*. In this book Hawkins identified astronomical alignments marked by the standing stones at Stonehenge. He proposed that the megalithic site was a sort of ancient computer calculating solar and lunar alignments, with the further possibility of its ability to predict eclipses. Hawkins, however, was not a historian, anthropologist, or archaeologist, and his proposals for Stonehenge flew in the face of the academic mainstream. In fact, the leading British archaeologist, Richard Atkins, rebuffed the work of Hawkins, publishing an article entitled "Moonshine on Stonehenge." The most respected British archaeologist of his time, Atkins declared that such alignments were impossible as the builders were nothing but "howling barbarians."

Time has proved Hawkins right, and not just about Stonehenge, but for the entire megalithic world where numerous astronomical alignments have been found all over the globe. This means of course that the builders of Stonehenge had a pre-planned design that emerged from a cult and culture wedded to the motion and measure of the stars. More important, and what should be obvious, is the fact that the actual construction of the site, like any grand megalithic site, required a great deal of skill, planning, resources, social and economic organizing, engineering, and so on. In other words, Stonehenge was not created by a bunch of howling barbarians but by a group of intelligent human beings working with the materials, techniques, culture, and metaphysics of the day. In most respects, these ancient builders were just like you and me.

Modern people tend to think of ancient thinkers as primitive—that somehow, people way back when thought fundamentally different thoughts that were simple and childlike. Like Atkins, these people tend to think of the people in the past as some form of "howling barbarian." The cause of this assumption is wed to the modern environment, which places a fabricated illusion of intelligence in the technology employed. When one digs up 4,000-year-old pottery shards and compares them to the computers, microchips, and space rockets of today, it is easy to assume we are far smarter. This is a false comparison, however. Take a modern stock broker, teleport him 4,000 years into the past, and see how well he does surviving off the land. There are many modern people, who, without their technical gadgetry, would be completely unable to function. Those "primitive" peoples amongst whom he might appear would consider him unschooled, uncultured, and intellectually deficient—in other words, a sort of "howling barbarian."

In my field of study, Howlers tend to take myth quite literally. When a myth says that the Earth was created out of chaos by the gods and rests on a turtle, they all believe that ancient human beings literally believed the earth was atop a turtle. Amongst this group you hear a great many pronouncements: "Those people back then all believed the Earth was flat," or "Without any real understanding of science, they believed the sun was a chariot pulled by horses." When one believes that most of the past was planted in a primitivism, which simply was the base for the evolution of the modern self, one tends to get a hyper-inflated ego. Modernity could be called the age of self-inflation. This book is not a social commentary, but it is again curious to me how the thought of the self is deeply connected with one's understanding of the past. We are in no small part a product of a temporal understanding of being which is surprisingly arbitrary.

The second group I call the Romantics. This group will ask me questions like, "How can we connect with the spirit of nature like the ancients?" or "Is there a way we can live these myths so we are not as violent?" and "What is it about monotheism (a.k.a. Christianity) that destroys the mythic spirit?" These people also tell me about a retreat their friend or neighbor went on where they re-enacted an ancient ritual in a sweat lodge or journeyed on a vision quest with a shaman, as if these activities were somehow implicit in the mythologies of antiquity. While the first group has completely marginalized the past, this second group has completely romanticized it. They assume that ancient peoples were in tune with all the powers of the landscape, less prone to violence or neurosis, and deeply spiritual. It is a Romantic Savage view of history that has always remained quite popular, yet has never hit the mark.

I am more reticent to tell these people that their assumptions are overreaching, simply because they seem filled with so much hope that somehow there is a way to obtain a greater connectivity and meaning in life from studying ancient myths and cultures. Nevertheless, I must point out that while ancient societies were connected to nature in a completely different way, they also over-hunted and deforested entire landscapes. Additionally, ancient societies freely practiced slavery, ritual prostitution, and human sacrifice. War was a way of life for them, as it is with us, and myths tend to be very violent. What these romanticists do not fully understand is that the human condition is the same in all places and in all times. Ultimately, the epistemology of joy for which they are reaching lies in the paradox that Buddha and Jesus taught: the way to the mythic Golden Age is only obtained either through the negation of suffering or through worthy suffering—but suffering is the constant.

One would hope that the third group would fall somewhere in the middle of the first two. My experience has been different. The third group tends to be a conflation of the first two. I call them the Conspirators. These people believe in a primitive past that is so over-romanticized that apparently only the aliens could have given us the pyramids and the myths. This paradigm says something about the modern mind; namely, it is deeply conditioned to believe that the ancient mind of the past was primitive. When great structures like the pyramids or ziggurats appear out of the sand, something other than human beings must have created them. Actually, the Romantic Savage view is similar in that it rests upon the idea of a supra-spiritual psyche that is wholly other and alien to the modern one, where deep insights are gained from mysticism, myths, eco-sensitivity, and practically any ancient Eastern religion—all of which are just outside the grasp of the Western imagination.

Even so, the topics of ancient history, myth, and religion have also flummoxed the scholars, who have picked every changing opinion available over the years, except for the extra-terrestrials. One suspects that if a grant or tenure were associated with E.T. that this exception might also disappear. I say this in slight jest, only to make the point that there is a horizon of the past rooted in our consciousness beyond which everyone gropes in the dark. While scholarship is the best method for investigating the past, scholars bring with them another set of problems.

I was keenly interested in a recently published article in the *New York Times* illustrating the profound difficulty scholars have with the interpretations of history and myth. The article entitled "*A Host of Mummies, a Forest of Secrets*" discusses a remarkable find in the Xinjiang region of China. A graveyard discovered in the Tarim Basin within the Taklimakan Desert has produced a series of mummified corpses whose preserved remains are in astonishingly good condition due to the arid climate and chemical makeup of the desert sand. Bewilderingly, the buried deceased are all Caucasian, of European descent, and their remains date back to nearly 2000 BCE.

Of even greater interest is the fact that the corpses were found buried in upside down boats covered with cowhide (Wade, par. 12). At each grave site was erected a wooden pole about thirteen feet tall: "Many had flat blades, painted black and red, like the oars from some great galley that had foundered beneath the waves of sand" (par. 11). Despite the boat within which each person was buried, the anthropologists at the site believe the tall oarlike posts are "gigantic phallic symbols" (par. 14). The blades of the oarlike posts have been re-deciphered as "symbolic vulvas" (par. 15). One anthropologist proclaims, "The whole of the cemetery was blanketed with blatant sexual symbolism" (par. 15).

A story attributed to Hermes Trismegistos relates how Aesculapius pleaded with King Ammon "not to let any of the sacred writings of Egypt be translated into Greek lest they become the football of rhetoricians and intellectuals who would not understand them" (*MJSP* 126). Little did poor Aesculapius know that it was not the Greeks he should have feared, but a host of modern scholars that have placed the entire ancient world on the head of a penis. Why should anyone consider that a forest of poles planted overtop boats and the buried dead be symbolic of giant phalluses? In my view, this scholarly interpretation neither marginalizes nor romanticizes the data, but represents an existential break rooted in the idea of self and history; in other words, it is an interpretation more closely aligned with the worldview of the Conspirators. Similarly, modern scholarship often projects a theoretical past of a modern making on historical data, and this scholarly construct is often the product of cultural ideologies, political fads, economic resourcefulness, and entrenched and departmental theories. We forget that the greatest resistance Galileo first had on his new ideas of the universe came not from the Church and the Papacy but from the university and its scholars who were well paid to teach the old and established cosmology.

One does not get very far in reading ancient myths before the realization strikes that what we are dealing with is a vast and ubiquitous wreckage of a bygone age. There are dozens of theories of what these myths mean. Curiously, I have found that competing theories may simultaneously be right while the most popular theories can be wrong. Joseph Campbell is loved by the Romantics (and I must admit I lean that way) but is often vilified by mainstream scholarship. Walter Burkert is representative of mainstream scholarship, and yet his own predispositions lead him to the erroneous conclusion that there was neither a belief in a resurrection nor an elevated status in the afterlife within the Greco-Roman mystery initiations. Burkert writes, "A redirection of religion toward other-worldly concerns, contrary to what is often assumed, is not to be found with the 'Oriental' gods and their mysteries" (*Ancient* 23-8). I find this conclusion astounding and even more problematic than Campbell's monomyth theory (that all myths emerge from a common psychic structure and adhere to a universal pattern). Meanwhile, the eminent *Encyclopedia of Religion* informs us that the origin of mystery religion initiation probably descends from the social initiations of a tribe or clan; like a great many encyclopedic entries, stuff is said without really telling us anything.

As one goes through the numerous scholarly sources—Frazier, Müller, Cassier, Harrison, Durkheim, Jung, Rank, Eliade, Lévi-Strauss, Campbell, Dubuisson—one senses an endless parade of ideas attempting to make sense of the puzzle pieces that are left behind. The problem is we only have a few hundred puzzle pieces to a ten-thousand piece puzzle;

thus, every theorist is rearranging these pieces in new combinations try-ing to produce some ultimate meaning from the past.

This is exactly how it should be. Much of what each theorist pro-duces is a result of the kinds of questions they put to the material; con-sequently, every approach is worth considering. In each approach there are probably questions posed which others have not contemplated. Every approach, including my own, is fraught with peril, and it is impossible to proceed without making some assumptions about the disparate material we have at our disposal. Given these points, I have often wished to pres-ent my own temporal context for the study of myth.

In answering the questions I receive, I find myself constantly trying to build a hook of understanding upon which to hang the answers I give. This book is an attempt to create a historical context through which one may consider ancient constructs embedded in myth, ritual, and culture. I have focused my material primarily on the Near East and Mediterranean, but only because our oldest written sources emerge from these lands and a great deal of scholarship has been done on these sources. My purpose is to show that what looks so strange to us about the past really derives from specific circumstances in which ancient peoples lived and which we have forgotten: the nature of orality and its epistemological consequences (epistemology is how we know what we know), and the nature of oral cosmology and how such people viewed the world and their place in it. People who live and think without writing will process information and interact with their environment in different ways. Literate people have forgotten how oral civilizations created and maintained calendars, or built their temples, or maintained any complex system of math, mu-sic, or science. Because we have forgotten these things, we assume they never existed.

In my first chapter I take on the Howlers, Romantics, and Conspirators. I explain that the ancient mind was no different in capac-ity or ability than the modern one. Despite excellent scholarly work that has corrected many flawed assumptions about the past, the idea of mental and cultural evolution is still deeply embedded in both popular and academic ideas. While there are great differences between the present and the past, the human past should not be seen as something radically different but as something radically the same. I show how many twentieth century histories derive from fundamentally flawed assumptions about the ancient mind, especially by examining the modern take of the history of science.

My second chapter discusses the cognitive consequences of orality and literacy. Understanding the nature of oral thinking is absolutely essential when studying the ancient past. People who do not read or write are not less intelligent than literate people, but they do organize information in completely different ways, with both keen limitations and curious potentials. One begins to see that the structure and nature of myths are products of the demands of orality. Additionally, the cultic and ritualistic nature of every ancient tribe or civilization is also a direct consequence of orality. While other scholars have addressed this topic, I hope to contribute a few new ideas when examining orality and its consequences.

My third chapter discusses the nature of oral cosmology. Ancient cosmology undergirds all ancient thinking, and in my view scholarly work on oral cosmology has been underwhelming. Ultimately, when many scholars think of cosmology they think of the spatial and mathematical models human beings have created to describe the visible universe; thus, ancient cosmology produced a geocentric cosmos. Actually, this is a modern definition of cosmology and it has little to do with ancient thinking. Ancient cosmology was ontological (the study of one's own being and its relationship with the environment) and not spatial or mathematical. This is the most difficult chapter of all, for I attempt to describe a way of seeing the universe that is utterly foreign to modern apprehension and does not easily fall within any of the theorists' models.

My fourth chapter deliberates on the interconnections between oral cult and oral cosmology. Cities and temples were built as scale models of the oral cosmos. Rituals amongst oral peoples often invoke some aspect of the manifest cosmos and often reenact cosmogonic events. Ancient religion and oral cosmology are inseparable. Any attempt to describe the myths and religions of antiquity outside of their own oral and cosmological contexts may result in an unnecessary and inflated caricature of history.

My final chapters examine a few myths in relation to the oral cult and cosmos described in chapters three and four. I have chosen the *Epic of Gilgamesh* as my starting point simply because it is one of the earliest myths we have recorded in our possession, with fragments of the epic cycle dating to about 2000 BCE. The journey of Gilgamesh is more than a swashbuckling adventure, but a profound commentary of the cosmos and man's relation to it. It also, in my view, establishes by cosmological analogy Gilgamesh's right to rule his city, for the rightful ruler must take proper measurements of the cosmic ideal in order to implement them into the rites of civilization. With this myth in mind, I also examine the myth complex surrounding the Labors of Heracles, which is a Greek adaptation of the Gilgamesh myth. The Labors of Heracles initiates our hero not only as a royal heir to kingship but more important as an heir to godhood on Olympus. You will find my conclusions a direct contradistinction to those of Burkert.

Finally, I examine a few founding myths in the Old Testament in the stories of Abraham, Jacob, and Balaam. I show how these narratives share many of the mythemes of the archetypal, cosmic journey implicit in the cultus of the oral age. Believers do not associate the Bible with mythology, though scholars have shown that Biblical themes overlap with other mythologies. What many scholars have not done, however, is link these comparative mythologies to the profound cosmographic formations of the oral world. Unfortunately, these comparisons find themselves on much more speculative footing. The temple cult of the Israelites was central to their tradition for nearly one thousand years but was extinguished not only from their religious ideals and practices but also from their scriptural cannon.

As one reads this work they will find that I am often poking holes in the ideas of mainstream ideology as applied to the past. I am very critical of how evolutionary theory has been adapted to the history of the mind. I am also very critical of many projections that historians of science have placed upon the past. I must state here that this does not mean I am critical of the modern theory of biological evolution or modern cosmological models. I am as entranced and ennobled by the revelations of modern science as any scholar. My point is that we are finite beings in an infinite universe; as a result, we will always be projecting our own ideas into the cosmos. Whatever our models of physics, our ultimate framework for understanding the universe is in metaphysics. This will never change.

I also confess that in creating a general context for the study of myth I am bound to craft universal categories for comparison. Entering the scholar's field one quickly recognizes that any general theory can be deconstructed by a particular example, just as any particular interpretation can be dismantled by a general theory. Scholars can never escape this paradox, for every particular example eventually gets wed with a universal theory that must explain it. In dealing with the subjects of myth and history, there will never be an end to arguing the points between universals and particulars. Additionally, it is impossible to generalize a swath of history some three thousand years long without making assumptions and errors. Recognizing the paradox of scholarship, and that in many cases only possibilities can be argued, herein I am not attempting to explain the meaning of myth but only its function within the domain of oral culture. I am not deciphering ancient myth. I am seeking its origins.

I hope by reading this book a person will have a new appreciation and view of the ancient world, its cultic constructs, and its mythologies.

Most of all, I hope by understanding more about our past we gain a refined appreciation for the ubiquitous human capacity to make meaning
of a constantly changing world. And with that meaning, perhaps we will
see anew the potential for the growth of mind and spirit in our relationship with the cosmos. In a modern world where hyper-materialism has
clouded our vision of the future, perhaps our way forward is a new look
into the past.

A Note on Sources

When people learn that I earned my degree in Mythological Studies at
Pacifica Graduate Institute, the home of the Joseph Campbell Archives,
they automatically assume that my interpretation of myth is Jungian or
Campbellian. It is not. This book is not about psychological archetypes.
While I deeply appreciate the contributions to myth studies these scholars have made, I disagree with Campbell's basic premise clearly stated in
his *Hero with a Thousand Faces* that myth is "psychology misread as biography, history, and cosmology" (256). I have the exact opposite point of
view: myth is precisely biography, history, and cosmology.

Adherents of Campbell insist that all mythic constructs emerge from
images autonomously produced in the human psyche. Campbell follows
the philosophy of Carl Jung, who believed that the storehouse of myth
derives from a "collective psychic substratum" that he called the collective unconscious (Jung and Kerenyi 74). According to Jung myth arises
from this collective unconscious through dreams, images, and fantasy
thinking. He believes myth motifs may exist within a cultural and cultic
system but cannot originate in a single tradition "since they may reappear anywhere, at any time, and in any individual regardless of tradition"
(Segal, *Jung* 64). Man is a myth-maker by nature. Jung and Campbell
are Romantics. They see archaic man as more in tune with his unconscious productions of myth. They also see modernity (especially Western

Modernity) as a sort of psychic break from the unconscious where the old myths no longer serve their ontological functions.

Campbell is not the only scholar to make such interpretive moves on the material. Structuralism replaces the "collective psychic substratum" of Jung with a collective hyper-stratum of relationships throughout language and society. It is an elegant ideological switch also rooted in theory to which the material of myth is applied. On this point, to be a comparative mythologist is really to be a comparative myth-theorist. In the past century there have been a score of theories interpreting myth, and one must know what the different interpretations and arguments contribute and deny.

One of the chief complaints against Joseph Campbell was his universalist approach. He could explain all myths around the world using one cookie-cutter press. This process often excluded the profound ethnic, geographical, environmental, social, and cosmological differences between cultures and their myths. On the other hand, Campbell's theory provided a rich field of inquiry and opened a vista for those dealing with the very difficult subjects of mind and psyche. Agree or disagree, his theory remains consistent, coherent, plain spoken, and for millions of people, relevant. Further, read Campbell's volumes of *The Masks of God* or his *Historical Atlas of World Mythology*, or peruse his personal archives filled with books copiously annotated by his probative hand, and one sees only the acumen of a top-notch scholar. My citations of Campbell are predicated on his solid scholarship.

I did much of my research at the library of Brigham Young University. BYU is home to the Center for the Preservation of Ancient Religious Texts, or CPART. This institution is digitizing the Dead Sea Scrolls, Herculaneum papyri, Syriac manuscripts, and many other ancient texts. I have quoted from Hugh Nibley, a leading and late BYU scholar, who spoke a dozen languages, read half a dozen dead languages, and lectured on ancient religion all around the world. Nibley received his doctorate from Berkeley in history and classics. He published scholarly articles in leading academic journals. Most of his popular BYU publications, on the other hand, were aimed at that particular student body, and his work to this audience is apologetic—a death nail to wider scholarly culture. Like Campbell, Nibley was a universalist, pouring the data into his own mono-Mormon theory, where every myth and ritual hailed from the ancient temple complex and a common ecclesiastical tradition. Nibley's brilliance is not to be disputed, however, and he has shown the connections between myth and ritual in many ancient cultures with an astuteness that is rare. Cautiously, while drawing from his resources and great thinking, I believe my own work counters many of Nibley's etiological arguments of myth on the basis of the structure of oral cognition and oral cosmology. Nibley's work, *The Message of the Joseph Smith Papyri: An Egyptian Endowment,* is a translation of Papyrus Louvre N. 3284, including comparative translations and commentary of other papyri such as the Egyptian Book of Breathings obtained by Joseph Smith through Michael Chandler in 1835, from which the book gets its title.

Finally as one reads this work, one will come to see that I liberally reference a work entitled *Hamlet's Mill* authored by Giorgio de Santillana, a professor of the history of science from MIT, and Hertha von Dechend, a professor of science at Johann Wolfgang-Goethe University. This acclaimed work also has its severe critics, and once again these authors tend to apply a universalist theory to myth, stating "whatever is true myth has no historical basis, however tempting the reduction, however massive and well armed the impact of a good deal of modern criticism on that belief. . . . Myth is essentially cosmological" (50). I actually am more closely aligned with this way of thinking than any other, though my conception of oral cosmology is different. Unlike these authors, I am not trying to prove that myth contained knowledge about the precession of the equinoxes, mathematics, geometry, or harmonics. I believe in fact that it did, and I address part of these connections in my first chapter. All of that is secondary for me, however, as I consider the really interesting information in *Hamlet's Mill* to be the cultic-cosmic connection in ancient myth, a connection the authors clearly understood.

I also liberally quote from a wide array of other scholars and cite translations of ancient texts from leading scholars. I have mentioned these three sources in particular because they exist just outside the center of the mainstream, which is exactly where one should be if progress in the field of myth studies is to be made. All these sources are the works of first-class scholars in their own fields. From them I did not form my opinions of myth, but only my sensibilities. From Campbell I first learned a passion for myth. From Nibley I converted to the myth-ritual school. From de Santillana and von Dechend I dispensed with the silly and soporific notion of mental and cultural evolution and have noted the numerous cosmological motifs in myth. After reading as many works from each of these sources as I could find, I discovered that I had far more questions than I had answers. What these sources really endowed on me was a deep-seated humility when viewing the past. We all know so very little. Many scholars do not speak that way, and in my opinion they are the most dangerous ones.

Regardless of one's sources, myth studies ever remains problematic. There is no universal key of interpretation. Or at least, that universal key belonged to an oral society rooted in a cosmology and cult system lost to the shadows of history. Indeed, the classical Greeks themselves constantly argued over the meaning of their own myths: to some they were history, to others they were biography, to others they dealt with the natural sciences, and to others still they were part of a ritual system of initiation. By the time most myths were written down they had already changed, and to decipher the meaning of oral myths from written texts is an oxymoron *par excellence.*

To study the ancient past, whatever the riddles it presents, is really to study one's self and one's relationship with the unrelenting cosmos. The decline of myth studies, folklore and religious studies, classical studies, and even the Western Canon of literature, is not, dare I say, a sign that we have discovered better things to think about. Sadly, it is a symptom of a teetering mind exhausted by the shallows of materialism. "It is a hard thing to get to the stars from the earth," wrote Seneca. This is a revelation to every age and to every generation. History has repeatedly shown that it is all woe and folly to the people who have stopped trying.

CHAPTER 1

MODERN THEORY AND ANCIENT HISTORY

History as Construct

History is often a philosophical reconstruction. Of course events really happen—dates, names, places, and movements are all important—but these are the bricks of history. The mortar that once held these bricks together can be very elusive to reconstitute accurately, the mortar being the thoughts, intents, and imaginations that originally created the bricks. When archeologists examine ancient cultures they are looking only at the bricks. The mortar has all dried up and blown away. Speaking of the unknown founders of Britain one eminent historian laments, "Their memorial has perished with them. Their lives, their loves, their hates, their speech, their manners, customs, and scheme of society, their deaths, their gods, all have faded as in a dream" (Campbell, *Occidental* 35).

Reassembling the archeological debris into a coherent whole requires a great deal of training: examining materials, manufacturing methods, art forms, languages, and so much more. The truth is, however, that all of the modern methods employed remain insufficient to reconstitute the ancient mortar in its entirety. No matter how well trained scholars are, they are restricted to fitting together the ancient bricks of the past using only the modern mortar of the present.

So much of the archeological record is admittedly monotonous and boring—little bits of pottery and clay, ash and bone, and periodically a figurine. It all requires a great deal of imagination to try to probe the *thoughts* behind the clutter. Yet no less of an imagination is required when facing the great cult centers of antiquity that have survived and remain so alien: "The first contact with the monuments of ancient Egypt always creates the same impression: the confrontation with another world" (*TK* 8). When one stands in front of the pyramids in Egypt it is as if one has stepped out of contemporary reality. It is not just Egypt that produces this sense of psychological awe. In fact, most of the great religious centers in early history produce the same mental discomfiture, as if one's intellectual horizon is not expanding but rather is being pushed in by a transcendent idea trying to get through. From Avebury and Stonehenge in ancient Britain to the ziggurats and mortuary temples throughout the Near East to the megalithic temples in Malta, the cipher city of Çatal Hüyük, or the exotic cave at Lascaux, the modern imagination is confronted with radically different ways of thinking altogether. In some respects, it is perhaps easier to work with clay bits and bones, for this at least seems far more terrestrial.

It becomes evidently clear just how otherworldly these ancient cult centers are when they are compared to their modern counterparts. In the West, perhaps the best one can do is compare the ancient monuments with some place like the Vatican in Rome, with its fountains, statues, pillars, and cathedral like halls. Of course, Rome has ancient roots, and something of the archaic past survives within its atmosphere, albeit its connection with the hoary past is fleeting, and for the most part what one sees is a sort of mythological bourgeoisie around every corner. Even further from the Vatican is the art and architecture of the modern megachurch, now completely de-mythologized and transformed into the apex of industrialized religious expression—the Coliseum—created in the manner of the true modern cult center: the stadium, the cinema, and the bureaucratic nave. Even when modern impetus seeks to recreate the ancient temple as a showpiece, it does no better than the Luxor in Las Vegas. Here is the modern imagination at work. When a seeker of the magnificent enters those glass doors he realizes immediately that he has been conned; what he gets is not the space of another world, but the apex of entertainment in the present one—which, as it turns out, is nothing but a billion dollar ash tray with a buffet line.

Historians, archeologists, and mythologists, however, are not just after the bricks; they are after the old mortar that once put it all together. *We want to know the life of the ancient mind*, for truly this should tell us something about ourselves, and the revelation of the self is a noble pursuit. Fortunately, or unfortunately, depending on one's point of view, the modern imagination has invented a catchall template from which all of ancient thought, work, and life can be reassembled. Our modern template is Darwinism. It is amazing that ever since Darwin our history books have never been the same. Ancient civilizations, whatever they were groping after with all their wits and strength, have been swept into the idea of cultural and intellectual evolution.

It is an idea proposed by Charles Darwin himself in his 1871 work *The Descent of Man*: "Differences [of moral and intellectual dispositions] between the highest men of the highest races and the lowest savages, are connected by the finest gradations. Therefore it is possible that they might pass and be developed into each other" (214). Applying biological evolution to the intellectual life, Darwin insists that through slow and often imperceptible gradations the "savage" develops into modern man. The thought is enticing, especially as it unites biology with psychology and history "by which all living and extinct beings are united by complex, radiating, and circuitous lines of affinities into one grand system" (*The Origin of Species* 157). It is the "one grand system" of such a theory that makes easy work of vast stretches of time known as ancient history and prehistory. Finally, here we have the mortar by which all the bricks of the past can be fashioned into one grand mosaic. This reconstruction molds order into the historical chaos by subjugating it underneath the triumph of modernity. Intellectual and cultural evolution is the metaphysical breath of life which infuses meaning into all those old shards of clay, from which, like a new Adam, modern man is born.

Ever since Darwin's claims, the professors of the human past have built onto this "one grand system" scheme. "We may, I think, apply the often-repeated comparison of savages to children as fairly to their moral as to their intellectual condition," writes Edward B. Tylor, the founder of modern anthropology. "The better savage social life seems in but unstable equilibrium, liable to be easily upset by a touch of distress, temptation, or violence, and then it becomes the worse savage life, which we know by so many dismal and hideous examples" (Tylor 31). It sounds so frightening and precarious, yet one cannot help but read current events in the postmodern age to see that everything Tylor is saying of the "savages" can be equally applied to large systems in the modern world. This interrupts our historical narrative, however, whose "standard of reckoning progress and decline is not that of ideal good and evil, but of movement along a measured line from grade to grade of actual savagery, barbarism, and civilization. . . . the result showing that, on the whole, progress has far prevailed over relapse" (Tylor 32).

Darwin, who never studied "primitive" cultures himself, has shown us the way. Tylor, who did study primitive cultures, took up Darwin's measuring stick and ran with it. Freud, who studied neither bones nor birds, adopted the same catch-all template for the human psyche, further opening this theoretical *Zeitgeist* not only for the outside world but now primarily for the inside world. Ever since this trio, the majority of theories addressing religion, myth, and history, or simply human activity, all follow suit. Spencer and Durkheim employed the Darwinian template for human society, Marx for the economy, Frazer for rituals, F. Max Müller for language, Lévy-Bruhl and Cassirer for mythology, and the list keeps going. It is all second nature now: animism, totemism, fetishes, taboos, magic, archetypes—these become the constituents of our mortar—all types of Darwinian thinking. We can now generalize any portion of history at any era by imposing the comforting, yet slow, linear gradation of intellectual evolution on any culture. The bits and bones and the great cult centers of history have all taken their place within this modern template.

The problem, of course, is that ancient categories of knowledge and ancient capacities of knowing are far more complex and familiar than has been assumed by our elderly scholars. It is also true, in recent decades, that modern scholars have revisited many of these assumptions in a far more critical manner. For example, Hugh Nibley notes of the ancient Egyptians that "the routine appeal to magic as a quick and simple solution to problems is more a game of modern scholarship than of ancient Egyptian religion" (*MJSP* 370). Herman te Velde quips, 'Levi Strauss has remarked that the term of totemism and likewise the concept of myth are categories of *our* thinking, artificial units, which only exist as such in the minds of scholars engaged in research, while nothing specific in the outside world corresponds to them any more' (cited in *MJSP* 370, italics his).

Constructs such as *magic* are far more ambiguous when viewed within the context of ancient culture. Stephen Quirke offers this critical examination of Egyptian magic:

> The [Egyptian] word *heka* denotes the assertive power by which creation originally unfurled and ever since has reinforced its existence. . . . *Heka* is often translated as 'magic,' but our word implies a rift between official and forbidden religious practice, and no such rift can be detected in ancient Egypt. The English word magic can mean wonder or enchantment, but it also carries the negative connotations of superstition and of practices

condemned by society. The very word was devised by the Greeks to denote foreign and suspect beliefs and rites, said to be practiced by the Magi who were vaguely thought to live somewhere in the direction of Persia, arch enemy of classical Greece. . . . By contrast the ancient Egyptian world knew no such concept for a marginal area of belief and practice. Our 'magic' equates with *heka* only in the sense that it evokes astonishment and awe. It singularly fails to convey the role of *heka* in Pharaonic texts and images. There . . . *heka* expresses a creative and protective power, a precondition for all life. . . . The primary meaning of *heka* remained the creative urge, a power beyond good and evil. (Quirke and Forman 23)

The Egyptian idea of magic was not modern hocus-pocus, but recognition that there remains a fundamental spark of life unfolding within and between components in nature in which humankind participates. Every animate thing belonged to a network of relationships extending from the heavens and into the underworld. Nature manifests principles emerging from this network. The Egyptians called this invisible source of life *heka*, and the entire framework of relationships *Maat*.

It is true that many Egyptians produced charms and spells to tap into this creative urge in order to influence change. Because of this, modern scholars have translated *heka* into the word *magic*, for everywhere in Egypt *heka* has religious undertones. It is also true that the recognition of a generative matrix of life interweaving all living things is a product of a highly observant, rational, critical mind, whose imaginative and analytic thought structures are wed to the concrete realities of those components in nature. *Heka* is a kind of quantum field theory for oral minds who do not have access to the hyper-abstract constructs that only literacy can produce. We are not dealing with a form of intellectual primitivism or pre-rational mysticism, nor does the scholarly label of sympathetic magic work either (that is, using objects to represent something or someone over which influence is sought); rather, we are being confronted with the very unique thought-structures of the oral mind.

Similar to the word magic, such modern concepts as totems, fetishes, anima, and taboos are modern constructions with modern ideologies overlaid upon them. These conceptions of modern scholarship often reduce the complexities of ancient thought to categories of pre-analytical-reason, pre-science, and proto-intelligence. Sometimes this Darwinistic view popular amongst the Howlers is imbued with semi-mystical thinking that is highly spiritualized and popular with the Romantics. Thus, in *The Civilization of the Goddess,* Marjia Gimbutas posits that European civilizations in pre-history were all matriarchal, benevolent, and egalitarian because they were run by women priestesses worshiping the Great Mother, a female deity of the earth. Overseeing such a matriarchal religion within a feminine spirit was akin to the Golden Age. Gimbutas writes: "It was the sovereign mystery and creative power of the female as the source of life that developed into the earliest religious experiences" (222). So much so that "the woman's ability to give birth and nourish children from her body was deemed sacred, and revered as the ultimate metaphor for the divine Creator" (223). Underneath the auspices of the divine feminine, there was no warfare for nearly three thousand years (viii).

According to Gimbutas, the remote past belongs to a pre-rational, pre-analytic age, not because ancient primitives had not learned to think yet, but because ancient females were supra-rational and intuitive, linked with the spirit of the landscape. It is a Romantic view of history. Like the Howling point of view, these conceptions are products of sheer oversimplification in accordance with Darwinian conventions, which, in some areas of modern thinking, are so ubiquitously employed that they have become assumed and subconscious.

It is not just general scholarship that works within these assumptions. The entire new age, UFO hunting, alien theorizing conspiratorial group falls into the same conventions. Thus, when facing the ancient cult centers of antiquity, they variously claim that the aliens built them, or that they were used as time portals or energy plants, all descended from a "primordial alien race of lizard people from the star Sirius B." Such intellectual claptrap is actually a product of Darwinian thought, for surely human beings could not have built these cult centers, let alone think the sophisticated thoughts necessary to build them. Some higher, extraterrestrial power must have done it.

Perhaps one of the best criticisms offered against these games of history-making comes as early as 1960 by Walter F. Otto, who, in his work *Dionysus: Myth and Cult*, deconstructs the Darwinian appliqué to myth theory. Otto notes that in order for any form of evolution to occur there must be, from the beginning, a completely whole organism in existence upon which the powers of evolution may apply. Otto asserts that when it comes to religious studies, scholars make the beginnings of a religious movement nothing but an abstraction; "At the beginning of the process called evolution there is, then, a mere Nothingness, and the concept of evolution has, consequently, lost its meaning" (9). And more penetratingly, Otto reminds us that no man prays to a concept (10) and that for the most part scholarship into the origins of religious thoughts invariably end up with circular and empty statements: "The questions of meaning and origin are always answered with vacuous formulations of religious viewpoints or sentiments which are supposed to have validity for all peoples and cultures" (12).

Otto sees that many historians and theorists have applied Darwin's "one grand system" to multiple areas of ancient thought and culture. Such stratagems are fraught with danger. For example, Darwin consistently applied his biological theory to every category of human experience with sometimes comical results. This is how Darwin explains the evolution of man and woman: "No one disputes that the bull differs in disposition from the cow, the wild-boar from the sow, the stallion from the mare. . . . Woman seems to differ from man in mental disposition" (*Descent* 234). Evolution is now going to explain the differences between man and woman; but note that it is to the *mind* that Darwin turns. "The chief distinction in the intellectual powers of the two sexes is shown by man's attaining to a higher eminence, in whatever he takes up, than can woman–whether requiring deep thought, reason, or imagination, or merely the use of the senses and hands" (*Descent* 234). Darwin goes on to explain why the man is superior to the woman in all these areas—which is practically every area—by noting how man must use all his faculties to win a woman, keep her, feed her, and protect her.

Proponents of Darwinism simply say that Victorian culture clouded his otherwise superb thinking in the biological realm, and in such cases as the sexes "he simply overreached." That is not true. Darwin did not overreach. He flatly got it wrong. He used his philosophical methodology of slow and minute adaptation and applied it to an area where it should have never been applied. If he could get it so wrong in the case of the evolution of the sexes, more specifically in the mental capacity of the sexes, where else could he have gotten it wrong? How about the evolution of mental capacity itself, regardless of the sex? If there ever was a prickly thorn in Darwinian theory, it has always resided in *consciousness*.

Darwin sought to overcome this hurdle by the same way he approached the evolution of the sexes—through small and minute changes and adaptation, man developed reason: "My object . . . is to shew there is no fundamental difference between man and the higher mammals in their mental faculties" (*Descent* 214). It is an incredibly brazen statement. Predictably, Darwin shows tendencies of many animals—for example, dogs, cats, and monkeys—to act with reason. Darwin continues, "Of all the faculties of the human mind, it will, I presume, be admitted that Reason stands at the summit. Only a few persons now dispute that animals posses some power of reasoning. Animals may constantly be seen to pause, deliberate, and resolve" (*Descent* 219). Thus, according to the meta-narrative, over long epochs of time, and through memory, curiosity, imitation, imagination, and finally reason, the mental life of modern Homo sapiens came about much the same way as the origin and evolution of biological life. The mind inched its way up very slowly from tadpole to primate to man. Furthermore, pre-historic man had a mind much like that of a child, as opposed to modern man, whose mind is at the apex of sophistication.

Aside from the difficulty of the very notion of consciousness, one can hardly believe Darwin's assessment that "there is no fundamental difference between man and the higher mammals in their mental faculties." Not only is there a fundamental difference, but also the difference is so great as to make the comparisons valueless. As Bruce Thornton puts it,

> No chimp buries its dead, or marries its mate in a communal ritual, or cooks its food, or worships a divine power, or writes a sonnet, or loves unconditionally. The crude behaviors that to some human observers resemble these activities are so remote from even the most primitive human community's social practices that they can be called "cultural" only metaphorically. And when one considers more advanced civilizations and their incredible alteration of the material world, the distance between ourselves and our primate cousins grows astronomical to the point that any resemblances become meaningless" (97).

Furthermore, there appears to be absolutely no small graduated steps to any of these processes. Either a being has sentient consciousness or it does not—all at once or nothing at all—with nothing between. This should be our first clue that the ancient mind—as far back as one can go—is operating on the same faculties as the modern one, the differences being culture, language, and their resultant metaphysics.

As such, one of the most recent myth theorists, Claude Lévi-Strauss, has eschewed part of the Darwinian paradigm. Of pre-literate peoples

Lévi-Strauss observes, "The way of thinking among people we call, usually and wrongly, 'primitive'—let's describe them rather as 'without writing,' . . . has been interpreted in two different fashions, both of which . . . were equally wrong. The first way was to consider such thinking as of a somewhat coarser quality. . . . The other fashion is not so much that theirs is an inferior kind of thought, but a fundamentally different kind of thought" (15-16). Lévi-Strauss rejects both approaches out of hand. Many of our historians insist that ancient thinking was childlike. Lévi-Strauss insists the complete opposite, for such people "are perfectly capable of disinterested thinking; that is, they are moved by a need or a desire to understand the world around them, its nature and their society. On the other hand, to achieve that end, they proceed by intellectual means, exactly as a philosopher, or even to some extent a scientist, can and would do" (16).

More to the point, "People who are without writing have a fantastically precise knowledge of their environment and all their resources. All these things we have lost, but we did not lose them for nothing; we are now able to drive an automobile without being crushed at each moment. . . . This implies a training of mental capacities which 'primitive' peoples don't have because they don't need them" (19). Where the modern mind can use an automobile or fly a plane, the ancient mind, having no need of these things, directed its attention towards its environment and held an incredible awareness of one's surroundings. So it is that Lévi-Strauss peels back over a century of thinking to firmly state that the human mind is exactly that—the human mind—capable of doing everything the mind can do, in any group and at any time, as long as the mind is intact. "It is probably one of the many conclusions of anthropological research that, notwithstanding the cultural differences between the several parts of mankind, the human mind is everywhere one and the same and that it has the same capacities" (19).

Many modern notions of the history of the mind are predicated upon a Darwinian metaphysics that actually is a refutation of the very experience of mind. Darwinian theory and methodology offers no explanation for the mind's irreducible emergence, nor is it a satisfactory backdrop for the mind of history or prehistory, leaving the mathematician Giulio Magli to describe the Darwinian take on cultural and mental evolution in history as a "ridiculous and fundamentally sloppy hypothesis" (4). Magli drives the point home: "So, avoiding schemas and preconceptions means completely and definitively accepting that there is no evolution in intelligence. The Romans were as intelligent as we are, as were the Egyptians. The same applies to the neolithic peoples, to the builders of the megalithic temples, to the artists of Lascaux" (264).

It must be noted that none of these scholars are criticizing Darwin's biological theory. As is often the case, theorists who resolve one aspect of a problem tend to use their solution for all other aspects of the problem, and sometimes for all other problems. Darwin was especially guilty of this, and the climate of the Secular Age has exasperated his initial errors. One must understand that biological evolution and mental evolution are not homologous. They are predicated on entirely different time scales and processes that modern science has yet to properly conceptualize. Giorgio de Santillana, a historian of science from MIT, and Hertha von Dechend, a historian of science from Johann Wolfgang Goethe University, have interjected a warning for the modern imagination to consider:

> The simple idea of evolution, which it is no longer thought necessary to examine, spreads like a tent over all those ages that lead from primitivism into civilization. Gradually, we are told, step by step, men produced the arts and crafts, this and that, until they emerged into the light of history. Those soporific words "gradually" and "step by step," repeated incessantly, are aimed at covering an ignorance which is both vast and surprising. One should

inquire: which steps? But then one is lulled, overwhelmed and stupefied by the gradualness of it all, which is at best a platitude, only good for pacifying the mind since no one is willing to imagine that civilization appeared in a thunderclap. (*HM* 68)

Mind, Writing, and the Construct of Science

While it is true that over the last forty years modern theorists picking away at the Darwinian cathedral of history have made many inroads, still, in popular books on myth it appears there has been no advancement at all. Even in college textbooks addressing myth there is often an evolutionary paradigm implied, if not flatly stated. Additionally, whole schools of thought are predicated upon the idea. The psychological theory of myth, for example, requires an evolutionary scheme in order to advance the idea that in the past the human psyche had not developed as rationally or materialistically; therefore, the conscious mind was more "in tune" with the unconscious and its archetypal messages. The theories from both Freud and Jung were entirely encapsulated in a Darwinian scheme. Post-Jungian theorists such as Edinger, Neuman, and Von Fronz have added little to the psychological paradigm in this regard. Post-Freudian theorists, such as Julian Jaynes, can never separate biological evolution from his concept of mind.

Yet, if the psychological theory of myth has been addicted to evolutionary metaphysics in its paradigms, modern historians of science have upped the ante, demanding, as if by scientific fiat, a form of evolutionary primitivism. Perhaps there is no better illustration of the modern imagination at work, using Darwinian mortar to put history together, than the writings of many of our historians of science who, curiously enough, cannot seem to leave ancient myth alone. Of course, true to the Darwinian outlook, peoples of very remote times were by nature incapable of anything resembling modern science, and for tens of thousands of years the struggling human mind gradually grew, step by step, until the modern mind was birthed. As everyone will tell you, it was the Greeks who were the first to separate themselves from the mythological mind and apply a rational mind to their world.

"It is generally agreed," writes Marshall Clagett in his classic work *Greek Science in Antiquity*, "that the learning of antiquity was digested in the Middle Ages and Renaissance to form the chief nourishment for growth of early modern thought. Thus early modern science grew out of Greek science and philosophy" (13). Modern science begins in Greece because, as the great Bertrand Russell casually explains, "What [the Greeks] achieved in art and literature is familiar to everybody, but what they did in the purely intellectual realm is even more exceptional. They invented mathematics and science and philosophy; they first wrote history as opposed to mere annals; they speculated freely about the nature of the world and the ends of life, without being bound in the fetters of any inherited orthodoxy" (3). In short, the Greeks were the first rationalists and therefore the first moderns as we employ the term.

It has been stated that the human brain has been in its present form for at least 200,000 years—with language coming in around 150,000 years ago, art and symbolism appearing 100,000 years ago, and a huge leap forward about 50,000 years ago with the appearance of ritual burials and complex hunting techniques. Fifty thousand years is a very long time to be waiting for the Greeks. What was everyone else doing in the meantime?

"Science as an orderly and rational structure," continues Clagett, "scarcely goes beyond the Greeks into the early history of man. Yet we should be aware of the countless centuries of man's activity before the inception of written records, as well as of the two thousand years or so of 'civilized' activity before the emergence of Greek culture" (15). Clagett summarizes the brief contribution to science that the Babylonians and Egyptians made, which boils down to observational astronomy, calendar making, and rudimentary mathematics and geometry. Yet even these areas of knowledge were employed only in concrete ways and were always attached to eschatology where the gods took center stage. Before the Greeks, there appeared to be little abstract thinking that forms the basis of modern scientific thought. Even so, Clagett glosses over one point: "with the invention of writing, possibly first in the area of Mesopotamia, about the middle of the fourth millennium BC, man stepped over the threshold of civilization" (17). No matter how large a step, however, the pre-Greeks were caught in another intellectual, maybe even pre-intellectual world: "But the sciences of astronomy, mathematics, and surgery did not advance so far in this period that they freed natural inquiry from the strong mythological and magical roots that lay deep in man's cultural past" (32).

Now we have it. The human race, for all those tens of thousands of years before the Greeks, held to an epistemology that was mythological and magical. So what does a mythological and magical mind think about? A more recent historian of science, Andrew Gregory, tells us: "Prior to science, there was technology. People knew how to do many useful things, without understanding quite why they happened, or why natural phenomena occurred. When they attempted to explain their world, it was in terms of myths and anthropomorphic gods" (Gregory 1). Gregory further explains that the creation of myths and gods was an attempt to explain the inexplicable by a pre-scientific mind. "A good example here is the daily passage of the sun across the sky. What do we see, and how do we explain it? To a pre-scientific society, the sun might well be a god driving his chariot across the heavens. Many primitive cosmologies supposed the universe to be hemispherical. There was a flat earth with a hemispherical bowl of the heavens above it. So the sun would disappear in the evening and reappear each morning, but what happened in between was a mystery–the subject of myth" (Gregory 2).

In another modern survey of ancient science we have this delightful approach: "When I try to see the Universe as a Babylonian saw it around 3000 BC, I must grope my way back to my own childhood" (Koestler

19). So now we perceive that mythological and magical thought might be something akin to childlike thought. Darwin and Tylor assure us this is so. "The world of the Babylonians, Egyptians, and Hebrews was an oyster," continues our historian of science, "with water underneath, and more water overhead, supported by the solid firmament. It was of moderate dimensions, and as safely closed in on all sides as a cot in the nursery or a babe in the womb" (Koestler 19). It sounds so sweet and innocent and childlike, as if the human mind, according to our Darwinist conventions, was still in embryo. According to these conventions, how could it not be? "Some six thousand years ago, [the] human mind was still half asleep" (Koestler 20).

Despite countless centuries of human beings thinking in mythological and magical ways a transition occurred in the mind, or as one of our historians asserts, "At some point, a new and more critical attitude came about. People began to reject myths and explanations in terms of the gods as arbitrary and fanciful. Instead, they began to use theories for which they could gather evidence and debate the merits. . . . Thunder and lightning were to be explained in terms of storm clouds, and not the anger of the gods" (Gregory 2). Please notice how our historian of science summarizes the transition from the mythological mind to the rational and abstract mind: "*At some point.*" Here are three words that can make any shadowy corner of obscure history sound like the cue for an opening act without really bothering to look behind the curtain. One must ask, at which point? More important, how did these ancient minds get to that point? For our historian the point of transition is, of course, the Greeks: "When and where this transformation occurred is relatively easy to pin down. The first steps towards scientific explanation were taken in ancient Greece around 600 BC. Prior to that, the Babylonians and the Egyptians had evolved advanced technologies, but had not progressed beyond mythological explanations" (Gregory 3).

It does not matter to which textbook of science one turns, for almost all say the same thing regarding the history of science: before the Greeks there were pre-scientific communities who attempted to describe the inexplicable in terms of gods and chariots, myths and magic, using minds that were half asleep. Notice the modern mortar being slopped between the scant bricks of pre-history. Being that pre-history constitutes ninety-nine percent of all human history, these very wide and all encompassing masonry strokes of our human past remain the definitive and authoritative account of pre-historic man.

These are grandiose assumptions predicated on so little material that one can only wonder why post-modern scholars have not been more critical? More inconvenient is the fact that not only does our vast historical tapestry have large empty spaces with insufficient material, but also there are portions that are completely out of place with no explanation at all. Let us return to the passing comment of Marshall Clagett, which is essentially similar to our last historian's explanation "at some point." Somehow, Clagett tells us, writing was discovered and civilization came about. Here is a sentence that should shake the foundations of all things we consider historical! Out of vast stretches of hunter-gatherer existence appears writing and civilization. Now that is a thunderclap.

The astute observer must ask the obvious question: "How did it happen? Especially with minds that were half-asleep?" Unfortunately, all this comes about three millennia before the Greeks. If only the Greeks had invented writing and civilization then we truly could have our "one grand system." Yet the Greeks did not invent these things; on the contrary, they were the inheritors of a long tradition which, by the way, was always trying to explain nature in a supremely rational way.

One would think that an investigation of the beginning of science, and with it the implication of the rational abstract mind required for modern theoretical approaches, would not begin with the Greeks but with the culture and mind that invented writing. If there was ever a transition in human history it was the turning point of writing: "Many scholars have pointed out that the alphabet is the miracle of miracles, the greatest of all inventions, by which even the television and jet-planes pale in comparison, and, as such, a thing absolutely unique in time and place" (*TC* 458). The emergence of writing has had more impact on human culture and civilization than anything else ever produced by the mind of our species. Writing allows for the projection of the human mind in all areas of life over vast spans of time and space. It allows for the exponential growth of standardization; hence laws, contracts, weights and measures, technologies, and liturgies can be set down before an ever-growing intellectual class in charge of promoting each of these areas throughout civilization. Indeed, as several scholars have pointed out, civilization and the ancient state cannot be separated from the advent of writing (Lundquist 192-93). Writing provides for the growth of knowledge in completely new ways.

For all these reasons and more, many scholars believe writing began with the needs of the state, and particularly with economics. Yet as Ian Shaw points out, "Most examples of early [Egyptian] writing are associated with the funerary cult and are not records of economic activities from settlements" (Shaw 81). Much of the earliest writing is religious in nature and one cannot help but see that the writing that expanded the power of kings and markets belonged to the cosmology of a hierocentric universe, for the gods also claimed writing as their domain. On a lintel in the great temple at Edfu is a depiction "showing four kneeling figures giving praise to the heavenly book descending to earth; hieroglyphs above their heads show them to represent *Sia* and *Hw*, or the Divine Intelligence and the Divine Utterance (the Word) by which the world was created" (*TC* 454). Here we have the Egyptian conception of the origin of writing—it is a gift from the gods descending from heaven.

More important, how did writing evolve? Like everything else regarding the ancient past, our theorists have applied Darwinian thinking. First, according to the standard conventions, was the pictograph. Early man drew a picture representing some thing. Indeed, early theories about picture writing held that such pictures are simple and easily read by any spectator viewing the picture. Others looking at the real complexities of picture writing have contradicted all of this now. Alan Gardiner writes, "True picture writing makes excessive demand upon the skill and ingenuity of the writer, and its results are far from unambiguous" (cited in *TC* 459). In other words the pictures are being used as symbols, the very basis of alphabetic writing. Furthermore, no two scholars can agree on the meanings of any of the picture writings, contrary to the oft-repeated mantra that early picture writing is easy to understand.

Did writing evolve, as Darwin would declare, by slow gradations and steps from pictures to symbols (like the clay tokens of which writing is supposed to have been the offshoot) to alphabetic script? Such thinking is implausible. As Nibley observes, "If writing evolved gradually and slowly as everything is supposed to have done, there should be a vast accumulation of transitional scribblings as countless crude and stumbling attempts at writing would leave their marks on stone, bone, clay, and wood over countless millennia of groping trial and error. Only there are no such accumulations of primitive writing anywhere. Primitive writing is as illusive as that primitive language, the existence of which has never been attested" (*TC* 454). In short, when writing appears (much like life and mind), it appears as a complete and complex system already fully formed. It appears in a thunderclap.

As such, the origin of writing is something upon which no one can agree. John Noble Wilford writes a summary of a symposium on the origins of writing held at the University of Pennsylvania in 1999. Wilford, a journalist writing for the *New York Times,* admits, "In exchanging interpretations and new information, the scholars acknowledged that they still had no fully satisfying answers to the most important questions of exactly how and why writing was developed. Many of them favored a broad explanation of writing's origins in the visual arts, pictograms of things being transformed into increasingly abstract symbols for things, names and eventually words in speech" (Wilford, par. 6). While many scholars believed the pictogram idea, some did not. Moreover, "their views clashed with a widely held theory among archeologists that writing grew out of the pieces of clay in assorted sizes and shapes that Sumerian accountants had used as tokens to keep track of livestock and stores of grain" (Wilford, par. 6). Now even the idea of market tokens serving as the source for writing lays in dispute. Finally, our news writer admits, "The scholars at the meeting also conceded that they had no definitive answer to the question of whether writing was invented only once and spread elsewhere or arose independently several times in several places, like Egypt, the Indus Valley, China" (Wilford, par. 7). In short, the origin of writing has no real answers, and all the Darwinian appliqué is really an attempt to cover over our ignorance, which is both vast and surprising.

Many historians of science insist that the mythological mind is completely separated from the rational, scientific mind. The Greeks were the progenitors of science because they were able to make complete abstract and theoretical statements about the world unattached to religious cult or gods. But what is writing if not the real beginnings of the abstract and theoretical? Early systems of writing turn out to be very complex with glyphs and symbols in composite relationships, situated in rows that can be read forward, backward, up, down, and around, by which sounds, thoughts, ideas, and complete intellectual constructs are represented. Individual symbols of writing may have multiple meanings, including numeric, geometric, cultic, and even astronomical correspondences. How could this all be put together by a mythological mind that is half asleep?

This problem only grows when one recognizes the sheer genius and complexity of early scripts. It is interesting to note the difficult trail modern linguists had to follow in order to decipher Egyptian hieroglyphs. Many assume that as soon as the Rosetta Stone was discovered translation of Egyptian from the Greek was a simple, straightforward process.

Nothing could be further from the truth. Scholars worked for long years in dead-end attempts, mostly because they did not perceive that the hieroglyphs *could be read in multiple ways* (e.g. phonetically and ideographically). It was not until Jean-François Champollion came along, with his knowledge of Greek, Latin, Hebrew, Chaldean, Syriac, Ethiopic, Arabic, and Coptic, that the true breakthrough of sign translation began. Even still, the process required a genius of intuition that neither the Rosetta Stone nor scholarly training could provide.

The standard explanation as to how Champollion deciphered Egyptian writing recounts his suspicion that the hieroglyphs held phonetic values. He collected the names of Egyptian royalty identified in the archaic script by the "cartouche," or circular "name-ring" that surrounded proper nouns. He compared an ancient Greek translation to some of these names and worked out the phonetic value for some of the hieroglyphs. Using this process as a baseline, Champollion was able to assign phonetic values to many of the individual signs of the script—and the process of translation had begun.

Why did Champollion suspect the ancient writing contained phonetic correspondences? Our illustrious scholar did not work in a vacuum and was using research from previous linguists trying to crack the code (e.g., Thomas Young and John Åkerblad). Perhaps more interesting, Champollion had a text in his possession recounting the words of Clement of Alexandria centuries earlier: "Those among the Egyptians who receive instruction learn first of all the kind of Egyptian letters called epistolographic; and second the hieratic, which is used by the hierogrammats; and finally the hieroglyphic kind. [There are two kinds of] hieroglyphic letters: one is curiological, making a first use of alphabetic letters; the other is symbolic" (*TK* 17).

Clement signifies that hieroglyphics can be read in two ways, one in the form of alphabetic letters (i.e., phonetically), and the other symbolically. Of this latter category Clement continues, "One literally represents the objects by imitation; another expresses them by trope (in a figurative manner); a third exclusively uses allegories expressed by certain enigmas" (*TK* 17). For example, the hieroglyphs could be read ideographically: a circle representing the sun and a crescent representing the moon. They could also be read as a trope: an arm holding a weapon meaning "combat" and an arm holding a jar meaning "offering." Or they could be read symbolically: an ostrich feather representing truth and justice because an ostrich is said to have an equal amount of feathers on each side of his body; or the Earth represented by Geb, the goose, because the male goose can actually lay an egg of which the Earth is a type. When Champollion applied his extensive knowledge of other languages to the script, with the Rosetta Stone before him, he still may have failed. The key to translation was not just the Rosetta Stone but also the essential idea presented by Clement of Alexandria that the hieroglyphs could be read in multiple ways–alphabetically, ideographically, figuratively, and symbolically.

Yet even our briefest of examples in the hieroglyphic signs brings up another point in this miracle of written language—many of the hieroglyphs (such as the feather or the goose) retain their meanings only because the writers of the script clearly knew the attributes, features, and habits or cycles of the natural world at an astonishing level. We are reminded of Lévi-Strauss's observation that "people who are without writing have a fantastically precise knowledge of their environment and all their resources." It turns out this acute knowledge was poured into the hieroglyphic script. The ibis, the hawk, the beetle, the serpent, and a host of other images all come complete with the ideas not only of the thing represented, but of their entire life cycle as observed by specialists. Lucie Lamy writes:

> Most of the plants and animals which are represented in the hieroglyphic writing are of southern, Nilotic origin; and Old Kingdom bas-reliefs show us that a great number of these species

were imported from the regions of the Upper Nile. . . . From other figurations we can see that these creatures were kept in vast aviaries and in large parks surrounded by high walls: the oldest known zoos, in which the Egyptians could study at their leisure the life and habits of the animals which they chose as symbols to figure in their writing. Each animal embodies a specific function, and it is for this reason that a particular animal was chosen as the attribute of a given divinity or of an abstract notion: a migratory bird, for example, the symbol and specific sign of *ba*, which we translate roughly as "soul." (Lamy 72)

It is not surprising, therefore, to find the foundations of the world's first apparent zoo in Hierakonpolis, Egypt, dating to at least 3500 BCE (Rose, vol. 63, I).

When we add images such as the Was scepter, the Ankh, the Djed pillar, the Uraeus, and the Ben-ben stone, we are seeing highly complex and intelligent correlations between the signifier and its meaning. In the case of the natural world, many of these signifiers have been corroborated by years, if not generations, of poignant observations on the one hand, and metaphysical projections of a highly intuitive kind on the other. It turns out that picture writing is both elegant and highly intelligent.

Cuneiform script—wedge-shaped characters produced in Mesopotamia—follows these same complex and multilayered patterns. The Assyriologist Jean Bottéro informs us that the Assyro-Babylonian script contains both ideograms and syllabograms, i.e., symbols and phonetics. The script takes on greater complexity when linguists realized that every phonetic value in a word *was itself a word* holding a complex of ideas and images in the minds of the original writers. This is all revealed, for example, in the fifty names given to Marduk in the *Epic of Creation*. When Marduk is called by the name *Asari*, we are given the explanation of the name: "Giver of agriculture, founder of the grid [of fields], Creator of cereals and flax, producer of [all] greenery" (95). Remarkably, one can derive this explanation from the individual phonetic constituents of the name: *a–sar–ri*. As Bottéro notes, "The fundamental and central value of the character *a* is 'water.' It seems that the [ancient] scholars referred to this 'water,' by an indirect way of reasoning, when they mentioned the grid (of the fields)" (95). The grid of the fields is the irrigation canals where water sustained the crops. Likewise, *sar* signifies cereals, flax, greenery, and production, while *ri*, or *rá* signifies "to give;" thus in the name *Asari* we have a complex of ideas which spell out the explanation given in the text.

Bottéro points out that every cuneiform character or phonetic sound has a constellation of meanings associated with it. They are determined by signifiers within the text or context within the spoken language. "The phoneme *du*, for instance, corresponded to a good dozen of signs which were different, but which referred to objects that were in their designations more or less homophonous, if not homonymous. *'Foot,' production, ruins, blow, goodness, to speak*, and still others were all pronounced more or less like *du*" (91). The ideograms in cuneiform become symbolic much as the Egyptian hieroglyphs are symbolic. The meaning is embedded in an archaic metaphysics: "the multi-valence of the signs, their polysemy as linguists would say, goes back in effect to the original pictography and to the obligation of organizing around each of them a 'semantic constellation' based on the things themselves and on their real or imaginary interrelations" (99-100). Like the Maat feather or the egg of Geb, an *a priori* metaphysics is infused into ideographic script: "However strange, even aberrant, such a vision of things, such a treatment of the signifying and the signified, and such a realistic and simple agreement between written signs and words and things may seem to us, they are nothing less than rooted in the very origins of the script" (100).

If so much can be associated with so little, how can the meaning of these ancient scripts be apprehended? When it comes to Egyptian hieroglyphs, for example, and despite the Rosetta Stone, and the genius of Champollion, the truth is a full understanding of hieroglyphs still eludes scholars, for *translation implies understanding*. Champollion transmitted technical aspects of the grammar and phonetics to an English equivalent of basic nouns, verbs, and determinatives. But what does any of it mean? Bruno Stricker admits of the Egyptian Book of Breathings, "The text is so pregnant that well-nigh every word, whether substantive, verb, or even preposition, possesses a hidden (*mystieke*) content. The mere business of translating, under such circumstances becomes virtually impossible. A translation can here be nothing more than a caricature" (cited in *MJSP* 62). Like the Assyrio-Babylonian script, every part of Egyptian writing abounds in a rich complex of meanings. Most of these meanings are hidden behind a cloud of mythological, cosmological, and liturgical epithets that can only be apprehended by the writers themselves within the culture and metaphysics of the writing.

Rolf Gundlach and Wolfgang Schenkel observed that "so far, no one has figured out a way to write Egyptian without hieroglyphics–which means that there are fundamental aspects of the system which still escape us" (cited in *MJSP* 51). Nibley observes, "To this day there is no agreement on the meaning of the most ordinary and familiar phrases in the religious writings" (*MJSP* 53). "It is more than a vast gulf of time that lies between us and the Egyptians—it is an insuperable wall of religion" (*MJSP* 62). The great Egyptologist Adolf Erman laments, "Religion is the *Schmerzenskind* of Egyptology. For half a century I have wrestled with it, and how little certainty has come out of it all! Everyone still invents his own Egyptian religion. . . . One might say that whatever we come up with is wrong, because the task is simply insoluble. I have never been able to escape from this verdict" (cited in *MJSP* 62).

Clement of Alexandria was right: much of the hieroglyphic writing was symbolic and associated with peculiar enigmas of Egyptian thought. Bottéro confirms this same realization with cuneiform script and its implied constellation of meanings. Remarkably, we have the words of an ancient Egyptian from the Eighteenth Dynasty on this very topic: "I was educated in the god's book and I looked on the tools of Thoth; I was prepared in their secrets and I delved into all their difficult passages" (Naydler 142-43). We also have the words of Amenemhet Surer, also of the Eighteenth Dynasty, as he declares himself the "master of the secrets of the divine words" (Naydler 143). The "tools of Thoth" and the "divine words" are hieroglyphs. In these passages we are given a glimpse of their true nature, for they contained "secrets" at the center of Egyptian ideology; thus the "difficult passages" are really a form of technical jargon employed by specialists.

What is the content of and context for this ancient, technical jargon? Is it all just a macabre fixation on death and the afterlife and religious bugaboo? Or was there a technical philosophy to be found, if not, dare we say, a form of science? On this latter question the agreement between modern orthodoxy is a resounding "No!"—despite the fact that our modern-day scholars have just confessed that they have no idea. Whenever these questions come up in academic debate the tendency is to relegate them to the pseudo-scholarship or alien conspiracy crowds.

The Paradox of Egypt

As a result, when it comes to the Great Pyramid at Giza, for example, the leading theories of solemn and dignified scholars are twofold: one, the greatest complexity of the object comes by way of social structure; and two, the pyramid is only a royal tomb with interior chambers that came about by accidental happenstance. On the first front, we are told, the greatest achievement revealed in the Great Pyramid is the social, economic, and political structures required for the building of the edifice. Indeed, large labor forces, foodstuffs, materials, payments, contracts, and schedules would be required to construct the tomb, along with the organizational and bureaucratic "paperwork." We are told that this is the true genius behind the pyramid. On the second front, modern Egyptologists assure us that all the interior spaces of the Great Pyramid came about one at a time as the builders recognized that they could keep building higher and higher chambers at a grander scale as they progressed. Thus, the underground chamber was meant as the original tomb, but after piling a million multi-ton blocks on top of this chamber, someone thought that an upper level chamber might be better. And after constructing the Queen's Chamber, they again wondered if they could create a higher tomb chamber to replace the one they just built. In short, the interior of the building was designed as it was built.

As utterly absurd as the Conspiracy crowd can be, the pronouncements of academia sometimes rival by sheer obtuseness the dialectics of common sense. It is certain that a considerable social and economic structure had to be in place in order to construct an object like the Great Pyramid. However, such a social structure did not appear overnight, but was already in place. It had to be in place to oversee the construction of previously built canals, temples, city walls, caravans, armies, fleets, large-scale festivals, and practically every other aspect of Egyptian civilization. It may be true that the construction of the Great Pyramid tested the limits of the organizational strata, created new relationships between nomes, and expanded organizational constructs beyond what they had been. A larger bureaucracy and social structure, however, cannot land a man on the Moon. Only determination, imagination, creativity, intelligence, and science can do that. Government may take a leading role in the project, but in the end it too must yield to the laws of physics.

One does not have to be an academic or a believer in aliens to automatically sense that the genius of the Great Pyramid lies in its engineering, geometry, and mathematics. Whatever its religious purpose or significance to the population, and whatever its proto-intellectual or mythological rationale, one thing is certain, serious and sober minds constructed it, working with all the science of the age. The builders had to assemble 2,200,000 blocks of stone, several of them weighing 70 tons, into an artificial mountain 40 stories high and measuring 230 meters square with a maximum deviation between measures being less than 20 centimeters. The entire structure was oriented to the true cardinal directions within three arc minutes, or one-twentieth of a degree, and crafted with a 51° 51' slope (1/7th of 360 degrees) retaining the dimensions of the Pythagorean triangle. Meanwhile, its interior chambers include small and precisely cut shafts hidden within the superstructure whose existence has never been satisfactorily explained. The best theory still concludes that they are aligned to specific stars central to Egyptian cosmology. The entire pyramid, therefore, is not only oriented to the cardinal points but also to specific stellar locales.

Not all the social-economic-bureaucratic machinations in the universe can construct only what a mathematician and engineer can. The suggestion that the interior chambers and shafts were built as afterthoughts during the construction is also ludicrous, as any carpenter or plumber can authoritatively explain, "You cannot put the trusses in the closet or install the drain on the curtains." Massive and complex structures have to be meticulously pre-planned and designed before construction begins. In fact, the suggestion that the building was planned as it was built contradicts the assertion that its greatest contribution to civilization was a complex managerial system. If the builders were repeatedly changing the design as it was built, there would be a profuse number of changes in the materials, labor, tools, and foodstuffs. The constant disheveling of design, materials, and labor is not solved by adding more middle-managers, scribes, and bankers to the payroll. The solution can only be accomplished through a precise building schematic, pre-planning, and clear-headed thinking.

Why do Egyptologists offer such understated theories? Because there truly is so much pseudo-scholarship in all things Egyptian that mainstream academics play it safe and dutifully follow the Darwinian demands of history. They believe that the Egyptians were pre-Greek and therefore possessed minds that were pre-analytical and wholly mythological. Because all of the precise measurement, geometry, and mathematics of the pyramids served only religious needs, we can put their skills into a different filing cabinet when we consider the history of science and thinking. Thus, the great historian of science Otto Neugebauer declares, "Egypt has no place in a work on the history of mathematical astronomy" (Magli 69) and that "mathematics and astronomy played a uniformly insignificant role in all periods of Egyptian history" (Neugebauer 71).

As already stated, Neugebauer is defining mathematics and astronomy under wholly modern conceptions. He considers "true" math to be only the kind that is analytical and abstract, and quips, "The mathematical requirements for even the most developed economic structures of antiquity can be satisfied with elementary household arithmetic which no mathematician would call mathematics" (Neugebauer 71-72). Like so many other scholars of his era, Neugebauer is essentially missing the point.

How does an orally trained society develop strict analytical and abstract mathematics? The question is like asking, how does a herring climb over the Andes? Or, how does an eagle swim the Atlantic Current? The assumptions behind all these questions are flawed. As we will discuss in the next chapter, orality gives structure to thought, but there are some things an oral mind cannot perform. Oral thinkers are not capable of analytical and abstract mathematics as employed by modern mathematicians. This does not mean, however, that oral thinkers are incapable of highly sophisticated thinking, even to a degree that rivals the greatest thinkers of any era. Neugebauer conflates the oral mind with primitive thinking, like all good Darwinists; thus, he never considers oral science for what it was, perhaps because he never expects to find a herring climbing a mountain peak or an eagle swimming a current.

A slight check on our own vision, however, can quickly change the scenario. Herrings really can climb over mountain peaks because such things exist under the water. Eagles can fly in currents because such things exist in the sky. It is our modern conceptions that are skewed. The mathematics built in the design of the Great Pyramid are based on basic geometric principles; on that point Neugebauer is right. Yet what are basic geometric principles? These are not self-evident, and years of serious and sober thinking are required to consistently place key geometric relationships within large stone structures. These relationships were not arbitrary, but mimicked invariant numbers embedded in observable astronomical and musical measures.

Household arithmetic did not build the Pyramid. The entire conception emerged from an oral cosmovision that appeared like a thunderclap on the historical horizon. In the words of Joseph Campbell:

> And then, with stunning abruptness, at a crucial date that can be almost precisely fixed at 3200 BC . . . the whole cultural syndrome that has since constituted the germinal unit of all of the high civilizations of the world [appeared]. . . . The new inspiration of civilized life was based, first, on the discovery, through long and meticulous, carefully checked and rechecked observations, that there were, besides the sun and moon, five other visible or barely visible heavenly spheres (to wit, Mercury, Venus, Mars, Jupiter, and Saturn) which moved in established courses, according to established laws, along the ways followed by the sun and moon, among the fixed stars; and then, second, on the almost insane, playful, yet potentially terrible notion that the laws governing the movements of the seven heavenly spheres should in some mystical way be the same as those governing the life and thought of men on earth. The whole city, not simply the temple area, was now conceived as an imitation on earth of the cosmic order. (*Primitive* 146-7)

The Great Pyramid has always been claimed to be one of the ancient wonders of the world. However, in between the stones lies the true miracle, for its construction required a cultural zeal akin to a form of cosmic Manifest Destiny and an intellectual gravitas seeking to push the limits of all the reason and science of the oral age. The mathematics of the Pyramid could not take a man to the moon, but that was not the intention. The mathematics of the Great Pyramid and scores of other sacred sites sought to bring the moon and stars down to man, where all macrocosmic processes were analogically copied in stone and ritual throughout the high civilizations of antiquity: "it can be said without exaggeration that all the high civilizations of the world are to be thought of as the limbs of one great tree, whose root is in heaven" (*Primitive* 149).

Several Egyptian texts inform us that the building of any temple complex followed proscribed rules that had been handed down from the earliest dynasties (*TK* 66-67). One of the first rituals done in the laying of a temple was the Stretching of the Cord ceremony; part of this is recorded at Dendera, "Watching the sky and at the celestial objects' rising movements, once identified the *Ak* of the constellation of the Bull's Foreleg, I calculated the angles of the temple" (Magli 85). The constellation mentioned is the Big Dipper, though the meaning of *Ak* is still unknown. Most scholars believe the term is related to the different positions of the Big Dipper around the celestial north pole throughout the year.

The essential founding of a temple begins by measuring and aligning it to true north. Yet this was just part of the process. An inscription at Abydos declares, "I have stretched the cord at the location of its walls. . . . Thoth was there with his books. . . . In order to establish the enclosure of its walls, Ptah-Tatenen measured the ground . . . thou wert with me in the form of Hunu [the neter of geometry], thy two arms held the mattock; thus the four angles were established as solidly as the four pillars of heaven" (*TK* 67). Another inscription at Edfu reads, "I have grasped the cord with Sefekht; my gaze has followed the course of the stars. My eye was turned toward the Great Bear, I have measured the time and counted [the hour] by the clepsydra, and then have I established the four angles of thy temple" (*TK* 67).

The constant references to "watching the sky" while constructing their temples places the Egyptian conception of sacred space squarely within a framework of cosmic harmony. The Great Pyramid's "star shafts" pointing to specific stellar locales adumbrates this point; as already noted, the building is not just aligned to the cardinal directions with uncanny accuracy but is also oriented to a cosmic grid central to the Egyptian cosmovision. For an oral mind such a cosmovision is the science of the age. Enormous resources and ingenious methods were used to calculate this science. For example, the curious and declining entry passage into the Great Pyramid illustrates an astronomical intention. The passage is only 3'6" wide by 3'11" tall, and it extends an incredible 345 feet into the subterranean foundations of the structure. It is slanted at 26 degrees exactly, and the eminent Egyptologist Ludwig Borchardt realized that by standing at its terminal end and looking up and out one would have the largest instrument ever built for measuring stars as they crossed the meridian (*TK* 68).

Astronomical calculations are not the only measures employed in Egyptian tomb and temple building. Harmonic ratios were also built into stone, whereby the ratios of the musical scale were prescribed in the overall architecture. One writer observes:

Significant points [in Egyptian temples] mark the intersection with transverse axes, the alignment of a central doorway, the position of an altar, the center of the sanctuary, etc. These significant points follow a precise arithmetic progression. In many of the best plans, these significant points are at harmonic distances from one another, and their distances from one end to the other express the figures of the Summation (so-called Fibonacci) Series. (Gadalla 116)

According to Egyptian temple texts, not only are the temples calculated with divine measures (i.e., geometry and harmony) and astronomical orientations, but they are also measured using time itself. Water clocks were utilized in conjunction with astronomical observations. Other writings assert the need to build temples on specific months, days, and hours, generally in accordance to key moments during the solar, lunar, or astral cycles. In many sacred sites, earth-sky relationships that were modeled within them had to be exact both spatially and temporally. The calendar was essential to the corpus of knowledge wed to the city-state and its engineering plans in a way that is unfamiliar to modern thought.

The fact that a host of mythological deities must show up at the founding of these edifices—all that have stewardship over an essential and sacred knowledge of measure and number—reveals that behind the masks of their religion a serious and sober logic existed. This paradox vexes modern interpretations of ancient religion. Thoth, Ptah-Tatenen, Hunu, and Sefekht appear not only with their ritualistic incantations, for which men like Neugebauer relegate them to the pre-scientific past of myth and magic, but they also show up with their books, tools, and measures, by which things like the Great Pyramid appear out of the sand.

When it comes to the Great Pyramid there are still three looming issues that have not been resolved. First, no Egyptologist can tell us what the Great Pyramid really meant to the Egyptians. In order to know this, we would have to know what all the chambers, halls, passages, and orientations signified; today only contradictory opinion exists. Second, no one can tell us how they built it. When judging the intellect of the mythological age, one would think this would be important.

Last, and most important, when it comes to something like the Great Pyramid we are faced with a dichotomy intrinsic in the blank portions of our historical puzzle. One would expect that such a complex building would require a pre-planned schematic. Yet where are the blueprints?

One expects layers of diagrams and building templates written down and reviewed at every stage of the project. No doubt written references were used, but in all the directions for building, we are given ritualistic imagery, not technical lists of materials and processes. The latter requires abstract thinking which Neugebauer is looking for but cannot find. The people who built the Great Pyramid, however, lived in the oral age of mythological tropes. Even with writing, it was the oral mind that built the pyramids.

If one contemplates this realization for a while only amazement and awe can result. How does one build something like the Great Pyramid without all the blueprints that modern architects would use? By all accounts, they used a rope, a rock, a stick, a series of chants, dances, and rituals, and an oral science of measure and number tied to astronomy and harmony. This is only one side of our dichotomy. The other side is the realization that hieroglyphic writing must have aided in the construction of the edifice as the increase in architectural complexity throughout Egypt coincided with the introduction and expansion of writing. If this is true then there must be another level of understanding behind the gods and their letters—a side that goes beyond solely religious considerations. The Stretching of the Cord texts assure us this is so. This also means that despite all of our modern translations of this ancient writing, there are fundamental aspects of it that have been permanently lost.

When we look at what is left of ancient Egyptian arts, crafts, industry, and civil planning, not to mention the use of metallurgy, irrigation systems, and engineering projects, what we see is a highly capable, rational, intelligent people—which not only contradicts the Darwinian paradigm, it renders it meaningless. In the end, it might come as a shock to us to realize that when the Egyptians built the Great Pyramid they were *not* saying, "Hey, look at us world; we are so religious." Rather, and more important, their imprint in the sand may have another message altogether: "Hey, look at us, all ye peoples of the earth, for we are the greatest intellectuals to have ever lived." It is somewhat comical to observe that in just a few thousand years these peoples have been relegated to the pre-rational past.

Myth and Reason

Egypt was not the only highly organized and intelligent, ancient civilization. The empires existing in Mesopotamia rival the complexities of Egypt. From ancient Mesopotamia we get such things as multiplication and square tables, a sexagesimal and decimal numeric system, and pre-algebra. We also discover ziggurats, libraries, and complex city planning. Everywhere throughout Mesopotamia we also find the gods and goddesses wed to astronomical and harmonic tropes.

We are told that the Greek Pythagoras was the first person to work out the numeric ratios of the harmonic scale and describe the world by using number. Not all is as it seems. The musician Ernest McClain, in a 1994 article entitled "Musical Theory and Ancient Cosmology" shares a startling insight about Babylonian myth that has gone essentially unnoticed. In many ancient scripts, characters and names have numeric values. It turns out that each god of the Babylonian pantheon has a numerical value associated with its name. These start with the sky god Anu, whose numerical value is 60. In a base 60 system, however, 60 also represents 1, which is a whole or starting point. The other gods have various values: Bel-Enlil is 50, Ea-Enki is 40, Sin is 30, Ishtar is 15, Marduk is 10. All this is well known, but what McClain shows is that if one divides these numbers into the base 60 (Anu), one gets the numeric ratios of the harmonic scale. Realizing this makes one also aware "how every element of Pythagorean tuning theory was implicit in the mathematics and mythology of [Babylon] for at least a thousand years, and perhaps two thousand, before Greek rationalists finally abstracted what we are willing to recognize as science from its long incubation within mythology" (par. 4).

While not all civilizations are equal, it is also true that there were similarly advanced groups spread throughout the ancient world, such as we also find in Crete, the Indus Valley, and ancient China. What separates modern man from ancient man is not intellectual capacity. One of the great divides between "us" and "them" is literacy. One must constantly be reminded that ancient civilizations were oral civilizations. Despite the presence of numerous hieroglyphic and cuneiform texts, most people could not read or write. Literacy was reserved for an initiated class of priests representing a minute percentage of the population. Even those who could read and write were still operating within the framework of oral thought discussed in the next chapter.

As already noted of the Egyptians, how does an oral society pass down its knowledge of higher forms of learning? How do oral peoples create, maintain, and pass down a solar, lunar, and stellar calendar? How do such people embed geometric and astronomical designs of high complexity within their architecture, without the use of massive blue prints, manuals, and books? How do they pass down knowledge of the basis of these things: the science of number, angles, ratios, measures, harmonics, and weights without writing?

This is no easy task, and these questions have been left unanswered and even unexplored by most historians of science. Contrarily, Giorgio de Santillana gives us something to consider:

Science, at all times, involves a technical language which can hardly be understood if it is not even recognized. Nobody can interpret farther than he understands, nor can anyone translate technical terms from an utterly foreign language if he is not first acquainted with the corresponding technical terms in his own. This should strike one as rather elementary. The vast amount of ancient Near Eastern and related "mythological" texts are at best obscure and ambiguous, often strangely incongruous. The most refined philological methods in the hands of expert philologists will yield only childish stuff out of them, if childish stuff is expected. Technical indications which would make clear sense to scientists go unnoticed or mistranslated. (*Origins* 11)

De Santillana writes several books and articles reconsidering the modern paradigm of ancient thought. His most popular work, *Hamlet's Mill*, which was co-authored with Hertha von Dechand, is a cornucopia of mythological fragments given cosmological interpretations. In another work, *The Origins of Scientific Thought*, de Santillana gives one example of what kind of technicalities Egyptologists miss when not familiar with astronomy:

To take a simple example: in an otherwise excellent and authoritative work on Egypt we find that the Sun, Amun Ra, stands in tradition as Egypt's first king, which shows Egypt's culture to have been sun-centered as all proper agrarian cultures are. But elsewhere the author has to admit that a still earlier god-king was Ptah, Lord of Memphis, the original capital of the 'United Kingdom' (Upper and Lower Egypt). He leaves us–and himself– to conclude that Ptah was another version of the Sun. Still, there is a demotic ostracon not to be ignored which actually states the star of Ra to be [Cronos], i.e. Saturn. We are led to suppose that the Sun had been superimposed on the original role of Saturn; the more so as astronomical cuneiform tablets call Saturn by the name of the Sun, Shamash, and as there is sufficient reason to take the Greek Sun for [Cronos] wherever he is spoken of as 'Helios the Titan.' Irrelevant, say the well-specialized philologists: it is only the matter of a late ostracon, and good method teaches us to discount anything late. Well and good, but they might have taken into account that Ptah, from the beginning, bears the title of 'Lord of the Thirty-Year Cycle.' It would be enough to show that, whether it be early or late, the ostracon is to the point. A check would have shown them that it is explicitly confirmed by Hyginus, Astronomica 42, and Diodorus 2.30.3. This in turn might have led them to discover many further remarkable connections which had been systematically ignored; e.g. in China (surely another agrarian state) Saturn was the Imperial Star. (*Origins* 11-12)

Behind the imagery of Ptah lies not just a religious but especially a cosmological metaphor. His title of "Lord of the Thirty-Year Cycle" analogizes him with Saturn, the planet that takes thirty years to complete one revolution in the sky as seen from Earth. Yet, his relation to Saturn is only part of the cosmology. As originator of the arts and crafts, Ptah was additionally known as the "Great Architect of the World," and his depiction as a mummified pillar is sometimes analogized with the axis of the world. He is often depicted standing on a plinth in the shape of the hieroglyph for *maat* or "truth," which is also recognized as the symbol for the cubit and measuring rod. Ptah has seven sons who help him fashion the world. We do not know how his seven sons aided him, but perhaps they are analogous to the seven stars of the Big Dipper whose observation and measure was central to the construction of the temples. Conceptually the construction of any temple was homologous to remaking the world. Ptah's arts and crafts were needed, but especially his numbers and astronomical measures. His cubit of truth is not only a measure of distance but also a measure of angle and degree as the temple is oriented to the sacred world (cardinal points, true north, and stellar locales). Behind the myth and religion of Egypt is not a proto-intellectual primitivism, but a highly rational cosmology radically different than our own and entirely predicated upon the rules of orality.

Ptah and his seven sons are not the only world builders in ancient myth. The Sumerian culture hero Gilgamesh founds the city of Uruk with the help of seven heavenly masters who are said to "sparkle in the sky." Gilgamesh employs these masters to build the seven walls of Uruk in accordance with the seven firmaments of the oral cosmos. It is truly remarkable that after Gilgamesh descends through the cosmic underworld to find the secrets of immortality and eternal life he returns to Uruk with Ur-Shanabi, the underworld boatman, to measure the walls and foundations of the city. No scholar has ever understood this passage in the surviving text, but we should be put on notice that the cosmic boatman is the only one who can verify the correct measurements of the temple and its city. We are dealing with a part of ancient cultus, similarly in Egypt, that required measures of both heaven and earth and that have been veiled in mythological tropes.

In Greek myth these cosmological connections survive. Cronos overthrows Uranous and Zeus overthrows Cronos. Yet, Uranous is the primeval matrix of creation and his name means *the heavens*. If Cronos is actually the planet Saturn we can see how he overthrows the heavens by cutting Uranous up during his thirty-year circuit as he moves through the ecliptic. Neither is Zeus a simple thunder god: his Roman name was Jupiter and his relation to the planet should be clear. In fact, in Aristotle's work, *On the Universe*, he clearly identifies Cronos with the planet Saturn and Zeus with the planet Jupiter. This entire conception most likely descends from Babylon, where Marduk, also a god of thunder, was represented as the planet Jupiter.

Embedded in these myths is an indication of a change of time reckoning: Jupiter overthrows Saturn, while a stellar cosmology implicit in the older deities gives way to a solar cosmology associated with newer gods. More important, the creator gods belong to a matrix of meaning extending well beyond religious considerations. Like the earliest scripts, each god and goddess comes complete with a host of inferences known only to the people who created them, many of those connections being linked with a technical language and skill rooted in the needs of the ancient state—for example, calendar making and temple construction.

We need not consider this observation without root within the technical language of ancient myth itself. There is just such an example of this possibility preserved by Plato in his work *Timaeus*. According to this dialogue, Solon, the wisest of the Greeks visits Egypt where an old Egyptian priest says, "And so also among your people the tale is told that Phaethon, child of the Sun, once harnessed his father's chariot, but was unable to drive it along his father's course. He ended up burning everything on the earth's surface and was destroyed himself when a lightning bolt stuck him" (22c). Our Egyptian priest recites the well-known myth, but then gives this incredible explanation, "This tale is told as a myth, but the truth behind it is that there is a deviation in the heavenly bodies that travel around the earth, which causes huge fires that destroy what is on the earth across vast stretches of time" (22c-d).

According to our ancient priest this myth is not about a historical figure, a psychological archetype, or part of artistic literature, nor is it about corn gods, fetishes, or magical thinking. Astonishingly, the myth of Phaethon is about "a deviation in the heavenly bodies that travel around the earth," where great destructions occur "over vast stretches of time." Who would have guessed? This myth is a reminder to check one's measurements, also implying that there is a science of measurement as well as a very long tradition of making those measurements. More interestingly, our priest tells Solon that this myth is not of Greek origin. "And so also among your people," the priest quips, indicating that the Egyptians must also have this myth. But where do we see it? Nowhere in Egyptian myth and language as we apprehend it, though it may be right in front of our noses.

What is being measured? Our Egyptian priest insists that those things being measured are bodies moving around the earth. One might instantly think of the planets, but one would have to remember that the Egyptians, as well as the Babylonians, were measuring *every* body that moved around the earth. These measurements included the times and seasons of every star rising and setting, as well as when those bodies rose and set with the sun (heliacal risings and settings). They also meticulously measured the orbits of the planets and their movements through the stars. Zenith transits and angular distances of the stellar orbs were also calculated. The entire model and scale of the visible cosmos was fastidiously recorded, mythologized, and ritualized. How does Phaethon relate to any of this? According to one of our historians of science, a chariot pulling the sun across the sky is nothing more than a mythological explanation attempting to describe the inexplicable.

Contrarily, a chariot puller such as Phaethon has an analog in the archetypal chariot helmsman known in Greek myth as Erichthonius. Erichthonius was the first man to build a chariot after the manner of Helios the Sun. His name means "one who is born from the earth," and thus suggests we should be looking for a terrestrial charioteer. Like a great many ancient connections in myth, being earth-born is a celestial affair. The original meaning of the word *Spring,* representing the new season after Winter, meant "to rise up from the ground." The impetus behind the idea was not primarily connected with a plant or pool of water that rises from the earth; instead, it referred to a star that rose up from the horizon (Worthen 178-79). The Sun is also born from the earth, and its birth is hailed upon a background of stars that change throughout the year. We should not be surprised to know that Erichthonius was always associated with a constellation in the sky. He was none other than the Greek *Entoxos,* "the holder of the reigns," which is the modern constellation Auriga, the charioteer. This constellation goes back far before the

Greeks into Babylonian and Akkadian star charts and is always associated with a chariot or charioteer (Olcott 63, 67).

This constellation is also associated with a goat. The brightest star in this constellation is a star of first magnitude, third brightest in the northern hemisphere and fifth brightest overall. Its name is Capella—the goat. Again, according to our Greek sources, this goat is the daughter of Helios and is the very animal that succors Zeus in the cave of nymphs after his birth. The goat's horn is the horn of plenty and its skin is the shield Zeus used to defeat the Titans. According to Euhemerus, this goat was also the wife of Pan who was ravished by Zeus and whose offspring was a boy named Aegipan (Condos 52).

Now what does a falling charioteer like Phaethon have in common with Zeus, or Pan, or a goat—especially as the goat is fundamentally linked with the sustenance and birth of a high god? The goat that nurtures Zeus out of his birthing cave is also the chariot rider that pulls the sun across the sky. In Phaethon's case, he is the earth-born charioteer that rises from the horizon and falls out of the sky when the sun goes askew in the heavens.

In ancient cosmology the world was defined by the movement of the sun across the horizon throughout the year. As one watches the sunrise, one notices that the sun does not rise on the same spot on the horizon. From spring thru summer the sun will drift northward on the horizon stopping at it extreme north position on the day of summer solstice. The sun will drift southward on the horizon stopping at its extreme southern position on the day of winter solstice. The midpoint on the horizon between these two solstices are the days of spring or fall equinox. This movement of the sun was imprinted in ritual. Entire populations of a city or country would gather together in great festivals to celebrate these specific days. The New Year was often the day of spring equinox or winter solstice when sacrifices, dramas, dances, and rituals were performed as they were seen as a cosmic representation of the recreation of the world.

If we looked up and observed the sky at the time of Solon and our Egyptian priest, we would see that the sun rose in the constellation of Aires, the Ram, on the morning of spring equinox. Zeus is often depicted in ancient art wearing a ram or goat skin. In this celestial imagery dramatized upon the horizon we see Zeus (as the sun) crawling out of his cave from his infancy to manhood to inherit Olympus as the sun rises into Aires. Yet when the sun arises out of the earth its light obscures the very faint stars that make up the celestial Ram, thus making it difficult to observe the zodiacal constellation in its role as Creator. Even so, Capella, the goat and charioteer, rises with Aires a little farther to the north and its light can be seen all the way past daybreak and into the early morning. In fact, Capella is the last star standing when all others have faded away. One judges the rise of the sun into the equinoctial colure of Spring (Aires) by watching the charioteer pulling the sun in its right course.

This celestial drama is not constant. Over several centuries the stars that receive the sun on the morning of equinox or solstice will slowly slip out of place and remain buried beneath the horizon as other stars take their place. This motion is called the precession of the equinoxes. Due to a wobble in the Earth's axis, not only do the stellar markers of equinox and solstice change, but the North Star also changes. The fact that Phaethon falls out of his course while pulling the sun strictly implies that Capella no longer is the chariot driver on the morning of spring equinox (Worthen 213-15). The star is no longer seen above the horizon at its appointed hour. According to this myth, Phaeton's seven weeping sisters spilled amber tears and were turned into poplar trees on the banks of the river Eridanus. These seven sisters are none other than the stars called the Heliades that sit above the constellation of a river. These stars were the equinoctial marker for the rising of the sun in Taurus on the morning of spring equinox centuries earlier. In the days of Phaethon they had changed their position on the horizon and were now the equinoctial marker at the heliacal setting, or as the Heliades set in the west at dusk.

This myth is exactly what the Egyptian priest referred to as tracking celestial bodies across the sky whereby great conflagrations are said to occur. These conflagrations are not always terrestrial. When stars are no longer in their place at sunrise (a destruction by fire) and no longer in their place at sunset and have been submerged under the horizon (a destruction by water), then the entire cosmic frame has moved and the earth is out of its peg. Suddenly, the chariot has run amok, the sun has fallen, and upon the shores of the Greek isles was heard the exclamation "Great Pan is dead" (*HM* 276). If this interpretation is correct, then the myth of Phaeton is about the shift of celestial coordinates in the sky due to the precession of the equinoxes. The discovery of this celestial phenomena is accredited to Hipparchus the Greek, but our myth points to an awareness of this phenomena many centuries earlier.

Ever since scholars such as Otto Neugebauer and Franz Kugler destroyed the Pan-Babylonian school of thought and with it the idea of myth as a higher form of metaphysics linked with observational astronomy, few scholars have cared to take a second look into such things. Armed with their impeccable credentials and their razor sharp, Darwinian rapiers, scholars like Neugebauer have fortified an impervious blockade to such thinking. They demand, as all good scientific method does, written documents and sources to prove the knowledge of such things, knowing full well that before the writings of the Greeks no such technical manual of mythology existed. In oral societies technical know-how is literally a secret of the trade, handed down directly from master to apprentice. To demand technical, written documentation from an oral age is to demand a diamond out of a turnip.

Mythological records can give us only hints and whispers. Whatever precious science and philosophy was to be had in the far off times before the Greeks was not written down. Like the herring and the eagle, oral science is not what modern scholars expect. A great many modern scholars therefore assume that no science existed in the age of myth. Nor do these scholars believe that any science could be encoded in temple architecture, liturgy, symbol, or sacred narrative. Complicating these matters is the state of the myths as we have inherited them.

The Greeks came to the fore at a very peculiar time in history, the so-called Axial Age. There is one tool the Greeks had that their forebears did not, and that was a fully phonetic and reductive alphabet (twenty-four characters) complete with vowel representations. They also lived in a time where thinking was rooted in writing. Literacy had replaced orality and *logos* had replaced *mythos*—at least to the degree that fully analytical thought predicated upon written texts was not only achievable but desirable. In the days of the Greeks, myth was already three-quarters dead and on its way out. The Greek scholastics never agreed on the function of myth: many interpreted myth as allegories of natural science, while others believed they were histories in narrative form, and still others thought they were fairy tales. Plato was ambiguous on the subject; he interprets the cosmogony of Zeus and Cronos in purely intellectual terms, though in propping up his argument he references an astronomical tradition (*Cratylus* 396b-c).

For the Greeks that we are familiar with, myth and science had become separate. However, that does not mean that myth was never science. As the Egyptian priest explaining the myth of Phaethon informed, "Ah, Solon, Solon, you Greeks are ever children. There isn't an old man among you. . . . Your souls are devoid of beliefs about antiquity handed down by ancient tradition. Your souls lack any learning made hoary by time" (*Timaeus* 22b-c). The Egyptian priest understood that his religious traditions had descended from generations of human activity embracing the high intellect that is the capacity of every human mind.

It may come as a surprise for our earlier historians of science to consider that the sun being pulled across the sky in a horse-drawn chariot is not just some game of a mythologist with a childlike mind describing the inexplicable. It turns out, aside from our charioteer, four horses most often pull the sun-chariot itself. This is not a fantasy image of a deity rolling across the sky, but of the four carriers of the sun throughout the year—the equinoxes and solstices. There are times when the sun-chariot moves by other means. For example, in the *Book of Enoch* in chapter 72 the sun moves in a chariot carried by the winds. Yet in this same passage we are informed that the sun rises and sets within a series of portals and windows, all within a specified cosmology. Our mythological minds are not creating fantastic tales of architecture, as our historians may want us to believe, but are framing a certain mind-set. The rising and setting sun is being measured against the background of stars which "receive" the sun and constitute the portals and windows. Although the *Book of Enoch* is a late text, it belongs to the ancient Hebrew tradition that is itself mired within the assimilation and dispersion of the Near East. Never at any time is the chariot of the sun a "simple-minded" thing.

We should never believe that all of the ancient star watchers, whose astronomical traditions must go back well before the third millennium BCE, considered the Earth to be flat. Plato reminds us there is a true Earth above the material one. This true Earth is nothing more than the Pythagorean cosmos, with its circling rivers of planetary orbits (*Phaedo* 107d-116a). The Flat Earth could be conceptualized as the ideal plane projected into space (*HM* 58), incorporating the Celestial Equator as it transects the ecliptic marking the point of equinox.

Nor did the ancient mythographers ever believe the world literally rested on an oyster, or a turtle, or an elephant, or on the shoulders of Atlas, or any other absurdity. All of these images resolve via intelligent tropes constructed by oral minds. For example, the Phoenician writer Sanchoniathon gives a Euhemerist view of the Greek gods. In his telling, Atlas was none other than the first Phoenician to lead a colony to Northern Africa. Atlas built a temple on top of a mountain where he studied astronomy. The mountain and the adjoining ocean were named after the man who had resolved the motions of the heavens and was represented by the Greeks as the being who held the Earth and cosmos on his shoulders (Maurice 99). Whether Atlas was a historical figure or not, our ancient writer could not help but introduce the concept of astronomy with this figure, and like our oyster and turtle, we are given a very small peek into an ancient mind-set that associated mythical figures with cosmic frames and cycles. Like ancient scripts, these images are all part of a technical jargon's meaning that has been obscured and broken over the ages.

Intellect and the Human Condition

Cautiously, when I say the "ancient mind," I am speaking only of those specialists who calculated the measures of the cycles of the sky and earth using math, geometry, and harmony, and encoded it all in the symbolism of myth. I am speaking of a small class of people, as de Santillana and von Dechend make clear: "the average Babylonian or Greek showed as little inclination to wonder at order and law in nature as our average contemporaries do. It has been and will be the mark of a true scientific mind to search for, and to wonder at, the invariable structure of number behind the manifold appearances" (61). I am reminded of Lord Raglan's response to H. J. Rose when the latter insisted that mythology was the product of a free mind playing with the imagination and poetically ascribing acts of nature to some superhuman being or demonic power. Raglan counters:

> Professor Rose's myth-maker must have been a very remarkable person. On the one hand, he could not have been an atheist, for then supernatural beings would have had no existence for him, and on the other hand he could not have been a believer, for then the freedom of his imagination must have been trammeled by the nature of his belief. This is no quibble; if a man believes in the

supernatural, he must have some beliefs about it, and if he has beliefs he cannot give free reign to his imagination. All men, both savage or civilized, are bound to accept, or possibly to reject, the beliefs of their day; to only the tiniest minority is it given to go even one inch beyond them. (93)

In short, the majority of people in the past may have been half asleep, as some of our scholars insist, but this reality is not the product of a Darwinian evolution of the mind. A great many people in our own day are half asleep. Modernity does not suffer from the lack of information as much as it is perplexed by too much trivial information. The cultural inundation of inconsequential things inebriates the mind into a half-conscious state. The quiet questions of the soul recede behind the cacophonous white noise of the audiovisual age. Consumerism replaces the cosmology of the sacred; the movie theater and sports stadium overshadow the consecrated grove and cathedral. We live in a world full of technological gadgets, yet nobody knows how they work. Meanwhile, the science of the ancient past was always connected to a metaphysics that was supposed to explain the universe, not through analytical theory, but from concrete objects and phenomena. Myth addressed both the natural world and also the transcendent world—the Real and the Ideal, the physical and the spiritual. Neither modern science nor modern culture has any inclination to do either, for modern science rejects the former and modern culture cannot even distinguish between the two.

Pulling the Darwinian plug from the modern conception of ancient history brings sobering realizations. Perhaps the foremost realization is an echo of what Lévi-Strauss has already observed of the human mind: it is "one and the same and that it has the same capacities" throughout time. We can add to this insight the constancy of *human nature*. Human beings, for tens of thousands of years, have been doing what human beings do, and will continue to do for tens of thousands of years. We eat and sleep and dream. We think and resolve and figure. We make love and write poems and create art. We war, deceive, and destroy.

"We must assume," writes de Santillana, "every age has minds of the order of Archimedes, Kepler, or Newton" (*Origins* 17). We can also rightly assume that every age is fraught with numbing violence and colossal ignorance. When we observe the ancient pyramids we are amazed. When we look at the ancient practice of human sacrifice we sometimes too easily attribute such practices to "primitive" cultures, forgetting that modernity has supplied such barbarity in profusion—the Holocaust to name but one example. The history of the mind is not a linear history. Each epoch has its "Age of Reason" and its "Fall." The apex of human reason is not modernity, but an uneven course of analogous magnifications of the mind between super-human spirits throughout history, few as they are. The human mind resides in a fractal universe where genius and ignorance coexist, and where authentic curiosity and moral courage are always something new.

CHAPTER 2

ORALITY AND LITERACY

Orality

Mind and language have been around since the first homo sapiens were formed out of the biological clay. Language is implicit within consciousness, and all human beings utilize language as the primary medium for thought. In the past five decades scholars have begun to analyze how language can structure thought. Oral cultures—cultures without writing—access different cognitive resources than do literate ones. Writing appears to have been invented some five thousand years ago. This means of course that most of human history has existed within orality. Despite such conspicuous history, modern and literate peoples have completely forgotten what it means to live in an oral world.

Walter Ong, in his book *Orality and Literacy*, observes that the oral nature of human language is permanent: "Indeed, language is so overwhelmingly oral that of all the many thousands of languages—possibly tens of thousands—spoken in the course of human history only around 106 have ever been committed to writing to a degree sufficient to have produced a literature, and most have never been written at all" (7). In modern times there are over 6000 spoken languages, but as Ong notes only some 78 have a literature (7). In modern linguistic charts, the Indo-European group shows just over 400 languages, with other language families listing far fewer. Of course, older languages within these charts are generally verified by the existence of texts. Like everything else in prehistory, our language charts suffer from an alarming lack of data out of which assumptions and generalizations must be made.

The division between oral and literate thinking is permanent. Eric Havelock, in his work *The Muse Learns to Write*, observes an "insurmountable barrier to the understanding of orality" (45). Oral constructs do not fossilize until they are written down, or when they have already ceased to be what they originally were (66). Indeed, the original oral network included epic poetry, chanted choruses, ritualized performances, music, and dance; consequently, all have disappeared from the surviving texts that utilized them (45).

From a literate point of view, observing the residue of oral cultures in ancient history has been problematic. Without writing, the study of ancient cultures comes only from archeological debris. As pointed out in the previous chapter, these scant bricks of history have been assembled with a Darwinian metaphysic that explains it all as simply primitive. The historians of science have noted a shift from "magic" to "reason" occurring "at some point." This modern appliqué has actually missed the point. The anthropologist Jack Goody has detailed the shifts from magic to science, from a "pre-logical" consciousness to a "rational" consciousness, or from the "savage" mind to domesticated thought. All are clearly explained as shifts from orality to various stages of literacy (Ong 28-9). Likewise, as Ong notes, the bicameral mind as explained by Julian Jaynes is more accurately described within this same cognitive shift (29).

When speaking about oral peoples we must be cautious to describe what we mean. A *primary oral society* is one that has no writing whatsoever: all the people of that society cannot read or write, nor do they have any concept of writing. A *secondary oral society* is one in which most people cannot read or write, but writing exists and is employed by the specialists of that society for various purposes. Even with writing, a secondary oral society employs oral strategies in all that they do. Writing does introduce intellectual abstraction, however, and a little bit of writing can change thought patterns. In other words, there is cognitive overlap where the oral thought processes discussed in this chapter are not only omnipresent in primary oral societies but also echo throughout the intellectual milieu of secondary oral societies in varying degrees.

It appears the Greeks had a crucial advantage for abstract thinking over their ancient neighbors because they employed a completely phonetic alphabet, which "favors left-hemisphere activity in the brain, and thus on neurophysiologic grounds fosters abstract analytic thought" (Ong 89). The Greek miracle is convincingly described by Havelock as the Greek literate revolution that was the basis for the creation of Greek literature and philosophy (1). The history of science begins in Greece because the Greeks appear to be the first rationalists in history. On the contrary, they were the first fully literate minds in history.

When Plato writes, "Is it not [in] reasoning if anywhere that any reality becomes clear to the soul?" (*Phaedo* 65c), we, with our modern, literate minds can find familiar ground. Thus, when Plato discusses the realm of pure forms and ideas, or philosophizes about the constituents of a virtuous state, or the dialectics of true philosophy, all in recognizable terms, we rejoice that people are finally reasoning things out in rational categories. All the more do we celebrate when seeing the prescient atomic theory of Democritus, or the ingenious mathematics and astronomical models of Eudoxus, the geometry of Euclid, and the technical brilliance of Archimedes. No wonder our historians of science have begun their analysis in classical Greece, where written documents prove a form of analytic thought that in many ways is very much like our own. In the words of F. M. Cornford, Greek philosophers "strike us as throwing off the vast symbolic visions of mythology, and walking, clear-headed, to see and touch real things. If we have a rational temperament, we feel at once a refreshment" (42).

At the same time, when we read a traditional cuneiform text we strain and blush over the imagery and wonder if we are observing a fertility chant or a burlesque poetry recital? For example, one hymn of Inanna declares, "What I tell you let the singer weave into song. . . . My vulva, the horn, the Boat of Heaven, is full of eagerness like the young moon. My untilled land lies fallow. . . . As for me, the young woman, who will plow my vulva? Who will station the ox there? Who will plow my vulva?" (Wolkstein and Kramer 36-37). Our probative anxiety only increases when we consider that in a creation text from Egypt, Osiris, who is also known as the Bull of Heaven, has the title of "mummy copulator," while Isis, who is also known as the Queen of Heaven, has the title of "vaginal river" (Doria and Lenowitz 9).

The Greeks write about cosmological theories and philosophic discourse: atoms, theorems, ratios, taxonomies, and history. The Babylonians write something about a vulva (technically, they sing about it, "let the singer weave into song"), which is also a horn, but also is the Boat of Heaven associated with the moon. The Egyptians write something about a mummy phallus and a vaginal river, but only in context of an act of creation and the soul's ascent to the sky. Is this just ancient and primitive fertility cult imagery, or a hyper-fixation on a religious death cult? Was Freud right after all, and all the overt sexual imagery in ancient myth and religion really does belong to a pre-rational, hyper-sexualized psyche?

No—rather we are simply experiencing that different lingual-cognition structures are employed by orally based cultures. Walter Ong notes that "the effects of oral states of consciousness are bizarre to the literate mind, and they can invite elaborate explanations which may turn out to be needless" (30). Elizabeth Wayland Barber and Paul T. Barber observe that the seemingly contradictory nature, concrete metaphor, and overall unintelligibility of ancient myth is a result of a permanent epistemological divide between orality and literacy: "The problem lies not in differing intelligence but in differing resources for the storage and transmission of data. Quite simply, before writing, myths had to serve as transmission systems for information deemed important; but because we—now that we have writing—have forgotten how nonliterate people stored and transmitted information and why it was done that way, we have lost track of how to decode the information often densely compressed into these stories, and they appear to us as mostly gibberish" (2). Ancient myth is a construct of oral cognition. Oral storage and transmission of data follows what Barber and Barber call "mytho-linguistic" principles and must be compressed "by any means possible until [the data fits] into the available channel: human memory" (3).

In this chapter I am going to explore several aspects of both oral and literate cognition. This discussion is not comprehensive. I am focusing on specific aspects of these cognitive systems in relation to ancient myth and knowledge. My approach may seem topically sporadic; it is. Ancient myth is a dead language and there is no Rosetta Stone to translate it. The first thing one must do is identify just exactly what "herring" and "eagle" we are describing, and what cognitive current and cultural mountain we are climbing. Hopefully we are conscious about our own literate assumptions and how they inform our own interpretations.

The Analogy Principle

The oral mind is rooted in the immediate and concrete experience of nature. When a literate mind wants to look up an idea, it goes to a dictionary or encyclopedia. An oral mind does not have these things, or even a conception of these things. The primary intellectual referents for the oral mind become the objects of nature. This statement is totally insufficient; however, as the oral mind does not objectify nature. In order to objectify nature into abstract principles, a person needs a layer of thought between him and his direct experience of nature. In literate societies, that layer of reflection between mind and direct experience is writing. Obviously, oral peoples do not have this layer of reflection that allows abstraction.

For example, a literate person will describe geometric figures as abstract shapes. We use words like circles and squares. An oral person, on the other hand, will identify a circle by referencing it to an actual object that is seen and experienced. Thus, oral peoples call a circle a plate, bucket, or moon; a square they will identify as a mirror, door, or house (Ong 50).

A literate person discusses the processes of the life cycle by introducing objectified principles: inception, genesis, fertilization, growth, and decay. An oral thinker can describe the same processes, but does so strictly within the noetics of orality. He will hand you a seed and say "Plant this in the soil. Make sure the soil is good soil. Pluck the fruit in summer. Sing the song and make the sacrifice in winter so that it may grow again." The oral thinker is perfectly capable of articulating the life cycle in the world, but he cannot separate that cycle from the things that manifest it. The plant *is* life. The plant *is* growth. The plant *does* fade. How will it grow again? Through the power of ritual song and sacrifice; because the rites, by analogy, participate via the characteristics of the vegetation.

Orality is permanently wed to concrete reality. Modern, abstract principles have their precursor in oral, concrete processes that are analogized through symbols, myths, and rituals. Mircea Eliade observes: "It is useless to search archaic languages for the terms so laboriously created by great philosophical traditions: there is every likelihood that such words as 'being,' 'nonbeing,' 'real,' 'unreal,' 'becoming,' 'illusory,' are not found in the language of the Australians or of the ancient Mesopotamians. But if the word is lacking, the *thing* is present; only it is 'said'—that is, revealed in a coherent fashion—through symbols and myths" (*CH* 3).

As can be seen from these examples, oral cognition relates the qualities of the environment to everything that shares those qualities. Thus, a circle is called both a plate (a manmade object) or the moon (a heavenly orb). Barber and Barber call this linguistic property of orality the Analogy Principle: "If any entities or phenomena bear a resemblance, in any aspect, [oral] people assume they must be related—where points of resemblance included form, behavior, cause, significance, or whatever" (35). Oral cultures know how a tree is planted and grows just as they know that there is a winter season. How do they ensure another spring? Through rituals that mimic the desired outcome: "one of the most famous analogical acts of the ancient Near East was the ritual 'sacred marriage', in which the king mated with the high priestess in imitation of the desired mating of the divine male and female principles of nature. The purpose, of course, was to promote fertility by analogical means" (36).

This structure of oral thinking explains the multivalent forms of ancient deities. Zeus was equally represented as a thunder god, a lightning storm, a planet, an eagle, and an oak tree (40). Zeus was the cosmic power that overthrew chaos, and the only thing potent enough in nature that regularly manifests this power is thunder and lightning. Zeus was also a kosmocrater, organizing time and space as he overthrew Cronos; thus, his representation as Jupiter. He could ascend to the heavens as an almighty being unencumbered by mortality, so was often analogized with the eagle. The oak is the mightiest of trees, and, coincidentally, was thought by the Romans to attract lightning. It does not surprise us then to find the priesthood of Zeus at Dodona using the leaves of the oak tree to make oracular pronouncements.

The Analogy Principle not only helps to explain the multiple representations of a single deity, but also the proliferation of multiple deities. Without a written record like a dictionary or encyclopedia, how does an oral mind catalog and separate all the different principles and dynamics of nature? Quite simply, the oral mind ascribes certain manifestations of nature, by analogy, to male and female rationales. Thus, something that inseminates at a cosmic scale, such as the sun, must not only be a god, but a male god (Shamash, Horus, Apollo, etc.). While that which gives birth, such as the earth, must not only be a deity, but a female deity (Inanna, Isis, Gaia, etc.). It is impossible, however, to ascribe all male and female manifestations in nature onto one image or being using only oral memory. Every different manifestation in nature must also have a divine will behind it. A different divine spirit is imprinted onto a pantheon of deities who not only organize the oral cosmos but also serve mnemonic needs. Polytheism and orality are wed.

Finally, the Analogy Principle also helps to explain the vocabularies of ancient languages. As already noted, a single Babylonian word could have an entire constellation of meanings, associations, or puns. Literate languages tend to have hundreds of thousands of words in their vocabularies, because every nuance can be described in writing and assigned its own vocabulary. Literate societies produce a proliferation of technical jargon. Oral languages, by contrast, have only a few thousand words in their vocabularies. Even with the introduction of writing, early scribes were still thinking inside oral demands, and the oral memory can only keep track of so many words. By sheer numeric reduction, single words in oral vocabularies, therefore, must have multiple meanings or associations. These meanings and associations come by analogy. The Hebrew word *dabar* not only means "word," but also "event." To say something is literally to bring it in motion. (Apparently, this analogy is completely lost in the modern world.) The Egyptian word *mdw* means "word," and also "staff or rod." For the Egyptians, the "word" has a meant action, but in the noetics of their oral vocabulary, the action of the word was represented by the authoritative figure giving it, thus the idea of a staff or rod.

Analogical thinking begins to explain the hymn of Inanna cited above. Inanna was the Queen of Heaven, most often represented by the planet Venus. As bride to the solar power, she was the symbolic genematrix of nature—her vulva is thus the earth that receives the solar semen and produces all living things. She is analogized similarly with a horn, the Boat of Heaven, and the moon. All these objects share in the perceived powers and phenomena where Inanna dwelt. The exact interpretation of these symbols remains problematic, in order to know what and why the creators of the hymn were thinking we would have to know all the analogical puns and relationships they assigned to their deity. Much of ancient myth and ritual is permanently buried underneath a long forgotten, oral network of ideas wed to an oral way of perceiving the universe.

Vertical and Horizontal Memory

Oral societies are of course limited by human memory. Without a way to permanently fix a complex idea, a technology that is most cogently supplied by writing, people have only mnemonic strategies to rely on. There are certain advantages and disadvantages with both oral and literate ways to retain knowledge. Plato, remarking on the advantages of oral memory, relates the story of Thoth and King Ammon. According to the traditional tale, Thoth, the Egyptian god of skill and craft, introduces writing to the Egyptians with a promise: "Here is something, once learned, will make the Egyptians wiser and will improve the memory." The Egyptian king sees this gift as something else, complaining that writing "will introduce forgetfulness into the soul of those who learn it: they will not practice using their memory because they will put their trust in writing, which is external and depends on signs that belong to others, instead of trying to remember from the inside, completely on their own" (*Phaedrus* 274c-275b). It is a perceptive complaint that oral thinkers persistently used. As late as 1477 CE, Hieronimo Squarciafico alarmingly warned that "the abundance of books makes men less studious" for it destroys memory and enfeebles the mind by relieving it of too much work (Ong 79).

In many ways, these complaints of the imposition of writing on individual memory are true. Herein lies a paradox: literate cultures have reductive individual memory, for they rely almost entirely on writing to keep their memories for them. Still, the permanency of fixed print allows for huge amounts of amassed knowledge. Writing allows for what could be called a *vertical memory*, where individual memory is reduced, but corporate memory, through print, can be unlimited.

Oral cultures, on the other hand, rely on what could be called *horizontal memory*, where individual memory is as expansive and broad as the natural landscape. The features they are memorizing are limited to only a few dozen vertical layers of technical know-how—the limit of natural memory. Oral peoples can never build a microchip or a space rocket, because these things take generations of fixed, typographic data, layered upon each other in successive adaptations and improvements. The technology to build a microchip requires several thousand vertical layers of experience and information. The oral mind simply cannot produce several thousand layers of memory. Oral cultures are homoeostatic; as Ong notes, "oral societies live very much in a present which keeps itself in equilibrium or homeostasis by sloughing off memories which no longer have present relevance" (46). Oral societies have to reduce the amount of new data they receive into their culture within preconceived channels of memory, "everything added to the corpus of stories to retell had better deserve its place, for it may be ousting something else. So first of all, the accounts to be transmitted have (and had) to be winnowed down to the most important" (Barber and Barber 154).

Horizontal memory is not primitive—it is oral. It can be fine-tuned to a degree that astonishes literate cultures. Walter Ong points out that Yugoslavian bards can reproduce a lengthy song after hearing it only once (60). Further, oral peoples can recite long, formulaic words and phrases verbatim, phoneme for phoneme, using mnemonic strategies (62). It is said that the Elder Seneca could repeat two thousand names in the order they were given, or recite hundreds of lines of poetry in reverse (Yeats 31). Bards in India can recite a textbook word for word by hearing it, and as one scholar notes, "It is said that if all the written and printed copies of the Rig Veda were lost, the text could be restored at once with complete accuracy" (McLuhan 93). An oral mind must be its own encyclopedia and can develop memory strategies that literate people think impossible.

Horizontal memory fixates on the traditions of a society, where it remains rooted. Horizontal memory is thus homologous with communal memory. Contrarily to corporate memory, which amasses huge amounts of data, communal memory is reductive, maintaining only the essential principles and concepts that protect and maintain the community. In oral cultures there are three primary forms of knowledge that are passed down from generation to generation. First, there are the traditions which provide a sense of values, ethics, and cultural norms. Second, there are also technical traditions and trade secrets, such as strategies for hunting, gathering, farming, and manufacturing. Finally, there are paramount religious considerations; for example, the created order and the required rites and sacrifices for the gods. Yet how does a vast and horizontal knowledge system get transmitted? Eric Havelock asks, "By what means can the general tradition be taught and commended to the population at large so that they can share it and live by it?" (75). His answer is in utilizing a language of action, where every tradition is put in story or artistic form so the entire community may participate: "Tradition in short is taught by action, not by idea or principle. For its teaching, oral societies have to provide suitable performance context attended by audiences who will be invited or invite themselves to share in what is on the one hand a language of specialists, yet on the other a language in which all to varying degree participate" (77).

Oral societies are playacting societies; horizontal memory must be performed. Only in the past several decades have scholars understood the breadth of this reality. A new look at ancient and sacred texts reveals that many of the phrases and verses were meant to be dramatized. M. Sylvain Lèvi believes that several of the hymns in the Rig Veda were the "remains of the earliest, and oldest, Indian dramatic creations, the beginning of the Indian Drama; and that the fragments could only be satisfactorily interpreted from the point of view that they were intended to be spoken, not by a solitary reciter, but by two or more *dramatis personae*" (Weston 26-27). Leopold von Schroeder believed many of the speeches in the Rig Veda to be part of the ritual culture drama, whose performance was for "stimulating the processes of nature" (Weston 26). Moreover, William Simpson notes, "In India the story of the origin of the Ganges as related in the Ramayana is evidently a derivation from ceremonial rites" (16). The ceremonial rites are linked with the passage of the dead into the next world and are performed during the days of festivities, which included drama and dance (16-17).

The correlation between drama and religious text reaches as far back as Egypt's earliest dynasties. Nibley asserts, "The Pyramid Texts themselves were placed on the walls of tomb chambers and passages to tell the priests what they should do and say at each particular station in the long ceremonies" (*MJSP* 96). Nibley cites Kurt Sethe, who believes that the text on the Shabaka stone was "a directive for people participating in a ritual play, whose lines are much longer and whose actions are much fuller than here indicated" (*MJSP* 96). Nibley also cites Joachim Spiegel who emphasizes that the "first half of the rites celebrated in the pyramid of Unas . . . took the form of a complete dramatic presentation . . . in the manner of a 'mystery play,' with stage, props, and actors" (*MJSP* 210). Eberhard Otto believed significant phrases in the much later Egyptian *Book of Breathings* were meant "as stage directions, indicating the instructions to the participants" (*MJSP* 247). William Simpson notes of the *Book of the Dead*, "From beginning to end the form is that of dramatic action; the Osiris—that is the deceased person—acts, and he speaks in a dramatic manner; and it is the same with the personifications that appear throughout the piece" (77). Theodor Gaster has shown similar patterns in the myths and texts (as dramas) of every major civilization of the Near East (85-103).

Horizontal memory follows a syntax of its own. Oral mnemonics requires redundancy, formulaic patterns, operational frames of reference, somatic gestures, narratives filled with monumental or memorable characters, fixed statements, ritual utterance, epic recitals, songs, and performances. Walter Ong asserts:

> Suppose a person in an oral culture would undertake to think through a particular complex problem and would finally manage to articulate a solution which itself is relatively complex, consisting, let us say, of a few hundred words. How does he or she retain for later recall the verbalization so painstaking elaborated? . . . The only answer is: Think memorable thoughts. In a primary oral culture, to solve effectively the problem of retaining and retrieving carefully articulated thought, you have to do your thinking in mnemonic patterns, shaped for ready oral recurrence. Your thought must come into being in heavily rhythmic, balanced patterns, in repetitions or antitheses, in alliterations and assonances, in epithetic and other formulary expressions, in standard thematic settings. . . . Serious thought is intertwined with memory systems. Mnemonic needs determine even syntax. (34)

These mnemonic demands of orality explain the stylistic features of ancient myth. Oral memory requires what Ong calls "heavy characters" who are outsized and heroic "not for romantic reasons or reflectively didactic reasons but for much more basic reasons: to organize experience in some sort of permanently memorable form" (69). Gods that are copulating with mortals and heroes and who fight outrageous creatures or perform impossible tasks with superhuman cunning or strength are the subject of myth because they are the product of mnemonic demands.

Songs, Signs, and Dances

The literate mind is rooted in visual thinking. We see words on the page and analyze ideas using those words. We "look up" an idea in a book. The oral mind cannot "look up" an idea. Rather, the oral mind is completely rooted in acoustics. Without writing, words become sounds. When sound becomes the basis of cognition, thought becomes rooted in dynamic relationships. Ong again notes that a literate-visual culture prefers immobility, "We often reduce motion to a series of still shots the better to see what motion is. There is no equivalent of a still shot for sound. An oscillogram is silent. It lies outside the sound world" (32).

Because all sound exists in dynamic form, always produced by motion, all things become wed in a continual network of creation and change. Because nature remains the intellectual referent for oral thinkers, sound and process cannot be separated from the things that produce them, or in the case of words, are produced by them. This is why the articulation of a ritual phrase in oral cultures is thought to be imbued with inherent power, for words have a creative assonance with the sounds of nature. Certain words or phrases mimic the sound, either literally or by analogy, of a buzzing bee, a fluttering bird, or a trickling brook. For oral minds, if the sounds are apperceptive, then the spoken word holds the same power as the functioning cosmos.

For example, the exhaling breath mimics the sound of a slight breeze. Breath is the key to life, but also to words; as a result, wind, breath, life, and words must all be connected. In ancient cosmologies, the world was centered within the four winds, for they were the breath of life from which creation emerged. In the New Testament, it is the Logos that creates the world: "In the beginning was the Word, and the Word was with God, and the Word was God. . . . All things were made by him; and without him was not any thing made that was made" (John 1.1, 3). For literate readers, these verses invoke an image of text and doctrine, a book of scripture, which is a sort of idealized schematic from which God forms the world. But the idea behind the phrase is not the written word, but the *spoken word*. God is the power of creation because he is in tune with it. His words and the processes of nature are homologous—the Earth is a song.

The idea of the spoken word creating the world is very ancient. One of the oldest texts found is a creation hymn known as the Memphite Theology, carved on the Shabaka Stone. The Stone itself dates to the eighth century BCE, but the grammar and syntax of the writing is argued to be centuries older. Part of the text reads: "the nine god company [of Ptah] stand before him grown into bodies of teeth and lips, [teeth are] the water seed of Atum, [lips . . .] the lithe spoke arms lifted from the mouth [of Ptah]" (Doria and Lenowitz 4). Each of the nine creation gods hold sway over a portion of nature, but in the texts they are analogized with the power of the mouth as "teeth" and "lips." Further, Ptah uses these powers to conceive of the god-word, which he utters creating the world, as the text declares, "all work and art were spoken into life" (Doria and Lenowitz 5).

The intellectual referents of the oral mind are the concrete realities of nature; hence this thought-world is accessed through the constant movement of sound. All objects in nature are thought to be alive with movement (the anima of nature). All speech becomes a form of action; thus, the Hebrew term *dabar* and the Egyptian word *mdw*. Likewise, the Egyptian word for "house" also means "stanza," that is, a musical construction. The Arabic *bait* follows suit, meaning both "house" and "stanza." Words are actions filled with power. Architecture is a harmonic construction, such as a song. For the oral mind, these analogies become literal; as a result, when building a temple, such as in Egypt, the founding is coronated with song and dance.

The acoustical nature of orality also informs its mnemonics. Things are better remembered when sung or chanted in rhythms, using direct experience with sound. The works of Hesiod and Homer were sung, and the Greek theater was full of singing and dancing. The oral community at large participates in ritual festivals imbued with sound as it reinforces thought and learning. The aural nature of oral mnemonics lasted all the way through the Middle Ages, where monks in their libraries often chanted or sung texts for memory purposes. The reading carrel was more of a singing booth, for the act of reading was still employed by the oral strategy of auditory memory, where information was remembered through sound (McLuhan 92).

Similarly to aural mnemonic techniques are the somatic strategies employed to aid memory. Ong notes that many oral peoples make string figures with their songs, manipulate beads, or tell their stories strictly to the music of drums and dance (66-67). Physical repetition and tokens become essential appurtenances to oral cognition. Henry Pernet, an expert on African ritual masks, notes that the creation of a ritual mask is wed to dance, as in the case of the Dogon, where participants don ritual masks and dance a liturgy that reenacts the creation of the world. Pernet quotes Marcel Griaule on the subject: "The society of masks is the entire world. And when it moves onto the public square, it dances the way of the world, it dances the system of the world" (61). So masks that not only represent the spirit or god which they prefigure but also symbolize "cosmogonic events of the greatest magnitude" (53) are wed to dances, which are the performance pieces of those events. Moreover, ritual masks can have multiple levels of meaning, depending on one's initiatory experience, a truth that extends into all of initiatory ritual (53). In short, the ritual mask is much more than a simple prop or costume effect—it is a memory key encoded with multiple layers of meaning. When combined with ritual dance, the ritual mask becomes a multivalent "lexicon" of culture meaning.

Furthermore, body painting and tattoos serve analogous functions as ritual masks and provide the same mental requirements of the mnemonic reservoir. It is no literary license when Herman Melville describes Queequeg, the faithful partner of Ishmael and a cannibal native of a foreign land, as having his body covered from head to toe with tattoos imprinted upon him by one of his people's seers. The tattoos were "hieroglyphic marks . . . a complete theory of the heavens and the earth, and a mystical treatise on the art of attaining truth" (399). This remarkable statement turns out to be the essence of ritual masks and their dancing societies.

It is strange for modern thinkers to believe that ancient cult dances had layers of information stratified within them. Some scholars have noted that the origin of the choral dance rests in ancient cosmology, where both Egyptian and Babylonian priests performed hymns and ring dances around the temple altars modeling the rhythms of the stars and planets (Backman 2, 16). To this day a cosmological dance is performed in front of the National Museum in Mexico City. It is a Maypole dance, of ancient origin, where six dancers circumambulate around the pillar or pole (*axis mundi*) fifty-two times while one plays music. The dancers, called the voladores, walk around the pole thirteen times, reverse their direction for another thirteen turns, repeating their turning march twice more indicating four cycles of thirteen rounds. Five dancers ascend the pole, the first voladore climbing to the very top where he plays the flute while the other four bind themselves to ropes at the "four quarters." In a marvelous athletic show, these four dancers hang upside down and descend from the pole by the ropes while swinging in the air around the axis another fifty-two times.

The entire spectacle is a cosmogony, and in the oral world dancing and calendar making are joined. The dancers at the top of the pillar represent the sun and its four carriers throughout the Mesoamerican calendar cycle of fifty-two years. These dancers also represent the five world ages at the center of the Aztec calendar. In another version of this dance there are only five dancers, all of whom ascend the pole, while four participants swirl downwards only thirteen times to the bottom from ropes, still retaining the sacred calendar number of fifty-two (4 X 13 = 52.) The eminent scholar of astronomy E. C. Krupp clearly links this aerial dance to the measurement of time cycles (209-11). John Major Jenkins links the fifty-two-year calendar cycle to a further astronomical measurement of tracking the sun-Pleiades conjunction at their zenith (82-83). The dance reenacts the cosmogony and does so through the numbers embedded in the performance. Most of the myth and symbolism of this dance has been lost, but we see how technical information can be encoded within such a dance.

Correspondingly, Athenaeus of Naucratis (2nd century CE) testifies that the entire doctrine of the Pythagoreans could be revealed in a dance (*HM* 118). The liturgical dance itself carried esoteric information. Hymn, music, motion, and the numbers of steps creates an instructive ensemble analogous to the central tenants that needed to be remembered. The song and dance become a memory key.

Not only are dances linked with calendric models, but they are especially employed within the cult mysteries associated with the cosmos. The cult dance is central in oral culture. One such example is provided by the Dogon's "resurrection dance," as explained by Ogotemmêli to the anthropologist Marcel Griaule. The dance originated at the beginning of the world and was revealed by the gods. According to tradition, the first such dance was done by the jackal, which was God's son. "God's son spoke his dance. His steps left traces . . . which indicated the meaning of his Word" (186). Those dance steps, as Ogotemmêli stated, were the representations of "God's roof, the inside of [God's] house, and the recess where the altar of the dead is placed" (186). The dance becomes a set of instructions on how one should move through God's domain. We find similar patterns throughout the oral world where priests and shamans analogically journeyed through the heavens by performing a dance (see chapter 4). In the case of the Dogon, the resurrection dance is explicitly related to the meaning of the "Word," so that the central idea of Dogon culture and cosmology cannot be separated from the dance that expresses it. Like Queequeg's tattoos that guided the art of obtaining truth, the cult dance was essential for teaching and transmitting truth in the oral age.

As literate peoples we have entirely forgotten the lengths to which oral people strove to map essential knowledge onto ordinary things. For oral people, every natural surface is a mental canvas, and very little is put to waste. Ceremonial clothing or tapestry is often imbued with cosmological symbols. Jewelry and tools are inscribed with symbols reciting mythological events. Surprisingly, there does not seem to be many arbitrary or utilitarian uses for living space; for the teepee, granary, hogan, and mound all served metaphysical and even cosmological purposes. Mountains, rivers, animals, and plants were incorporated into mythological tropes. Myths themselves were networked within the tokens, dances, and ceremonies of oral civilization. This is not to say that everything in the ancient world was imbued with mnemonic layers stratified in myth and rites. Nor is it true that every oral participant knew the true meaning of the cult songs and dances. It is to say that oral cognition and literate cognition are of a different order, and many of the consequences of orality remain unseen.

The Silence Principle

There is another mytho-linguistic principle worth noting; Barber and Barber call it the Silence principle. This principle is quite simple, "What is never said may eventually be forgotten entirely" (19). This should seem quite obvious. Upon reflection, one must ask in an oral society, "how much is never said?" It turns out, quite a bit. The reductive nature of oral vocabularies requires multiple meanings or associations for each word in the vocabulary; however, no ancient writer wrote down in dictionary style all the associations and analogies used in their language. This was something they believed everybody already knew. A millennia later, the oral economy of linguistic analogy and association had been completely forgotten, making the most simple and formulaic phrases in ancient texts impossible for modern scholars to understand. No one really understands what the Pyramid Texts meant to the people who wrote them. We certainly understand the themes: death, resurrection, celestial ascent, and deification. That is about as far as we can go.

The Silence principle spreads even further into the frame of orality. Direct social pressures contribute to knowledge loss. As Walter Ong explains, for example, when the market for an oral genealogy disappears, the genealogy itself also disappears (66). Oral language is so formulaic and conservative that when social upheavals occur—such as in migrations, war, or new technologies—old words, phrases, or even rituals may be repeated without the participants understanding what they mean (Ong 63; Barber and Barber 22). Additionally, many ancient cult practices held religious taboos forbidding the disclosure of information. To that end, the culture-requirement of secrecy has done its job, for a great amount of information has been permanently lost. The myth and cult constructs associated with the Greco-Roman mystery religions and revealed during private initiations were forbidden from public discourse. Likewise, the Pythagorean School was known for its knowledge and skills, but also for its guarded secrecy. As a result, we know neither the true extent of the eschatology nor the technical know-how of the mystery cults or the early schools. Just so, the name of the Hebrew god was so sacred that it could not be uttered; to this day no one knows how to pronounce YHWH.

This last point sinks deep into oral consciousness. For the modern mind, a sign of true intelligence is in writing what you know. In academia, for example, there is a repeated mantra, "publish or perish!" The sentiment is simple: if you are not writing and publishing you are not really thinking. Oral culture has the exact opposite understanding; writing is not so much a taboo as it is an intellectual handicap. For centuries people steered away from writing not because they could not understand it, but because they did not trust it. They sensed that once you removed meaning from the direct object to which it is attached then you could make anything mean everything, and subsequently, nothing. The sentiment was simple: if you *are* writing and publishing you are not really thinking. This entire dynamic is revealed in Plato's story of Thoth and King Ammon, where the king believed writing would lead to stupidity.

This distrust of writing and the consonant understanding of oral thinking (that the integrity of meaning is wed to the direct object as experienced in nature) lies at the heart of ancient philosophy and science. Clement of Alexandria warned that the sacred things of deity were only entrusted to speech and never to writing (Weston 135). We hear this and think of the ancient religious cults, forgetting that the sacred things of deity also and especially included the sciences of number and harmony. There were secrets in nature that had to be parsed out, but they were to be kept secret. The neophyte learning them had to experience them through direct observation and ritual performance of symbol, song, and dance. They were never to be written, and in many cases there were severe punishments for the improper disclosure of sacred knowledge. In ancient culture the mantra was not "publish or perish;" it was rather "if you publish you will perish." Due to the intentional taboo of writing, the great philosophical and scientific traditions of ancient history are permanently lost behind the tumbling tells of mythological debris.

It took nearly three thousand years after the invention of writing for the human experience to develop into fully literate consciousness. It is impossible for us to fully realize how the invention of writing changed civilization—but there was a change—from orality to literacy, from mythos to logos. This change not only altered the capacity for king and state to expand, but more critically, it altered the very structure of thought. The ancient mind did not "evolve" with writing, but it did learn how to store, process, and associate information in new ways, and this change had enormous consequences. The transformation from mythos to logos did not happen overnight—it was uneven and periodic, and it covered only certain portions of a culture's population. Even after the introduction of writing, ancient cultures existed for numerous centuries utilizing an oral mind set. The transition from primary and secondary orality into full literate consciousness took hold in Classical Greece:

> It does appear that the Greeks did something of major psychological importance when they developed the first alphabet complete with vowels. [This] crucial, more nearly total transformation of the world from sound to sight gave ancient Greek culture its intellectual ascendancy over other ancient cultures. The reader of Semitic writing had to draw on non-textual as well as textual data: he had to know the language he was reading in order to know what vowels to supply between the consonants. The vocalic Greek alphabet was more remote from that world. . . . It analyzed sound more abstractly into purely spatial components. It could be used to write or read words even from languages one did not know. . . . Little children could acquire the Greek alphabet when they were very young and their vocabulary limited. . . . It appears that the structure of the Greek language, the fact that it was not based on a system that was hospitable to omission of vowels from writing, turned out to be a perhaps accidental but crucial intellectual advantage. (Ong 89)

Orality and Religion

The difference between orality and literacy has another consequence that pervades all of our assumptions about the study of myth. Many textbooks discuss myth in the context of ancient religious beliefs and practices. This is appropriate as myth and religion are synonymous. This connection becomes a sticking point for many historians of science who assert that the age of myth was an age of religion and magic, and that science is a product of reason and logic. According to them, science could not come about until the Greeks began separating religious beliefs from observation and experimentation.

This ubiquitous meta-narrative is a creation of the secular age. As already pointed out, religion and magic did not build the Great Pyramid. While the Great Pyramid was used for religious purposes, concepts like "religion" and "magic" cannot build any physical structure. Further, the separation of "reason" from "religion" is wholly a secular idea. Throughout the ancient world and all the way up to modern times, universities were religious institutions and observation and experimentation were never antonymous to religious belief or faith. As proof of this, Isaac Newton had one of the greatest scientific minds in human history; his master-piece *Principia* may very well be the greatest book on mathematics ever written. What many history books fail to mention is that Newton wrote more on religious subjects than on all of his topics in mathematics and the sciences combined.

In the ancient world there was no separation between science and religion. In fact, there was no such thing as "religion." It may come as a shock to know that the idea of "religion" is created only by the literate mind. To repeat, *religion is a category of literacy*. Amongst oral people there is no epistemological separation between different fields of knowl-edge. There is only existence and reality, and oral people's seek to mimic cosmic reality in all that they do, whether it be for the needs of the state, agriculture, human reproduction, or whatever. Where horizontal and communal memory are the cognitive contexts for knowing, concepts like religion, science, art, and history all belong to the same corpus of epistemology. In other words, to offer a ritual sacrifice and to add a series of fractions together for market or architectural needs are activities that do not belong to different fields of knowledge. Planting and harvesting, constructing temples and tombs, sex and birth—these are repetitions of cosmic functions. Technology and mathematics are often employed to accomplish these acts, but only the literate mind separates technical functions from social and biological relationships. The oral mind makes no such distinction.

Remember, in an oral world there is limited objectification of concepts into abstract principles; oral cognition is rooted in concrete reality. The word religion is an abstract concept. Oral peoples did not have this concept. The Greeks, Romans, Egyptians, Babylonians, and every other "high civilization" in antiquity had no word that corresponds to our notion of religion; nor did the Native Americans, Polynesians, Aborigines, or any indigenous tribe of oral thinkers.

In modern times the idea of religion is employed broadly and inconsistently: it is equally applied to a church; a belief of faith; a superstition; a dream or vision; a ritual or custom; a social tradition, organization, or behavior; and a personal or collective psychology. In *The Western Construction of Religion* Daniel Dubuisson cites prominent philosophers and theologians who provide definitions for the concept of religion. He sums up over two centuries of authoritative explanations in four words: "An absence of criteria" (63). As the word is presently used, its only clear demarcation is what it is not—secularism. Some scholars have suggested that the modern usage of the idea of religion only took shape as it arose sympathetically with the idea of secular humanism.

Dubuisson's critique is more exhaustive: "Just like the notion itself, the most general questions concerning religion, its nature and definition, its origins or expressions, were born in the West. From there, they were transferred, much later and at the cost of daring generalizations, to all other cultures, however remotely prehistoric or exotic" (9). Dubuisson notes that the concept of religion is first introduced within a literary domain and its conceptions only find coherence in written texts: "[religion] is the exclusive and original creation of the first Christian thinkers writing in Latin" (24). The notion of religion was grafted onto the Latin word *religio* (which originally referred to the public oaths and ordinances of the Roman cult of the state) and its new conception was the result of an "audacious textualization" by the earliest Christian writers who were demarcating their beliefs from the pagan cults of their day (24-30). Like the demarcation of religion versus secularism, the first Christian use of the term *religio* "was defined from the very outset by its claim to difference, by its opposition to all other cults, and by its separation from all that [it] was not" (24-5). Dubuisson reminds us that "religion" was a creation of late and literate processes of Western culture.

How do we study cross-historical myths and religions when the categories and concepts we use to quantify our data are modern fabrications with no parallels in the ancient world? It is a dilemma that cannot be overcome and is why Eric Havelock and Walter Ong state that we can never fully understand the world of orality. This innate schism between orality and literacy reveals itself in the very idea of religion. This schism is patched by the intellectual mortar of Howlers, Romantics, and Conspirators; or worse, according to Dubuisson, by anthropologists whose use of religious anthropology "often represents only the secularized and rationalized version of it that has been gained as the result of analytical work that consists, in essence, of putting the fantastic in parentheses" (20).

If oral cultures do not have the concept of religion, what are they doing with all their sacrifices, myths, and rituals? As stated, the oral mind does not have a layer of reflection between it and its experience of nature; therefore, proper action in this material realm is the reproduction of cosmic processes as revealed by nature and reproduced within human life. For oral peoples "nature is a hierophany," writes Mircea Eliade, "and the 'laws of nature' are the revelation of the mode of existence of the divinity" (*CH* 59). These laws were absolute and descended from the heavens: "Life on earth is to mirror," Campbell adds, "as nearly perfectly as is possible in human bodies, the almost hidden—yet now discovered— order of the pageant of the [heavenly] spheres" (*Primitive* 150).

Oral minds readily observed that nature reveals universal principles and functions. A seed is planted in the ground where it sprouts, grows into a tree, produces fruit and more seeds, and dies. The earth does the same in its seasons. During different seasons certain animals and birds migrate, while different plants grow and die. Everything is connected. The central question in such observations is *what causes these things to happen?* Without an electron microscope, the oral mind perceived that the laws of nature were a product of divine functions—invisible and universal processes that were at the root of all living things. *Reality resided in the invisible cause and not in the material product.* Remarkably, these invisible causes were associated with certain parts in the sky (see next chapter); they were also associated with different male and female deities. With such a cosmovision, right living was thought to be a ritual re-enactment of these invisible laws in daily life and in yearly cult festivals.

The modern concept of religion often seeks what is usually termed *transcendence*: rising above the profane and obtaining that which is holy or sacred (variously defined by different cultures). This modern sense of transcendence is individual and interior—a disciple of the religious life can rise above the mundane through personal meditation, prayer, right thinking, and right living. The literate mind seeks *orthodoxy*—thinking and behavior that conforms to the established and written rules and laws. Oral peoples, on the other hand, appear to strive for a *divine descendence*: bringing down the powers of the sacred, invisible principles from their celestial abode into the human realm. This sense of the sacred is communal and exterior; it resides in the entire tribe, clan, or city that gather at public festivals performing rituals that reenact the cosmogony and analogically reshape the world. The oral mind seeks *orthopraxy*—re-enacting the principles of the cosmos through ritual.

Oral societies are communal, thus their cultural ideals tend to devalue the needs of the individual against the needs of the community. This is a difficult concept for many in the modern West to understand. Western culture is predominantly an individualized culture. We have the attitude of: "I want what is best for me. I can achieve either financial or spiritual success through hard individual effort." This thinking endows itself on the religious ethos. For Christianity, the Holy Spirit is that power of God that speaks to the individual disciple. While there are group encounters with the Spirit, salvation is largely an individual affair. Jesus is a personal intercessor. This ethos is a product of literacy. People who read most often learn through individual study. Literacy creates the environment for interiorized thought that is self-reflective. As a result, it is personal prayer, personal meditation, and personal discipleship that gets one to enter into a relationship with one's personal god.

In oral societies the reverse is often true. It is the tribe, clan, or city that is to be served first. Worship is a public function enacted through public rituals for public ends. It is only in this context that prearranged marriages and caste systems make sense, and for most of human history such things were the norm. Oral eschatology is also communal and oral salvation seeks communal integration. This is why most ancient societies had some form of what is called ancestor worship. This aspect of ancient culture seems idolatrous to western religions, but only because literacy introduced a very steep sense of individualization. Oral peoples cannot imagine an eternal life outside of the ancestral collective. The ancestors are the archetype for the living community. It is the ancestors who bless, who give boons, and who look out for the living. Indeed, oral systems are polytheistic systems and the gods also belong to a divine clan. As a result, it is communal worship, communal ritual, and communal sacrifices that allows for the collective to gain a relationship with the divine community.

Oral peoples are just as concerned with ethics and morality as literate society. For them the ethical and moral life is living in accordance with the laws of nature. In Egypt, this idea was conveyed by Maat, the goddess of truth, justice, and the proper order of the cosmos. Every Egyptian had to face the goddess Maat in the afterlife. At death the soul would descend into the Hall of Judgment, where the person's heart was weighed in the cosmic scales against her—an appropriate metaphor as Maat was also a representation of balance. If the heart caused the scales to dip out of balance then it was consumed in the dark recesses of the underworld.

Maat is represented in the scales of justice as a single feather. How could one's heart be measured against a feather? What was being weighed was not ounces or pounds, but the essence of being one had become whilst living. Often a priest would hold a feather next to the nostrils of the sick: if the feather fluttered the breath of life was still within the patient. The cosmic feather of Maat, by analogy, tested the breath of life within the essence or soul of the individual. The feather was also the material manifestation of flight as well as the power to move between realms (earth and sky). By analogy the feather of Maat appears to have represented to the Egyptians the invisible foundations of the material cosmos that causes things to be set into motion. The symbol seems to hold a hierarchy of puns: the feather engendered from an egg is analogous to consciousness gestating from Maat; the feather is to the power of flight as the heart is to conscience; the bird is to the sky as the soul is to the heavens. It is a very elegant conception that is equal to any modern religious notion of transcendence, but a conception placed squarely within the material universe embracing the invisible laws of life.

Egypt was not the only ancient civilization to have such conceptions. In India, right living was termed Dharma, the unseen order of the cosmos made manifest in the social good. In China the same conception was utilized under the word Tao. In Greece, the goddesses called the Moiria held the same function as the Egyptian Maat. They were connected with destiny, law, order, truth, and the structure of the universe. In a funerary papyri of a Greek soldier we find these elements necessary in the afterlife as they provide not only wisdom but also the breath of life (see Cornford 12-21; Betegh 39, 200-2, 267).

These conceptions of living in accordance with cosmic laws are foundational in oral societies. These cosmic laws are always expressed in myths. Oral societies seek to re-enact their myths in their rites so as to align all human action in accordance with the first moment when creation sprang forth and all things were running in harmony. Mircea Eliade reminds us that ancient ritual systems derived their meaning only by "reproducing a primordial act, of repeating a mythical example" and that these mythical examples are an "imitation of a celestial archetype" (*CH* 4-5). The rituals associated with the calendar, or the marriage of a man and woman, or the construction of a shrine were all analogical repetitions of the primordial act of creation. "Man is contemporary with the cosmogony," continues Eliade, and his myths and rituals "project him into the mythical epoch of the beginning" (*CH* 22). Joseph Campbell concurs, noting that effective rituals in the oral world were "experienced not as references but as presences. They render[ed] visible the mythological age itself." (*Primitive* 179).

Oral cognition places the mind in direct relationship with nature. The Romantics claim that this form of thinking is more holistic and can lead to harmonious living between land and people. Every cognitive system, however, can find expression in extremes. The same oral constructs that sought to relive the moment of creation through the direct experience of nature led many cultures to such practices as human sacrifice. Campbell notes, "Groups of a hundred souls or so do not require the murder of their finest sons and daughters to enable them to cohere. This flowering of rites derived from a cosmic insight—and one of such force that the whole sense, the formal structuring principle of the universe, seemed for a certain period of human history to have been caught in it" (*Primitive* 178-79).

This cosmic insight was a literal re-enactment of the process of creation through death. Many early myths describe the creator gods sacrificing themselves so that life may begin or be renewed. Often these gods were analogized with the sun—the giver of life. The sun is born every morning and dies every night. This cycle is seen to exist within life-giving processes in nature, such as the birth and death of animals and plants upon which humans survive. Life therefore is a product and synthesis of this same cosmic cycle. Proper human action becomes a ritual recitation of those very processes. The act of human sacrifice appears to be the most extreme end of analogical thinking, where the offering of the most cherished living thing (or one's social and political enemy) is a re-enactment of the sacrifice of the gods and of the daily and annual birth and death of the sun.

One example of all these oral concepts can be found in the cultural traditions of the Aztecs. The New Fire Ritual was a re-enactment of their creation myth. According to this myth the previous world age had ended in a cataclysmic flood: "there was water for 52 years and then the sky collapsed" (Fernández 21). In the midst of this desolation the Mexica gods gathered to reignite the fires of life and begin a new age. Two gods, Tecciztecal and Nanahuatzin stood before the sacred fire; Tecciztecal retreated before the scouring heat of the flames, but Nanahuatzin "made an effort and closed his eyes, and rushed forward and cast himself into the fire" (Séjourné and Nicholson 75). Nanahuatzin was consumed but also transformed through self-sacrifice into the Fifth Sun depicted in the center of the Aztec calendar. He restored light and harmony to the world below.

According to the Aztec cosmovision, every fifty-two years human sacrifices were made in similar fashion to re-ignite the cosmic fire and stave off world cataclysm. The sacrificial victims were often fifty-two years old and the time leading up to the fifty-two year mark was filled with insecurity and fear (Read 125). In preparation for the New Fire ritual, "all fires were extinguished, all wood and stone statues of gods kept in people's homes cast into the water, and all cooking utensils and fire implements thrown away. Everything was swept clean and all rubbish disposed of" (Read 125). All things of the previous order were discarded in preparation for the creation of a new heaven and new earth. Darkness descended upon Mexica civilization in cosmic re-enactment of the end of the previous age: "Everywhere people perched on rooftops in the darkened valley; no one was touching the ground. All watched for the fire to be sparked above on an isolated mountaintop called Uixachtlan" (Read 125).

This mountain was known as the Hill of the Star (Jenkins 82). The star in question is actually a star cluster known as the Pleiades. The priests performing the ritual did so only when the Pleiades reached its zenith at midnight. Were the Pleiades to reach the zenith before or after midnight all believed the world would end (Jenkins 83). At the moment of the Pleiades' zenith a sacrificial victim was laid upon an altar on the Hill of the Star and his heart was cut out. In his gaping chest a new fire was built that consumed his flesh. The new fire was started by a fire drill, which image is the Aztec representation for the ceremony itself. The victim's heart was fed back into the flames and once his entire body was consumed a faggot from this fire was taken and distributed throughout "all the regions of Mexica dominion" to rekindle the fire of civilization and to birth a new age (Read 126). The ritual ended with feasting and celebrating, and more human sacrifices, as the communal fires were rekindled from the sacrificial heart bathed in the starlight of the Pleiades.

The New Fire ritual is complex. According to Kay Read, no theory is sufficient to explain adequately the phenomenon (128). Read herself explains the ritual in terms of a cosmic meal: "Death necessarily is accentuated in an eating environment such as the Mexica's, because for one thing to eat, another must die" (136). As the Aztecs must eat from the resources of nature so also nature required sustenance from the Aztecs, allowing a "dynamic exchange to occur in what is an ecological balancing act" (136). In this view, the idea of human sacrifice is an ecological exchange: the cosmos feeds the community and therefore the community must feed the cosmos.

Read's thesis focuses on the biological cycle of eating a meal. This interpretation is acceptable only inasmuch as it is a reflection of oral consciousness seeking to mimic all cosmic processes. The Aztecs are ana-logically recreating the world by re-enacting a creation myth in accor-dance with heavenly cycles. The Pleiades was the celestial archetype or divine function of creation and was the source of the invisible cause of creation. The rising of this star cluster indicated the best time to plant crops, and there was widespread belief that these stars regulated the sea-sons. Further, in Aztec culture the Pleiades was a constellation called the Crowd or Marketplace, and represented the heavenly center or zenith. As these stars rose in the sky, life was born anew on the earth. Below it was the constellation of the Fire Drill, composed of the stars forming the Belt of Orion (Brundage 61).

The Aztecs ritually repeat their creation myth. The ritual must be done exactly as the gods did it; therefore, it must be done at the right place (The Hill of the Star), and in the right way (every detail of the myth is repeated), and at the right time (at the zenith of the Pleiades). The sac-rificial victim takes the place of Nanahuatzin, who sacrifices himself into the fire and is reborn as the Fifth Sun. The fire from his burning corpse is used to reignite civilization. All these processes occur underneath a measured and prescribed heavenly order. As the Pleiades represented to the Aztecs the heavenly zenith and the source of new life, sacrificing a victim to the flames as this heavenly archetype rose in the sky meant that all the powers of that archetype would descend to earth and re-fertilize the new age. Repeating this ritual every fifty-two years in a nationwide festival kept the axle of heaven running smoothly. The invisible laws of nature were repeated so that civilization would also run smoothly—crops would grow, animals reproduce, and the human order would exist in cosmic equilibrium.

No matter how bizarre such a conception of things is to the modern mind, this remains the structure of thought in the oral age. As we examine the highly varied and complex ritual systems of the "mythological age," we begin to see that the modern idea of religion is replaced by the myths and rituals of the cultus, maintaining all the necessary customs and beliefs for its society. In these ritual systems there is no separation between what would be called religious and secular, or for that matter metaphysics and science. The gods served all needs and all forms of knowledge. Calendars, music, numbers, markets, governments, and all other areas of knowledge were all synthesized together in one corpus of being seeking to live the heavenly order on earth. The modern division between these areas of knowledge has no parallel in the ancient world. Each branch of knowledge is really nothing more than a function of some invisible principle of the omnipotent cosmos who has one divine source.

Oral Cult as Memory Theater

Orality and polytheism are necessary partners of cognition. For example, every cycle in the oral world had a deity associated with it, as is noted in the Egyptian scheme by Tom Hare: "Here, 'polytheism' was a manifestation of geographical and social diversity, a way of relating the local community to intangible forces important to that community, such as the change of the seasons, the cycle of the river, the processes of growth and decay, human life and death" (163). Myth and ritual were synthesized into great festivals that not only propitiated the gods, but maintained the calendar, conjoined its participants with the agricultural cycle, and sustained social cohesion as ritual initiations were done in concordance with the biological cycles of puberty, menstruation, and child-birth. Participants worshiped these deities, but the deities themselves are mandatory. The oral mind must divide the cosmos by its functions and cycles and assign to it a pantheon of identities by which these functions and cycles can be recollected on mnemonic grounds alone.

Oral information processing is so dependent on memory strategies that every available resource is employed to aid in the recollection and transmission of data. Formulaic phrases and patterns, heavy and heroic characters in narrative, chanted rhythms and poetical meter, and musical instruments playing to ritual songs and performances are all part of the oral, memory reservoir. There were other implements to aid memory, as Yeats notes, "the ancient memories were trained by an art which reflected the art and architecture of the ancient world, which could depend on faculties of intense visual memorization which we have lost" (20). The "art and architecture" of the ancient world was an integral part of the mnemonic library. McLuhan reveals that this kind of memory aid was used through the Middle Ages, where medieval cathedrals were the "books of the people." The art and sculpture in the cathedrals reminded illiterate worshipers of the stories and scriptural passages. Manuscript illumination served comparable needs as the colorful or gilded ornamentation in books did more than decorate the pages, but served mnemonic purposes (108-9).

In a small known chapter in Renaissance history, the connection between architecture and memory is firmly established. Guilio Camillo was an Italian philosopher, a contemporary with Copernicus and Kepler, and was one of the most famous men in the sixteenth century (Yates 135). His work was extolled by leading Renaissance intellectuals as being within the genus of the Seven Wonders of the World and was grouped with the philosophies of Hermes Trismegistus, Pythagoras, Plato, and Pico della Mirandola (Yates 140).

What was Camillo's remarkable contribution to the new age? Unlike Copernicus and Kepler, who had used printed texts to fashion a new phenomenology of the sky, Camillo used images and texts to fashion a phenomenology of the mind. Camillo built a memory theater. Literally, Camillo constructed an enclosed amphitheater filled with images, statues, drawers, and files. The stage was the focal point where one stood. The seats had been replaced with a multi-tiered edifice engineered with an entire network of images and designs, each referencing some ancient work, science, or philosophy. Contained within associated drawers and files were volumes of written speeches and treatises illuminating every area of human knowledge. A contemporary of Camillo states, "[Camillo] pretends that all things that the human mind can conceive and which we cannot see with the corporeal eye, after being collected together by diligent mediation may be expressed by certain corporeal signs in such a way that the beholder may at once perceive with his eyes everything that is otherwise hidden in the depths of the human mind" (Yates 137).

Camillo made a library for the mind, using mnemonic strategies and images as his "card catalogue." Interestingly, Camillo's theater was built on the foundations of ancient cosmology predating the geocentric one that Copernicus would reform. Camillo's theater was divided into three tiers, representing the celestial, material, and lower worlds. These tiers in turn were predicated upon seven levels each representing a planetary sphere as well as a field of ancient philosophy. Each tier and level had pillars and gates, which further divided the metaphysical universe according to neo-platonic and even cabalistic thought. We are not dealing with a vision forged from modern thought projected onto the Renaissance and the Scientific Revolution, but with the thought of these eras as they really were—deeply mired in a synthetic idea of the universe where the microcosm was every bit as important as the macrocosm. Kepler earned his keep, after all, not by teaching math and astronomy, but by creating astrological charts for his employers.

The idea of Camillo's theater was simple. If one familiarized himself with each image at each level, he could create a memory network in his mind that would be the primer to recall every aspect of the known cosmos, as Frances Yeats explains: "But his memory building is to represent the order of eternal truth; in it the universe will be remembered through organic association of all its parts with their underlying eternal order" (142). Each level ascended from First Causes through the orders of creation. In turn, each heaven was associated with a field of philosophy. Collected written works associated with that field were contained in drawers by their images. Camillo was so adroit with his memory theater that he could stand, and like a human computer, spout off thousands of different sources and citations of the leading thoughts of men, past and present. Camillo's memory theater was truly an astounding marvel.

Ironically, Camillo's great contribution to Renaissance art has been entirely forgotten. Typographic print made his contribution to the sciences nearly irrelevant and his memory theater has been utterly lost to the mind immersed in print. We have forgotten that many such memory systems were employed through the Middle Ages. Giordano Bruno is generally described as being burned at the stake for his cosmological theories. Contrarily, Bruno was found a heretic by his close association with the occultism that was employed within his own memory theater. Bruno created charts and images, in printed form, mired within the older pagan cosmology, where the Hermetic universe served as his memory primer (Yeats 285). Robert Fludd also constructed a memory theater using a cosmological template (Yeats 317). All of these men were intellectuals who had incredible and even superhuman capacity of memory. They were not born prodigies, but had trained their memories using mnemonic techniques. In all cases their memory systems were tied to a conception of the heavens, and in the case of Camillo, to an actual architectural library of the mind.

Camillo's memory theater was a new application of an old idea. For centuries through the Middle Ages scholars had used an instruction book on rhetoric attributed to Cicero that taught the art of memory. The memory strategy utilized in the *Rhetorica ad Herrenium* involved thinking of a well-known place, such as a building, and placing in each part of that building an image of one thing to be remembered. Jerome Lettvin explains:

> Probably the only written work available to us about the ancient arts of memory is the *Rhetorica ad Arrhenium*, improperly

attributed to Cicero. Here we find prescriptions for remembering things. We are instructed, for example, to imagine a walk through a temple, quiet and alone, during which we keep several feet from its wall. The argument that we wish to remember becomes associated with a sequence of things we see on the walk within the temple; and indeed the English word "topic" drives from *topos*, or place—a topic is the place in the temple to which we have attached an idea in the course of our walk. In effect, the temple comes to embody a kind of cross-mapping, in which something that we wished to remember superimposes itself upon something that we already knew very well. The temple is thus a stable and well-known ground on which the new set of facts is arrayed: the temple serves the purpose of a theory, to the extent that you can derive from a theory a great many facts, that, though seemingly unconnected, can nevertheless be related by the mapping you have made. We have, therefore, an art of memory in which a well-known universe can serve as a ground upon which other universes can be mapped. (133-34)

This kind of memory system is much older than Cicero. The earliest attribution of a codified system of memory is given to Simonides of Ceos (6th century BCE), who was supposedly the first Greek to invent topical mnemonic techniques. Such attribution is grossly misplaced; indeed, the entire oral world relied heavily on mnemonic strategies for the transmission of knowledge. Lettvin believes the foundation for such mnemonics was rooted in ancient myth: "For myths are more memorable the more things one can map on them. And there is for me a great poetic quality in a language whereby the relations of animals to each other, people to each other, the heavens to the earth, the gods to humankind, can all be worded in about the same way, until finally, by a single set of sentences, I can remember all of the universes as if they were maps of one another" (135).

Nor is the idea of a "temple walk" as the basis of memory original to the Greeks. It is a strategy hoary with age. As it turns out in advanced oral civilizations throughout the Near East and Mediterranean from at least the third millennium BCE, the ancient temple space was the memory theater for the entire culture. As already discussed, in order to pass down the most important information to each generation in an oral world, that information had to be layered within a language of action. The dances, dramas, ceremonies, festivals, and myths were not independently created to describe one idea or principle as if each dance was a book from a library describing a different subject. On the contrary, this language of action in oral civilization is incorporated into a synthetic whole at the center of the civilization's identity. The dances, festivals, temples, and myths constitute a cultus that has regular rhythms scrupulously overseen and followed by the educated caste endowed with the culture's knowledge. It is an oral civilization's cultus rooted in its sacred center that is, for all intents and purposes, the memory theater of that oral society. Annual festivals and perennial myths become the "well-known universe . . . upon which other universes can be mapped."

Orality and History

How much memory can be amassed? Even with the implementations of the cult the oral mind maintains only a few-score layers of vertical memory. Whatever information is kept in the memory theater must deserve its place. This brings up an issue of critical importance: how do oral peoples keep a history within the limitations of oral cognition?

Literate histories have more than a few-score layers of memory written into them. Good histories, like good modern science, require thousands of layers of information annotated by journals, minutes, events, reports, and charts. Obviously oral peoples do not have these things, and crafting a long and detailed historical exegesis is impossible. On the other hand, oral peoples create lists. They can memorize hundreds and even thousands of names in their genealogies. A list of names, however long and complex, is not a literate history. On this point Eliade observes that the literate reader of history is confronted with a dilemma: "The ahistorical character of popular memory, the inability of collective memory to retain historical events and individuals except insofar as it transforms them into archetypes . . . poses a series of new problems" (*CH* 46). These problems come by way of literate renderings of oral histories. Perhaps there is no better example of this quandary than traditional Biblical interpretation, as English scholar Margaret Barker makes clear, "The death blow to mythology was dealt by those who made the myths into history. We still have problems with Adam and Eve to this day as a result!" (*Gate* 180).

In oral societies real and historical details of a person or event lasts in the memory for about a century. A grandfather can tell a grandson about his experiences. The grandson eventually tells his grandson what he has learned. After that, the initial teachings of the first grandfather may degrade. To maintain historical continuity persons or events that must be remembered are placed within a specific memory theater set up for them—myth. Oral peoples have a set of narrative templates. These templates are products of their cult and cosmology; in other words they are associated with the rituals and festivals that are constantly maintained and familiar to everyone. People of renown are placed within these templates and their stories are mythologized so that they can be remembered for generations. This process is reversible, so that when a particular teaching must be transmitted a myth is told rooted in historic fact. Eliade observes, "the historical character of the persons celebrated in epic poetry is not in question. But their historicity does not long resist the . . . action of mythicization" (*CH* 42). Eliade reminds us that myth is not the first stage of the development of oral history, but the last (*CH* 43).

Was the Earth literally created in seven days? According to a literal, historical, and most of all literate interpretation of the Bible, the answer is yes. For centuries faithful Christians have advocated the historicity of such absurdities that grow at the turn of every page: Noah really did put two of every animal in the ark; Joshua really did stop the sun in the sky; Samson really did kill a thousand Philistines with the jawbone of an ass; and Jonah really did dwell for three long days in the belly of the whale. In all fairness, this is not a Christian problem, but a literate one. Believing Christians interpret the Bible literally because literate minds conceive history in this way.

Literate people of other faiths do the same, as many faithful Muslims take all the passages of the Koran literally and historically; just as many Hindus historically interpret the Mahabharata. While many academics find this amusing, they often fall into the same trap through the back-door. Misunderstanding the cultic or cosmic analogies in myth, scholars often interpret them literally for the people who produced them. Thus, they believe that all those people back then really did believe a horse and chariot pulled the sun across the sky or that the earth rested on a turtle. Further, with the same fundamental literalness many scholars deny any historicity to mythical figures. For decades Bible academics argued that Jesus was nothing but an apparition of fable and folklore. More ironically, scholars are often guilty of interpreting their own theories as literal history. After all, which is sillier: believing that the earth was created in seven days? Or that ancient peoples making a grave site affixed wooden oars to inverted boats so as to represent a parade of penises propped to attention, and the blades of those oars as open vulvas ready to receive the dead? Somehow the first notion is seen as sheer lunacy while the second is viewed as common-sense education. Even when there is clear reproductive symbols at ancient grave sites, the analogy is not to sex, but to the function of sex—cosmic rebirth.

The dilemma remains in cognitive systems. Oral peoples mytholo-gize history. Literate peoples historicize myth. Another way to put this is to realize that in oral societies there really is no such thing as pure history or pure myth; the two are often homogenized into a single cult system of narrative and ritual. An example of this process can be seen inscribed on a wall at the Temple of Luxor in Egypt. A great scene is introduced in stone spanning the entire entry pylon and known as the "Battle of Kadesh." In this scene pharaoh is depicted surrounded by his enemies in a battle that was indeed historical; the Egyptians fought the Kheta at Kadesh at the bend of the Orontes River during the fifth year of the reign of Ramses II. Even though the battle is a historical reality, the content and positioning of the "historical narrative" on the wall is peculiar.

In the first composition, Ramses is shown enthroned, facing west towards sunset, while in front of him there is another depiction of him charging into battle in his chariot. Behind him, however, he is again depicted, larger than life, enthroned and facing towards the east, a rela-tionship not without significance: "In the first composition, the king's east-west direction is comparable to the daily precession of the sun; seat-ed and drawing his bow, and smaller than he will next be shown, the king symbolizes the setting sun. In the second image, the west-east direction symbolizes the nocturnal path of the sun and its battle against the adver-sary: night" (de Lubicz, *Sacred* 127-28).

According to the depiction, the battle soon goes sour and the Egyptian king is surrounded by the enemy hoard. Indeed, at the hour of midnight pharaoh finds himself separated from his army divisions and facing the enemy all alone. In this darkest part of the battle the king invokes a prayer:

I invoke thee, O my father Amon! Here I am in the midst of great multitudes of people whom I know not; all nations have joined themselves together against me. My numerous soldiers have for-saken me, not one of my charioteers has looked around for me, and when I call out to them, not one of them harkens to my voice. But I believe that Amon is worth more to me than millions of soldiers, and hundreds of thousands of chariots, more than a myriad of brethren or youths, were they all united together! The work of many men is nothing. Amon surpasses them all! (de Lubicz, *Sacred* 129)

After the king's prayer, at the seventh hour of the night, the entire situation is reversed. Ramses is now identified with Amon and suddenly all of his enemies collapse before him, even as the pharaoh rises from the darkness of night and conquers his enemies with the rising sun (de Lubicz, *Sacred* 130-32). There really was a King Ramses and he really did fight at Kadesh, but if we take this scene literally (a.k.a. purely histori-cally), then we are led to believe that Ramses single-handedly destroyed thousands of his enemies with nothing more than a chariot and a prayer. The entire historical episode has turned into a radical piece of political propaganda. However, there is an internal logic to the sequence of events as presented, and rather than political propaganda, what we are being shown is something of a far more meaningful and esoteric nature.

Pharaoh confronts his enemy facing west while the sun sets. During his battle pharaoh is thus symbolically descending below the horizon, and indeed, at the darkest moment within this netherworld journey, at the seventh hour, the king finds himself alone and hopelessly outnum-bered. The seventh hour just so happens to be the darkest moment of the netherworld descent in the Egyptian funerary texts, the passing of which shows the initiate begin to rise back up with the sun out of the under-world. Ramses, passing the darkest hour, rises again with the sun upon the horizon victorious over all his enemies. The entire historical vignette is thus analogized with the netherworld journey of the sun.

Myth and history have met, not at odds with one another, but as complements to a fully logical scheme. In modern times we call this kind of historical narrative "cheating." Modern historians want only the facts, and this kind of analogizing, no matter its cultic or cosmological background, is not purely factual, and therefore of no use. On the contrary, myth deals with ultimate realities and relationships, for those are the things that oral historians want to pass down to every generation. Pharaoh gains power over his enemies because he is cosmic man (*anthropocosmos*), one who can descend the celestial axis with his soul intact. Like Gilgamesh, Herakles, or Moses, our hero has seen the other side of the veil and has returned to found the rites of civilization and even lead it into battle against evil forces. This historical vignette is more than history, it is *trans-history*. It is not only about a historical event but also and primarily about light and dark, good and evil, and the true source of one's power and authority.

Like oral science, oral history is not what literate minds want or expect. We quip over "household mathematics" and smile at outlandish tales while forgetting the elegant symmetry the oral mind achieved in its construction of the above and below, of time and space, of myth and history. We want our herrings in the water and our eagles in the air, only distantly aware of the mountain standing in the deep and the current swimming in the sky. These paradoxes will always challenge our interpretations of myth and history.

Literacy and Transformation

From a modern literate point of view it is impossible to fully understand the oral world. What I have done is walk around its circumference occasionally poking holes in the walls of our own misunderstanding. It is possible, however, to examine how an information-processing revolution can change civilization. In more recent history there was such a revolution introduced by the creation of the printing press. Some scholars insist that the printing press not only changed civilization but also was the beginning of the era we call modernity (Toulmin 5). In discussing this invention and its consequences, we may use this transformation of information processing as a template and project backwards what may have been similar consequences with the introduction of writing. If the invention of the printing press helped to create modernity, then the invention of writing itself may have been a necessary precursor for the creation of the hieratic city-state and the first political empires.

It should be noted that the first printing press was actually invented by the Chinese (7th century CE), who also invented our modern form of paper (2nd century CE). The Chinese printing press was composed of wood blocks upon which were carved the text or images to be printed; the blocks would be dipped in ink, much like a modern stamp, and then pressed on paper. By the 11th century CE the Chinese also invented a movable type printing press using porcelain tablets. This press had limitations, for the size of the tablets and the artistry of the carved or painted characters was highly prohibitive for the production of books. The greatest limitation was the Chinese alphabet itself, which unlike the English alphabet was composed of thousands of characters. To obtain full literacy in 11th century China was a full-time job for scribes, chosen from youth, and employed for specific administrative purposes.

The printing revolution in Europe came by way of the Gutenberg press (15th century CE). This machine was predicated upon the screw press used to press cloth, though adopted with the ingenious innovation of a metal alloy, movable-type alphabet, that made printing fast and efficient for its day—a true technological marvel. Because European writers were using reductive alphabets (English, Latin, Greek, German, and French all have less than thirty letters) and because the alloy characters were small and movable, books could be made relatively quickly, inexpensively, and in great numbers. Books that once took months or years to hand copy, or print using blocks, could now be manufactured by the thousands in just days or weeks.

In *The Printing Revolution in Early Modern Europe*, Elizabeth Eisenstein shows how European presses changed civilization. She begins, "As an agent of change, printing altered methods of data collection, storage and retrieval systems, and communications networks used by learned communities throughout Europe" (xiv). It sounds rather dry until one begins to consider the breadth and depth of the tentacles that formed the printing revolution. Let me cite several passages that will part the curtain just a little:

> The difficulty of making even one "identical" copy of a significant technical work was such that the task could not be trusted to any hired hands. Men of learning had to engage in "slavish copying" of tables, diagrams, and unfamiliar terms. The output of whole editions of sets of astronomical tables did not merely "intensify" previous trends. It reserved them, producing a new situation which released time for observation and research. (18)

> During the first centuries of printing, old texts were duplicated more rapidly than new ones. On this basis most authorities conclude that "printing did not speed up the adoption of new theories." But where did these new theories come from? Must we invoke some spirit of the times? Or is it possible that an increase in the output of old texts contributed to the formulation of new theories? (42)

> Much as maps from different regions and epochs were brought into contact in the course of preparing editions of atlases, so too were technical texts brought together in certain physicians' and astronomers' libraries. Contradictions became more visible,

divergent traditions more difficult to reconcile. The transmission of received opinion could not proceed smoothly once Arabists were set against Galenists or Aristotelians against Ptolemaists. Not only was confidence in old theories weakened, but an enriched reading matter also encouraged the development of new intellectual combinations and permutations. . . . Increased output directed at relatively stable markets, in short, created conditions that favored new combinations of old ideas at first and then, later on, the creation of entirely new systems of thought. (44)

Yet Copernicus's life (1473-1543) spanned the very decades when a great many changes, now barely visible to modern eyes, were transforming "the data available" to all book readers. A closer study of these changes could help to explain why systems of charting the planets, mapping the earth, synchronizing chronologies, codifying laws, and compiling bibliographies were all revolutionized before the end of the sixteenth century. In each instance, one notes, Hellenistic achievements were first reduplicated and then, in a remarkably short time, surpassed. . . . Typographical fixity is a basic prerequisite for the rapid advancement of learning. It helps to explain much else that seems to distinguish the history of the past five centuries from that of all prior eras. (78)

As communion with the Sunday paper has replaced churchgoing, there is a tendency to forget that sermons had at one time been coupled with news about local and foreign affairs, real estate transactions, and other mundane matters. After printing, however, news gathering and circulation were handled more efficiently under lay auspices. . . . The displacement of pulpit by press is significant not only in connection with secularization but also because it points to an explanation for the weakening of local community ties. To hear an address delivered, people have to come together; to read a printed report encourages individuals to draw apart. (94-95)

As long as texts could be duplicated only by hand, perpetuation of the classical heritage rested precariously on the shifting requirements of local elites. Texts imported into one region depleted supplies in others; the enrichment of certain fields of study by an infusion of ancient learning impoverished other fields of study by diverting scribal labor. . . . Systematization came only after the humanist impulse could be combined with new features supplied by print culture. (125, 127).

Eisenstein makes many more points, but these are sufficient to show the powerful transformations of the printing revolution. One of Eisenstein's points is very instructive. During the period of the Enlightenment numerous new theories were emerging. Where did they come from? Eisenstein hits the mark when she poses, "Must we invoke some spirit of the times? Or is it possible that an increase in the output of old texts contributed to the formulation of new theories?" The profusion of older texts in European scholarly society did in fact create new combinations of ideas upon which innovations in theory and science could be made. In fact, during the Enlightenment era, Europe was gathering all the old Greek texts they could find to translate and print. There was a surge in new ideas predicated on older Greek ideas.

It is interesting to note that Copernicus's great work, *De revolutionibus orbium coelestium*, is a strange composite of heliocentric philosophy mixed with Ptolemaic science. The first few pages of this celebrated work begins with the resolute hypothesis that the sun is in the center of the universe. The planets, including the Earth, orbit around the sun, and the Earth itself turns on its own axis. This is all true of course, and revolutionary in 16th century Europe. The problem is after the first few pages Copernicus's book quickly devolves into Ptolemaic stratagems of cycles and epicycles, so by the time Copernicus is done he has completely blurred his own theory—and he knew it. In fact, while several history books insist that Copernicus reduced the number of epicycles in the Ptolemaic system, he actually added to them, making the old system even more cumbersome.

Copernicus was not a professional astronomer: he received his academic training in law and medicine. He had a passion for cosmology; however, and he spent decades making notes on astronomical observations. Curiously, Copernicus proposed his heliocentric theory very early in life. An obscure manuscript he authored entitled *Commentariolus* appears in a library inventory list in Cracow dating to 1514, thirty years before the publication of his masterpiece. The small tract, according to the inventory, discussed the possibilities of a heliocentric system. It is the inventory that is dated to 1514, not the manuscript itself, which must have been written even earlier and presumably would have been formulated earlier still. This fact suggests that Copernicus formulated his heliocentric theory before many of his own astronomical observations. His main heliocentric theory seems formulated from his desk and not from some observatory. So one must ask the question, where did Copernicus get the idea of a heliocentric system, especially as he had no idea how to prove such a system? The answer is simple—from ancient texts. This is proven in Copernicus's own words:

I therefore went to the trouble of reading anew the books of all philosophers on which I could lay hands to find out whether someone did not hold the opinion that there existed other motions of the heavenly bodies than assumed by those who taught the mathematical sciences in the schools. And thus I found first in Cicero that Hiketas had held the belief that the earth moves.

Afterwards I found [in] Plutarch [it is actually psuedo-Plutarch] that others have also held this opinion. (Koestler 207)

Of greater interest is the citation Copernicus gives:

But others hold that the earth moves; thus Philolaus the Pythagoriean held that it revolves round the Fire in an oblique circle like the sun and moon. Herakleides of Pontus and Ekphantus the Pythagorean also suppose the earth to move, though not in a progressive motion, but after the manner of a wheel, turning upon an axle about its own center from west to east. (Koestler 207)

Copernicus had access to ancient texts that had been reproduced and printed as part of the printing revolution. Surprisingly, many of these ancient texts had already posited either a heliocentric or pseudo-heliocentric system. The particular genius of Copernicus was not mathematical or observational proofs of a modern heliocentric theory, as much as it was a rewriting of the Ptolemaic system within the context of an effusive and persistent searching through numerous texts as he traveled and worked in different parts of Europe. Copernicus read Greek, Latin, Italian, German, and Polish, and searched a wide variety of book collections, libraries, and multilingual texts. His work shows a remarkable familiarity with a variety of texts and sources including religious and mathematic literature, an acquaintance with "place names and calendars, of ancient chronologies and coins" (Eisenstein 208), and a knowledge of ancient and contemporary writings.

One example of the widespread research Copernicus was able to do exists in two peculiar geometric proofs included in his book and without which his work could not have been constructed. The geometric proofs are original to Europe, and one must therefore imagine that Copernicus must have devised them himself. Curiously, as one scholar has noted, two Islamic astronomers whose works had already been published much earlier established these very proofs. More tellingly is that Copernicus's proofs are labeled identically to the earlier Islamic publications: "Any geometric theorem has the various points labeled with letters or numbers, at the discretion of the originator. The order and choice of symbols is arbitrary. The German science historian Willy Hartner noted that the geometric points used by Copernicus were identical to al-Tusi's original notation" (Teresi 5). The suggestion is that Copernicus copied these proofs, wholesale, from Arabic sources. This does not imply plagiarism, for in the beginning of the print era there was no such thing. It does imply a thorough review of newly available sources from which Copernicus was working.

Copernicus was a sort of master librarian at keeping notes, over years of his life, as he built up an edifice of ideas and sources. His heliocentric theory and proofs arose from the pages of books with his actual observations reinforcing his pre-formulated theory. This same dynamic existed within the works and theories of Johannes Kepler. One is reminded that the Hellenistic virtuoso of astronomy Eratosthenes (3rd century BCE)—who calculated the circumference of the earth, the tilt of the earth's axis, and the distance of the earth to the sun and moon and who established an early system of latitude and longitude—was himself the librarian of Alexandria. One wonders how much of his work was based off access to both old and contemporary texts that were being catalogued in that massive gallery of ancient knowledge? One also wonders what his sources may have been? More tantalizingly, was the origin of those sources only from Greece?

In any case, there could be no modern age without the printing press. In five centuries, more was learned and debated than in the previous twenty. This took place mostly because the nature of the communication and information network had completely changed, as Eisenstein notes:

"Typographical fixity is a basic prerequisite for the rapid advancement of learning." Vertical memory had been introduced into Europe, where there was a marvelous expansion of texts that exponentially brought more information, ideas, and people into the debate. Point by point, we see that scholars had more time for new research and argument; therefore, they could compare and contrast previous theories at a level never seen before. They could view internal strengths and weaknesses of given theories and debate them on their merits within an ever-growing circle of participants. Perhaps most important, a form of information permanency was finally established transcending the economic/political/social/religious needs and wants of a very small group of people in possession of hand-copied texts. In short, the more books and the more participants, the more information will spread and a greater potential will grow for new ideas.

The conglomerate affect of new materials and ideas produced another cultural consequence, as Eisenstein notes: "Insofar as memory training and 'slavish copying' became less necessary, while inconsistencies and anomalies became more apparent after printed materials began to be produced, a distrust of received opinion and a fresh look at the evidence recommended itself to all manner of curious men" (194). This distrust fueled further inquiry and testing of not only old theories but also of many unexamined cultural norms. Print culture and the spirit of testing the old and asserting the new combined to underwrite what would become known as the Reformation. Various writings of Martin Luther sold over 300,000 copies throughout Europe, and "Protestantism surely was the first to exploit [the printing press] as a mass medium. It was also the first movement of any kind, religious or secular, to use the new presses for overt propaganda and agitation against an established institution" (148).

The printing revolution helped change the religious geography and continued to do so well after the Catholic-Protestant split. As already noted, there were unforeseen consequences of the printing press, such as the decentralization of the community from the church. Given enough time in the modern world, the press really has replaced the pulpit. The transformation is not finished, as now the Internet is making the press obsolete. Not to be outdone, video and audio mediums may even replace the use of the written word. All of these transformations have enormous consequences, many of which remain unexamined, and few seem to be positive for critical thinking. Such is the nature of an information-processing revolution; many changes of thought and information patterns occur—but are they all progressive?

It is impossible to imagine the Scientific Revolution occurring without the printing press. Of course, the Information Age and the Digital Age could not even be conceived without it. If so much can change with the introduction of a new way to process, record, and store writing, what could change with the introduction of writing itself? Similar consequences must have followed the invention of writing, though on a completely different scale. In the least, the intellectual class (i.e., the temple priests) could also exponentially enlarge the knowledge base and market transactions with the permanency of the written word. Without a printing press there were certain limitations: everything did have to be written by hand, which meant a constant training school of scribes with various competencies. Judging from the tens of thousands of clay tablets that have been discovered in Mesopotamia, and the prolific amounts of texts from Egypt—and knowing so little of it has survived—we can guess that the ancient world was also filled with the written word. Indeed, the Library of Alexandria in the third century BCE contained at least a half million scrolls (Casson 36).

One must consider how writing impacted the building of large cult centers like the ziggurats and pyramids. Enormous amounts of materials, inventories, labor, food, and wages would have to be organized, often over long distances at a colossal scale. Contracts and decrees of every sort involving every sector and building stage would have to be kept. Perhaps even the geometric designs, angles, and measures—let alone weights and formulas calculating the movement of large blocks over long distances horizontally and vertically—must have required some written medium for constant checks and re-checks in a structure's progress. While oral conventions were employed, the introduction of writing must have increased the capacity for larger scale projects. It is curious that within a few centuries after the invention of writing the great ziggurats and pyramids begin to appear. Even the old megalithic rings, such as Stonehenge, are refashioned at a grander scale. Are such correspondences just coincidental?

The invention of writing must have also contributed to increased complexity within governments, markets, agricultural planning, and other social structures. With the invention of writing much more could be done in a shorter amount of time. We come to understand this reality when we see thousands of clay tablets whose contents are:

> lists and inventories of possessions; accounts of receipts and issues; of objects in storage or on hand; records of the regulations of communal life; price indices; international treaties and private agreements involving all imaginable types of transactions; sales and acquisitions, loans and deposits, marriages and "divorces," dowry agreements, wills and inheritance divisions, adoptions and contracts for nursing or for apprenticeship; official or private letters; commemorative and dedicatory inscriptions; property marks, etc. (Bottéro 20)

These tablets reveal a complex and networked civilization. No doubt oral civilizations can also be complex, but writing allows for the increase in networked complexity; the introduction of writing expanded the social and economic products of those networks. Ian Shaw, in his *Oxford History of Ancient Egypt*, makes a similar observation:

> The Early Dynastic Period [of Egypt] was a time of consolidation of the enormous gains of unification, which could easily have failed, when a state bureaucracy was successfully organized and expanded to bring the entire country under royal control. This was done through taxation, to support the Crown and its projects on a grand scale, including expeditions for goods and materials to the Sinai, Palestine, the Lebanon, Lower Nubia, and the Eastern Desert. Conscription must presumably also have been practiced in order to build the large royal mortuary monuments and to supply soldiers for military expeditions. The use of early writing no doubt facilitated such state organization. (87-88)

Writing also restructures thought (Ong 8). I cannot stress this last point enough. The ancient mind was linked with its information medium. Every category in an oral mind is localized in the temporal world. The dictionary or encyclopedia of an oral mind thus becomes nature. The development of a phonetic alphabet alters the imaginative resources of an individual. As David Abram notes, letters in a phonetic alphabet "do not exist in the world of ordinary vision" (112). The earliest scripts are pictograms or ideograms directly linked with a physical object or process in nature. Phonetic scripts are linked to thoughts only; therefore, are autonomous to the real world. This autonomy and timelessness creates a "reflexive awareness" which is analytical. Abram shows how the Greek word *psychê* is used by Homer to signify the invisible breath that animates a living body, but is used by Plato and Socrates to describe "the aspect of oneself that is refined and strengthened by turning away from the ordinary sensory world in order to contemplate the intelligible Ideas, the pure and eternal forms" (113). There has been a shift in meaning from the direct experience of breathing to the indirect observation of thinking; "the Socratic-Platonic *psychê*, in other words, is none other than the literate intellect, that part of the self that is born and strengthened in relation to the written letters" (113).

The consequences of information-transformation are not just progressively linear but are also multi-dimensional. For example, the transference of cognitive resources from the direct experience of nature to the inner world of the mind permanently changes one's relationship to nature. In literate cultures writing is the layer of reflection between the thinker and the direct experience of nature. While this layer of reflection helps create abstract and analytical categories in a vertical memory system, it also acts as a barrier to the living breath of life inherent in the actual experience of nature in a horizontal memory system. Again Abram notes, "If we no longer experience the enveloping earth as expressive and alive, this can only mean that the animating interplay of the senses has been transferred to another medium, another locus of participation" (131). The new locus is the written word. The old locus was not just nature, but one's "attunement or synchronization between [our] own rhythms and the rhythms of [nature]" (54). The immediate effect of this transition is obvious: oral cultures live in nature, literate cultures use it.

Information systems also create economic patterns, as certain resources are utilized in an information network depending on the medium. Ancient cultures had an economic ecosystem centered on the cultus of its civilization. The temple complex and its priests served as the market nexus where trade, art, and manufacturing were found. Manuscript culture creates an economic ecosystem around the perpetual training of scribes and the local dissemination of information specifically for the people who can afford it. Print culture changes that economic ecosystem towards mass markets and mass marketing. Today we live in a post-literate, audio-visual culture. The economic ecosystem is created around television, cinema, and the Internet. Indeed, the budgets of some modern films now exceeds the gross domestic product (GDP) of some poorer countries. It is an old adage that people, business, and ideas will follow the money. The money, however, is a product of communication flow and information networks.

How people communicate is intimately linked with how they think, work, and believe. There are enormous consequences to oral, literate, and post-literate ways of thinking. For the most part these consequences remain unseen and subconscious. This should be a lesson for us, for what seems so primitive and obscure in the ancient past is really nothing more than the outcome of oral consciousness. Aside from the technological marvels that can only be created in vertical memory systems, much of the "primitivism" we see in the past is nothing more but the projection of our own literate biases upon an imaginary world of our own making.

Conclusion

The earliest scripts are still very much attached to the oral cultures that produced them. Whoever invented writing was a genius. But where did they get the idea in the first place? When we look at the early scripts of cuneiform and hieroglyphs we see that simple images and phonemes can be loaded with a constellation of associations and meanings. Why create such ambiguity within the system? The advantage of writing is the opportunity for clarity and meaning in any given mark. Of course we understand that writing does not appear *ex nihilo,* or out of nowhere. It shows up predicated upon an earlier tradition of information processing that had been operating for millennia.

Even as the printing press could only come about with the written script, writing itself must have been predicated upon a previous system of information management, a system originating in an oral society. When we look at the earliest writing we must be peeking into the internal gear-works of that previous system. I think we might rightly assume that such a system bestowed its imprint, its style, its prerogatives, and preju-dices upon the first scripts, for the earliest writers would have used what was already familiar as they made their first bold steps. When we look at oral societies we see that information processing is very important and always occurs in a series of rituals abounding in mythological tales. Myth and ritual are the x-rays of the first written scripts: the skeleton that birthed a new creation we have improperly called the beginnings of civilization.

If ritual masks and tattoos can communicate an entire "library" of truth to its participants, then the earliest scripts must have done like-wise. As such, the translation of the earliest Egyptian hieroglyphs and Mesopotamian religious texts must still be in its infancy, for the initial scripts would be attached to a grand metaphysical network implicit in the cultus of its particular civilization. As Nibley observes of Egyptian hieroglyphs, for example:

> Everyone knows that the Egyptians called hieroglyphics the "divine words" and that they were meant to conceal, if not to mystify; they know also that in the most important passages the scribes often resorted to cryptograms and even spoke to each other in code language when they discussed them; it is not too much to say that the religious texts are written in a *Metasprache*, or metalanguage, to use Erik Hornung's expression, a special *Initiationssprache*. The words used on the higher level could only be understood in their true sense by the initiated. Everything was in code, the nature of the gods concealed "by a cloud of epi-thets," referring to mythological or cultic situations which only the instructed understood; the cultic images are not portraits, but "ideograms" that must be interpreted. (*MJSP* 126)

It should be clear from this realization that to interpret the mythologies outside the context of the ancient *cultus* in which they were forged is a near futile task. At best, we can derive only pieces and fragments of ancient thought by studying the myths alone or the surviving symbols and archaeological remnants in concordance with those myths. The ancient songs, dances, and rites associated with them are lost. The most critical pieces are missing, and in their absence modern theorists have supplied their own mortar to put the remaining pieces of this grand, wrecked system together again. The cohesive vision of that mortar has been and often remains a Darwinian view of history and mind; as such, it is a foregone conclusion that most theorists would never even bother to look for a complex technical language within the superstition, magic, totems, taboos, fetishes, and the ubiquitous fertility emblems that have filled our college textbooks for well over a century.

It is perhaps a step backwards to define myth as the oral imprinting press of pre-literate people. The definition uses a literate metaphor for an oral category. Then again, a literate metaphor may be the only way to describe the function of myth in oral societies to a literate audience. An imprinting press is a mnemonic device, which like the actual printing press, can establish a permanency of information using imaginative motifs, images, and narratives. These can be used to entrench and store information which must be retrieved as quickly as one can pick up a book. One image, motif, or narrative is bestowed with multiple layers of meaning all connected together in a sort of mental mainframe, whereby a host of ideas can be remembered.

If myth is the oral imprinting press of pre-literate people, then ritual is the "ink" of that press, the residue in which the content of the mythic medium congeals. "The rites were representations of this accord, in a way comparable to those formulae of modern physics through which the modes of operation of inscrutable cosmic forces become not only accessible to the mind but also susceptible to control," writes Campbell. "They are physical formulae; written, however, not in black on white of, say, an $E=mc^2$, but in human flesh" (*Primitive* 179). Myth and ritual are not adolescent fancy. In their original form they belonged to the mnemonic library of oral minds seeking to resolve the problems of the day with the materials at hand.

Myth is sacred narrative because all aspects of the oral cosmos existed within a frame of sacred time and space. Every action-principle of nature, such as genesis, gestation, birth, life, and death, was associated with a deity whose role was analogous to their name and implicit in the self-organizing cosmos that unfolded in every season. The stars, planets, sun, and moon; the waters, trees, fields, and flowers; the birds, mountains, and human beings—all became the constituents of flowing legends and epics in a grand tapestry of metaphysical thought. Myth was the technical language of the oral age.

Finally, who were the first minds to fashion the use of myths and rituals to transmit information? Who were the first mythographers that employed intuition, observation, and analogical thinking, and conceived their systems of myth? Who calculated the necessary instructions of the seasons, calendars, animal behaviors, migratory patterns, and agricultural practices—let alone the principles of life and death and the cosmos? Might I suggest that with the superhuman spirit that invented writing, the first myth-makers were of an order of mind equal to any human our historians prize—Einstein, Newton, Kepler, Plato. They were a group of people at the very edge of history—people that we know nothing about and to whom we owe everything.

CHAPTER 3

ORAL COSMOLOGY

The Problem

Principles of orality are invaluable when investigating features of myth and polytheism, but these principles lead us to perhaps the strangest construct of ancient thinking—oral cosmology, the meaning and relationship between the individual and his *cosmic* environment. In my view ancient cosmology is the focal point of oral philosophy and is essential for the understanding of the ancient mind. One does not study ancient myth and religion for very long before being confronted with a stunning metaphysical expanse of symbols and rites saturated with cosmic themes. The mythological strata is so impregnated with these themes that it is certain that celestial phenomena is the primary archetypal reservoir of oral cognition.

This realization brings up another more intractable problem, for modern literate culture has switched its cognitive model. We prefer abstract ideation no longer attached to the daily concrete manifestations in material phenomena. Literally, the modern mind has severed itself from its immediate experience of nature, but especially of the heavens, and this has profound consequences. Nothing can illustrate this point more lucidly than an example shown by Jay Leno of *The Tonight Show*. He went to the campus of UCLA during a graduation ceremony to ask some very simple questions dealing with astronomy. Leno posited his questions to college graduates, most with bachelors and some with masters degrees. One of the questions asked was "How many moons does the Earth have?" Surprisingly, the answers ranged from three to nine. Another question was "How long does it take for the Earth to make one complete orbit around the sun?" "About three years," replied someone wearing a university graduation cap. Perhaps Leno edited out the scores of people giving the correct answers?

Yet another example illustrates the depth of the problem. The modern world is under the constant thrum of electric lights that produce what modern astronomers call "light pollution." The night sky can no longer be seen in detail within or near urban areas. This fact is verified by the electric blackout that occurred in Los Angeles during the earthquake of January 17, 1994. As the 6.7 earthquake hit at 4:37 in the morning, thousands of people scampered outdoors to escape shaking and falling debris. Because of the blackout, people who had lived in the city all their lives were confronted with a vision they had never seen: the stars, including the bright white band known as the Milky Way stretching across the sky. In fact, hundreds of phone calls flooded the Griffith Observatory over the next several days as people called, many quite alarmed, asking what was the cause of the strange lights in the sky (Krupp, *Negotiating* 76).

One has to travel several hundred miles away from urban light sources to see a true black sky. In the United States there are few such spots left. In Hong Kong with billowing dust clouds produced by automobiles, factories, and coal burners, not only is the night sky permanently obscured but so also is the day sky. Add to these facts the constant environment of modern life—the cubicle, the classroom, and the office, with the infinite flickering light and white noise of media screens and devices. One begins to wonder about the epistemological consequences of such an artificial environment? How does one experientially think of the universe when one is permanently separated from it by a layer of artificial technology? How does this dynamic affect our perceptions of reality?

Modernity has not escaped the consequences of its own form of cognition. Herein lies another paradox. Literacy has a layer of reflection between the thinker and its object where objectification and abstraction of ideas can occur. This creates ever more complex levels of classification and organization where a vertical memory system is built. On the other hand, this layer of reflection also acts as a barrier to the direct experience of nature. The higher a civilization's vertical memory system, the further its consciousness drifts away from the base of its creation. Not only are modern peoples severed from basic awareness of the sky and its cycles, most of them have no idea how the food appears in their grocery stores.

Additionally, the higher the vertical knowledge system is, the greater amount of specialization is required, thus profoundly reducing one's awareness of other important fields of knowledge while simultaneously reducing or eliminating outsiders from engaging in various branches of knowledge. Modern cosmology is an excellent example of this, as today's cosmological paradigms have become so dense with mathematical theories and technical jargon that the complex mental machinations of cosmologists have become an end unto itself. The layperson is left entirely out of the debate in an increasingly adventitious universe while cosmologists are left speaking to an ever-narrowing body of selves. Ancient cosmology explained the universe to the entire community, while the modern community has become cosmologically illiterate.

Our point of comparison is not the anxieties innate in these worldviews, but in the cosmovision itself. The ancient oral world related to the cosmos in significantly different ways. Sometimes those ways seem so remote and incomprehensible; as a result it is far too easy for educated modern people to place these differences in a completely different box labeled "primitive." Oral cosmology was not primitive. It was oral. Our misunderstanding comes about because we have changed our basic thinking strategies from orality to literacy. Ancient cosmology had its own high demands, as de Santillana and von Dechend explain: "Yet, it was a prodigiously vast theory, with no concessions to merely human sentiments. It, too, dilated the mind beyond the bearable, although without destroying man's role in the cosmos. It was a ruthless metaphysics" (*HM* 6). This chapter seeks to articulate the epistemological considerations of a culture's cosmology, including our own, and how its consequences explain differences between modern and ancient forms of thinking.

Modern Cosmology

According to modern definitions, cosmology is the study of the origin and structure of the universe. However, modern cosmologists no longer gaze at the sun, moon, or Milky Way. In fact, modern cosmologists rarely look at the sky at all. Modern cosmology belongs in the archetypal reservoir of literate, abstract ideation; therefore, it takes place inside the laboratory and math cubicle. Modern cosmology is strictly mechanistic, and it focuses primarily on the "big universe"—the chemical and energetic makeup of stars and galaxies, the Big Bang Theory, and so on. We call this universe a *macrocosm*. There are also little bits that compose the universe: protons, neutrons, quarks, leptons, and such, all lumped into a field of study called particle physics or quantum mechanics. The little universe that makes up the big universe is called a *microcosm*. In modern terms the microcosm is the skeletal foundation of the macrocosm: one builds upon the other.

This definition of cosmology is specifically modern and is fixated upon two underlying assumptions. First, the modern conception considers the universe as an assemblage running on physical parts and material forces. For the modern macrocosm, this view constitutes a cause and effect relationship between a primordial atom's expansion via a Big Bang and a multi-billion year course of evolution that produced our galaxy, solar system, sun, and earth. The material universe is like a machine, and modern cosmologists want to discover the formulas, ratios, and theorems that describe its cogs, gears, and uncanny timing. This can be done because the universe is unalterably obeying the architecture of natural laws.

Second, and perhaps most important, modern materialists are certain that they have separated science from religion and cosmology from eschatology (the theological considerations of death and ultimate destiny). Modern cosmologists pejoratively classify ancient cosmologists as astrologers. They believe that the ancient world was mired in another kind of thinking that was primitive and religious. They believe their own cosmology is not religious, because they wear lab coats instead of frocks and do their work in laboratories and math cubicles instead of cathedrals. They do not care about the sun chariot and its horses—they are working on quantum field theory, string theory, multi-verse theory, space-time geometry theory, and so on. They use highly complex mathematical models in all their theories without reference to the will of the gods; therefore, they believe they are practicing true science as opposed to pseudo-science. There is no place for anything religious in modern cosmological matters.

There is a problem for the materialists and their modern cosmos. It turns out to be the same problem that has existed in every cosmology throughout history—an underlying *fundamentum* that is so subtle that it is frequently overlooked. What the modern definition omits from its parameters is the very thing one must be aware of when studying cosmology: it is not a science, it is an epistemology. What we think about the universe, its origin and structure, turns out to be the box that contains our imaginations. This point cannot be overstated: *a civilization's ultimate framework of cultural imagination is its own cosmology.*

It is the construction of a theory, especially a cosmological theory, that turns science into metaphysics. This is especially made clear when one modern cosmologist defines his field of study this way: "Maybe more so than in any other field of physics, cosmologists construct fantasy worlds which they hope may have some bearing on what we observe"

(Ferriera 10). How can this be justified from a strict, scientific point of view? Our modern cosmologist continues, "The hope is that, like Albert Einstein, by stretching our imaginations but at the same time remaining firmly entrenched in basic principles, it will be possible to explain many of the unanswered questions in cosmology" (Ferriera 10).

The modern positivist focuses primarily on the "firmly entrenched basic principles" that are made up of formula and proofs and says all the universe can be explained in this way. Much like history and myth, all those "firmly entrenched basic principles" have to be strung together in a dot-to-dot construction that encompasses a wider area of ideology that may not be justified by those basic principles. They are strung together into "fantasy worlds." In order to create a fantasy world one must already have a cosmology in mind. This means modern cosmology is a product of a philosophical cosmovision already firmly established. This is the way it has always been. Pythagoras believed the center of the universe was a fiery cube. He had very good reasons to believe this. Aristotle believed that the Earth was the center of the universe, and all his data fit this model. Johannes Kepler believed that the distance between each planetary sphere could be represented by the geometric ratios of the platonic solids. It was an elegant idea and completely wrong. Albert Einstein's relativity equations could predict an expanding universe; however, Einstein did not believe in an expanding universe and so he created a cosmological constant incorporating his new formulas into his pre-established ideas. Every cosmologist pours his observations into a fantasy world crafted by the intellectual tender of the age.

Cosmologies are produced by inductive methods, and as Steven Gimbel has pointed out, "any finite set of data will have an infinite number of mutually exclusive hypotheses that can be inductively inferred from them" (113). That is to say, any finite set of observations can be explained by an infinite number of theories that describe them.

Cosmologists will never run out of descriptive fantasy worlds, because, like historians, they will never have enough puzzle pieces. This is why, according to Karl Popper, all scientific discovery "is impossible without faith in ideas which are of a purely speculative kind" (16) and that all scientific observation statements are really "interpretations in the light of theories" (McGee 30).

The Big Bang Theory is an excellent example of this process, as it is a very useful tool to describe several features of the observable cosmos, but admittedly it is also a theory that begins in mid-sentence. Not one modern cosmologist, astrophysicist, or math-theorist can definitively say anything about the where, what, or when of the original singularity from which the universe expanded. Many competing assumptions of a highly philosophical nature must be made before the formulas and schemas begin to apply. What we have with the Big Bang Theory is really not a conception of the origin of the universe, but a statement about the evolution of the universe after the origin already occurred. The same is true for the human microcosm, as biological theoretical-constructs only apply after life appears. Every cosmology begins just one step after "In the beginning," and this is why all cosmologies are "interpretations in the light of theories."

Ancient cosmology was not pre-science. It was oral science. The oral mind does not theorize observations into abstractions like the literate mind. That does not mean that the oral mind cannot theorize. It does, but it theorizes using concrete relationships. When either a benevolent or terrible event occurs at the same time that a certain star appears on the horizon, there might be a correlation. Within this context, those ancient astrologers were doing the exact same thing as our modern cosmologists, yet only within the oral universe. They observed, recorded, measured, and modified their observations of the above and below in an attempt to describe a universe which fit the data. However, the data was poured into a pre-established cosmovision—a fantasy world crafted by oral cognition. Whatever their religious concerns, the astrologers always thought they were doing cutting-edge science.

Cosmology and Society

Cosmologies underwrite our collective imagination. As a result, all cosmologies have social consequences. It should not surprise us to find that our attitudes of the universe are reflected in the ideas of ourselves and vice versa. This observation is no slight quibble. Agrarian societies, whose produce is a correlate with the power of the sun, tend to live under monarchal governments, where kings and emperors are the political embodiment of the celestial order. This kind of social order was manifest until the Industrial Age. Stephen Toulmin, in his book *Cosmopolis*, points out that in eighteenth-century France, "the key force in society was the monarch's 'solar' power to control (and illuminate) the state's activities. The Sovereign supervised the Court and the royal agencies, and influenced the actions of the nobles and gentry directly: those of the lower orders or 'masses' followed suit indirectly. . . . Social stability depended on all the parties in society 'knowing their place' relative to the others" (133). Toulmin asserts that the model of the monarch was "cosmo-political" and "to the extent that this hierarchy mirrored the structure of nature, its authority was self-explanatory, self-justifying, and seemingly rational" (133).

As Nicholas Campion smartly points out, the notion of the political monarch was challenged in the 18th century "when radicals seized on Isaac Newton's gravity, in order to argue the consequence—that all human society, being an integral part of the cosmos, must also be governed by one law, kings included" (*Astrology* 2). The popular and philosophical arguments for "natural law" were synchronous with the novel discoveries of the new cosmic order. "All such views" writes Campion, "are versions of what I term the Cosmic State, the application of cosmological theory to political ideology and the management of society" (*Astrology* 2).

What Campion has called the "Cosmic State" is what I have termed the *cosmological imagination*. My definition of the term extends beyond socio-political ideology, for the cosmological imagination is the genus of epistemological considerations—it is the resource from which we frame our ideas about being. Not only does the cosmological imagination underwrite the socio-political structure, but also for a literate society it defines the relationships between such things as religion and science and creates context for all our ideas about history.

A new look into history shows that the supposed tensions between religion and science, for example, are products of a tension formed within the new cosmology of the Scientific Revolution and the age we call "Modernity." Toulmin demonstrates that this conflict is an anachronistic reading of the facts: "Before the Reformation, Christianity had little investment in doctrines which natural science had any reason to dispute. What scientific innovation went on, for example, at the hands of Albert the Great or Nicolas of Cusa, was exposed to few theological constraints. . . . The alleged incompatibility of science and theology was thus a conflict *within* Modernity, which arose as the growth of experience gave scientists occasion to question beliefs used by Counter-Reformation Catholics and Protestants alike *after* 1650" (144).

Toulmin argues that the birth of the Modern Age came about through a series of historical upheavals occurring over a few centuries, including the invention of the printing press and the mass distribution of texts, the European discovery of America, the Thirty Years War, the Little Ice Age, the Great Reformation, and the birth of heliocentrism and a new cosmology. These events converged in a sort of existential challenge to the old ideas of the divine authority of king and church. Blood, famines, and social-religious division struck at the foundations of traditional community, and society itself was at risk of dissolution. As a reaction, several great thinkers like Rene Descartes and Wilhelm Leibniz sought to create a philosophy based on the sure foundations of logic and observations. These philosophies were synchronous with the newly argued order of the cosmos. Descartes and Leibniz wanted a "one grand system" where the mathematical laws now seen as operating the universe could be replicated in human thinking and society.

The oral mind of antiquity sought to perfect society by replicating cosmic functions, in all their varieties, in their rites and festivals. The Modern Age starts as the literate mind sought all-inclusive intellectual principles. The repetition of the cosmogony was replaced by the recitation of universal law. The literate mind calls the former "religion" and the latter "reason." Toulmin points out, however, that this new form of universal orthodoxy was the driving force behind social persecutions: "The theories at issue in the attacks on such men as Servetus, Bruno, and Galileo did not involve long-standing matters of medieval theology: they all turned on the novel assumptions about the order of nature that made up the scaffolding of the modern world picture. Far from perpetuating 'medieval' intolerance, the condemnation of Galileo, Bruno, and Servetus represented cruelty of a specifically 'modern' kind" (144). Applying "natural law" to the social sphere and to the authority of human institutions created a basis for cosmic control over social and environmental chaotic forces. It turns out that universal law was thought to endorse the universal Church, no matter how inflexible that law might be.

With the introduction of Einstein's relativity theory, social-political forms have marched in step with the cosmic idea and cultural relativity has become ensconced in the modern psyche. $E = mc^2$ has a corollary in the social equation $E^2 = MC$: the social estate is a confluence of competing ethnic and economic exactions (E^2) given authority through the doctrine of Multi-Culturalism (MC). The great advantages of this ideology have been the recognition of different cultures and belief systems, the increase of civil rights for minorities, economic safety nets for the poor, and other social programs that seek to redistribute power and wealth through the entire social organism. Like all cosmo-political systems, there are also down sides: cultural relativism homogenizes all values while ironically splintering universal rights and wrongs into fragments of self-interest; the comprehensive rule of law eventually transforms into tribal claims to truth.

Because modern cosmology is predicated on a cause-and-effect universe running on physical parts and material forces, modern culture sees itself the same way. If the universe is a machine, so is everything else. This idea is self-perpetuating. The artificial layer of technology between us and nature soon becomes our entire relationship with nature. It is easy to believe the universe is only a machine when one learns about it by reading words on a machine. The modern cosmological imagination seeks to incorporate the individual—its psyche, mind, and social behaviors—within its formulas and ratios. Modern biologists are developing gene therapies for the purposes of bio-engineering. Medical doctors believe that the right formulae of prescription medications can cure any ailment. Modern sociologists and politicians believe they can perfect society by applying "scientific methods" to social behaviors. Everything can be organized, created, and controlled.

Whether it be solar monarchies, institutions predicated on "natural law," or social relativity manifested through multi-culturalism, societies reflect their unique cosmovision within the social sphere. One day, our current view of the Big Bang universe will change. No one knows how or what the new ideas will be. What is certain, though, is when the ideas of the universe change so will the culture and structure of society. These frames of thinking and being march in step with one another. When one realizes this one can look at the past and perhaps consider history from a cosmological point of view.

Ancient Cosmology

For long decades scholars have examined how ancient people's viewed the universe. In most history books on science, ancient cosmology starts with the perfunctory glazing of the mythological age as a precursor to the real stuff: Greek material, then spatial and mathematical descriptions of the earth and sky. While this approach is perhaps obligatory for the modern mind researching in his cubicle, it says absolutely nothing about how oral people's saw the universe for thousands and perhaps tens of thousands of years.

In the broad cultural milieu of the ancient world a completely different cosmovision was held in the minds of our myth-makers. The cosmology of the past did not see the universe as a machine, nor as a laboratory beaker filled with arbitrary energies and forces. More important, is the central fact that ancient cosmology was not affixed to the macrocosm. Whether the planets orbited the sun or the earth was less important than what the planets foretold about human life and revealed about divine nature. The impetus behind the cosmic curtain was not the question of how the little universe builds the big universe, or how the physical laws operate the big universe; instead it was the question of how the big universe influenced the little universe, how the grand cosmic scheme manifested itself on the earth below. Life in all its myriad appearances was only a reflection of a conflagration of energies from an omnipotent source.

Oral cosmology was not rooted in abstract particle physics, nor was it learned about by reading words on a machine. *It was rooted in the principles of genesis; life, death, and rebirth were the processes that needed to be examined.* People observed these processes by watching the daily manifestations revealed in the sky and reflected on the earth. The ancient microcosm was fashioned from the concrete observations found within nature and in the resultant notion that the life cycle of man was analogous to the grander cycles surrounding him, and thus the microcosm became synonymous with *anthropocosmos* (man as the ultimate manifestation of the universe).

It is the philosopher Jacob Needleman who perceives the essence of ancient cosmology when writing, "We have misunderstood the cosmological schemes of the past. What we call 'geocentrism' was never meant to establish the earth merely as the spatial center of the great universe, but principally to communicate its place as an intersection of primary and secondary cosmic purposes and forces" (19). Needleman continues:

> It is geocentrism, without the idea of microcosmic man, which modern science rejected. But a purely external geocentrism was never the whole meaning of this idea in the ancient world. It is only we, who have lost the idea of the microcosm, who see it that way. But taken with the idea of the microcosm, geocentrism reminds us that objective reality contains many kinds of influences that can act upon us, that there is a scale of being to which man is born would he but search for it as diligently as he pursues the satisfactions of external life. (28)

Humankind was part of a grand, celestial fabric—a "scale of being" whereby all the processes in heaven were reflected on the earth below, especially within the human soul. Instead of spatial mechanics, oral cosmology was grounded in cosmic relationships. Oral cosmology is first and foremost ontological; it places the individual observer in the center of the cosmic stage of process.

How is one to diagram such a cosmology? It turns out that many such diagrams of the oral cosmos were made. They tend to be labeled as religious icons and mythological bric-a-brac, however, and are often skipped in our history books of science as the real precursor to the Greek literate revolution in science and philosophy. Let us examine a few of these older conceptions of the cosmos.

In 1907 a silver platter was discovered in a Roman cemetery at Parabiago, near Milan (see figure 1). It weighed almost eight pounds and was just over fifteen inches in diameter. It is believed that the plate was a lid for a funerary urn. Its dating is uncertain, but stylistic clues place its manufacture somewhere between the 2nd and 5th centuries CE. Depicted on the plate is a series of religious symbols placed in a cosmic setting. Strictly speaking, these cosmic images are set within a funerary and cultic context (that's why this platter does not make it into our history of science books). One can view these images for the principles they represent, however, and begin to see how people not interested in abstract ideas or a technical cosmos perceived their universe.

On the Parabiago Plate the Mother Goddess Cybele rides her lion chariot through the heavens. Above her, the chariot of the sun (pulled by horses) and the moon (pulled by bulls) fly in their orbits, while below her Oceanus emerges from the waters with a water-nymph. Above Oceanus are four small figures, each representing the seasons, the winds, and the cardinal directions. Surrounding Cybele are her attendant dancers who dance the rhythm of the heavens. Sitting next to Cybele is none other than Attis, the central figure of a mystery cult promising rebirth after death. This grandiose parade marches towards the Tree of Life depicted as a serpent entwined obelisk. Before the obelisk is the circle of the zodiac surrounding the god Aeon, who is holding a mighty staff (the axis of heaven) and is being born up above the horizon by a god.

Figure 1. Parabiago Plate, Lid for Funerary Urn

Large, round lid found in a Roman cemetery. The depiction on the plate reveals the ontological cosmos of the mysteries of Cybele. Cybele is a *kosmokrator*, or one who organizes the cosmos. Surrounding her are various images representing certain aspects of the universe. The Sun, Moon, and Seasons are all personified as aspects of a functioning cosmos that endows the cycles of death and rebirth on all material things. Cybele and Attis represent the mystery of resurrection as revealed in the seasonal cycles. The god Aeon represents the invisible forces that underwrite all material phenomena. (Illustration by Lynde Mott, original image in Vermaseren, Plate 53.)

Here is the ancient cosmos in total. We do not see a schematic of heavenly spheres, geocentric or heliocentric diagrams, or the universe stuffed into the shapes of the platonic solids. What this cosmology is trying to show us is the probing mysteries of life and death. The seasons, the heavens, the sun and moon, and the watery course of Oceanus are all cyclical powers reigning in the sky and corresponding to cyclical manifestations on earth, including the agricultural cycle, the natal cycle, the menstrual cycle, and even the cycles of the weather. Everything on earth was influenced by the powers above. In the Parabiago Plate, these archetypal powers frame the experiential world and coalesce around Cybele, Attis, and Aeon. Each of these figures are central to the "fantasy worlds" of ancient cosmologists, for each of these deities represented the secrets of the life cycle.

Cybele was a mother goddess imported into Greece from Phrygia. She was a religious deity with various cult centers where adherents worshiped, but she originates from the oral psyche as a *cosmic principle of the life cycle in nature*. As a mother goddess, she symbolized the mystery of conception and birth: "She is the transforming medium that transforms semen into life. She receives the seed of the past and, through the miracle of her body, transmutes it into the life of the future" (Campbell, *Goddesses* 25). She also represented the powers of life over death and was made equal to the Greek goddess Demeter. Cybele was often depicted enthroned next to Demeter in the underworld where both goddesses equally shared their role as cosmic mother, "out of which the light of life is to spring forth again in an ever-rotating cycle" (Vermaseren 10). Cybele's throne in the underworld is well deserved, for only in the underworld were the keys of life and rebirth kept. All life emerges from darkness, as the plant climbs out of the soil or as the stars ascend above the horizon. In some aspects, the underworld was nothing more than the principle of the womb of the mother goddess, wherein the divine spark of life could find the egg from which new life would grow.

Cybele is only one form of the mother goddess. By late Roman times this divine mother was called the Goddess of Many Names. Jane Ellen Harrison notes that Hera, Demeter, Athena, Aphrodite, and Artemis are all representations of different aspects of this same goddess (*Mythology* 49). In the *Metamorphoses* of Apuleius she is identified as the Mother of the Gods, Minerva, Venus, Diana, Proserpina, Ceres, Juno, Bellona, Hecate, and others (Vermaseren 10). All of these goddesses were different manifestations of the same cosmic principle. Jane Ellen Harrison observes that the male gods on Olympus were approached with prayer, praise, and presents, but the great Mother was "approached by means that are magical and mysterious" because she possesses the mysteries of life (*Mythology* 49).

This was certainly the case in Egypt where Isis and Nephthys are dual personifications of the mother goddess, one representing the heavenly mother and the other the earthly one (*MJSP* 163). In the Egyptian scheme Osiris is Lord of the underworld. He takes center stage in the mystery drama of rebirth. He was slain, but through proper initiation and living in accordance to Maat, he may arise anew. While Osiris appears to be the central figure of the mystery rites, it is actually overseen entirely by the goddess, whose womb is the *deus ex machina* that saves the climactic action from complete oblivion. Repeatedly in the funerary texts and vignettes the major characters of the liturgical pageant show up performing all their prescribed duties: Osiris is killed and rises, Anubis guides, Thoth records, Horus aids and fights, Atum, Re, or some other version of the solar god breathes new life into the dead, and so on. Never far away from all these scenes, however, is a representation of the mother goddess who oversees the entire operation from beginning to end and is the key to cosmic rebirth.

Cybele is also associated with new life and resurrection through the image of her male partner Attis. The rebirth of Attis was celebrated yearly during a mystery festival. Much like Jesus Christ, Attis was slain and through the mystery of resurrection reborn from the tomb. Oral people's well understood that all processes in nature manifest in dualities: light and dark, hot and cold, wet and dry, male and female. While the great mother was the personification of the gene-matrix in nature, the miracle of birth requires a male counterpart in the process. The womb requires semen, as the earth requires sun and rain. Every mother goddess had a male consort who represented the scintilla of life that blossomed in the underworld womb. Attis is a mythological figure synonymous with the Babylonian Dumuzi, the Egyptian Osiris, the Persian Mithras, and the Greek Dionysus. All of these deities were associated with death and resurrection, and all were central to the idea of an ordered cosmos. The fourth-century pagan philosopher Sallustius wrote, "The story of Attis represents an eternal cosmic process, not an isolated event in the past. As the story is intimately related to the ordered universe, we reproduce it ritually to gain order in ourselves. We, like Attis, have fallen from heaven; we die mystically with him and are reborn as infants" (Freke and Gandy 256).

All this talk about life and death, goddesses and gods, wombs and sparks of life seems terribly religious, but we must remember that the ideas of "religion" and "science" are modern inventions with no real parallels in the oral world. A modern cosmologists may roll his eyes at this discussion, insisting upon his theorems and formulas as the only proper way to describe the cosmos. An oral philosopher would simply point to a woman and a man and note that all of their biological functions are manifestations of cosmic processes. The oral philosopher does not state these observations with abstractions; however, and only describes them as experienced, assigning to them a pantheon of divine identities representing the invisible powers behind the working universe. In this sense, Cybele is more than a mother goddess, she is a *kosmokrator*, who, like Mithras, "represent[s] the organization of the cosmos in its entirety" (Ulansey, *Origins* 117). She represents the first causes by which life came into being. According to Sallustius she and her consort are "eternal cosmic [processes]." The fact that Cybele and Attis also provided a way for a soul to be reborn in the next world does not diminish their role as *kosmokrators*—rather, it defines it.

Here we see just how linked ancient cosmology and eschatology really are. This link is directly imaged in the figure of Aeon, the god of space and time. He is always shown surrounded by the zodiac: a series of constellations circumscribing the horizon and forming the "world disc." In many depictions he is associated with a serpent, lion, and eagle wings. These are the same iconic elements found in the Greek sphinx that was placed most commonly at tombs. We find further similarities in the Mithraic sphinx guarding the paths of the dead in the Mithraic temples, and the Hebrew cherubim standing watch in the Israelite Holy of Holies. These images actually have corollaries in the constellations, where the man, serpent, lion, and bull are representations of Aquarius, Scorpio, Leo, and Taurus. These constellations contain the four Royal Stars that quarter the horizon and define space and time. By watching these stars rise and set, calendars and festival cycles were regulated. More important, from fragments of esoteric lore handed down to us we discover that each of these constellations was associated with a celestial path for the dead. Aeon becomes a representation of the revolution of the celestial orbs, the frame of time and space, and the secrets of life and death manifest on earth and hidden in the stars.

In the Parabiago Plate two small creatures sit below the great god Aeon—a grasshopper and a lizard. Why on earth would a grasshopper be associated with the organizing principles of the cosmos and the great deities Cybele, Attis, and Aeon? Egyptian funerary texts give us the key, as the deceased often encounters or is represented by a grasshopper in the underworld. In the *Pyramid Texts* Pharaoh ascends to the sky as a grasshopper (§890-2). In the famous judgment scene in the *Book of the Dead* the deceased declares his worthiness to all the gods of judgment and to the cosmic order of Maat by insisting he has entered the Field of Grasshoppers (*BD* 125). A grasshopper is sometimes depicted under the scales of Maat during the weighing of the heart (*MJSP* 159). Both in ancient Crete and Egypt the grasshopper stands at the entrance to the underworld as guide of the dead (*MJSP* 160).

These images associate the grasshopper directly with the dead, rebirth, judgment, the underworld, and (through Maat) the entire cosmic order. His appearance on the Parabiago Plate is well deserved. According to Nibley, "What makes the grasshopper a special representative of spiritual reality is not so much its uncanny power of negotiating empty space [flying in the air without wings] as its unearthly and immortal voice" (*MJSP* 160). Nibley points out that the Egyptians knew the grasshopper could still sing even if its sound organs were removed. He also points out that the grasshopper's song is attuned to the sun and the temperature of the air, as is its life-cycle: "It has been found that grasshopper eggs always hatch either at dawn at twenty-two degrees Celsius or at sunset at eleven degrees Celsius, thus establishing that uncanny relationship between the life-cycles of sun and grasshopper of which the ancients seem to have been aware" (*MJSP* 160).

Like the grasshopper, the lizard has similar associations; it too basks in the sun and regrows its tail. Both motifs are representations of death and rebirth connected with the sun. Both creatures are physical manifestations of various cosmic powers: resurrection, flight, and an eternal voice. Both sit below Aeon, the god of time and space. The implication is simple: if one knows the correct cosmic relationships that Aeon represents, then one can find rebirth in the eternal world, and one's soul can rise with the sun to inherit eternal life. Aeon becomes an image of the microcosmic life cycle endowed by macrocosmic laws; therefore, he is the template of the unfolding cosmos.

The soul, as microcosm, is the highest confluence of heavenly powers, and therefore has within it the seed of all other manifestations in nature. Oral minds seek to parallel these natural manifestations within consciousness itself as a way to refine and perfect the soul. If a cricket can sing without a voice and fly without wings, surely a disembodied soul can speak and move as well. This is why Sallustius says, "As the story [of Attis] is intimately related to the ordered universe, we reproduce it ritually to gain order in ourselves. We, like Attis, have fallen from heaven; we die mystically with him and are reborn as infants."

Due to the structures of oral cognition, oral cosmology is almost the opposite of a literate and abstract view of the universe. Put in another way, the modern macrocosm is heliocentric, *but the modern microcosm is wholly and completely geocentric.* Man is born of the earth and returns to the earth, and his relationship with the earth is total—*anthropocosmos* has become *anthropopergamentum* (man as dirt without an eternal soul). The modern imagination is so ensconced in this form of microcosmic geocentrism that its consequences are no longer self-evident, yet the consequences of this ideology are ubiquitous and inform all the theories of modern cosmology. While it was Copernicus, Kepler, and Newton who conceived the new age, it was actually Darwin who birthed it. Charles Darwin is the chief cosmologist of our time, for he reinvented the microcosm, permanently separating man from the unfolding cosmos and ensconcing the modern cosmovision in purely materialistic terms.

Ancient geocentrism served a different scale of being. It turns out that the Earth was not really the center of this scale as much as it was its bottom—the place to which physical matter descended. In ancient India and Greece, the Earth was a way-point where the soul was refined towards its greatest end with knowledge and suffering. As Thomas McEvilley observes, souls who failed to transcend the mortal sphere were reincarnated over long ages back into the earthly sphere (98-99). Rebirth into mortality was dreaded (99). The ultimate end of the soul was to transcend the gross, physical matter of the environs of the Earth and to ascend into the heavens as an immortal (101).

One chief view of the ancient microcosm was the idea of the soul escaping the material realm and being sealed to the imperishable, eternal realm. This form of geocentrism obviously serves a completely different idea of cosmos, one that is not just mechanistic and spatial, but primarily ontological. In this sense, the ancient macrocosm was geocentric, *but the ancient microcosm was heliocentric, in that a man or woman could join the sun on its way to the realm of fixed stars to gain celestial immortality and self-hood.* Thus declares the *Pyramid Texts* in the third millennium BCE, "The King travels the air and traverses the earth. . . . Those who are in the firmament open their arms to him, the King stands on the eastern side of the celestial vault, there is brought to him a way of ascent to the sky" (§325-6). "O my father the King, raise yourself on your right side, . . . that you may be pure thereby as a god. Go up as do the messengers of Re, for your hand will be taken by the Imperishable Stars and you shall not perish" (§2182-3). It is a grandiose sentiment that finds echoes in the Orphic gold plates, the *Mithras Liturgy*, and all the mystery religions. This heliocentric microcosm endures all the way to at least the fifth century CE where Macrobius affirms that "complete blessedness" in "a place in the sky" (*Commentary* 10.4) is assured for all those who are able to tread the celestial highway with its attendant gates (*Commentary* 12.1-16). Centuries later Dante would revivify this scheme, albeit within a different context, in his *Divine Comedy*.

This imaginal microcosm pervaded throughout the ancient world, including within cultures that apparently did not believe in a blessed afterlife. Journeying through the sky to discover the source of all manifestations on earth was essential to run a balanced and harmonious society. Gilgamesh must journey through the cosmos to rule his city. His trials against the giant Humbaba and the Celestial Bull belong to the cosmological constructs of the day, where the king received his authority from celestial archetypes, the king himself being the chief archetype—*anthroposcosmos.* Only after Gilgamesh descends through the underworld is he allowed to return to Uruk and measure out all of its walls and dimensions with Ur-Shanbi, the underworld boatman. It is Gilgamesh who restores the rites of civilization from the ancient ones, and apparently does so after his celestial escapade. Gilgamesh earns the right to rule his city by obtaining knowledge from the heavens.

We find a homologous situation in ancient Israel, where Ezekiel obtains his prophetic authority through a hieratic tour of the universe. He sees the Earth in its celestial context, quartered by the four winds and guarded by the fiery cherubim, who are also synonymous to the Aeon and the Sphinx. This same heavenly journey appears to be assigned to the Israelite high priest. In Isaiah chapter 22 the high priest is named Eliakim—a name that means *God shall cause to ascend.* He is given the keys of the temple and apparently his priestly authority by being "fastened" to the "nail in a sure place" (Is. 22.20-24). This nail is the North Star, and in oral cosmology the Big Dipper and pole star are associated with the heavenly throne of the gods. It appears that the high priest analogically ascends to this throne as he enters the Holy of Holies.

Contrary to many textbook assumptions that the mythopoeic mind believed in a literal, mechanistic, geocentric cosmos, it is not until the Greeks that such a universe was espoused and debated. Eudoxus (410-355 BCE) appears to be the first Greek to adopt the homocentric planetary spheres, while Anaximander (610-546 BCE) is our earliest source for a pseudo-geocentric model. By the time of Aristotle (384-322 BCE), the geocentric universe had been embedded in the cultural imagination of the West, leaving Ptolemy (90-168 CE) to work out its mechanics in his great work *Almagest,* which would serve as the cosmological mainframe in the Arab world and throughout Europe until the so-called Enlightenment. In any case, a literal geocentrism hales from a Greek tradition, the very tradition Copernicus would oppose by looking for different views within the Greek literature.

More important, even while geocentrism was popular among the educated Greeks, it was not a universal cosmological model; for example, among the late Jewish and early Christian sects co-habitating the Ptolemaic world there is no clear evidence for belief in the Ptolemaic cosmos. As Peter Schäfer makes clear, "I am not convinced, however, that the very fact of a multiple-heaven scheme in our texts necessarily points to the adoption of the Ptolemaic model" (260). The texts that Schäfer refers to are early Christian and apocalyptic texts, which swim in an ancient structured universe that is quite different than the geocentric one. "The problem is not so much that the planets are put in one or two heavens, or that the heavens are not planets. Much more disturbing is the fact that in none of these texts do the heavens actually encircle the earth. . . . Our texts remain much closer to the ancient Near Eastern/biblical model than to the new discoveries of the Graeco-Roman world" (260). Schäfer concludes, "There is no real evidence in the texts surveyed so far that the Jews and Christians of the first few centuries CE adopted the Ptolemaic model of the cosmos" (260-61).

Schäfer draws a connection between the early Christian universe and the Near Eastern universe. So what was specifically the Near Eastern macrocosm? Near Eastern cosmology presented a three-tiered cosmos— Heaven, Earth, and the Underworld. These levels were also divided into various layers, usually seven, each with various correspondences to each other. The seven levels of the heavens corresponded to the seven planetary spheres: the sun, moon, and the five visible planets to the naked eye (Mercury, Venus, Mars, Jupiter, and Saturn). This cosmo-planetary scheme, with the seven heavens and corresponding underworlds, "goes farther back than Indian and Iranian culture, namely to the most ancient Near East, whence India and Iran derived their idea of a 'cosmos'—a cosmos being in itself by no means an obvious assumption" (*HM* 123).

These cosmic layers were connected by the Earth's axis that was analogized in myth by the symbol of a tree, pillar, or mountain. This cosmic axle was not only the connecting point between the planes of cosmos, but in the terrestrial sphere it was the *fundamentum* around which the universe churned and creation emerged. Instead of a singularity expanding in a Big Bang, the oral mind perceived the *axis mundi* as the frame of the universe. It was a cosmic umbilicus linked to the eternal circuit of life and death, drawing its creative powers from both the upper and lower heavens and manifesting them upon the earth between.

Oral cosmology takes a radical turn from modern conceptions of spatial layers or mechanistic wheels. Were ancient cosmology just another way to imagine a material schematic, either geocentrism, celestial spheres, or three-tiered axis cosmology is comprehensible because one can actually observe features in the earth and sky that can be logically constructed into these metaphysical frames. Most historians of science treat ancient cosmology in this way—as a product of a rather primitive consideration of a spatial orientation of the heavens. Once again the point must be made that ancient cosmology was predicated upon the microcosm and a scale of being linked to the cycle of life and death. Spatial or mathematical mechanics was neither the primary purpose nor the chief demonstration of oral cosmology. Rather, the oral mind sought to ritually reenact and reconstruct celestial archetypes in the material world.

Celestial Archetypes

For someone living in a pre-industrial and pre-literate world, and whose primary intellectual referents are the manifestations of nature, the vision of the sky is the most remarkable and ubiquitous landscape instilled in the eye of the mind. In such a world the sun and moon are stunning presences whose cycles palpitate to the heartbeat of life itself. The full light of the moon can be as radiant as the sun at night. Its phases are a sort of celestial metronome measuring out time and space with precision. In almost all mythologies the moon is female, for her phases are an archetypal signification for all biological processes: new, waxing, full, and waning are consonant with birth, youth, maturity, and decay.

The sun's light and heat are omnipotent powers filling the sky. Its risings and settings are never exactly the same. The sun not only drifts across the horizon north and south during the year, but also it is always accompanied by a new canvas of color and image at the moment it appears and disappears, as if the entire dome of heaven were a symphony tuning for a performance, its magnum opus being the revelatory rhapsody of *fiat lux*. Its presence is also an archetypal signification for power, light, life, and order. In nearly all mythologies the sun is male, for its penetrating radiance vivifies the world, fecundating every spot capable of growth, and harmonizing the life cycle within its seasons.

The sky holds more than the sun and moon. It is filled with stars, and in a truly black sky these stars are a breathtaking tapestry of light with profound variation, color, and brightness. The stars also have cycles, shifting on the horizon during the year. On the day of spring equinox one group of stars appears on the horizon before and after sunset, and on the days of summer and winter solstice other groups of stars appear respectively. The most spectacular vision of the starry sky is a large band of white light stretching from horizon to horizon and filled with iridescent clouds of nebulosity known as the Milky Way. From the point of view of an observer on earth this band of light is the visual plane of the lateral axis of the galaxy; as one looks at the Milky Way one is looking through the center of the galaxy. Experientially this river of light is as poignant and omnipotent as the sun and moon. Its image dilates the mind and one can get lost in observing its broad and deep luminosity. Perhaps for these reasons the Milky Way in myth is always portrayed as a river or body of water encircling the earth, as if the earth were a deep shore amidst celestial tides. In many cosmogonies the earth arises from waters. Many scholars point to terrestrial phenomena as the intellectual primer for these myths; for example, the annual rising of the Nile in Egypt causes new and fertilized soil to appear. While true, few scholars seem to sense that the archetypal primer for this image is heavenward.

Finally, there are five bright objects that all follow the same path in the sky. These are the "wanderers" or planets, and with the sun and moon, they move in their own clockwork rhythms. Venus is the brightest object in the sky (besides the sun and moon). Venus and Mercury are never seen far away from the sun. Jupiter is the second brightest planet and takes twelve years to complete one circuit around the path of the wanderers (called the ecliptic). With Mars and Saturn, each of these bright objects were mythologized into various deities that held certain stewardships (i.e., functions) over the earth. The path on which they tread followed what would be called the Zodiac. In myth, this stellar path may have also been analogized as a river, for at certain times of the year a very faint band of light can be seen marking the ecliptic and rising from the horizon intersecting the Milky Way. This light is called the Zodiacal Light. Two constellations stand at the junction where the ecliptic meets the Milky Way: Taurus and Scorpio. In myth, these areas in the sky are often depicted as gates to the heavenly world. In Babylonian astrology, these two constellations may have defined the real celestial axis, measured by the Zodiac and the path of the planets.

In consonance with the heavenly designs are a host of other rhythms manifest on earth, including migratory patterns of birds, animals, and even insects, which follow yearly periods, as well as agricultural cycles, which bloom and decay with an attuned frequency to the rising and setting celestial orbs. Oral thinkers immersed in the immediate experience of nature astutely observed the synchronous relationship between the heavens and the earth. It appears that from prehistory the oral mind perceived celestial manifestations and patterns as the archetypal source for all processes on earth. The Neoplatonist philosopher Proclus describes this mindset: "Observing that all things form a whole, [certain ancient thinkers] laid the foundations of hieratic science, wondering at the first realities and admiring in them the latest comers as well as the very first among beings; in heaven, terrestrial things according both to a causal and to a celestial mode and on earth heavenly things in a terrestrial state" (Corbin 105). "As above, so below," declares a late Hermetic text, but the sentiment describes an oral cosmovision haling back millennia.

"For archaic man," Mircea Eliade writes in *Cosmos and History*, "reality is a function of the imitation of a celestial archetype" (*CH* 5). In Iranian cosmology, Eliade continues, "every terrestrial phenomenon, whether abstract or concrete, corresponds to a celestial, transcendent invisible term, to an 'idea' in the Platonic sense" (*CH* 6). Accordingly, there is a visible sky, but also an invisible celestial sky. There is the visible earth, but it corresponds to a celestial earth. Every virtue, prayer, and rite has celestial correspondences (6). This cosmological perspective pervades oral culture. We find the exact same conceptual world amongst the Iroquois Indians, who believe that heaven is populated by the Ongwe, a term that "stands for the images of all things which later existed on earth, i.e., an image of the houses, an image of the trees, and of all the animals" (Von-Franz 38). The Ongwe are seen as living beings, and many are identified with constellations in the sky and are the celestial abode of pure forms.

So it is that specific stars and constellations were thought to be the repositories of the invisible functions displayed in nature. Clive Ruggles notes that many cultures believed that quartz was really an emanation of moonlight, while the Barasana natives believe their Caterpillar Jaguar constellation has an earthly counterpart in the caterpillar (Campion, *History* 29). At the same time Caterpillar Jaguar rises in the sky earthly caterpillars made their cocoons for transformation. These numerous cocoons would drop out of the trees and provide an additional food source for the natives during the rainy season (Krupp, *Beyond* 254). For the Native American Pawnee, Venus and Mars were the parents of the first people, and when the two planets rhythmically came together in the sky they were imprinting the model of parenthood upon the people. For them the Pleiades represented not only the change of seasons but also the idea of being "united." Thus, when the Pleiades heliacally arose, group festivals would unite the people in their annual rites. The aborigines of Australia believe that the source of being exists in Dreamtime, where "people are related to stars, stars are related to animals, animals are related to the land, and all are related to the invisible beings who are everywhere and who 'sang' creation into existence" (Campion, *Astrology* 24-5).

The idea of the celestial world being home to pure forms from which material phenomena descend reminds us of Plato's allegory of the cave. According to Plato, there is a realm of pure forms existing in the regions above, and all that we perceive on earth below are nothing but shadows of these forms (*Republic* 514a-e). While Plato makes these forms the pure ideas of reason and philosophy, they are in fact wed to the idea of cosmic archetypes. In his *Phaedo*, Plato takes his followers on a tour of the cosmos. If one ascends above the sky, one sees "the true heaven, the true light and the true earth" (110a)—meaning that there is a true heaven above the manifest one, and a true earth above the one upon which we stand. In this realm of celestial archetypes exists a place of "all true knowledge, visible only to intelligence," where one is "delighted at last to be seeing what is real and watching what is true" (*Phaedrus* 247c-d).

Plato's cosmology was not new, as Walter Burkert points out, but drew from "older contexts beyond provincial borders" contained in wisdom texts and cosmogonic myths. "The hypothesis or suspicion that Greek philosophy was not an original invention of the Greeks but copied from more ancient Eastern prototypes is not a modern one," writes Burkert, for Aristotle, long ago, had already made the argument (*Babylon* 50). Truly, every mythical motif and allusion contained in Plato's works teeter with meaning and is connected to the ancient storehouse of thought wed to an oral cosmology hoary with age. Conversely, as some scholars have noted, every myth containing a Platonic structure belongs to the same cultural storehouse. As Eliade summarizes, "Plato could be regarded as the outstanding philosopher of 'primitive mentality,' that is, as the thinker who succeeded in giving philosophic currency and validity to the modes of life and behavior of archaic humanity" (*CH* 34).

Plato's realm of pure forms is a Western restatement of an Eastern mythological mindset. In the Chinese *Tao Te Ching* we read, "Man's law is from the Earth; the Earth's from Heaven; Heaven's from the Tao. And the law of the Tao is its being what it is" (Campbell, *Primitive* 29). There is a hierarchy of being whose source is the Tao. Tao is often translated as "The Way," but like a great many ancient words it has a multitude of associations that are difficult to interpret. Here, the translator says "the law of the Tao is its being what it is." It is like saying Tao is simply what is. Tao is the source of Heaven, Earth, and Man. Like Maat and Dharma, Tao is not only the proper order of the universe, but the very structure upon which that order rests.

Understanding that for the oral mind everything below has a source from something above reorients our gaze towards mythological matters. The problem, of course, is that most of the philosophical connections oral societies perceived between celestial and terrestrial types have long been lost or obscured. Nevertheless, oral ontology rooted in cosmic archetypes remains the key. Suddenly, a stone sky is not so unusual. Anaximenes declared that the constellations had been written on a heavenly, crystalline sphere, which is very similar to the Assyrian conception of the gods engraving the stars on a sky of jasper. Even as quartz was an earthly manifestation of the light of the moon, so also was highly polished jasper an emanation of the celestial sphere, and thus was prolifically used in amulets and royal seals. The stone sky would not fall down on one's head, as a rock drops from one's hand, simply because it was the sky itself that was standing on the stone.

The cosmogonies of the ancient world must be placed within this oral framework, and our interpretation of them must be reevaluated. Our modern understanding of the cosmos is materialistic and spatial, so when ancient creation narratives speak of heaven and earth we attribute this to ancient thought on a geocentric scale model of the cosmos. Something is deeply awry with our conceptualization, as archaic languages have no word for "world," but only terms enumerating the constituents of the world, which primarily include heaven and earth (Burkert, *Babylon* 61). These constituents, however, are not arranged spatially, but ontologically. It is curious that the biblical creation narrative uses the plural for heaven, *shamayim*, "In the beginning, God created the *heavens* and the earth" (Gen. 1.1). How many heavens are there? And how are they related to the earth? Is there a "true heaven" above the one we see? Is there another earth beyond our physical senses from which the material world was made? What does this mean?

The Hebrew word *shamayim* denotes a duality, and thus conveys a heaven above and a heaven below. With the material realm, these heavens frame the three-tiered cosmos: heaven, earth, and underworld. These heavens are often divided into seven firmaments, and in Hebrew commentaries such as the Midrash there are always seven firmaments. It turns out that in the Hebrew cosmogony these heavens were consonant with the seven days of creation, so that the heavens and the earth were "in tune" with each other. Notably, the creation of the earth culminates in the formation of man "in God's image" (Gen. 1.27).

This creation account cannot be read in segments, but must be seen as a synthetic whole. God starts with a series of heavens where archetypal reality resides, creating layers of being until a material realm is formed. The earth is a manifestation of the heavens. In the center of the material realm is Man, who is really *anthropocosmos*, the paramount manifestation of the heavenly order. In other words, there is a "true Man" above the material one who resides in the "true earth" and "true heaven." This true man is God, and God, heaven, earth, and Man are a continuum of being that share co-equal roles in the creation drama. It is difficult to create a concrete hierarchy of being in this order. If Man is the paramount manifestation of the heavenly order, than the heavenly order must also be the manifestation of Man, and our entire modern conception of ancient cosmology as a spatial order is wrong. A late Arabic creation myth (we often deal with late sources as they are the ones which are written down) reveals the problem of our conceptual framework:

> Know that when God had created Adam who was the first human organism to be constituted, and when he had established him as the origin and archetype of all human bodies, there remained a surplus of the leaven of the clay. From this surplus God created the palm tree. . . . Now after the creation of the palm tree, there remained a hidden portion of the clay from which the plant had been made; what was left was the equivalent of a sesame seed. And it was in this remainder that God laid out an immense Earth. Since he arranged in it the Throne and what it contains, the Firmament, the Heavens, and the Earths, the worlds underground, all the paradises and hells, this means that the whole of our universe is to be found there in that Earth in its entirety, and yet the whole of it together is like a ring lost in one of our deserts in comparison with the immensity of the Earth. And that same Earth has hidden in it so many marvels and strange things that their number cannot be counted and our intelligence remains dazed by them. (Bloom xiii)

There is much to say of this beatific vision, but central to this creation account is the fact that Adam is the celestial archetype of all manifest things. The hierarchal order has been reversed, and it is the cosmos that was created from the clay from which Adam was formed. In this context the cosmos is created from the remnant of Adam's clay, a remnant the size of a sesame seed, so Adam stands above the created order as its template. What connects Adam and the heavens is a palm tree—or the Tree of Life. This is a representation of the axis of heaven whose roots sink deep into the abyss and whose branches rise high into the realm of fixed stars, spanning all of creation. It is a conception that spans all of ancient cosmology, though in various forms. In Buddhist cosmology the term universe was written in Sanskrit as *loka-dhātu*:

> It refers to a place that has come into existence through the *karma* (actions and their enduring results) produced by living beings. The universe is also maintained by karma and disintegrates through the action of karma. . . . The term *universe* came to have such a strong connotation of human life and destiny that it almost ceased to connote the universe as a spatial entity. (Sadakata 25)

It is also clear from the Arabic account that our modern conception of the Earth is not the same as the ancient conception. Expressively, Earth seems to be a technical term, part of a mythological jargon that had entirely different connotations than a blue speck of dust in a sea of billions and billions of stars. The Earth is homologous to Man, for the Earth too encompassed all the heavens: "this means that the whole of our universe is to be found there in that Earth in its entirety." Earth is not a spatial entity, but a plane of existence that stretches through the heavens, is marked off by the heavens, and is manifest through *karma* or the clay of Adam, which is the substance of human-being perpetually becoming through the heavenly axis.

The mythological Earth is not a planet or a disk; it is a nexus. It is the sticking point manifest amidst heavenly archetypes. A clue to interpretation might be given by Plato when he actually describes the cryptic and technical term Earth in his *Phaedo* (107c-114c). Similarly to the Arabic creation myth, the Platonic Earth is "nothing but the Pythagorean cosmos" surrounded by Oceanus and other swirling, cosmic rivers that Numenius of Apamea described as the planetary spheres (*HM* 188). There is a "dry earth" above the celestial equator and a "wet earth" below it, so that the "waters above" and the "waters below" are really cosmic regions, which have terrestrial manifestations. The Earth itself being an amalgamation of cosmic forces and relationships, "this means that the whole of our universe is to be found there in that Earth in its entirety."

If there is a true Earth above the material Earth, and this Earth is a cosmic disc embedded in the Pythagorean cosmos (and thus this "flat earth" could be said to be the celestial equator extended into space), then what are we to make of the true heaven above the material one? Anaximander's geocentric schema resides within this metaphysical frame, for according to Anaximander, the Earth was a conical cross section floating in space. The stars, sun, and moon were actually appearances caused by holes in the celestial spheres through which the light of the "true heaven" cascaded through. The issue of the true heaven becomes more complex. Our first clue in understanding this true heaven does not reside in an ancient geocentric view of the heavens, but in an ancient heliocentric view that I have been citing the entire time. This heliocentric view is ontological. Our first look into its philosophic scope is appropriately delivered by Copernicus, who studiously read through every book and manuscript on cosmology he could find. Copernicus writes:

> I therefore went to the trouble of reading anew the books of all philosophers on which I could lay hands to find out whether someone did not hold the opinion that there existed other motions of the heavenly bodies than assumed by those who taught the mathematical sciences in the schools. And thus I found first in Cicero that Hiketas had held the belief that the earth moves. Afterwards I found in [Pseudo] Plutarch that others have also held this opinion. I shall put down his own words so that everybody can read them:

But others hold that the earth moves; thus Philolaus the Pythagorean held that it revolves round the Fire in an oblique circle like the sun and moon. Herakliedes of Pontus and Ekphantus the Pythagorean also suppose the earth to move, though not in a progressive motion, but after the manner of a wheel, turning upon an axle about its own center from west to east. (cited in Koestler 207)

Copernicus read a document written by Psuedo-Plutrach (3rd to 4th century CE) citing Philolaus the Pythagorean (4th to 5th century BCE) and Heraclides of Pontus (4th century BCE). These latter writers had both claimed different motions for the heavens than the geocentric cosmos adopted by Aristotle and Ptolemy. Unfortunately, like all good historical mysteries, the original writings of Philolaus and Heraclides are lost, and all we have are fragments and quotations from other writers citing them. This frustrating scenario generally pervades all of our sources.

Heraclides of Pontus was a student of Plato and was a contemporary with Eudoxus. What is known for certain is that Heraclides asserted that the earth rotates on its own axis, just as Copernicus had read. Heraclides also believed that the planets of Mercury and Venus rotated around the sun on epicycles, anticipating the system of Tycho Brahe some two thousand years later (Gottschalk 81-2). Furthermore, several late writers attribute a heliocentric theory of the heavens to Heraclides, but no known fragment or early source explicitly states the case; we must assume that either later theories and ideas were placed upon Heraclides' science or that there was another tradition that has been lost from our sources.

More compelling, the Pythagorean Philolaus is cited by Copernicus as one of the early Greek philosophers who believed in a heliocentric system; in fact, the Copernican system was originally called *Philolaica* after this Greek philosopher (Kahn 26). The problem with the cosmological system of Philolaus is that he makes the Earth orbit not the sun, but a central Fire; all the planets including the sun revolve around this central Fire. In other words, there is a second sun around which the heavenly spheres rotate and from which our own sun receives its light. Aristotle in his *On the Heavens* articulates this strange cosmology:

> As to [the earth's] position there is some difference of opinion. Most people—all, in fact, who regard the whole heaven as finite—says it lies at the center. But the Italian philosophers known as the Pythagoreans take the contrary view. At the center, they say, is fire, and the earth is one of the stars, creating night and day by its circular motion about the center. . . . The Pythagoreans . . . hold that the most important part of the world, which is the center, should be most strictly guarded, and name it, or rather the fire which occupies that place, the "Guard-house of Zeus." (cited in Temple, *Crystal* 271)

Many scholars have wrestled over this idea attributed to Philolaus. It is clear that these early Greek thinkers were using mathematics and understood the Earth to be moving in a circular orbit (unlike Aristotle and Ptolemy). Yet disappointingly, the system described by Philolaus does not seem to correspond to any kind of real scientific observation, leaving most commentators on this teaching to acquiesce, "despite the presence of some genuine technical knowledge . . . the system of Philolaus taken as a whole seems less like scientific astronomy than like symbolical speculation" (Kahn 26).

This disappointment derives from strictly modern cosmological thinking. Philolaus is not teaching a mechanistic phenomenology of the sky but a scale of being in which the cosmos participates. This second sun is the heaven above the heavens and the source of all material manifestation. It is the *apeiron*; the realm above the fixed stars, the heavenly abode beyond Plato's cave, the super celestial region of Orphic cosmology. It is called the Guardhouse of Zeus, and this designation was also known by other names: "the Hearth of the Universe, . . . the Tower or Watch-tower of Zeus, the Throne of Zeus, the House of Zeus, the Mother of the Gods, the Altar, Bond and Measure of Nature" (Heath 164). And further, "in this central fire is located the governing principle, the force which directs the movement and activity of the universe" (Heath 164). Pindar assigns to this archetypal region of the cosmos the home of immortals and the blessed dead: "But, whosoever, while dwelling in either world, have thrice been courageous in keeping their souls pure from all deeds of wrong, pass by the highway of Zeus unto the tower of Cronos, where the ocean-breezes blow around the Islands of the Blest" (Sandys 25). Here, the tower of Cronos is analogous to the Guardhouse of Zeus, while the "highway of Zeus" is a river path which ascends to it. Pindar details water imagery when he mentions "ocean breezes." One highly suspects, therefore, that the "highway of Zeus" is actually the Milky Way and that the tower of Cronos is a second sun around which the Earth and its heavens orbit. This supercelestial region is the location of the "Islands of the Blest."

Not surprisingly then, elements of this cosmography appear in Mithraism, one of the leading religions in ancient Rome. David Ulansey notes that in Mithraic iconography Mithras is always portrayed *separately* from Helios. Mithras was consistently labeled "the unconquered sun," *sol invictus;* the fact that these two gods are not synthesized but complementary, for Ulansey shows that the Mithraists believed in the existence of two suns ("Mithras" 161). Ulansey calls the second sun the hypercosmic sun. It exists above the fixed stars. Ulansey also tracks the tradition of this hypercosmic sun from Plato to Philo and Plotinus ("Mithras" 164-65). The object of Mithraism was to ascend through the cosmos and join in the realm of the hypercosmic sun. This fact, for Ulansey, solves two puzzling depictions in Mithraic iconography. Mithras is always shown slaying a cosmic bull in the tauroctony. Many scholars agree that this bull is in fact a representation of Taurus who sits at the intersection of the Milky Way and ecliptic; however, the depiction of the bull in Mithraism is facing in the opposite direction from the actual constellation. Ulansey believes that the Mithraic depiction is viewed from "outside the cosmos," from the "hypercosmic" perspective ("Mithras" 168). This would also explain the imagery of the rock-birth of Mithras. Mithras is depicted being born out of a rock inside a cave. A snake often entwines the rock. The cave itself is an image of the heavens as seen from the inside. The rock-birth scene depicts Mithras emerging out of the heavenly cave as seen from the "hypercosmic" perspective ("Mithras" 168-69). According to this ideology, Mithras is *sol invictus* because he is a depiction of the hypercosmic sun around which the sun of our solar system orbits. He is the lord over the Watch-tower, the cosmic altar which is the source of the earthly creation; thus, Mithras is the ruler of the Moirai—the Fates, and oversees the entire operation of the celestial spheres (Ulansey, *Origins* 86).

If Heraclides did teach a heliocentric system, no doubt it was a heliocentrism belonging to the microcosm and not the macrocosm; Man was the thing who could ascend to the Central Fire in heaven. Actually, a few fragments from Heraclides strongly suggest that his heliocentric universe was akin to that of Philolaus. Heraclides' cosmology also contains three tiers, though his identification of these celestial levels is very interesting, "the sphere of the fixed stars belonged to Zeus, the spheres between it and the sun to Poseidon and those below the sun to Pluto" (Gottschalk 99). In this context the familiar division of sky, ocean, and underworld is not on the Earth but is describing a celestial cosmography. Heraclides also mentions three celestial roads and gates upon which the dead travel: one is near Scorpio, one by Leo, and another by Aquarius

(Gottschalk 99). One cannot help but notice that these celestial figures form the composite image of the Greek sphinx (and the gnostic Aeon and Hebrew cherubim). This context is highly suggestive that the sphinx represented the multiple paths of the dead. We are also informed that one of these roads leads to the outermost heaven, while the other two appear to sojourn to some other state of being akin to damnation or purgatory (Gottschalk 99).

It is clear from the writings of Heraclides that the middle heaven, the space between the sphere of fixed stars and the Sun, is located in the Milky Way (Gottschalk 100). In this case, Poseidon is the god of the sea because he is the god of the celestial ocean arcing over the sky and intersecting the ecliptic at the gates or ports of heaven—Scorpio and Taurus/Gemini. The location below the Sun appears to be the "Heavenly Hades" (Gottschalk 101). This sphere would include the realm of the dancing planets. The Moon is critical in this ladder of ascent as it becomes the waypoint or "resting place of the soul on the penultimate stage of its upward journey" (Gottschalk 102). According to Heraclides, the souls of the dead rise to the Milky Way, apparently through the planets. Souls that are ready for apotheosis (deification) ascend out of the Milky Way into the super-celestial realm, which is the *apeiron* of Anaximander, the tower of Cronos for Pindar and Philolaus, or the hypercosmic realm of Mithras. Souls that have not purified themselves sufficiently to leave the wheel of rebirth fall back down from the Milky Way, through the ladder of the planets, and are reincarnated on Earth for another bio-revolution (Gottschalk 102-03).

It is Plato that reminds us that the transcendent end of conscious being is to transform into a philosopher. One must remember that in Greece the idea of *philosophia*, the love of knowledge, originated from a particular kind of knowledge—knowing how to escape the wheel of rebirth in this world and entering into the cosmic dimensions above (McEvilley 100). For Plato, true knowledge is found only by ascending to the "region above the heavens" into the super-celestial sphere. Many oral societies placed the gods in this realm. Plato placed the origin of true forms in this realm. Ptolemy turned it into a mechanical sphere.

Finally, if there is a true earth and a true heaven, then there probably is another conception of the underworld—the third level of ancient cosmology—that transcends our modern notions of a pit or cave where the dead fall. Corresponding to the celestial archetypes of the oral mind, the underworld was an astral region in space linked to the axis of heaven. It was called the "underworld" because it was a world beneath this one, the framework beneath material phenomenon, the source of true form and life; in this sense, it was a mirror image of the celestial realm. One must come to understand that the underworld of ancient cosmology was neither subterranean nor only the abode of death. It was the opposite of material existence and was both the gate out of that existence (through material death) and the spring of its source (through material birth). This idea is expressly embedded within the Egyptian psyche, as W. B. Kristensen notes this connection, "The ancients [believed] that all that lives and all that grows is the result of an inexplicable and completely mysterious co-operation of heterogeneous factors. . . . Life and death appear to be irreconcilable opposites: yet together they form everlasting life. Neither predominates; they alternate, or more aptly they produce one another" (cited in Piankoff 29).

According to our scholar, when the Egyptian sun sank down into the underworld it was not dying, but returning to its source, "What was meant is evidently that the sun, when it goes down, does not die but reaches the hidden fountain of its life. Becoming or arising is the nature of Khepera" (cited in Piankoff 30). The underworld was also called "the land of life" because here was the seed soil for material creation; therefore, "'the land of life' is a frequent name for the nocturnal abode of the sun. Absolute life has its home in the realm of death" (cited in Piankoff 30). More importantly, such a conception of the underworld did not belong only to Egypt, but to ancient thought, "[This] totality of life and death was the mystery at the center of all mystery religions" (cited in Piankoff 29).

Both in Egypt and Babylon, terms and images relating to the underworld were always associated with the sky. This is especially clear in Egyptian cultus, where there are over 370 different astronomical terms employed in the funerary texts (*HM* 73). There are over thirty-seven terms for the word *heaven* alone, each with its own nuance and cosmographical relationship that is left up to the translator to attempt to figure out or to ignore (*HM* 73). This same ambiguity exists for the Egyptian words for *underworld*. The underworld was never meant to be underground or the permanent abode of the dead despite the insistence of some scholars. Nibley writes:

> Indeed, in [the Book of Breathings] it is never unequivocally stated that the dead is in the underworld at all! This is because every term denoting the underworld is ambiguous. . . . On the other hand, the terms denoting heaven and celestial exaltation are quite clear and unequivocal. While in early times, as Hornung notes, the afterlife is depicted *only* in heaven and not beneath the earth, from first to last heaven remains the preferred residence. (*MJSP* 347)

According to Hornung, the Egyptian gates to the netherworld were always located in the "seam or juncture in the east and west where heaven, earth, and underworld came into contact with each other and where intercourse between the spheres is possible" (cited in *MJSP* 107). While Egyptian terms such as *Rosetau* clearly indicate the heavens, they also refer to the necropolis (Walton 317). *Duat* refers to the east and *Imhet* refers to the west (Walton 317), yet these are cosmographic terms, for one enters the heavens in the seam or juncture on the eastern and western horizons where the sun rises and sets. "For the Egyptians, then, the afterlife was entered by ascending to the sky to join the gods, particularly the sun god in his journey across the sky" (Walton 318).

There are no Mesopotamian funerary texts that give a direct comparison, but the cylinder seals and kudurru markers are full of the same allusions to a heavenly netherworld that is the abode of the dead. Gavin White, in his book *Babylonian Star-Lore*, has reconstructed the Babylonian astral scheme using these seals and markers. In the Babylonian planisphere and in the northern reaches of the sky by the Milky Way sits a sphinx panther, which guards the entrance to the celestial underworld (37). A constellation of an ark or boat sits by one of the celestial gates to transport the souls of the dead (37). On the opposite side of the sky we find the other celestial gate marked by the constellation Orion or True Shepherd of Anu, who has been struck down by a mace as one who walks the path of the dead (compare Osiris and Orion) (31). Remarkably, the Babylonian constellations associated with the journey of the dead follow the Milky Way (36).

The Milky Way as the abode of the dead is a universal theme in antiquity. As early as the *Pyramid Texts* we find that the Milky Way is central to the journey of the dead: "Ahoy, Ferryman! . . . Behold, I have come and gone, for I have reached the height of the sky, and I have not been opposed by the Great Ones of the Castle of the Mace, who are on the Milky Way" (§946-50). This theme is repeated in the *Book of the Dead*: "I will not enter the place of destruction, none shall bring me offerings of what the gods detest, because I pass pure into the midst of the Milky Way" (*BD* 176). The Babylonian planisphere shows that "the Milky Way itself was either directly envisioned as the pathway of the dead or that each of its myriad stars was thought to represent an individual soul on its journey to the afterlife" (White, *Babylonian* 36).

In Hindu the name for the Milky Way was *Chhayapatha*, "the path of the shades of the dead," as well as *Somadhara*, "the stream of soma" (Krupp, "Negotiating" 86). This latter term links the quest for immortality by the initiated dead with the Milky Way. Orphic and Pythagorean doctrines always located the dead in the Milky Way (*HM* 242). The tradition enters Gnosticism where in the *Apocalypse of Paul* souls are gathered at the river of milk (Copeland 154). The northern Voguls identified their high god with the title of "Guardian of the World" and imaged him as a swan leading the dead through the Milky Way (Krupp, "Negotiating" 83).

This latter motif finds resonance in Plato's *Republic* where Orpheus turns into a swan (10.620a). Zeus also descends to the Earth as a swan, impregnating Leda, who births the twins Castor and Pollux, the Dioskouroi. The first priest of the Eleusinian Mysteries was named Eumolpos meaning "good singer," and his emblem was the swan (Kerényi 52). This imagery is highly suggestive of celestial archetypes, for there is a swan that swims down the Milky Way in the constellation Cygnus. Next to Cygnus is Lyra, the celestial lyre of Orpheus. The Dioskouroi are Gemini, the celestial gate to the Milky Way. These motifs intimate that the Eleusinian mystagogue, like the Vogul high god, was the swan who used music and song to lead the dead through the Milky Way.

The Milky Way was imaged in myth and cultus as a celestial river that needed to be traversed via an ark or boat past guardians and gates. Yet this was only part of the ancient cosmography. The Milky Way itself was part of a grand celestial landscape that separated the high heavens and the realm of Hades—both of which were located above and below the celestial river respectively. Heraclides has mentioned that the realm below the Milky Way belonged to Hades, and it is truly curious that in many myth systems the constellations south of the Milky Way seem to belong to the celestial underworld. It is quite remarkable that the Maori of New Zealand claimed that the way to the underworld began at Rigel, the foot of Orion, the starting point of the river constellation Eridanus (*HM* 210, 261). It is a tradition repeated in the *Book of Hermes Trismegistos* where one entering Hades leapt from the same celestial foot (*HM* 261). It is hardly coincidental that in Greek myth both Jason and

Heracles sail to the underworld on the Eridanus where they obtain the Golden Fleece and golden apples respectively; one suspects that these golden objects are analogous to the secrets of life and death buried deep in the underworld realm.

In summary, Heaven, Earth, and Underworld were interconnecting layers of a scale of being. The true source of all manifest powers in material creation resided in the "true heaven," "true earth," and "true underworld." In order to understand these celestial archetypes, one had to have access to them. In an oral society, one gained access to these archetypes by analogically journeying through the stars.

The Celestial Journey

In the first century BCE the Roman philosopher and statesman Cicero wrote a treatise entitled *On the Republic*. Much like Plato's own work, *The Republic*, Cicero sought to describe the constituents of a great and enduring civilization. Also like Plato, Cicero eventually turned to cosmology, where the paradigms of the eternal realm are offered as archetypes for the material one. In his concluding book, Cicero wrote of the eternal nature of the soul.

In classical dialogue form we are introduced to a man named Scipio, a Roman tribune and grandson to the great Publius Cornelius Scipio Africanus, conqueror of Hannibal. The younger Scipio has a dream in which his grandfather appears and gives a sort of guided tour of the cosmos. The grandfather promises that souls who live an upright life filled with honor and duty to the commonwealth will be given a passport into the sky where they will enter a circle of illustrious light known as the Milky Way. Further, Scipio the younger is taken on a grand tour of the interceding space between the Earth and the Milky Way; that is, the seven heavenly spheres with their musical harmonies and proportions. Additionally, the nature of cyclic time is revealed, so that eternal space and time are shown in their cosmic context. At the conclusion of the dream the grandfather states:

> But if you will look upwards and contemplate this eternal goal and abode, you will no longer give heed to the gossip of the common herd, nor look for your reward in human things. . . . Know, therefore, that you are a god if, indeed, a god is that which quickens, feels, remembers, foresees, and in the same manner rules, restrains, and impels the body of which it has charge as the supreme God rules the universe; and as the eternal God moves a universe that is mortal in part, so an everlasting mind moves your frail body. (7.5-8.2)

Four and a half centuries later, a pagan by the name of Macrobius Ambrosius Theodosius wrote a treatise on this dream entitled *Commentary on the Dream of Scipio*. This work became an authoritative discourse on cosmology and theology and was read throughout the Middle Ages. One fascinating aspect of Macrobius's work is his discussion of the descent and ascent of the soul that can either sink into or arise from the material realm. In order to do this, the soul makes an astral journey through portals and gates identified as constellations. There are roads and boundaries through the constellations. The celestial escapade begins in the Milky Way, and the soul's genesis into material birth starts where the zodiac and the Milky Way intersect (12.5).

The dream of Scipio is not an isolated vision. Cicero's work is predicated upon the writings of Heraclides of Pontus, who in his *Empedotimus*, wrote of a similar vision where the true nature of the heavens and the ultimate fate of the soul is revealed. As already mentioned, Heraclides asserts that the true division of space by the Olympian gods is astral: "the sphere of the fixed stars belonged to Zeus, the spheres between it and the sun to Poseidon and those below the sun to Pluto" (Gottschalk

99). There is also a Heavenly Hades that is demarcated from the realm of Pluto and is clearly identified as the Milky Way. According to this cosmography the Milky Way is a celestial path that transcribes the entire heavens above and below the earth. Within it "the souls of the good make a tour of the heavens during the intervals between their earthly lives," observing all the wonders of the cosmos (Gottschalk 101).

Heraclides is not the source for this kind of writing either. As already noted, Plato also writes a treatise entitled *The Republic* wherein he details the celestial voyage of Er. Er was the son of Armenius who was slain in battle and ascended through the heavens. Er goes with a great company of departed souls to "a marvelous place, where there were two adjacent openings in the earth, and opposite and above them two others in the heavens, and between them judges sat" (10.614c). These openings are the seams or junctures on the horizon that the dead are born into and arise out of from material existence. The dead also tour the heavens learning its structure and powers (10. 616a-621d).

Parmenides, the "father of philosophy" and the founder of the School of Elea, writes a poem called *On Nature,* which describes the essential nature of being and appearances. Remarkably, Parmenides declares his authority of the knowledge he bears by describing his ascent through the astral world. He describes a cosmography of gates and pathways that "reach up into the heavens, filled with gigantic doors" (Kingsley 53). These doors open and close with keys held by Themis, the bride of Zeus. The Greek poet Pindar identifies her as one who knows the celestial way. Similar themes are found in the intellectual *mise en scène* of the Pythagorean school (Bonnechere 172). The early Greek schools were taught in the manner of the mysteries and within a precinct that was a model of the cosmos.

The birth of Western rationalism and civilization presented a radically different cosmology in which the soul took center stage. The early Greeks are credited with the first advances in what today is called modern and Western thinking, yet they still had one foot firmly planted in the oral cosmos. Understanding the source of true forms and the nature and relationships of the heavens was critical for the philosophic mind. Parmenides and Pythagoras both declared their authority to teach because they had seen the heavenly realm. Plato and Cicero use celestial archetypes as a basis for creating the virtuous state. With Heraclides, they promise a blessed afterlife if one knows the way through the heavens. An astral journey is the central motif underwriting the authority to teach, the model of the perfect city, and a template for the ascension of the dead. The Greeks did not invent this celestial voyage, they inherited it. As already mentioned, Egyptian and Babylonian sources also reveal that the celestial journey was used to reinforce the power and authority of the king, to found the city with its temple and cult, and to establish an eschatology for the dead.

In almost every mythological system the *axis mundi* not only ordered the universe, but most significant, also provided a path where an initiated few could climb up or down and through the cosmos. This journey was essential for understanding and administering processes on earth. In other words, in order to apprehend the true root of created manifestation one had to analogically journey to the heavenly source. This journey of the initiated to climb up and down the axis of heaven, journeying on the rivers of a celestial earth, descending through the underworld and climbing into the super-celestial sphere *lies at the core vision of ancient oral cosmology.*

This cosmographic journey was ritually reenacted in different contexts in many ancient cultures. Vestiges of it survive in the rites of kingship and fertility festivals, of shamans and healers, not to mention features of it found in the Greek schools, oracle temples, and healing centers. In many cosmographic systems, climbing up the axis meant passing through two great gates, crossing a broad river, and surpassing the seven planetary circuits. This journey was mythologically represented with the motifs of boats, ladders, gates, and rivers. Climbing down meant traversing the underworld, which was never meant to be seen literally underground; in fact, the underworld was in the sky, and it was the only place where the true secrets of life and death were found.

We are reminded that eschatology cannot be separated from ancient cosmology. Consciousness and cosmos were apart of the same scale of being. The end of that scale, in many traditions, was apotheosis (deification) in the supercelestial realm. In order to obtain full consciousness one had to dwell with the gods in their true heaven. An old oracle of Apollo expounds this view:

> *The path by which to deity we climb,*
> *Is arduous, rough, ineffable, sublime;*
> *And the strong massy gates, through which we pass*
> *In our first course, are bound with chains of brass.*
> *Those men the first who of Egyptian birth*
> *Drank the fair water of Nilotic earth,*
> *Disclosed by actions infinite this road,*
> *And many paths to God Phoenicians show'd.*
> *This road [the] Assyrians pointed out to view,*
> *And this the Lydians and Chaldeans knew.* (Thomas trans. 296)

The path to deity is an astral road. It is full of both terrors and wonders. There are many gates that must be passed, for the initiates declare that "in our first course" they encounter gates of brass. Where are these brass gates? No immediate location is sure, but in most celestial cosmographies the journey through the astral realm begins in the underworld. The Greek historian Hesiod, in his *Theogony*, provides a description of the threshold between the upper and lower worlds where Night and Day rise and set from a sub-celestial chamber: "Next to that [Atlas] stands holding the broad heaven firmly upon his head and untiring hands, where Night and Day approach and greet each other as they cross the great threshold of bronze" (25). The horizon is the brass gate to the other world. The prototype of this gate remains the regions of Tartarus around which a "brazen barrier is driven" crafted of high walls but also of bronze doors (24-5). These brass gates were constructed by Poseidon. Perhaps this last detail is only a curiosity, but Heraclides has already stated that Poseidon was the god of the Milky Ocean and that the Milky Way itself was associated with the Heavenly Hades.

The hymn of Apollo cited above identifies the Egyptians as the discoverers of this stellar path. It also recognizes that the Phoenicians, Assyrians, Lydians, and Chaldeans knew this celestial way. This knowledge was transmitted to the Greeks from older sources, and we see echoes of it within the writings of Greek philosophers and statesmen. The full cosmographic construct appears in Greece within the institutions known as the Greco-Roman mystery religions (see next chapter). A close examination of these religions shows that a hieratic journey through the sky was essential for understanding the cosmos and one's relationship to it.

In oral cultures the deceased often had to complete a panoptic journey through the sky. One record of such a journey survives amongst the Chumash Indians. Bryan Penprase, in his book *The Power of Stars*, gives a summary:

> Perhaps the most interesting journey described in Chumash sky lore involves the journey of the souls of departed people as they rise to the sky. Departed souls were believed to rise into the sky at the edge of Chumash territory . . . and there began a journey along the Milky Way. As they arrived to the sky they were greeted by the "Widows," a group of stars known to the Chumash as "Wit" (or Land of the Widows) in the European constellation of Cassiopeia. The widows were eternally youthful and bathed themselves in a shallow pool and did not eat, but

instead inhaled their food. After leaving the widows, the souls crossed a deep ravine and encountered giant ravens who pecked out their eyes. The dead would replace their eyes with one of the many poppies that grew in this part of the sky. The ravine mentioned in the story might be associated with the stars within Cepheus and Lacerta. After the harrowing encounter with the raven, the dead were confronted with the formidable Scorpion Woman, known as "She Who Thunders" and represented by the stars of Cygnus. Scorpion Woman blocked their path and the souls had to get around her to cross a large body of water, which in the sky is the Cygnus Rift, a dark area of the Milky Way. The souls crossed this water over a very narrow bridge where huge monsters would taunt the souls and attempt to get them to fall off the narrow bridge. Only after crossing this frightful gauntlet of challenges did the souls reach their final destination, knows as "*Shimilaqsha*" or "Land of the Dead." The path of these souls is visible on any clear night and the final destination is the brighter of the two parts of the Milky Way past the Cygnus rift, near the constellation of Aquila. (67)

The Chumash sky journey is remarkable for its similarities with other myth systems. Of peculiar interest is the narrow bridge that spans an impassable body of water and is surrounded by monsters inhibiting the traveler's way. Much of the same features appear in Egyptian religion, and an impassable sea in the underworld is a universal myth motif. We find all these images in a Zoroastrian text where the deceased must cross the Chinvat Bridge, which is fashioned like a sword. It too spans impassable waters and is surrounded by terrible guardians (Boyce 82-83). This entire complex of images descends to early Arthurian literature, for in Chrétien De Troyes' *The Knight of the Cart* Sir Lancelot enters an enchanted land by crossing a terrible sword-bridge guarded by ferocious lions.

The true primer for these images remains the celestial journey through the sky. The bridge and the waters had parallels in the heavens. They in turn were part of the underworld journey, which was also located in the sky. Native American mythologies abound with these kind of tales, and they were part of the myth-ritual systems of their respective tribes. The Navaho myth cycle *Where the Two Came to Their Father* is perhaps one of the best preserved (though fragmentary) examples. The title comes from the name of the myth, but the myth was at the heart of Navaho ritual. Before Navaho warriors were about to engage in military action they would gather and perform this myth. It often took five days. The myth follows a pair of heroes journeying through the cosmos, returning to their father's house located in the sky. It is evidence enough that the Navaho were being given correct, ritual instructions on the way to the next world—an auspicious endowment to be given the night before battle.

Remarkably, the beginning of the myth starts with the creation of the world and the first peoples. The order of the heavens are established, stars and constellations are given significations, and participants are made to understand that their ancestors really belong to the star-world. Their true heritage descends from the eternal realm. When the tribal medicine man revealed this story to Western researchers, he blessed them with understanding, disclosing the central eschatology of the rite when declaring, "I am Changing Woman's Son! . . . I am the one that lives on forever. Everything is beautiful. Everything is beautiful. Out of my mouth, beauty, and around me, beauty. I AM EVERLASTING MAN!" (Oakes and Campbell 11). The medicine man created sand paintings picturing stages of the journey. The myth, rite, and paintings are really no different in theme or grandeur than the Egyptian *Pyramid Texts*; or for that matter, the words of another heavenly sojourner, who, after his resurrection from death, explained to the very first witness, "Touch me not; for I am not yet ascended to my Father: but go to my brethren, and say unto them, I ascend unto my Father, and your Father, and to my God, and your God" (John 20.17).

Changing Woman is nothing but the personification of the Great Mother Earth, who constantly reveals the eternal cycles of life and death in her seasons. Specifically, Great Mother Earth has two sons, Monster Slayer and Child Born of Water, and these are the two heroes in the myth being performed. What is the object of their quest? To ascend to their father in heaven. In order to do this they must go through extraordinary trials. First, they must reach the end of the world guarded by Sand Dune Boy. The heroes can only pass him by using songs. Of course, Orpheus can only pass Cerberus with his music and hymns. Attis passes to the next world by performing songs and dances for its guardian. The Egyptian dead must pass Aker, and then obtain the Nemes Crown whilst performing choral hymns.

Surpassing the edge of the world the heroes enter "the zone beyond mortality, where death becomes rebirth" (Oakes and Campbell 70). The road through this veil is so perilous the heroes need a guide. Spider Woman comes to their aid, giving them secret knowledge for their journey. They must surpass the proper entrance to the next world called "Rock That Claps Together." It is a curious motif, especially as it has an exact parallel in the Greek Symplegades or Clashing Rocks, which were said to be the entrance to the underworld.

Finally, the heroes come to an impassable sea. The only way across is to climb four mountains, but this journey is also filled with other terrors. Again, the myth sounds like a retelling of the Babylonian story of the hero-twins Gilgamesh and Enkidu, or even the Greek Herakles and Iphicles. The twin heroes represent the twin aspects of nature: male and female, the heavenly and underworld realms, light and dark, immortal and mortal. There are many variations of these dual-heroes throughout myth, including Castor and Pollux, Prometheus and Epimetheus, Romulus and

Remus, Tagaro and Suquematua, Hunahpu and Xbalanque, and the list goes on.

After overcoming all obstacles, the heroes enter the domain of the Father or the House of the Sun. They are given new identities (their skins are changed), and they return to the mortal world with the experience and wisdom of Everlasting Man—knowledge that can only be obtained in the heavenly realm. The end of their journey is summarized by the final sand painting of the myth: "the picture of Sky Father and Earth Mother surrounded by the horizon of the sacred colors, eternally enwrapped in the world-engendering embrace. This is a picture of the soul, because, mythologically speaking, the microcosm is a precise reproduction of the macrocosm" (Oakes and Campbell 83).

The guide that helps the heroes or the deceased through the celestial realm is a central part to this cosmology. Numerous examples can be given of the steward of the stellar path. In Egypt the knower of the way was Anubis, who guided the dead in an astral journey. There were a retinue of guides often accompanied by the "unwearying stars" (the planets) and the "Imperishable Ones" (the northern circumpolar stars). Mesopotamia had similar astral guides called the Anunna, led by the heavenly Igiggi, and in textual variants of the Gilgamesh cycle these are the stewards who lead our epic hero through the celestial realm. The prototypical celestial guide is the prehistoric shaman, whose original prestige and authority derived from his "knowledge of the way." Guilio Magli reminds us that the shaman is the designated mediator between the three worlds—upper, lower, and middle. "Shamans usually carry a wooden stick, sometimes topped with a carved symbol, often a bird. The stick symbolizes the axis, the same axis that anyone could trace by stretching an arm out to the celestial North Pole, but one that only he can pass along" (292-93). More explicitly, the shaman as "knower of the way" can pass through portals in the sky known only to him by means of his "cosmological maps, which encompass the whole universe; there are many examples of the maps, from all over the world, usually sketched on skin or carved upon rocks" (294-95).

A prime stewardship of the shaman is "guiding the souls of the deceased to the abode of the dead, as he also escorts the souls of sacrificed animals to the sky" (*HM* 122). Much like the journey of the dead for the *mystai*, the trek is dangerous, for the shaman must "fight hostile spirits, and/or rival shamans, and tremendous duels are fought. Both combatants have with them their helping spirits in animal form, and much shape-shifting takes place" (*HM* 122). We are reminded of the celestial voyage of the Egyptian dead where much of the same drama occurs. De Santillana and von Dechend note that the role of shaman is identical to Near Eastern tradition: "The shaman climbing the 'stairs' or notches of his post or tree, pretending that his soul ascends at the same time to the highest sky, does the very same thing as the Mesopotamian priest did when mounting to the top of his seven-storied pyramid, the ziggurat, representing the planetary spheres" (*HM* 123).

Astonishingly, it appears that no matter where we turn in the ancient past and among oral cultic societies, this same figure, mystagogue–gnostic–shaman, keeps showing up with the same powers and offices for its tribe, clan, or group. The Native American medicine man, the Indian guru, and the Japanese miko are not only healers and oracles, but especially "knowers of the way." This way is always the road that runs between different worlds; especially to the high heavens where all the secrets of the universe are kept and where all true knowledge of human-being is to be gained.

Because our modern understanding of oral cosmology has been reduced to spatial and mechanical models, we have forgotten the ingenious categorizations of oral thinking and their ontological cosmos. These served multiple purposes, including and perhaps principally psychological ones. The practitioners of the Navaho myth prepared themselves for battle by reciting their heavenly myth. The warriors now became an incarnation of Monster Slayer, and the battle to which they marched took on archetypal significance as a battle between the cosmic forces of good and evil. Like King Ramses, who learned the secrets of life and death giving him power over his enemies, the Navaho ritual reinforced the majestic sense of the origins of life and the fate of the soul as it journeyed through the next world.

At the center of oral cosmology is the ritualized celestial journey. Because these all appear mythological, magical, and supremely religious, modern scholars discount any real scientific knowledge obtained by this kind of oral categorization of celestial phenomena. It is true, this kind of rationalization does not fit the definitions of modern science, despite the fact that these mythic journeys belay a measured and calculated cosmos. It is also true that if one is going to journey through the stars finding their archetypal secrets, one must have some notion as to which stars hold which secrets. What is so surprising is that oral peoples did not invent this journey arbitrarily, but had identified, through close observation and metaphysical speculation, close heaven-earth correspondences. Some stars represented the entrance to the underworld, while others represented the source of wisdom, or the essence of community, family, and council. Some stars represented divinity, some the loci of death, and others rebirth.

An oral mind trained in the learning of his ancestors could gaze at the heavenly orbs while reciting myths through song and dance and recall the collective wisdom of the tribe. It is highly probable that the celestial journey was the "temple walk" of oral minds embedding their most profound truths and insights in mnemonic shrines within the stars. Oral cosmology was a memory theater; similarly to Guilio Camillo's cosmic stage, the myths and rituals of the celestial journey taught each participant to "perceive with his eyes everything that is otherwise hidden in the depths of the human mind." As stars rose and set the people would know when to plant, when to harvest, when to hunt and travel, or when to sing and dance. They would also learn whence life came, how it came, and where it ends. Nature, economy, society, war and peace, marriage and child rearing, and the ultimate questions of life and death—these were the objects of oral cosmology.

Yet more impressive is the profound metaphysic of human origins and destiny embedded in these ritual tales. The profound yearning for enlightenment in the life of the Buddha and the sweeping and radical ethics revealed in the life of Jesus Christ are not a complete break from pagan primitivism after all. Each of these later systems of thought were predicated upon an earlier and oral era where the ultimate expression of being was Everlasting Man. Here was the true man standing above the earthly one. One could gaze only at his shadow in material form. To know the true self was to strive towards the enlightenment and ethic as revealed in the cycles of nature and the canopy of the heavenly orbs. In the words of Joseph Campbell:

> From the high symbolism of the Emperor of China, the Buddha, and the Christ, to the simple legendary motifs and complex cer-emonial references of [*Where the Two Came to Their Father*] may seem a far cry. But it is only the element of the unfamiliar that conceals from us the truth that here, under these strange names and manners of worship, there exist and threaten even to speak to us the old figures known from our nursery days and days of early prayer: the ageless presences of the myth of man. They are carry-ing here, as everywhere, the infallible wisdom of their deep life source. It was only the unfamiliarity of the costume that made us believe, for a moment, we were among exotic strangers. (Oakes and Campbell 61)

As strange as playacting a heavenly journey is to modern thinking, and no doubt a little bemusing to modern cosmologists, for the oral mind this was the ultimate expression between the relationship of consciousness and reality. Man and cosmos were sympathetic. They could be analogically connected through ritual. For the oral mind, where nature is the primary referent for knowing, a re-enactment of a celestial voyage in a liturgy performed during key points in the stellar and agricultural cycle placed man in the center of the cosmic stage. With one hand in the furrows of the earth, and the other clutching the fingers of the gods, microcosmic man pulled the two realms together in both a physical and psychological harmony. This analogical act was, for numerous millennia, the religion, science, reason, and calculation of the oral imagination. It was the fantasy world crafted by both astute observation and a metaphysics that also dilated the mind.

A Flat Earth in the Sky

Repeatedly in popular and academic texts we are informed that ancient cosmology was constructed around a flat earth. It is the immediate and wholly cognizant awareness of the rhythm of the sky that quickly dispels a sense of a flat earth, despite the flat ground one is standing on. In the old days people were guided by the stars when traveling long distances. It does not take long for a traveler to notice how the dome of heaven changes as one journeys north and south. The easiest guiding point to see north of the equator is the North Star; this star is fixed, does not rise or set, and is the point that all other stars dance around in the night sky. This is why this star has been called the "North Nail," "World Nail," or "nail in the sure place."

Curiously, if one is at the equator, the North Star (presently Polaris, but this star changes over time) sits low on the horizon. If one travels north this star slowly climbs in the sky, so that its angular distance from the horizon increases the farther one travels. If one were to travel all the way to the North Pole, the North Star would be directly overhead. Furthermore, if one travels south of the equator, then the North Star, that fixed object that never rises or sets, suddenly disappears below the horizon. Concurrently, the farther north and south one sojourns the larger the difference in the rising and setting times of all the stars. While breaching the equator, one is constantly seeing new stars rise ahead and old ones disappear behind. This phenomenon cannot be explained by a flat earth, and can only be explained by a spherical one.

We know such observations were made especially by maritime cultures. One example is given to us by Herodotus as he relates a story about Phoenicians who sailed around the horn of Africa. Upon returning they reported that the position of the sun in the sky had changed during their voyage, so that at noon "they had the sun on their right—to northward of them" (4.42-3). Herodotus states that he disbelieves this observation because our historian lived north of the equator, where the sun at noon is always due south and to the left if one is facing west. The Phoenicians reported that the sun had changed positions at midday, to the right and north. This proved that they had actually made the trip, for such an observation only occurs south of the equator.

Such observations are only a subset of the whole when navigating the seas, as Allan Chapman expertly explains: "For if one sails the oceans, certain things sink into one's broader awareness—such as the realization that when sailing over the horizon, a ship's hull disappears first, and the flag at its mast-head disappears last. And should one then climb a cliff, or the mast of one's own ship, one can see the departing ship's hull reappear above the horizon, only to slip away again" (78). Added to these observations are features of solar eclipses, where the same solar eclipse is visible at 9:00 a.m. in Spain, but noon in Athens, and 1:00 p.m. in Egypt. If one lived on a flat earth there would be no differences in the time of observations (78). Or the observation that during a lunar eclipse, when the sun sets on one horizon and the full moon rises on the other, the shadow that falls across the moon is always curved (78). Again, such features are impossible to explain with a flat earth cosmology.

Modern scholarship declares that the discovery of a spherical earth belongs to the maritime Greeks. The Greeks are attributed the discovery of a spherical earth because they are the first plainly written source in history to describe earth as a sphere. Fair enough, but this does not mean they are the first to apprehend the earth as a sphere. Any traveler observing the heavens over long distances, on land or sea, would note changes in the celestial landscape that would intimate a spherical earth.

Did ancient people journey long distances? The fact is that trade routes, migrations, and nomadic travels were far more complex and long distanced in the ancient world than has been previously thought. Maritime trade from the Mediterranean to the northwest coast of India was established as early as the mid-fourth millennium BCE (McEvilley 1-2). Caucasian populations had settled as far east as modern-day China by 2000 BCE (Barber 18). Similar population movements also occurred in Japan at equal and earlier dates (Yoshida 29-43). A few centuries later, grave goods at Mycenae contained objects that originated in Mesopotamia, Syria, Egypt, Nubia, Anatolia, northern Europe, and Afghanistan (McEvilley 4). At this same period, Egyptian beads were buried in the burrows at Salisbury Plain (*MJSP* 258). By the middle of the second millennium BCE full east-west contact along the whole of Eurasia had been achieved (McEvilley 4). Compellingly, scores of depictions of functional boats have been found in prehistoric rock art throughout coastal Europe (Görlitz 90-109). It is truly curious that the earliest accounts of both Sumerian and Egyptian tradition assert that the first settlers of both lands arrived on boat.

While many of these facts are verified by archeological discoveries, certain other finds have been pushed aside by mainstream scholars because the data no longer fits the conformed theories of dispersion routes. Japanese ceramic wares dating to 3000 BCE have been found in Ecuador, while Asian cotton and mythological figures carved into gourds dating to the late second millennium BCE have been discovered in Peru (Campbell, *Flight* 96). Traces of nicotine and cocaine have been discovered in Egyptian mummies (Balabanova 6-21). Inexplicable parallels exist between Eurasian and Mesoamerican calendar astrological systems (Kehoe 47). Mesoamerican art reflects indigenous ethnic features, but also displays Asian, African, and Caucasian traits in numerous carved figures—racial characteristics that require intellectual somersaults to explain away.

Hundreds of similarities in vocabularies, myths, rituals, and cultural patterns are found in both hemispheres, making arguments for inventionism (the idea that different cultures invent similar words or symbols autonomously) problematic at best. Even if we discount trans-oceanic voyages as a viable method of contact and assert that dispersion followed land routes before the melting of the last Ice Age, then we must also be aware that such massive migrations across continents would have produced an awareness of changing landscapes—terrestrial and celestial. If a people who have set up their calendars, festivals, rituals, and planting seasons based off certain stars rising and setting at particular times, find themselves in a different land, north or south of their origin either by trade journey or migration, then they will certainly notice the change in the position of the stars overhead, and perhaps the introduction of new stars altogether. Again, a flat earth cannot explain such observations, and I think we can rightly assume this awareness existed far before the Greeks.

So why do so many ancient cosmologies all seem to say that their originators believed in a flat earth? Babylonian, Egyptian, Greek, Indian, Chinese, and Germanic mythologies all have either an explicit model of a flat-disk earth or an implicit association. The latter is the case for Egypt, where the mythological world emerged and is surrounded by the circle of the waters, as if the earth were a disc. This imagery is identical to the flat-earth disc of the Greeks, surrounded by Oceanus. We know that this idea is not rooted in pure spatial logistics. In Plato's account, Man as *anthropocosmos* appears as part of the cosmological scheme, for Oceanus was known as the primeval psyche of the world. In Orphism, Oceanus was also called Chronos, as in Time, and is described by Pythagoras as the psyche of the universe (*HM* 189). Typically, Oceanus is described as representing terrestrial waters, especially as the ocean surrounding the world of the Greeks. Plato's Oceanus, however, resides in a heavenly context. It is the largest river that flows around the earth; therefore, it can be reliably imaged as nothing other than the Milky Way—the place where conscious souls dwelt, descending and ascending on rivers through the hollows of the Earth. The mythological earth is not so much a spatial disk formatted by primitive thought as it was a stage upon which all celestial influences ran, like tides from a cosmic ocean breaching the material shore.

In the *kai-t'ien* model of ancient Chinese cosmology the earth was also flat, slightly domed, and square. Many flat-earths turn out to be square. In the *Satapatha Brāhmana*, an eighth century BCE Indian text, the heaven, earth, and Hindu temple are all square. Building the temple required square bricks in resonance with the square earth, "Now this earth is four-cornered, for the quarters are her corners: hence the bricks are four-cornered; for all the bricks [of the temple] are after the manner of this earth" (Menon and Filon 69). In this context the earth was entitled *Chatur-antha*, "bordered on all four sides" (Menon and Filon 69). A square earth makes sense if one considers that the primary method of spatial orientation on land is by the four compass points: north, south, east, and west. These are said to be the four corners of the earth.

The cardinal directions are only one aspect of the square earth. The earth is also squared by the movement of the sun across the horizon during the year. The sun's extreme north position on the horizon is the summer solstice; its extreme south position is the winter solstice. Between the two are the days of spring and fall equinox. On these four significant days throughout the solar year different stars appear on the horizon where the sun rises and sets. These stars oppose each other in the dome of the sky, so that the flat-earth is measured and quartered by the ecliptic. One could say that there are terrestrial cardinal directions (north, south, east, and west) as well as celestial cardinal directions (summer and winter solstice, spring and fall equinox).

The earth being squared by the heavens is an important feature in flat-earth cosmology. The Hindu god Indra was lord of heaven, and he is often depicted holding in his hand the Vajra, a four-cornered thunderbolt. Like Zeus, Indra is a thunder god who organizes the cosmos. His thunderbolt is a representation of the square earth and heaven. Menon and Filon believe that this square thunderbolt symbolizes the opposition of the winter and summer solstice and that the thunderbolt is actually connected to the ecliptic. This interpretation coincides with John S. Major's description of the flat-earth of Chinese cosmology, which was nothing but the solstitial and equinoctial points on the horizon projected onto the celestial equator (Major 133). In this conception, the flat-square-earth of antiquity was actually the integration of the horizon with the sky and its moving celestial bodies. The real flat earth was the equator extended into space (the celestial equator). This earth was transected by the plane of the moving planets (the ecliptic). Where the celestial equator and ecliptic intersect are the equinoctial points of the year, and with the solstice points, they form the square heaven and earth on the horizon.

The Hindu astrologer often represents the cosmos by drawing a large square in the dirt with a stick. He subdivides this square by quartering it (see figure 2). This quartered square represents the earth and its cardinal directions. He will subdivide this square again, making a grid of sixteen units. By brushing out the center four squares the astrologer creates a border of twelve squares that represents the ordered cosmos. Each one of these twelve squares is called a "house" and in late astrology they represent the twelve signs of the zodiac. By placing a stone or shell in these "houses" as a representation of a planet one can measure time and space in a simple calendrical and astrological model. The twelve squares of this cosmic grid not only represent the zodiac, but also have multiple associations, "the scale of 12 squares could be associated with the number 12, and with the astronomical periods of 1 day consisting of 12 double-hours, or 1 year consisting of 12 months, of Jupiter's period of 12 years. Very probably the astrologer's faith in these fundamental numbers helped them to fix these periods, small fractions being neglected as due to errors in observation" (Menon and Filon 42).

The astrologer can subdivide the grid of twelve squares again by halving each square. Wiping out the central area and leaving only the border the astrologer obtains a frame of twenty- eight squares. This number corresponds to the number of days in the sidereal period of the moon. Each of these units are now labeled "lunar mansions" and can be used for lunar calendars and astrology. By placing a stone or shell in these squares one can track the movement of the moon through the ecliptic or the location of a star in relation to the moon, whether the star is visible or not. Finally, by dividing this grid in half again, one obtains a grid where the border squares number sixty, and this method of calculation and representation may be the origin of the sexagesimal system used in antiquity (Menon and Filon 38).

By using a stick, drawing a square, and using simple division by halving each square, one creates a progressive series of grids that reveal a remarkable synchronicity to solar and lunar cycles. By placing a rock or shell in the different squares as a representation of either a star or planet, a priest or shaman can begin calculating relationships in the sky necessary for time keeping. For an oral mind, the flat-square earth is not a primitive conception of a planetary model; rather, it is a referent to the ordered and created cosmos in which the earth participates that has been calculated in a diagram at one's feet.

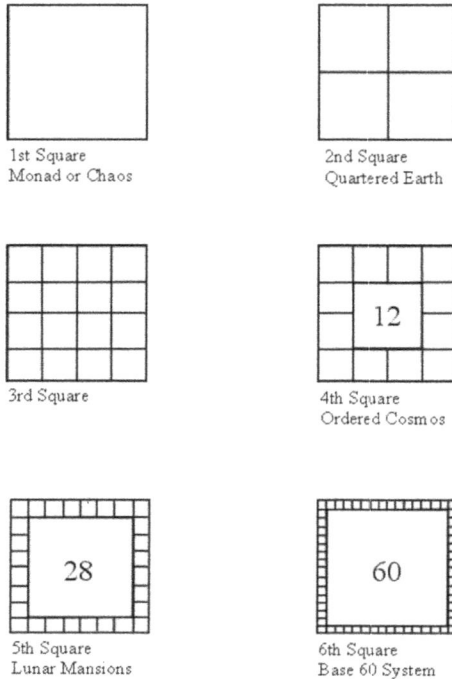

1st Square
Monad or Chaos

2nd Square
Quartered Earth

3rd Square

4th Square
Ordered Cosmos

28

5th Square
Lunar Mansions

60

6th Square
Base 60 System

Figure 2. The Cosmology of a Square and Flat Earth

Hindu astrologers represented the earth and cosmos by drawing a square on the ground. They would divide the square into four, and then divide each additional square into four again. After a series of divisions, and by wiping out the center squares leaving only the perimeter intact, they would obtain 12, 28, and 60 squares. These were used to define cosmic relationships between earth and sky. The very first square represented the initial point emerging out of chaos or the cosmic monad from which all things emerge. The first divided square of 4 represents the four corners of the established order. The 12 squares represented the zodiac, while the 28 squares represented lunar mansions. It is suggested that the sexagesimal number system, or base 60 system, was conceived in this way. (Illustration created by the author.)

The Hindu earth was entitled *Chatur-antha*, "bordered on all four sides." This conception was linked with the construction of a square temple using square bricks. As best as we can figure, the square temple is perhaps the best planisphere of oral thought. All early buildings are rooted in square architecture. The Egyptian pyramids were originally constructed from square mastabas. Babylonian ziggurats were all built on the template of the square and the cube. Hindu and Chinese temples follow suit. Many temples show solar, lunar, and stellar alignments. If a modern anthropologist were transported back in time to the fourth or third millennium BCE, and if he were to ask an ancient priest to explain his conceptual model of the cosmos, that priest would probably point at the temple, tomb, pyramid, or ziggarut, and say "that is the universe." Of course, the priest would also be thinking of his rituals, songs, and dances which harmonized the movement of sun, moon, and stars with social and agricultural cycles. The priest would be thinking of his festivals, sacrifices, sacred numbers, and esoteric philosophy behind his cosmology, all of which served to explain the processes of life and death and the invisible forces behind material manifestation. The modern anthropologist, on the other hand, would simply record in his journal, "The primitive believes the universe is a square."

The oral cosmos is wholly experiential. The literate cosmos is abstract and technical. This does not mean that oral cosmology does not include very technical data. It is just that the data is not expressed in technical terms. Perhaps the origin of the three-tiered oral cosmos— heaven, earth, and underworld—derived from the direct observation that the celestial vault changed as one moved north and south on land and sea? As one crossed south of the equator strange things happened. New stars appeared southward as one journeyed in the same direction. The North Star —considered to be the throne of heaven and top of the world axis—was no longer visible! Even as all the north circumpolar stars rotated around the North Nail, so did the southern stars move around a central void. The sun changed its position in the sky at noon. Noontime shadows also changed their direction. Combine these observations with other changes keenly noted by the oral mind: such as the change in trade winds and currents; the migratory path of different species of birds and butterflies, or the differences in periods of daylight depending on one's latitude. If an oral person traveled above and below the equator he would notice both celestial and terrestrial changes that represented a sort of reversal. The upper celestial world and the lower terrestrial world harmonized on the geography of earth; earth was not so much flat or square as it was a cosmic reflection.

Perhaps the three-tier oral cosmos derived from an oral conception of the moving sky. All stars south of the ecliptic were considered the underworld. The frame of the flat earth was really the squared points on the horizon where the celestial equator and ecliptic met. This frame was surrounded by the Milky Ocean and capped by the north and south celestial poles. Perhaps the oral cosmos was framed by the agricultural cycle. The underworld was the seed; the middle world was the sprout; the heavenly world was the fruit. Perhaps the oral cosmos was framed by the biological cycle. The womb was the tomb, and the tomb was the womb. Birth, life, and death were only a copy of the rising and setting sun and moon. Perhaps the oral cosmos was analogized to the female maturation cycle. Youth, adulthood, and old age resonated with prepubescence, puberty, and menopause. Perhaps the oral cosmos was defined by an esoteric philosophy of the eternal soul that originated in the heavens. The underworld was the south celestial pole. The heavenly world belonged to the north celestial pole. The journey between the two included astral roads and gates that ran through the entire heavenly sphere.

The truth is all of these phenomena informed the oral conceptions of the universe and cannot be imprinted within a technical diagram in a modern text. Technically, oral people do not label the earth as "flat" or "square." Remember, the oral mind rarely has a word for "square" or "circle." They label such figures from an actual object in nature. A circle is called a "moon" or "plate" while a square is called a "door" or "house." The labeling of a "flat-earth" comes by way of a literate mind projecting abstract concepts onto oral categories. Modern conceptions of ancient cosmological models are deeply skewed. We are constantly misappropriating the positions of the herring and the eagle based off literate patterns of thinking. Our history books are filled with numerous diagrams of the "old cosmologies" showing flat disks or squares surrounded by mountains with a solid sky on top and waters underneath. M. A. Orr offers a warning about these diagrams and our interpretations of them, "All these theories and guesses may seem to us very crude and fanciful, and we may compare them to the eager questioning of intelligent children, too impatient to consider whether the answers given are satisfactory explanations or no. But we must remember that all we know of the early cosmogonies is from allusions and descriptions by later writers, who often—like Aristotle, for instance—only quote to condemn" (Orr 57).

Oral cosmology was transmitted orally. This should be obvious, but the consequences of this fact are often overlooked. Our understanding of ancient cosmological systems are given us by literate authors who have already misapprehended the oral sources. What we have today are only fragments of myths, art, rituals, and artifacts that must be interpreted by scholars who cannot agree on basic terms but might agree on flawed premises. The situation is even worse when realizing that until only recently anthropologists and ethnologists began investigating the cosmological systems of indigenous tribes, and this after most of the cosmology had already been lost. Von Del Chamberlain wearily admits, "Those of us interested in attempting to analyze indigenous astronomical knowledge can site example after example in which opportunity knocked and the ethnologist opened the door only a crack, peeked through, then closed it without inviting celestial information to flow into the treasure house of the ethnographic record" (1). There are many reasons why modern investigators missed this knowledge. The modern literate mind is severed from anything but nominal awareness of celestial cycles. Many scholars cannot frame the questions needed to probe oral cosmology. Additionally, in oral tribes there are no words for "astronomy" or "cosmology." One begins forming a cosmological understanding only by direct initiation into the system.

For the most part, the oral cosmos has faded like a dream. For many historians of science, it has been obliterated within the idea of cultural and intellectual evolution. We now have the Hubble Telescope and the Chandra X-ray Observatory, supercomputers and space rockets, calculus and astrophysics. Why bother with a solar chariot and its four horses? What I have attempted to show is that the human mind is always trying to probe meaning from its environment. Cosmology in every age seeks to explain reality. It is very tempting to look at pictures from space telescopes and believe we have a better handle on things. In many areas we do. We must always remember that the data coming from these modern tools must be incorporated into a pre-established cosmovision—a fantasy world—which will highlight a certain awareness of facts at the expense of others. "To our ancestors Nature presented herself in her naked, beautiful and awful majesty;" writes Rasmus B. Anderson, "while to us in this age of Newtons, Millers, Oersteds, Berzeliuses and Tyndalls, she is enwrapped in a multitude of profound scientific phrases. These phrases make us flatter ourselves that we have fathomed her mysteries and revealed her secret workings, while in point in fact we are as far from the real bottom as our ancestors were" (28).

Ancient cosmology came up against the great wall of being—the mystery of life and death. It did not solve the mystery, as no cosmology can. It simply tried to replicate the processes which revealed the mystery on earth. The ancient astronomer built a pyramid in an attempt to probe this mystery. His temple was the telescope into the mind. The modern astronomer, on the other hand, has focused his telescope on material and abstract forces. This has not changed anything. The mystery of life and death remains, standing just beyond the horizon and imposing questions that are both beautiful and terrifying. For some, staring into a modern telescope is simply an escape from gazing into that other cosmos, the one that sees breath, psyche, and soul as the object of the stars.

CHAPTER 4

CULT AND COSMOS

Temple, City, and Cultus

Ancient Near Eastern civilizations were hierocentric, founded around the temple (*TC* 15). The ancient temple was the *omphalos* or *axis-mundi* of the world, the hierocentric point of creation that gave the ancient state its authority and prestige (Lundquist, "Legitimizing" 181). The temple was the *imago caeli*, the image of heaven (Assmann 17), and the meeting point of all three cosmic regions—heaven, earth, and the underworld (*CH* 14). The temple was the replication of the cosmos and in the words of Schwaller de Lubicz, "a confrontation with another world" (*TK* 8). Babylon was the hieratic city-temple whose name literally meant "gate of the gods," for here was the place where the gods had descended to earth (*CH* 14). The temple as heavenly gate reaches all around the world, for we find similar themes and designations all over the globe.

The etymology of *temple* is very important on these points: the word comes from the Greek root *tem*, meaning *to cut*, and refers to the cutting of two perpendicular lines; therefore, the temple was the *quadrata* or cross, a cosmological symbol existing millennia before Christianity. The cross was a symbol for the square-earth or the cardinal points of orientation that defined sacred space—terrestrial and celestial. It is the Roman writer Varro, in the first century BCE, who first uses the word *templum* to denote the temple as a sacred space aligned to the four cardinal points.

While the word is relatively late in its construction its methodological basis was the *idée fixe* of the archaic age. To mention that the pyramids and numerous Egyptian temples are aligned to the cardinal points is obligatory. One must also remember that many such edifices were raised and aligned to the rising and setting of certain stars, confirming that in many traditions the entire "landscape" of the sky was central to the idea of temple and sacred space. "The temple in particular—pre-eminently the sacred place—had a celestial prototype," writes Eliade, pointing out that the designs for the Hebrew tabernacle and Gudea's temple in Lagash were revealed by the gods and predicated on a celestial order (*CH* 7). The temple is the *template*, a synonymous word, or map of the heavens in which ritual was the measure and gesture that mortals could make to transport themselves through the planes of heaven and earth.

In Egypt, the idea of the *temple* was wed to the idea of a *ship* that sailed through the heavens (Griffith 21-25). The Egyptians painted wings on their ships and placed temple shrines within them. More important they imagined the Nile river as a heavenly waterway, with various scholars assigning its astral identification to either the Milky Way, ecliptic (Griffiths 20) or, as per Hyginus, to the constellation of the river Eridanus (Condos 105). Whatever its stellar correspondence, it is of prime importance that when the pharaoh sailed upon his winged holy ark down the Nile he was actually reenacting the celestial voyage in the sky. Both in Egypt and Greece holy relics were carried from temples and shrines within boxes denoting ships, and one Greek word for temple, νηός, "is identical to the genitive singular of νηῦς, 'ship'" (Griffith 24). We cannot ignore that the object of Greek mystery initiation was to reach Μακάρων νήσοι, a term that translates to *Isles of the Blessed*. The word Μακάρες is of apparent Egyptian origin (Griffith 32-33), and its imagery remains the same as in Egypt: the initiated arrive at the celestial garden via an ark or ship. As Drew Griffith assays, this idea of temple and heavenly ship had many connections in the past:

The equation of temple and ship gives special point to the fact
that as helmsman of Olympus, Zeus sits high on the benches
in what ancients rightly saw as a seafaring metaphor. Ships and
parts thereof made common dedications, like the prows (*rostra*)
displayed in the Roman forum, usually at temples, and Christian
lore says that Jesus, who like the Egyptian ferryman of the dead,
Mahaf, was a fisher of souls, taught from the boat of Simon Peter,
the Rock on whom he would build his church. The central part
of a sanctuary to this day is called the "nave," from the Latin for
ship. (25)

In other words, the ancient temple was seen as either the connecting point
of the three worlds, or as the vessel that sailed through those worlds. The
temple-ark was a heavenly ship sailing through celestial waters.

Temple liturgy cannot be separated from the space in which it is
performed. The sacred space is the point where true transformation takes
place, and, according to Eliade, it is the point of orientation that founds
the sacred world (*Sacred* 22). More important, the temple is a template
of ancient thought. No matter where we turn, the central ordering of the
universe via the rites of the sacred space exists amongst oral peoples in
the mythologic age and beyond. The Babylonian ziggurats, the Egyptian
pyramids, the Greek oracle centers and temples, ancient megalithic rings
and mounds, ceremonial hogans, tepees, granaries, and grave mounds—
all show a remarkable homology, broadly speaking, in form and function
across cultures. In the least, the form of all these structures is a replication of the cosmos while their function remains the constant renewal of
benevolent, cosmic powers.

The sacred world was founded by the construction of a sacred center.
Natural forces eroded the sacred world and presented a threat to the civilized state; therefore, the sacred world had to be periodically re-founded
in seasonal rites and festivals, where the king was re-enthroned and the

land was re-consecrated and re-made into the original garden of paradise. The locus of this re-founding was the temple, and the means by which the world was renewed was ancient ritual—reenacting the original deeds of the gods or offering sacrifices and services towards them ensured the perpetuation of the cosmic order. These rituals had to be enacted in the right place (the temple), in the right way (mimicking the original acts of the gods), and in the right time (for example on New Year's Day or other celestially significant periods throughout the year). Thus, calendar making, astronomical measures, and astrological considerations were always wed to the rites of oral society—sky and rite remain inseparable.

The temple founded not only the sacred world but also the ancient city. The Greek *polis* referred to a specific kind of social order that was a living synthesis to the grand system of nature—the *cosmos* (Toulmin 67). The city, rightly ruled, was a reflection of the universe, rightly maintained, in its annual cycles and seasons. This fusion between city and cosmos is pre-Greek. In ancient Mesopotamia, the city and the cosmos were synonymous: "the cosmos found its ultimate ordered state in the city. The world could not exist at any meaningful level without cities" (Walton 275). Temples could not be built outside of cities (Walton 277). The temple was the template of the cosmos that founded the city-state and ruled over the extension of all human activity within its sphere. "The founding of the state amounted to the same thing as the founding of the cult" (Walton 277); thus, we find the seven heavenly masters (the Igigi) as the founders of Uruk (*EG* 1.21) and the entire *Epic of Gilgamesh* as the city's claim to power and prestige as its national hero treads through the spheres of cosmos.

This idea was also rooted in Egypt, where the city was the primordial habitation of the gods (Walton 276). The city preceded the actual creation of the sacred world, whose rising in the primordial hillock could only occur through the founding of the temple in its city (Assman 25). The Egyptian ideogram for "city" was a circle divided into four quarters, each quarter reflecting the plan of the entire universe. Every royal city in India was built after a celestial prototype (*CH* 9) in which city, temple, and cosmos became united. Not surprisingly then, in ancient China the entire countryside was called the Celestial Kingdom (Toulmin 67) for the city, palace, and temple were a reflection of the heavenly order: the Emperor's decrees were the Mandate of Heaven (Toulmin 67) as the Emperor brought the beneficial cosmic powers to root in the land as its intermediary.

In Egypt the entire land was also a sort of Celestial Kingdom. Egypt was divided into forty-two nomes or districts, each with its founding city and temple. In the *Book of the Dead,* forty-two judges guard the way against an unprepared initiate. These judges were a reflection of the forty-two nomes or townships existing throughout Egypt. Each town was itself a representation of a celestial loci, for each "bore a name of mystery and reflected the region of the holy dead" (Adams 63). Eliade states that "in Egypt places and nomes were named after celestial fields: first the celestial fields were known, then they were identified in terrestrial geography" (*CH* 6). City, cult, and cosmos, all associated with the path of the dead, were united in a cosmovision that employed city planners and engineers to replicate this grand cultus in the sacred buildings and structures of the living. This Egyptian cosmovision would last as far as the Hermetic tradition. In *The Asclepius,* attributed to Hermes, these relationships are made clear: "Knowest thou not Ascelpius that our land is the image of heaven, the representation on Earth of every celestial ordinance? Our land is the temple of the world" (cited in Harrison, *Cauldron* 75).

A new field of study has cropped up in the past few decades known as archaeoastronomy, the result of archaeologists and astronomers having repeatedly found significant celestial alignments within ancient structures or standing stones. Most of these alignments were first noticed with the rising sun on the morning or evening of solstice or equinox (as at Stonehenge). Additional alignments have been found with the cycles of the moon (as at Chaco Canyon). Even more interestingly, significant alignments have also been identified with specific stars in the sky (as in the Great Pyramid). What is truly astonishing is that not only were significant temple structures aligned with points in the sky, but that the temple structures themselves also represented certain points in the sky. And not just the temples, but also the entire geographic landscape. The terrestrial Nile was a heavenly waterway whose proper identification was probably not exclusive to the Milky Way or the constellation Eridanus, but may have belonged to both. According to Eliade, in Mesopotamian beliefs the Tigris was identified with the star Anunit and the Euphrates with the star of the Swallow. While all the Babylonian cities "had their archetypes in the constellations: Sippara in Cancer, Nineveh in Ursa Major, Assur in Arcturus, etc." (*CH* 6). "When we come to the technical fabric of Mesopotamian cosmology," writes Campion, "it is difficult to generalize over a 3,000-year period, but, it is clear that all parts of the cosmos were linked to each other, so that each star or region of the sky might have a terrestrial counterpart, and vice versa" (*History* 40).

What was the purpose of this heaven-earth correspondence built into land and stone? Campion notes that the stars were "co-opted into the emerging bureaucratic political order" where astrology and calendar keeping were the requirements of the day (40). One has to consider the oral strategies required in calculating the highly complex fabric of heaven and its moving bodies. On mnemonic grounds alone, many memory aids would have to be built to organize the hundreds of stars in every direction and in their seasons. What better way to aid the memory than to build on the ground what was to be remembered. It appears that Camillo's memory theater had its precursor in the cosmology and cultus of the ancient *polis*. In the oral world, the cultus of a culture was its memory theater, and all the festivals that were kept in rhythm with cosmic cycles had to be overseen by those who knew them. The priests and priest-kings recreated the oral cosmos on earth in ritual, architecture, and myth, as these constructs never appear to be separated in the ancient world. The power and authority of the king and his priesthood thrived on his celestial authority rooted in celestial archetypes recreated on earth.

Even in nomadic tribes such heaven-earth correspondences have been found, where natural land features replace brick and stone temples as representations of the stars. For one example, the Lakota tribe based their nomadic travels not just on following game or in rhythm of the seasons, but especially on heaven-earth relationships. Ronald Goodman, in his essay *Lakota Star Knowledge*, recounts the sacred journeying of this tribe, "During the three month period from spring equinox to summer solstice the Sun travels through four Lakota constellations. Three of these stellar groups are connected by oral tradition to specific places in the Black Hills. By synchronizing their arrival at each of the three sites to the entrance of the Sun into the corresponding constellations, the people were following the Sun's path on Earth" (143). Their nomadic journey's were not arbitrary, and like the high civilizations of the Near East, these people also sought to reinvigorate the powers of the world through ritual and sacred space, "Furthermore, from being at the right places at the right times and doing the appropriate ceremonies, the people received spiritual power from *Wakan Waste*, the cosmic powers of good. This stellar power . . . was especially focused through the Sun to certain sites on Earth as it passed through the constellations correlated with those sites" (143).

Every sacred loci—terrestrial and celestial—had a myth and ritual associated with it. The myths served to explain the primordial origin of this heaven-earth relationship, while the ceremonies re-enacted some portions of the myth. Central to Lakota culture and cosmology are the several myths surrounding "Fallen Star," a primordial and stellar ancestor of the tribe:

> Long, long ago, two young Lakota women were out one night looking at the stars. One young woman said, "See that big

beautiful star. I wish I could marry it." The other woman said the same about another star. Suddenly, they were transported into the star world, and there these two stars became their husbands. The wives became pregnant. They were told this star world was theirs but also warned not to dig any wild turnips. Eventually one of them did, and as she pulled out the turnip, a hole opened in the star world. She was able to look down and see the Earth and even her own village. She became homesick and decided to return to Earth. She braided more and more turnips to make a rope and let herself down through the hole. But the braid didn't reach the Earth, and she fell. The crash killed her, but her baby was born. The baby was raised by a meadowlark. Since meadowlarks spoke Lakota, the baby, now named "Fallen Star," grew up speaking it too. (Goodman 142)

Fallen Star returns in other myths to help the people of the Lakota tribe. So when a "red eagle" appears stealing girls and killing them, the tribe prays to Fallen Star, who appears and destroys the eagle and turns the slain girls into the seven stars of the Pleiades. Fallen Star is often associated with the motifs of celestial ascent: in another story he saves a brother and sister from a bear by raising them atop Devil's Tower in the Black Hills, a sacred landmark with a celestial archetype in the Lakota constellation of *matotipila* (incorporating the stars Castor and Pollux). Later, a bird returns the children back to earth.

The sacred star groupings of the Lakota are where the ecliptic intersects the Milky Way through Taurus and Gemini, and the stars central to Lakota cosmology include Rigel, Sirius, Castor, Pollux, Procyon, and the Pleiades. It is a remarkable coincidence that these are the same stars that occupy the celestial underworld in myths and cosmologies around the world. If dispersion is not the root of these similarities, then we must assume that many people all around the globe recognized the great importance of this area in the sky. The similarities between myths and cosmologies could be explained as the similarities required in every oral group to keep a calendar in rhythm with the seasons, animal migrations, weather, and similar environmental patterns, where the heliacal rising or setting of these stars coincided with specific heaven-earth phenomenon. Because the cycle of the celestial bodies are the same everywhere around the globe, similarities in myth and ritual can be explained if we attach them specifically to cosmological models welded to the motion of the stars.

Still, this does not explain the similarities of the esoteric nature of these systems. In many such cosmologies, there are hints of the soul's celestial journey through this portion of the sky to obtain authority or immortality. The journey becomes a grand, celestial escapade with multiple motifs and rites that cannot easily be explained by calendric models. Because these systems were kept oral and secret, our knowledge of them is extremely limited. What little we do have speaks to an amazing metaphysics attached to oral cosmology and *anthropocosmos*, the micro-macro-cosm interrelated between heaven, earth, and man.

In the Lakota myths of Fallen Star we find elements of the mortar that once affixed the bricks in Lakota culture. The Lakota are descendants of the stars. Their real home is in the star world. Fallen Star is an ancestor who imbues the tribe with celestial powers. By ritually re-enacting the stories as well as the movement of the sun through these stars they achieve harmony. The smoking of the Sacred Pipe ceremony, for example, had a celestial archetype. The Sacred Pipe itself was a correlation to the stars in Aires, the spoon which carried the coal that lit the pipe was a correlation of the Big Dipper, and the coal itself was the earthly embodiment of the Sun (143). The smoking of the Sacred Pipe "was a cosmic ritual to rekindle the sacred fire of life on Earth. The higher powers, using stars and the Sun, performed a celestial Pipe ceremony to regenerate the Earth" (143). Ronald Goodman summarizes all of these relationships:

> Reflecting on what has been delineated so far; the stars were the visible scriptures of the people at night, and the related land forms were the visible scriptures during the day. Both night and day the people walked between sacred stories written in the sky and on the Earth which, through the mediation of Fallen Star, taught them how to establish an authentic relation to the sky, *Skan*, "the one who moves whatever moves." . . . For the Lakota, spiritual power was achieved by living in harmony with the stellar macrocosm. The entire spring journey was a ceremony which attempted to mirror on Earth what was happening in the spirit world. Lakota star knowledge together with the oral tradition was a ritual artifact of attunement. The nomadic life of the Lakota can be fully understood only in the context of their stellar theology." (145-46)

Returning to the Old World of Greece and Mesopotamia, we find similar connections where temple and city are the earthly manifestations of celestial archetypes. Such connections are found in the Boeotian city of Thebes that was destroyed by Alexander the Great. Thebes was one of the oldest and most powerful cities in ancient Greece. It is awash in mythological associations that rival the lore of ancient Troy. Some of the greatest kings in Greek myth, such as Cadmus, Amphion, and Oedipus, are directly associated with this city. Immortals are also related with the Greek Thebes as the wives of both Heracles and Dionysus hale from this city. Of greater interest is the leading etymology of "Thebes." It is a Greek transliteration of the Egyptian *Ta Apet,* or the temple of Apet, which becomes *Thebai*, the city of *Thebes*. The temple of Apet is in the Egyptian city of Thebes. This Egyptian city was named "Thebes" by the Greeks, who saw a similarity between their Boeotian city and the Egyptian one (Strudwick and Strudwick 10). The secret chambers within the Temple of Apet are a model of the cosmos and reflect the celestial journey of the dead (see below).

The Greek Thebes was a model of the cosmos. It was built as a circular city (Brown, *Semetic* 112). Ancient writers often commented on its seven city gates; for example, Sophocles repeatedly identifies Thebes with its seven gates, having his chorus sing, "From that day on we called you king, we crowned you with honors, Oedipus, towering over all—mighty king of the seven gates of Thebes" (*King* 1328-30). Eteocles declares Thebes as "the seven-gated town" (Euripides, *Phoenician Women* 748). The greatest statement from our playwrights comes from Euripides' *Bacchae*, where the *mystes* Pentheus gazes with new vision after his mystery initiation: "I seem to see two suns blazing in the heavens. And now two Thebes, two cities, and each with seven gates" (918-20). This incredible statement indicates that Thebes was in fact built after a cosmic prototype; the second city seen by Pentheus is the true form from which the earthly Thebes was modeled—each with seven gates. The Boeotian city of Thebes was a model of the heavenly city. Pentheus also sees two suns, and based off our discussion in the previous chapter we understand why—his vision only makes sense within the oral cosmos.

According to later writers, such as Nonnos, each of the seven gates of Thebes was dedicated to a heavenly sphere. The northern gate was dedicated to the Moon. The second or northeastern gate was dedicated to Hermes or Mercury. The eastern gate was dedicated to Aphrodite or Venus. The southern gate was named Êlektôr, the Sun. The western gate was dedicated to Ares or Mars. The northwestern gate was dedicated to Zeus-Bêlos, or Jupiter. The seventh gate was dedicated to Cronos, the "High-Celestial," the planet Saturn (Brown, *Semitic* 140-42).

The celestial design is manifest in another Greek fragment wherein the Greek writer Armenidas is cited, informing us that the acropolis or temple of the city was named Μακάρων νήσοι, "The Isles of the Blessed" (Brown, *Semitic* 139). This fact brings up the second leading etymology of the word *Thebes* which is *têboh* or *tâbût*, referring to an ark or ship (Brown, *Semitic* 139). Each etymology qualifies as a candidate simply because each etymology is a pun of one another. The only way to get to the Heavenly Isles was in the Heavenly Ship. Temple, city, and ship are homologous. When we put these pieces together, then, we have a statement by Euripides declaring that the city itself was modeled after a heavenly prototype. It has seven gates, which are convincingly related to the planetary spheres. Its central temple is named the Isles of the Blessed that was the location of the Throne of Zeus or the Tower of Cronos, or the second sun around which the heavens revolved. The fact that Euripides also mentions this second sun in context of the city of Thebes is revealing. The city itself may have been analogized with that of an ark or ship; this is the heavenly ship that sails to the Isles of the Blessed. One would think that if the ancient Greek world universally believed in the homocentric spheres articulated by Aristotle and Ptolemy, then the ancient Greek cities might have been built within the model of the universe orbiting the Earth. According to our pieces and fragments, the Greek Thebes was a model of a more ancient cosmos.

There are other interpretations of the data. Earlier writers identify the gates of the Greek Thebes not with the planets but with the different sections of the town. Still others state that the gates were constructed by Apollo's lyre. This founding myth is probably our best confirmation of the heavenly design. According to the Greek tale, the walls and gates of Thebes were created by Amphion, who took a heavenly harp and strummed it; the music from this celestial lyre caused rock and stone to move and form the city. It is fairytale imagery, and the myth is often taken as a fairytale itself. When one understands that the city, temple, cult, and cosmos are all synonymous, one begins to see the cosmogonic imagery in the myth. The original music of the spheres belonged to the choral dance of the temple builders, who founded their cities in concert with a heavenly design. The Egyptian temple builders also showed up with their songs, chants, and hymns, as well as with their numbers and measures attuned to the sky. The story of Amphion and his heavenly lyre creating the walls and gates of Thebes most likely relates to the song and dance performed by its architects who danced the city into existence using celestial archetypes as their blueprints.

The celestial template of the Boeotian Thebes was imported into Greece. There are numerous reports of seven-gated or seven-walled cities being built in the ancient Near East, each with planetary connections. Herodotus informs us that King Deioces compelled the Medes to build him a great city, Ecbatana, built with seven concentric walls: "The circles are seven in number, and the innermost contains the royal palace and treasury. The circuit of the outer wall is much the same in extent as at Athens. The battlements of the five outer rings are painted in different colours, the first white, the second black, the third crimson, the fourth blue, the fifth orange; the battlements of the two inner rings are plated with silver and gold respectively" (1.98). The different colors of the walls correspond to the different celestial, planetary spheres, linking city with cosmos. Not surprisingly, according to de Santillana and von Dechend, this seven-walled design with its colors and planetary associations was the template from which the great city of Ninevah was also built (*HM* 239-40). Going back even further, we find the great Sumerian city of Uruk, home of Gilgamesh, built by seven wise men with seven great walls (*HM* 300-01). This time the symbolism stretches beyond the planets and is associated with the entire celestial sphere. The seven wise men appear to represent the seven bright stars of Ursa Major (*HM* 301). The walls themselves represent the planets, while the sister city of Uruk, Eridu, is a representation of the great star in the south, Canopus (*HM* 301).

In brick and stone we are getting hints of a grand cosmological scheme. As already mentioned, the city itself was a model of the central temple upon which it was founded; thus, the Babylonian ziggurats were often built in seven levels. The famed Tower of Babel was built with such a design: seven tiers leading to an eighth shrine at its apex (Herodotus 1.181). The great ziggurat of Nabu was called "House of the Seven Bonds of Heaven and Earth" and was painted with seven colors conforming to the planetary scheme (Menon and Filon 128-29). Yet another ziggurat was named "Temple of the Stairway to Pure Heaven," where the word translated as "stairway" refers to the passage between heaven, earth, and netherworld (Walton 121-22). Interestingly, there were no interior chambers in Babylonian ziggurats as there were in Egyptian pyramids. This meant that the ritual space of a ziggurat was in fact the exterior stairway that scales the structure (Walton 119). The ziggurat was the stairway of the celestial ascent, and like the pharaoh sailing down the Nile in his heavenly ship, the Babylonian kings ascended through the heavens upon the stairs of their temples.

The Hieratic City in History

How far back does this cosmological tradition of heaven and earth go? It is a curious question with limited sources for answers. Scholarly tradition places the birth of the cosmological city and temple in the late fourth millennium BCE. This view is accurately presented by Joseph Campbell, "and then, with stunning abruptness, at a crucial date that can be almost precisely fixed at 3200 BC . . . there appears in this little Sumerian mud garden [Mesopotamia]—as though the flowers of its tiny cities were suddenly bursting into bloom—the whole cultural syndrome that has since constituted the germinal unit of all the high civilizations of the world" (*Primitive* 146). This "germinal unit" was the hieratic city, or "the form and concept of the City of God conceived as a 'mesocosm' (an earthly imitation of the celestial order of the macrocosm)" (*Primitive* 148). In this view, the hieratic city was "the highly conscious creation . . . of the mind and science of a new order of humanity, which had never before appeared in the history of mankind; namely, the professional, full-time, initiated, strictly regimented temple priest" (*Primitive* 146).

Temple, city, and priest lie at the foundations of civilization. Cultural and economic resources are all rooted in this hieratic complex. As Nibley points out, the temple and its cult served more than governmental purposes, for the need to convert various forms of wealth into acceptable offerings produced an "active banking and exchange in the temple court," while the first coined money appears in a temple context (*TC* 23). Associated with the temple and cult rites were all the accouterments of civilization, and it was the temple that served as the intellectual, economic, and artistic storehouse of the community. It was the priests who kept the writings, histories, and calendars. It is quite remarkable that the birth of the first cities coincides with another highly conscious creation of the mind and science of the age—writing. The now semi-literate priests measured the heavens and performed geometric and mathematical calculations, all with writing as an aid. They also created poems, songs, dances, and performances, and crafted mythic narratives incorporating the whole of the cult within oral and written parameters. Meanwhile the temple precinct encouraged the production of art, sculpture, figurines, and architecture, while the cult festivals brought together whole societies in cultural, economic, and social exchanges. In short, it is the temple and its cult that lies at the foundation of civilization (*TC* 25).

While the first mud brick cities and temples emerge at this time, it does not naturally follow that the cosmology behind these "germinal units" that mirror the universe originated in the same period. As E.

A. Wallis Budge reminds us, neither the Sumerians borrowed from the Egyptians nor the Egyptians from the Sumerians, but rather the cult systems of both peoples derive "from some common but exceedingly ancient source" (Raglan 116). The dating of the hieratic city to 3200 BCE is only a dating of the "bricks of history" and not necessarily the mortar that assembled them into the first cities. The hieratic city did not appear *ex-nihilo*, but was predicated on a much older system.

In point of fact, it is amazing that Egyptian religion appears in a thunderclap. From the earliest times the Egyptian cultus with its rites, myths, temples, and cosmological structures appears fully formed and functioning. Lucy Lamy observed, "The predynastic remains from the Nile Valley already reveal a high degree of culture and an unquestionable seeking after perfection in craftsmanship. But nevertheless, the sudden appearance with the First Dynasty of a complete civilization utterly defies all our notions of evolution" (68). Comparing early stone edifices in Egypt with even earlier mud brick structures, Lamy sees a process of long-term connections that hail from prehistory, "[brick structures] were in turn copied from elaborate tents which had preceded them. The tent implies nomadism, and raises the perennial question of the origin of the race of the Pharaohs" (68). The Egyptians themselves insisted that their rites and myths hailed from the Companion of Horus. These were the mythological patriarchs who, according to an inscription in the Temple of Dendera, lived in an epoch 40,000 years old (Lamy 68).

Even in nomadic cultures writes Hugh Nibley in *The Ancient State*, "The first cities are now believed to have arisen around sacred shrines of which the city itself, then the whole land, and finally the entire earth was thought to be an organic extension" (41-42). Similar to Lamy, Nibley sees the first shrines as tents: "It has also become apparent that the shrine or temple, which in time sought to draw all things into its orbit, always made its first appearance as a tent" (42). Egypt is not the only civilization that emerges from proto-cultic nomadism: "The archaic ritual tents of the Pharaohs have their exact counterparts in the cult-huts of the Mandu, which in turn have been shown to be identical in form and function to the earliest reed shrines of Mesopotamia as well as to the oldest Indo-European tent-shrines" (42). Nibley summarizes the whole situation:

> And if the first temples were tents, the first cities, whether in Asia, Africa, or Europe, were camps. That fact is the key to the whole problem of the Holy City or hierocentric state, according to Korvin-Krasiński's observation: "The quartered pattern of the world and space with the cultic shrine in the center as representing a scale-model of the entire creation, is actually incomparably older than the world capital," having its origin "in the ceremonial camp," from which the pattern passed over to the city by way of the great Megalithic ritual complexes. (42)

The great Megalithic ritual complexes are now thought to be part of a long and old tradition linking sky, rite, and landscape into a cultic ensemble dating back millennia. For example, the main sarsen circle built at Stonehenge dates to about 2500 BCE, while the blue-stone circle only dates to about 1800 BCE (Aveni 64). Yet, the oldest Aubrey Holes that founded the site date to at least 2900 BCE (Aveni 64). More interesting, as early as 1864, Edward Duke suggested that Stonehenge belonged to a complex of megalithic sites consisting of seven rings representing the planets and surrounding the great Solsbury Hill (Aveni 64). Recent scholarship sees Stonehenge as belonging to a landscape of multiple megalithic sites, and somehow relates to the journey of the dead. The much older Newgrange has now been dated to at least 3200 BCE (Harrison, *Cauldron* 40). It is not only astronomically aligned but specifically serves as a cultic doorway of the dead and their passage between the worlds (Hadingham 51-53). Other architectural features of surrounding megalithic sites date to 3600 BCE (Aveni 79). We are now numerous centuries before the building of the great pyramids in Egypt; nevertheless, the Egyptians themselves claimed that their temple tradition with its journey for the dead derived from the "Senior Ones" and haled from the megalithic age (*MJSP* 258). Astonishingly, Ernesto Schiaparelli, discoverer of the tomb of Queen Nefertari, also made note of the remnants of a giant stone circle found at Heliopolis, six hundred meters in diameter, but whose remnants have long since vanished (*MJSP* 257).

In the July 2006 issue of *Archaeology*, Ulrich Boser writes an article entitled *Solar Circle* that shakes the foundations of all our simplistic notions of the origins of rite and cult. Boser notes that within the past few decades archaeologists have now discovered the remnants of hundreds of henges throughout Austria, Germany, and the Czech Republic all dating between 4800 and 4500 BCE—all with the same architectural features: "a concentric ditch, a palisade, and two or four gates equally spaced around the perimeter. There were no buildings or homes within the enclosures, and they were typically located on a hill" (31). These henges represent "the first monumental architecture in the world" (30) and utilize a "clear architectural concept" (31): a *templum*, standardized throughout ancient Europe. What were they used for? Archaeologist Peter Biehl assures that they were used for "sophisticated astronomy" (33). Stäuble believes they served multiple purposes, including "marketplace, town square, and temple" (33), while Francois Bertemes insists they were cult sites for rituals (33).

I assert that they are all correct as the ancient temple shrines, constructed first as tents, then as wooden henges, and finally developing into grand stone structures, were the organizing element of prehistorical civilization—the *fundamentum* around which the ancient state was established. Whatever the age of the mythological patriarchs, the origins of the cosmological city and its cultus are far more complex than simple assertions about psychological or social needs. In academic textbooks today we are informed that cities evolved through the processes of agriculture, cultivation, and the domestication of animals, where hunter-gatherers could no longer roam but had to stay put to grow their crops and herds. The impetus behind this instruction is an evolutionary model of technology and techniques, where the city becomes a product of pure social, agricultural, and economic factors. The problem with this model is that it contradicts the very nature of human consciousness, which applies meaning and order onto everything it does. Whenever one finds civilization in the oral age there is already a pre-established cult and a sacred center, and the impetus behind this center is primarily a cosmological construct where social, agricultural, and economic factors are important but secondary. Meaning and order come first, gardens and walls second. Eliade notes that in many archaic cultures when a territory is first taken and a settlement established, "rites are performed that symbolically repeat the act of Creation: the uncultivated zone is first 'cosmicized,' then inhabited" (*CH* 10). When the Scandinavian colonists first settled Iceland, the cultivation of the land was ritualistic, the repetition of the primordial act of Creation: "By cultivating the desert soil, they in fact repeated the act of the gods, who organized chaos by giving it forms and norms" (*CH* 10).

In establishing a created order out of chaos, a point of origin must be erected; therefore, the first act in inhabiting a new land is to make an altar, pillar, or temple whose symbolic value is the establishment of the cosmic order on the earth. This point becomes the navel of the world; it is linked to the three-tier cosmos and is the *axis-mundi*. It is from this center that all the powers of chaos can be controlled, and is done so through the rites of the cultus. Only after this moment of consecration of the land to the higher order can agriculture and herd tending begin.

Oral cosmology rooted in celestial archetypes is much older than the hieratic city. It was birthed in ages past and took shape within the nomadic tent and the prehistoric wooden henge. The cultural revolution that began the first city-states in Mesopotamia is not a starting point in history, it is an inexplicable chapter referencing the part of the book that has been torn out. For decades scholars have stated that the few primitive tribes in existence today are a reflection of the state of humanity for countless centuries before the birth of civilization. One prominent scholar offers this warning: "The point is this: that what we observe as 'primitive' conditions are, with very few exceptions . . . only what is left of the rise and fall of past higher cultures; what appeared to be a universal steady state of superstitions from which thought grows is only the common denominator to which decaying civilizations run in the end" (de Santillana, *Origins* 10).

Cult and Cosmic Journey

For many ancient cultures, the greatest secret nature revealed was the processes of death and rebirth. It seems that all the creative, philosophical, and rational consciousness of the Egyptians was poured into discovering the process the soul might undertake to find eternal life. They were not the only ones, and the central question of life after death remains prominent across cultures and throughout history. In the ancient Near East and the Mediterranean, many different cultic expressions emerged in an attempt to recreate the process, by ritual analogy, of being reborn. The dramatization of myths and the central ontological expression of the celestial journey underwrite much of these ancient cult systems.

The eminent Egyptologist Gaston Maspero held the view that the Great Pyramid itself was not solely a tomb, but a mystery temple where the chapters of the Egyptian *Book of the Dead* were ritually reenacted by initiates in the different chambers and hallways (Adams 29). Ernest Palmer informs us that "no class of images occurs with greater frequency in the [*Book of the Dead*] than those which refer to some building" (Palmer 29). Repeated references to a "northern passage," "southern passage," "hidden lintel," and various gates, doors, and staircases refer to the celestial cosmography of the afterworld journey for the Egyptian dead (Palmer 29). These references are analogous to the actual passages, gates, doors, and stairs built in temple space, either literally or metaphorically, for the initiate to tread through while re-enacting a ritual journey through the cosmos.

We are repeatedly told that no hieroglyphs exist in the Great Pyramid, but as Marsham Adams pointed out as early as 1905 there is one glyph carved deeply into the lintel of the outer main entrance: that of the Horizon of Heaven (Adams 33-34). To enter into the dark passageway of the pyramid was to descend below the horizon in an underworld descent where the initiate declared to the gatekeepers, "May you give me a path that I may pass in peace, for I am straightforward and true" (*BD* chpt. 15). Here "The God" replied, "You shall ascend to the sky, you shall traverse the firmament, you shall associate with the stars, who shall make acclamation to you in the Sacred Bark" (*BD* chpt. 15). According to this view, the Great Pyramid is the perfect synthesis of the oral requirements of civilization. It was the temple that founded the city and the cult, it represented the cosmos, and it was a stage where Pharaoh reenacted the cosmographic journey of the dead.

It is well known that Egyptian temples and tombs were models of the Egyptian cosmos. In oral cosmology, this cosmos is rooted in the life cycle and the microcosm of man. George St. Clair observes, "Tombs were constructed on the model of the world of night, and the constellations of the sky were figured on the ceiling. The ceilings of the pyramid chambers were sprinkled over with stars. *These surroundings indicated the region which must be traversed.* The deceased, having undergone the rites of the Opening of the Mouth and the Eyes, was supposed to be reanimated; and after being equipped with formulas and amulets, the same as Osiris had been, he set forth to seek the Field of Reeds" (St. Clair 470). The Egyptian initiate found resurrection by journeying through the heavens to the celestial source of life.

An example of temple, cosmic journey, and oral cosmology is found in the already mentioned Temple of Apet, at Karnak, in the Egyptian city of Thebes. The temple was built in the fourth century BCE and modified by Ptolemy III and again by Ptolemy VIII a few centuries later. This temple is interesting for our discussion as it is the source of the leading etymology for the word *Thebes* used by the Greeks. As already mentioned, *Ta Apet,* the temple of Apet, becomes *Thebai*, the city of Thebes.

Apet is the hippopotamus goddess who was known by related titles, including Opet, Ipet, Ipy, as well as Taurt and Taweret. In Theban mythology Apet was the mother of Osiris, that is, the gestational matrix who caused Osiris to be reborn in the netherworld. In the *Pyramid Texts* we hear the deceased exclaim: "O my mother [Apet], give me this breast of yours, that I may apply it to my mouth and suck this your white, gleaming, sweet milk. As for yonder land in which I walk, I will neither thirst nor hunger in it forever" (§381-82). Apet's heavenly milk is a form of "the waters of life" whereby the deceased may travel in the celestial netherworld fully sustained.

In the *Papyrus of Ani* Apet is synthesized with Hathor, the Heavenly Mother, who resides "in the Bark of Millions of Years; a resting place for him who has done right within the boat of the blessed; who built the Great Bark of Osiris in order to cross the water of truth" (*BD* chpt. 186). In the vignette of this portion of the papyrus Apet is shown standing before the heavenly mountain of Hathor holding a torch in her right hand and an ankh sign and Sa in her left. These symbols often accompany Apet: the torch is to light the way through the underworld; the ankh is the promise of life and vivification; the Sa is a reed life-preserver worn by river travelers, that is, Apet gathers up the worthy out of the waters and places them in the "Great Bark of Osiris."

Apet herself is more than a hippopotamus, but a sort of watery sphinx-like creature—an amalgamation of hippopotamus, human, crocodile, and lion. Her name, like all things Egyptian, appears to have multiple allusions to which translators have made several attempts, including "harem," "favored place," and "great one" (Wilkinson 184). De Lubicz notes that the root of Ipet, *ip*, signifies "counting" or "enumerating" and links the idea of numerical measure with the function of gestating (*TK* 37). The synonymous name Opet signifies a "secret chamber" referring to the chambers in her temple (Rubalcaba and Cline 154). These chambers become a cultic-cosmic womb in which the deceased is reborn. At the temple at Dendera and on the ceiling of the tomb of Seti I, Apet becomes Nebet-akhet, "mistress of the horizon," and is shown as a northern circumpolar constellation corresponding to our Draco and Little Dipper. Wilkinson writes, "in astronomical paintings . . . she is frequently depicted holding a mooring post—sometimes in the form of a crocodile—to which is tethered one or more of the northern, circumpolar constellations in the form of an ox [Ursa Major]" (Wilkinson 184-85; see figure 3).

Apet was a constellation often depicted holding a mooring post. In some depictions she holds two mooring posts, a dagger and a crocodile. These mooring posts represent two stars or regions. Exact identifications are uncertain, but many scholars believe they represent the celestial north pole and the pole of the ecliptic. These stars were used to maintain a seasonal calendar and were utilized in the operation of Egyptian water clocks. If her name refers to numeric gestation, then it is well deserved as she is a celestial archetype with an apparent stewardship over time. Time, however, is not a mechanical moving of parts—it is a *function* that manifests only through the life cycle. Like the Lakota *Skan*, Apet is that invisible force "who moves whatever moves," and like the Gnostic Aeon, she represents the microcosmic life cycle endowed by macrocosmic laws. She is a representation of the revolution of the celestial orbs, the frame of time and space, and the secrets of life and death manifest on earth and hidden in the stars.

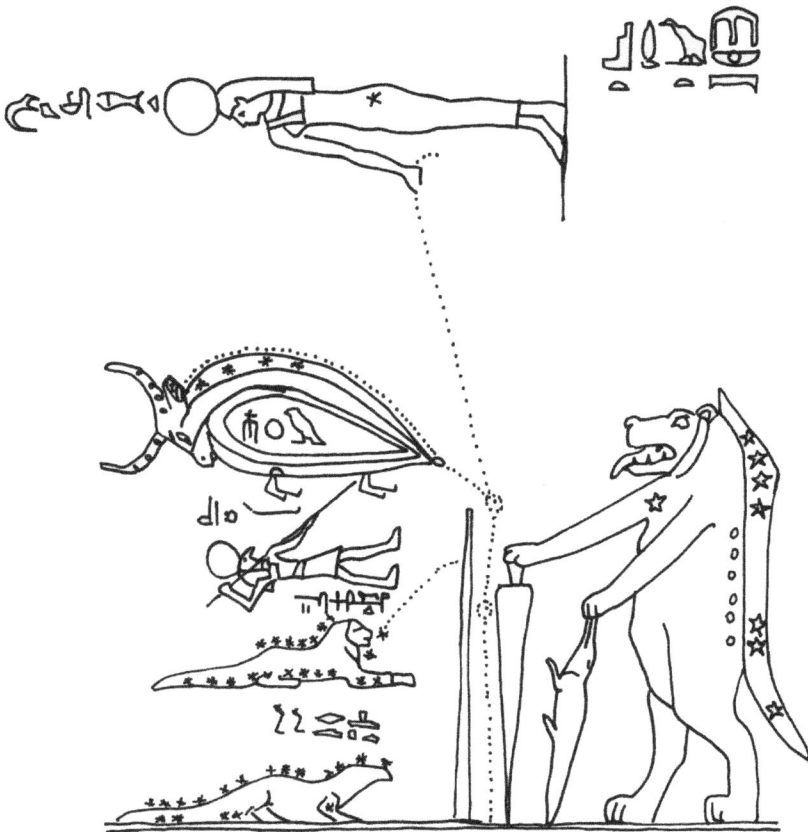

**Figure 3. Apet as Northern Constellation Depicted
in an Egyptian Tomb Painting**

The goddess Apet is portrayed as a hippopotamus, often with a crocodile on her back. In this tomb portrayal she holds two mooring posts, believed to be the northern celestial pole and the pole of the ecliptic. Apet herself is analogous to the modern day constellations of Draco and the Little Dipper.

Like all Egyptian symbols, esoteric meanings and cultic puns associated with this goddess have been permanently lost. (Illustration by Lynde Mott)

Her imagery of a water-sphinx is peculiar on this point; the iconography of hippopotamus and crocodile would tend to direct one's gaze to the southern aquatic constellations. The Egyptians had a constellation of a crocodile, for example, that eventually became the stars forming the serpentine Hydra. The hippopotamus and crocodile are creatures who can both submerge beneath the waters and at the same time bask in the sun on dry land. Perhaps her mooring posts do not just represent two northern stars, but may infer the two chief ports in the sky—the north and south celestial poles. Her imagery belies the notion of life breathing underneath the waters, and it is between the celestial poles in the cosmic waters that all life processes are manifest. From at least New Kingdom times, the Great Feast of Opet (Apet) was held in Thebes celebrating the renewal of Amun and the king's right to rule. The feast coincided with the heliacal rise of Canopus (Conman 16); this star represented the celestial south pole. Another great festival entitled Amun's Entrance into the Heavens was celebrated when Canopus rose acronychally (rising in the east as the sun set in the west). Could the imagery of Apet and her two mooring posts relate to the two celestial poles? No one knows. There is a vast cloud of cosmological puns behind this deity's name and iconography, the exact interpretation of which has been permanently lost.

Whatever her astronomical allusions, Apet is a Heavenly Mother who births the soul from the waters of the netherworld. Her temple is the ultimate expression of cosmic rebirth, and her three "secret chambers" that form her holy sanctuary represent a unified, cosmographic theme (see figure 4). In the northern chamber the deceased is shown on the lion couch being resurrected; his legs are rising up as Isis and Nephtys oversee the gestation process unfold. The deceased is none other than a youthful Osiris. Above Osiris is the god Amun-Re transformed into an ithyphallic *ba* bird. The union between Amun-Re and Osiris is the central mystery behind resurrection and the function of the gestational matrix of Apet. With the aid of the divine goddesses Isis and Nephtys, the deceased is promised new life.

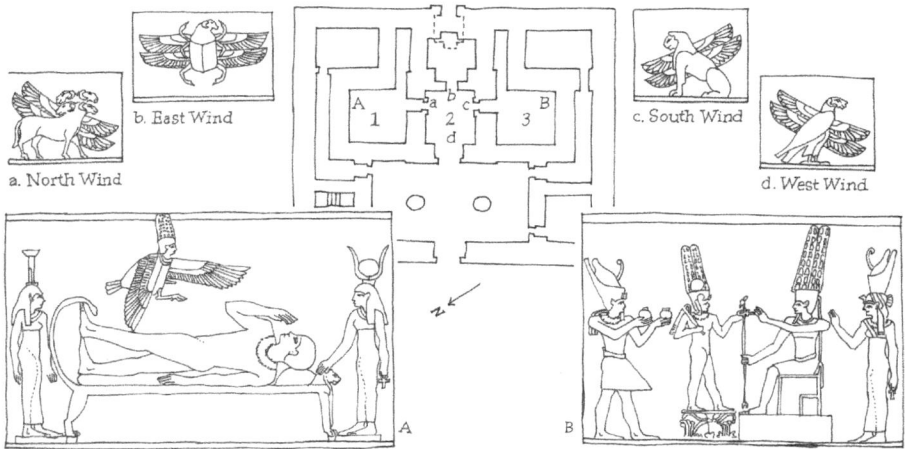

Figure 4. Temple of Apet (Opet, Ipet), Karnak, Egypt

Constructed in the fourth century BCE, the Temple of Apet was central to the yearly Festival of Apet. Apet is translated as "favored place" while Opet is translated as "secret chamber." The chamber in question is actually the three chambers in the chapel of the temple. In the north chamber Osiris is seen on the lion couch being raised from death. In the central chamber there are four archways marked by the Four Winds. This chamber represents the cosmic journey the soul must take in the afterlife. The south chamber shows scenes of enthronement where Osiris is given a crown, scepter, and ankh. Here is depicted the entire life cycle and mystery of the microcosm: life, death, and rebirth associated with an astral journey and exaltation. (Illustration by Lynde Mott, original image in Nibley, *Approach* 271).

In the central chamber there are four doorways marked by hieroglyphs representing the four winds. Here are the four cardinal directions and pathways of celestial ascent whereby the soul travels through the cosmos—west, east, north, and south. The Egyptian canopic jars in which the organs of the deceased were placed were also representations of the four sons of Horus. They not only represented the four winds and cardinal directions but also the four bright stars of the bowl of the Big Dipper in the celestial north. This chamber adumbrates the celestial journey that the deceased must undergo in order to find eternal life in the hereafter. In the southern chamber there are multiple scenes of enthronement where the soul, successful in its cosmic journey, receives the staff of power and the ankh of life. The initiated now sits in a verdant garden resting from his perilous journey and crowned with immortality. The secret chambers of Apet reveal the mysteries of Osiris. It is a mystery cosmography where the individual faces death and darkness in one chamber but through proper ritual and esoteric knowledge is revived. Resurrection unfolds as the deceased travels through the four corners of the cosmos finding the secrets of life and death in the stellar south and the throne of immortality in the stellar north. Victorious in this journey, the initiate now sits enthroned in a state of exaltation.

The Celestial Journey and the Greco-Roman Mysteries

By the sixth century BCE the Mediterranean world was rooted in mystery religions. Thrace was the homeland for the Dionysian and Orphic mysteries, which quickly spread all over Greece. Attica was home to the Eleusinian mysteries, while Samothrace and Andania held similar cults. Phrygia was home to the mystery cult of Cybele and Attis, Syria to Aphrodite and Adonis, while traditionally Persia was the source of the Mithraic mysteries. Egypt held the mysteries of Osiris, Isis, and Serapis. Every major city that the Apostle Paul proselytized in was home to some mystery cult: Antioch to Adonis, Ephesus to Attis, Corinth to Dionysus, while Tarsus, Athens, and Alexandria each held similar cults. This close association between the widespread mystery cults and Paul's missionary journeys perhaps explains the mystery terminology filling portions of Paul's letters (Freke and Gandy 162-63). The Roman Mithras cult had spread wherever Roman legions had sojourned; in fact one can determine the extent of Roman imperialism simply by locating the remains of the Mithraic temples found within the frontier camps of the legions (Willoughby 27). So it is that Willoughby writes, "It would not be a mere rhetorical figure if one were to designate the religious history of the Mediterranean world in the early imperial period as the age of the mysteries" (27).

Although the root of *mysterion* is *myein*, the word *mystery* itself refers to something that is veiled, something that can only be learned through an initiatory process by a guide or mystagogue. A mystery religion is a religion where one is initiated into a hierarchy of doctrines or ideas through a series of secret rites within a secluded precinct. The object of the secret initiation is "the revelation of the Mystery of Man" (Weston 145), or as Reitzenstein summarizes the central tenet of the mysteries, "the doctrine of the Man, the Heavenly Man, the Son of God, who descends and becomes a slave of the Fate Sphere: the Man who, though originally endowed with all power, descends into weakness and bondage, and has to win his own freedom, and regain his original state" (cited in Weston 146).

Like the cosmology of Heraclides, the teachings of the mysteries intimated that the soul descended from the heavens and could re-ascend to its heavenly source through proper ritual knowledge. It appears that a mystery religion offered an initiate, man or woman, a liturgical re-enactment of the journey of the Heavenly Man or God-man through the spheres of cosmos. The whole idea being that if one was given the right instructions, the correct rites, and lived up to the moral and philosophical tenets they represented, then one was given power to tread through the cosmos after this life and gain either immortality with the gods or at least a blessed life in the garden of paradise serving the gods. By Roman times it is the former concept that seems to have predominated. According to Franz Cumont, the tenet of the mysteries was the guarantee of "celestial immortality" (Ulansey 86-87). This is an idea supported by the *Mithras Liturgy*, whose own text declares itself an ΑΠΑΘΑΝΑΤΙΣΜΟΣ, a "Ritual for Immortalization" (Betz 1).

In ancient Greece mystery initiation was crucial. On this point there are numerous witnesses. Pindar writes, "Happy is he who, having beheld [the mysteries], descends beneath the earth: he knows the end of life and he knows the Zeus-given beginning" (Kerényi 39). Sophocles writes, "Thrice happy they who go to the world below, having seen these mysteries; to them alone is life there, to all others is misery" (Willoughby 63). Plato asserts, "whoever arrives in the underworld uninitiated and unsanctified will wallow in the mire, whereas he who arrives there purified and initiated will dwell with the gods" (*Phaedo* 69.c). Isocrates declares, "Those who share this initiation have sweet hopes for the end of life and for all future time" (Willoughby 63). Aristophanes has his chorus of initiated *mystai* sing, "To us alone is there joyous light after death, who have been initiated and who lived in pious fashion as touching our duty to strangers and private people" (Willoughby 64-65). Aristophanes' Trygaeus is desperate for initiation, "I must be initiated before I die" (Fellows 108), fearing the darkness that awaited without it. Cicero observes, "in the *initia* we recognized, just as the word indicates, the principles of life, and from them we obtained a basis not only for living happily but also for dying with better hope" (Kerényi 39).

The object of mystery initiation was a celestial ascent out of the underworld and into a heavenly realm, as is alluded to by the Roman Hippolytus: "after men have been initiated into [the lesser Mysteries] they should cease for a while and become initiated in the Great, Heavenly,

Mysteries—for this is the Gate of Heaven, and this is the House of God, where the Good God dwells alone, into which House no impure man shall come" (cited in Weston 147). This journey in the afterlife was filled with gates, guardians, obstacles, and terrors. One needed a guide, as Plato assures us, "We are told that when each person dies, the guardian spirit who was allotted to him in life proceeds to lead him to a certain place, whence those who have been gathered together there must, after being judged, proceed to the underworld with the guide who has been appointed to lead them thither from here" (*Phaedo* 107d-e). Plato insists that this underworld path has many forks and crossroads, and this is why a guide is needed. He also declares his knowledge of these things is from the observance of sacred rites and customs (*Phaedo* 108a).

The sacred, secret road through the axis of heaven was wed to the mystery of immortal life. The initiates at Eleusis traveled the "Sacred Way" during their ceremonies, performing hymns, dances, and rites that guaranteed a blessed afterlife. Albert Cook observes that the word *elýsion* is related to the word *elýste* which literally means "a way," and comments, "We must suppose that the Greeks recognized a definite 'way' from earth to heaven, along which those honored by the summons of Zeus might pass" (36). The leader of the mystery rites was called a mystagogue, though Max Pulver notes that his special office was that of an ὁδηγός, "the guide to the upper world" (191). His special stewardship was to lead the worthy upon the "sacred way," which the Orphic gold plates analogously identifies as reserved only for the initiated who would tread the celestial highway whereby they would "become god from man." Pulver writes, "Initiation is an act of decision before the entrance [to the upper world], and then it becomes a way, a long way–as is Gnosis" (191).

"Initiation into a mystery cult such as that of Mithras," writes the well-known Manfred Clauss, "enabled one to acquire knowledge of all the secret lore, prayers and rituals which guaranteed that the initiate's soul would one day find its way to the sphere of the fixed stars" (141).

Contained within Mithraic shrines are images which all correspond to astronomical stations and gates for the initiated to pass on his way to meet the Father God, even Mithras himself. Images of a lion, serpent, scorpion, bull, raven, cup, sun, and moon fill temples and are engraved on ritual artifacts. All these images are analogous to the celestial under-world of Mithraism located in the constellations of Leo, Hydra, Scorpius, Taurus, Corvus, and the Crater. Mithras is a kosmocrater: the rock from which he is born is a representation of the heavens, and the Mithraic caves or shrines in which the initiations took place also represented the heavens (Clauss 65). Even the seven initiatory grades within Mithraism are somehow related to the seven planets (Clauss 132-33), suggesting a heavenly ascent as the neophyte earned each of the successive and higher degrees. In the Mithraic mosaics from Ostia there are representations of seven gates associated with the seven planetary spheres, but also with the zodiacal constellations, as well as the seven grades of Mithraic initiation (Betz 136).

This cosmography is only reinforced by the *Mithras Liturgy*, a con-troversial Greek fragment found in the Paris Magical Papyrus, translated by Hans Dieter Betz, and whose context is rooted in magical incanta-tions but whose subject matter is entirely placed within the frame of Mithraic cosmography. In this text the initiate is given instructions on how to make the celestial ascent through prayers and rites. A celestial as-cent it is, as the deceased makes his way to the high celestial realm: "You will hear nothing either of human or of another living being, nor in that hour will you see anything of mortal affairs on earth, but rather you will see all immortal things. For you will see the divine constellation on that day and hour, the presiding gods arising into heaven, and others setting" (Betz 51). The deceased has arisen in the afterworld only to see the gods imposing their powers while they rise and set; the gods in the afterlife are therefore the stars (Betz 142), and knowing one's correct relationship to them becomes critical as one journeys with them. Indeed, the initiate himself declares, "I am a star, wandering about with you, and shining forth out of the deep" (Betz 52).

Our mystery cosmography similarly shows up in Orphism within the famed Orphic gold plates—tablets of gold found buried with Orphic initiates whereon instructions for the celestial ascent were written. Many of the tablets were found on the mouths of the deceased, as if they were the oral passports through the netherworld. Others were found clutched in the hands of the dead as a token and passport through the underworld. On one tablet we read:

> Thou shalt find to the left of the House of Hades a spring,
> And by the side thereof standing a white cypress.
> To this spring approach not near.
> But thou shalt find another, from the Lake of Memory
> Cold water flowing forth, and there are guardians before it.
> Say, "I am a child of Earth and starry Heaven;
> But I am parched with thirst and I perish. Give me quickly
> The cold water flowing forth from the Lake of Memory."
> And of themselves they will give thee to drink of the holy spring,
> and thereafter among the other heroes thou shalt have lordship.
> (Guthrie 172-73)

On another tablet we read: "Thou art become god from man. A kid thou art fallen into milk. Hail, hail to thee journeying the right hand road, By holy meadows and groves of Persephone" (Guthrie 173). Still another tablet adds to the details listed above, "And indeed you are going a long sacred way which also other *mystai* and *bacchoi* gloriously walk" (Burkert, *Greek Religion* 293).

As Susan Cole points out, the collection of Orphic gold tablets has grown so large that the categories of similarities have become as important as the categories of differences. The Orphic gold plates share repeated celestial themes: a journey, a path, an initiation, guardians, a spring of water, the crossing of water, a great tree, and a celestial garden. Cole writes, "In one way or another, the texts assume that eligibility [for privileged status in the afterlife] was established by ritual and confirmed after death by recalling or reciting esoteric information that could have been learned only through that ritual experience" (201). The privileged status Cole speaks of refers to a celestial ascent indicated by the initiate declaring, "I am child of Earth and starry Heaven," as well as declaring that he or she was a "kid" or lamb who has fallen into milk, which likely indicates the Milky Way. Much like the *Mithras Liturgy*, the Orphic dead tread through the cosmos with the stars as a star on their way to the high celestial sphere of the supreme god(s).

The later Gnostic tradition borrows from this same cosmography. Jorunn Buckley reminds us "gnosis is linked with a secret initiation-ritual closed to outsiders," whose contents included "types and names," which were needed for salvation (573). Yet these "types and names" belonged to a special path. The title of a gnostic leader was *gnōsis tēs hodou* and meant "knowledge of the way" (*HM* 131). It is the cosmographic way of all mystery initiation: "The 'Way' which had to be learned by heart is that which leads outwards-upwards through the planetary spheres, past the threatening 'watchtowers' of the zodiac to the desired timeless Light beyond the sphere of fixed stars, above the Pole star: beyond and above everything, where the unknown god (*agnostos theos*) resides eternally" (*HM* 131).

The pagan defender Celsus declared that this celestial path was not only a pattern in the mysteries but was also central to early Christian belief, "Now Christians pray that after their toil and strife here below they shall enter the kingdom of heaven, and they agree with the ancient systems that there are seven heavens and that the way of the soul is through the planets" (Hoffman trans. 95). Perhaps this gives new light upon the saying of Jesus, "I am the way, the truth, and the life, no man cometh unto the Father but by me" (John 14.6). Jesus is also a type of mystagogue teaching an individualized moral path, "Because strait is the gate, and narrow is the way, which leadeth unto life, and few there be that find it" (Matt.7.14).

Where did the Greco-Roman mysteries come from? This question has engendered a great deal of scholarly debate. Jessie Weston notes that the worship of Adonis dates only to 700 BCE, but the rites associated with the worship hail from Phoenicia and extend back a millennia earlier (Weston 40). Carl Kerényi reminds us that the Greeks considered the mysteries of the Kabeiroi age old (Kerényi 44). Excavations of shrines find nothing earlier than the eighth century BCE, but the rock altars themselves hail from extreme antiquity (Kerényi 44), while the mysteries of Samothrace belonged to the aboriginal population (Kerényi 46). Madeleine Jost informs us that according to an inscription on the Parian Marble, the Eleusinian mysteries hail from the fourteenth century BCE (Jost 153). Robert Brown shows that the rites of Dionysus came early to the Greeks and that their origins were lost in antiquity (*Dionysiak* 89). Burkert asserts that the rites of Dionysus originate in prehistory, though his assimilation to Osiris may be as late as the sixth century BCE (*Babylon* 73). Walter Otto, on the other hand, notes that the rites of Dionysus were pre-Greek and were always associated with the rites of the dead (Otto 115-18). Martin P. Nilsson tracks the myth of Heracles and his acquiring of immortality with the journey to the celestial Hesperides, identical to the Elysian fields: "This idea is pre-Greek. The inference to be drawn from this fact is that a cycle of Labors was already formed and provided with its natural and logical end in the Mycenaean age" (Nilsson 214). From the beginning, the myth-ritual school noted that neither Greek myth nor Greek rite can be accounted for by Greek thinking: rather, they hail from a prior time and older sources (Harrison, *Art* 3).

The Greek historian Herodotus insisted that the Greek mysteries haled from Egypt (2.171-72). While many modern scholars have discounted this claim, the similarities between these mystery religions and the funerary constructs found in Egypt are numerous. R. Drew Griffith, in his work *Mummy Wheat,* argues that the words *Eleusis* and *Elysium* (of the Eleusinian mysteries) are of Egyptian origin (13-16). Griffith also shows that the underworld goddesses Demeter and Persephone hale from Egypt (77-78), as well as the concepts of nectar and ambrosia (68-69). Plutarch claimed that the rites associated with Dionysus were parallel to the rites of Osiris in Egypt (13.2, 35.1). Walter Burkert points out that the initiates' journey in the underworld depicted in the Orphic gold plates have a precursor in the Egyptian *Book of the Dead* (*Babylon* 87).

Like the hieratic city, the rites of the afterlife are lost behind the curtain of time. Nibley points out Egyptian initiation into the afterlife existed from the very first dynasty and that its origins lay in prehistory (*MJSP* 20). These rites, according to Alexandre Morret, were "only an imitation of the rites of the 'first time'" (*MJSP* 104). This "first time" is a mythological era akin to the primeval age when the gods first raised the primordial hillock and placed man on the earth. The Egyptians themselves claimed their mysteries came from "hoary antiquity" (*MJSP* 26); in this we hear an echo of the complaint the Egyptian priest gave Solon when he declared that the Greeks were children and did not know the ancient traditions handed down from the dawn of time (*Timaeus* 22.c-d). The fact that this priest links these traditions with measuring the orbs in the sky is remarkable.

Like so many other things in history, pinning down the exact origins of the Greco-Roman mystery traditions is impossible. Many unanswerable questions come into play: As Egypt is the most likely source, where did Egypt get their mysteries from? How far back do these traditions go? How did they change? From orality to literacy? From the fourth millennium BCE to the first? From Egyptian culture into Greek? All that can be said with certainty is that by the sixth century BCE these traditions were rooted throughout the Mediterranean. The distinctive ideas of Orphism, for example, are mentioned by such early Greeks as Herodotus, Plato, and

Euripides. According to some traditions, the Orphic movement introduced the rites of Dionysus, yet the relations between Orphism and the mysteries of Dionysus have always been blurred. Because the initiations into these cults were kept with guarded secrecy, no one knows exactly what they entailed. We have only hints and whispers—a few puzzle pieces—a few bricks. By what mortar shall we put them together? In the spirit of Herodotus and Plutarch, Egyptian cosmography is most likely the correct context.

The theology of Orphism is hinted at in the cult object known as the *Orphic Alabaster Bowl* (see figure 5). This artifact was part of a private collection in Leipzig, Germany. Found in the Mediterranean region its exact origins are unknown. Due to the artistic style of the figures and the Greek grammar employed in the inscription on the outside of the bowl, the object is dated to the first few centuries CE. Hans Leisegang, in his essay "The Mystery of the Serpent," gives the most comprehensive interpretation of the piece.

The Orphic Alabaster Bowl displays sixteen figures, men and women who are nude and make ritual hand and arm gestures. They circle and face a winged serpent that is twined around an egg-shaped omphalos. Leisegang asserts that this object is a "unique representation of a cultic scene, a *dromenon* of the jealously hidden Orphic mysteries" (195). Participants in the mysteries were often initiated in the nude. This was not a sexual rite; rather, the one seeking transcendence had to face reality with no artifice—literally one was to stand naked in the presence of god. The serpent and omphalos are symbols of rebirth, the goal of initiation. The various hand and arm gestures were part of the rites and were physical expressions of making oaths. The new initiates in the cult of Mithras were greeted by special handclasps and were called *syndexioi*, "those who were united by a handshake" (Clauss 152). In modern times "signing the dotted line" is committing to a promise. In antiquity, hand and arm gestures, as well as handclasps and handshakes, were synonymous with invoking a prayer or taking a vow.

Figure 5. Orphic Alabaster Bowl

The Orphic Alabaster Bowl is part of a private collection in Leipzig,
Germany. This cult artifact depicts sixteen initiates who are nude
and perform ritual hand and arm gestures. The initiates surround
a winged serpent entwined upon an omphalos, symbol of cosmic
creation and ascent. The partial inscription on the exterior of the bowl
signifies that these ringed neophytes are circling through the celestial
vortices, presumably with the round dance of mystery initiation.
(Illustration by Lynde Mott, original image in Leisegang, plate I.)

Leisegang reconstructs the inscription on the outside of the bowl from a surviving Orphic fragment, "Hear, thou who [turnest forever] the radiant sphere of distant motion [that runs round the celestial vortices]" (201). Leisegang continues, "This is an invocation of the celestial force which moves the outermost sphere encompassing all the other spheres of heaven. This celestial force . . . is designated by the names of Zeus, Dionysus, and Helios" (201). In Orphic cosmology there were seven celestial spheres (each sphere represented by a planet), which in turn operated under the grand cosmic sphere that was the domain of the gods. All the spheres of heaven, therefore, moved upon the pistons of a super celestial region that was the source of true form and being. Leisegang continues, "This distant sphere, which encompasses the actual heavens with the planets and their orbits, is here the sphere of Helios and at the same time of Zeus-Dionysus who created and engendered all things out of himself. . . . Side by side with the scientific cosmology of the Greeks there was another [cosmology] in which the sphere of the sun surrounded the whole starry firmament" (202).

The cosmology displayed is that of the second sun or "true heaven" discussed in the previous chapter. The entire visible cosmos was a manifestation of light emitted by the Sun God standing in his Tower at the source of all life. The Roman Emperor Julian mentions this cosmology in a brief recounting:

Some say then, even though all men are not ready to believe it, that the sun travels in the starless heavens far above the region of the fixed stars. And on this theory he will not be stationed midmost among the planets but midway between the three worlds: that is, according to the hypothesis of the mysteries. . . . For the priests of the mysteries tell us what they have been taught by the gods or mighty daemons, whereas the astronomers make plausible hypotheses from the harmony that they observe in the visible spheres. It is proper, no doubt, to approve the astronomers as well, but where any man thinks it better to believe the priests of the mysteries, him I admire and revere, both in jest and earnest. And so much for that, as the saying is. (cited in Leisegang 202)

Julian's description reveals an existing tension between two competing cosmologies, that of the mystery priests and the differing hypothesis of the Greek astronomers. Much like the tensions between Creationists and Darwinists of today's era, the two competing cosmologies were rooted in an entirely different set of metaphysics that sought to explain the universe. Of critical importance, however, is the fact that this older debate was rooted in the very structure of the universe itself, while the current debate is predicated in the processes of DNA and ecosystems. The differences in these tensions can be explained as the transition of intellectual resources from ancient macrocosm to modern microcosm.

The Orphic Bowl depicts initiates in a round presumably circling through the gates of initiation, the gates being the celestial spheres or "vortices," which are passed through in a cosmic ascent as man journeys through the heavens to his cosmic source. Leisegang writes:

In the course of the mystery rite, the mystai have been led "the upper way" (ὁδός ἄνω); they have attained to the supercelestial region (ὑπερουράνιος τοπος), like Parmenides hastening away from all things earthly in the chariot of the sun; like the "immortal souls" in Plato's *Phaedrus* "standing on the outside of heaven [ἐπὶ τè τοῦ οὐρανοῦ νότῳ]; and the revolution of the spheres carries them round, and they behold the things beyond"; and like the souls in the inscriptions on the golden medallions of Thurii, which were put into the graves of the Orphic dead, who "enter the wreath of heaven," who "from mortals become gods," and who call themselves "sons of the earth and the starry heavens." (212)

The Orphic Alabaster Bowl is similar to another ritual artifact known as the Pietroasa Bowl, an Orphic sacramental bowl made out of gold and dating to the same era as the Alabaster Bowl (see figure 6). This bowl was discovered with twenty-one other artifacts in the town of Pietroasa, near Buzau, Romania. During the First World War all these pieces were taken to Moscow and melted down for their precious metals. The engraved depiction of the bowl was preserved, however, when it was lent to an English museum in 1867, where it was photographed and reproduced with a mold. Like its alabaster contemporary, nothing is known of the origin of the piece. This bowl also shows sixteen figures surrounding a central omphalos atop which is seated a figure, the Magna Mater, holding a grail or cup.

Each of the sixteen figures is somehow related to the mystery journey. The first figure is none other than Orpheus, who holds a fishing rod with a fish at his feet. The imagery is one of initiation into the processes of resurrection. Joseph Campbell, in his *Creative Mythology*, compares this imagery to several other fish motifs in Assyrian, Hindu, and early Christian iconography with the same theme of resurrection (13-5). Campbell similarly shows that the other figures follow a cosmographic and liturgical logic, "Having been drawn to the mystic gate by Orpheus's fishing line, the neophyte seen at Station 3 commences the night-sea journey, sun-wise around the bowl. Like the setting sun, he descends in symbolic death into the earth and at Station 14 reappears to a new day, qualified to experience the 'meeting of the eyes' of Hyperborean Apollo at Station 16" (15). In other words, the figures in the round imply an underworld descent represented by such figures as Demeter, Kore, and the Lord of the Abyss. This descent turns into a celestial ascent represented by Dionysus-Sabazius and the twins Castor and Pollux. If the initiate is successful in his cosmic journey he ends at the "summit of heaven or in the supercelestial region as on the alabaster bowl" (Leisegang 256), depicted as Apollo with his musical lyre. The fact that the Great Mother sits in the middle of the bowl holding a sacrament cup also indicates the promise of resurrection (via the Mother) through initiation (via the cup).

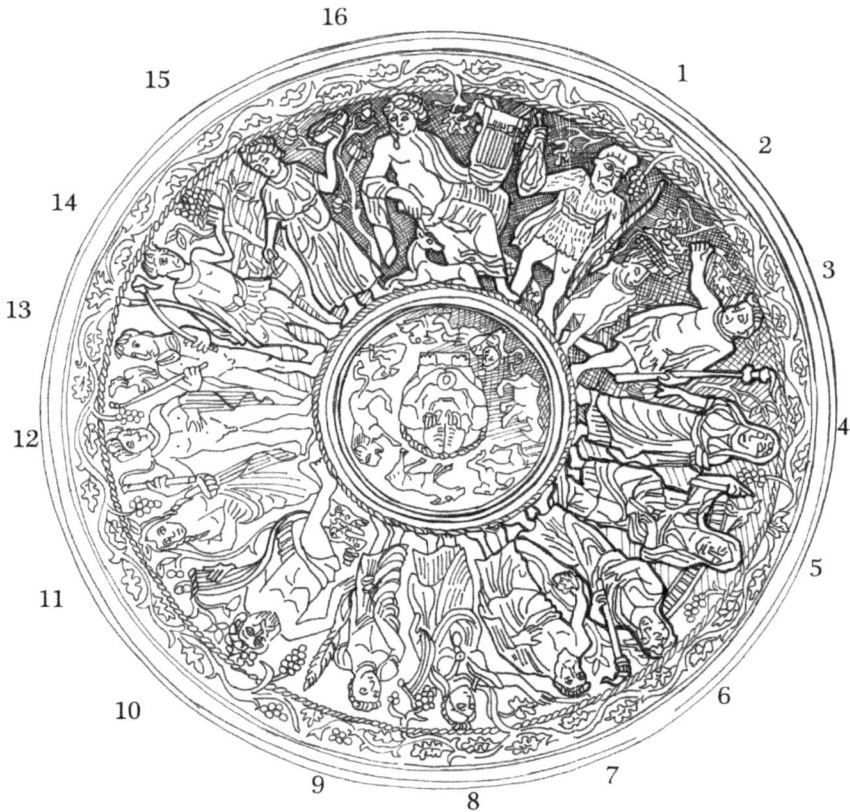

Figure 6. Pietroasa Bowl

An Orphic sacramental bowl made out of gold and dating to the first few centuries CE. The identification of some of the figures is unknown and generally attributed to some aspect of mystery initiation as *mystai*. Leisegang identifies the figures thus: 1)Orpheus, 2) Pluto, 3) Mystes as torchbearer, 4) Mystes as carrier of pail and bowl, 5) Demeter, 6) Persephone, 7) newly initiated mystes, 8) Tyche, 9) Agathodaimon, 10) Lord of the Abyss, Ptah, 11) Dionysus-Sabazius, 12) Castor, 13) Pollux, 14)A mystes, 15) A mystes, 16) Apollo. (Illustration by Lynde Mott, original image in Campbell, *Creative Mythology* 10.)

Both the Alabaster and Pietroasa Bowls intimate a ritual cosmography where initiates reenact a journey through the cosmos to obtain immortality. In the first piece the initiates are in a round swirling within the celestial vortices indicated from the inscription. In the latter object each of the figures represent some portion of the journey, where underworld descent, celestial ascent, and the high summit of heaven are represented by corresponding figureheads. Leisegang demonstrates that both these bowls belong to a cultic genre where in different traditions similar iconography appears. In an Etruscan oil lamp we find sixteen figures in a circle and within a ritual context representing the heavens (245-7). In an eight century CE Christian Eucharist platter the same cosmography is displayed, where the Virgin Mary and baby Jesus replace the Magna Mater, and a chorus of heavenly angels fill in for the initiates (259-60).

The object of mystery initiation was rebirth in the next world. There is a very brief description of initiation in the mysteries of Isis written by Apuleius in his classic work *The Golden Ass*. A man named Lucius is transformed into a donkey, the lowest and basest beast of burden. In order to return to his human state he must be initiated into the mysteries. He undergoes several preparatory events which slowly transform him back into a human. The actual mystery initiation is cryptically reduced to only a few sentences, "I came to the boundary of death and after treading [Persephone's] threshold I returned having traversed all the elements; at midnight I saw the sun shining with brilliant light; I approached the gods below and the gods above face to face and worshiped them in their actual presence" (11.23).

Lucius has made an arduous journey through all the elements (water, fire, air, and earth). This is a theme in other Greek mysteries as the Orphic underworld contained elemental rivers which one also had to traverse (Eisler 204). The initiate of the *Mithras Liturgy* must make the same elemental passage (Betz 50, 56). At the lowest point of his journey Lucius sees the sun shining at midnight. This is the same motif as the Hyperborean Apollo in the Pietroasa Bowl. The midnight sun is the noontime sun in the underworld; when it shines in its splendor the process of rebirth is completed. This moment had a parallel in the ritual initiation known as *epoptes*, the moment of true seeing where the divine mystery was revealed. Lucius sees the gods "face to face" and is thus invited into their presence. Lucius has transformed from an ass to a man, from an initiate to a god. Not surprisingly Lucius is given a new garment, an Olympic robe "of fine linen" and "colorfully embroidered" to depict images and creatures from another world. He is also crowned and given a blazing torch, "Equipped thus in the image of the Sun I stood like a statue while the curtains were suddenly pulled back and the people crowded in to gaze at me" (11.24). He stands wearing the garment of the gods as an image of Helios himself.

If we compare this cult imagery to that of the Orphic Bowls, and in turn compare each of these to the secret chambers of the Temple of Apet, we find a remarkable homology in cult and cosmography. The Egyptian dead and the Orphic neophyte enter the dark halls of rebirth at the gate of the underworld. They travel through the cosmos. Victorious, they find peace in the garden of paradise, crowned with glory and kingship, dwelling with the gods.

One final artifact will show that the journey through the cosmos was essential, not just for immortality, but for gaining any secret the other world held. In the mid-nineteenth century, an antiquities dealer named M. Péretié purchased a bronze plaque in Hama in Northern Syria. It was found by a peasant in Palmyra. The bronze plaque, known as the Péretié Plaque, is Assyrian and dates to the early first millennium BCE (see figure 7). Almost nothing else is known about it. When it was first examined by nineteenth-century scholars the universal interpretation was that it represented the gate of the soul in the Assyrian underworld (Simpson 121). One scholar writes about the artifact, "People may differ as to the significance of this or that detail, but no one will deny that the plaque is religious and funerary in its general character, and that, whatever may have been its purpose, it is as a whole connected with the memory and worship of the dead" (Perrot and Chipiez 349).

Figure 7. Péretié Plauqe, Assyrian Bronze, Front & Back Side

Cult scene depicting the three tiers of the Assyrian cosmos: Underworld, Earth, and Heaven. From bottom to top we see each stage of the universe one must trespass in order to ascend the celestial axis. The seven lion-figures in the atmosphere are the seven celestial guardians performing a processional dance. We find parallels of this cosmography in Mithraism and the Mysteries of Persephone, as well as early Christianity. The seven gates of Ninevah each held a guardian statue much like these on this plaque. The back of the plaque holds an Assyrian Sphinx, who oversees the entire cosmic frame. (Original image in Simpson, 120; copyright free.)

Modern scholars have deconstructed this view. The Péretié Plaque is no longer seen as a representation of the afterlife or the gate of the soul; rather, it is now interpreted as a magical amulet depicting a healing scene for the sick (Black and Green 181). Modern scholarship has rewritten the general view of Mesopotamian afterlife as one of bleakness. Jeremy Black and Anthony Green write in their dictionary of Mesopotamian gods, "The conditions of 'life' in the underworld were thought, with few exceptions, to be dismal in the extreme. The Sumerian dead fed on dust and scraps and lived in darkness. This is amply documented in the Sumerian poem 'Gilgameš, Enkidu and the Nether World' . . . where Gilgameš asks the ghost (*gidim*) of Enkidu about the underworld" (28).

Whether the plaque depicts the deceased rising in the afterlife or a sick person arising from the doctor's couch, the cosmic context is the same. In order to live again, or to be healed, one must know the proper celestial archetypes of rebirth. For this reason, the plaque depicts the Assyrian cosmos. On the front of the artifact, reading from bottom to top, we see a central, lion-headed goddess kneeling on a horse. The horse in turn kneels in a boat that sails on a river. The goddess is Lamaštu, a terrifying visage who holds serpents in her hands, has whelps suckling her breasts, and bears donkey-dog ears perched atop hairy skin. She is the demon-goddess of the underworld and was thought to be the harbinger of disease and miscarriage. If she represents disease, then the medical interpretation of the plaque is appropriate. Lamaštu is very similar to the Greek Erinyes or Furies, however, who also were demon goddesses of the underworld and were also thought to bring miscarriages. They specifically judged the deceased and determined if they had kept their oaths whilst living. In other words, both a funerary and medical interpretation can be applied to the figure. To her left is a masked priest who has a serpent tail and taloned feet, in resemblance of a sphinx-guardian. To her right are a series of glyphs which relate to offerings and tokens whose full significance is unknown. This panel depicts the underworld, where the horse is a psychopomp, the ark is fording the river that separates the worlds, and the goddess is the central underworld figure of death and passage. The masked priest holds his right arm to the square in a ritual gesture, while the offerings and tokens on the right refer to the necessary accouterments for some ritual.

In the panel above the underworld we see a figure lying on a ceremonial bed or couch attended by two officiating priests garbed in fish skins. To their right are two lion-headed figures in ritual poses, clasping hands and raising their arms to the square. A third figure witnesses the ritual actions of the two leonine attendants, who are not only in a ritual pose but whose legs are open indicating movement, perhaps signaling a ritual dance. Of further interest is the person on the altar-like bed. His body is wrapped, as if deceased, though his arm is raised indicating that he lives. These appear to be funerary garments, perhaps arguing for the funerary interpretation of the image. The garment of the priests proves they can move between the worlds; even as fish dive into the dark waters (as evidenced by the fish swimming in the underworld river), so do the fish-clothed priests, themselves images of Oannes or Ea, hold authority to descend into the underworld and to re-ascend with its secrets.

The next panel shows seven guardian figures with raised arms and lion heads, all performing a processional, ritualized dance. These are the guardians of the upper world, the attendants of the celestial gates, against which no one can pass without the correct ritual knowledge obtained by descent into the underworld. They are analogous to the seven leaders of the Anunnakkū; this latter group are the fifty attendants of Gilgamesh who aid the hero in his descent through the underworld. In one tablet we read: "Then came 'The Warriors,' all sons of one mother—they were seven in number . . . . In heaven they sparkle, on earth they know the path, . . . may they show him the way" (*EGHA* 36-49). They also show up on the ark of Ea as it crosses between the worlds. An ancient hymn declares, "Seven times seven lions of the field occupy its deck. . . . Its house, its ascent, is a mountain that gives rest to the heart. . . . May the ship before thee cross the canal! May the ship behind thee sail over its mouth! Within thee may the heart rejoicing make holiday!" (Simpson 135).

These seven celestial stewards show up numerous times, across cultures, and always in the same context: the seven gatekeepers of Inanna, the seven "bright ones" of Osiris, the seven celestial pole lords of Mithras, the seven celestial guardians in the book of Revelation, and the seven handmaidens of the Gnostic Sophia—all sparkle in heaven and are all knowers of the way through the celestial axis. Of acute interest is the last Gnostic example, where in the *Acts of St. Thomas* we read: "She [Sophia] is surrounded by the seven bridal attendants chosen by herself. Her handmaidens are also seven, dancing a ring dance before her" (Backman 16). The seven guardians are dancers because they are the stewards of the dancing planets which circumambulate around the throne of god. We shall have more to say on this subject below.

Finally, the top panel of the Péretié Plaque depicts the celestial heavens, with glyphs for the sun, moon, and stars, as well as other symbols relating to the Assyrian cosmos. On the back of the plaque is a great Sphinx whose leonine head peers over the top as the ultimate guardian of the universe and its secrets. In short, this plaque not only shows the Assyrian universe, with its underworld, mid-world, and celestial world, but it shows this universe in a cultic context, with a guardian Sphinx, priests, offerings, tokens, and dances, and where the person on the altar-bed is wrapped in the cloth of the deceased but whose arm is raised because he is being raised up and through the celestial axis.

How very similar is this scene to that of the priests of Pharaoh who offered at the altar of the heavens prayers, hymns, and dances that allowed the deceased to ascend: "The doors are opened because of those whose seats are hidden; arise, remove your earth, shake off your dust, raise yourself, that you may travel in company with the spirits, for your wings are those of a falcon, your gleam is that of a star, the night demon will not bend over you . . . . Cross the sky to the Field of Rushes, make your abode in the Field of Offerings among the Imperishable Stars, the followers of Osiris (*PT* §747-9). Pharaoh must ascend the celestial axis by raising himself up from his mortal grave. He passes hidden seats or gates, moves with guardian spirits as a star, crosses the celestial waters where the dark forces of the cosmos (the night demon) are blocked from denying him passage because he is among those who are "knowers of the way." He finally settles in the north celestial realm with the gods. This is an identical visual theme to the Péretié Plaque, and for that matter, to both the Orphic Alabaster and Pietroasa Bowls.

If the plaque is an amulet for healing magic, as modern scholars insist, then one is reminded that the healing centers in Greece were also mimicking the mystery cosmography of an earlier age. One obtains the powers to heal and the office of a healer only by traveling through the cosmos, obtaining the secrets of life in the underworld, and ascending on high to become a *Physikos*. The fish-skinned priests prove they have power over life and death because they are able to descend into the underworld with their fish garment. The dancing lions indicate that the upper world has also been breached. Either way, the man on the ceremonial bed plays the role of a *mystes* who has reached into the beyond via rites of the cult.

Cult and the Heavenly Chorus

The seven dancing lion figures in the Péretié Plaque brings us to another inexplicable feature of myth and cult. In a version of the *Epic of Gilgamesh* entitled *Gilgamesh and Huwawa A,* our Babylonian heroes are given a gift from Utu, the god of heaven, to help them defeat the terrible giant Huwawa. This gift is fifty warriors (called the Anunna or Anunnakkū) who are guides to the cedar forest. These fifty warriors are led by seven nobles who are called the Igiggi, an untranslatable term. The description of these seven heavenly leaders is worth noting:

> *Then came "The Warriors," all sons of one mother—they were seven in number.*
> *The first, their eldest brother, had the paws of a lion and the claws of an eagle.*
> *The second was a slithering snake,*
> *The third was a dragon-snake,*
> *The fourth rained down fire,*
> *The fifth was a noble snake that . . . in the upland,*
> *The sixth was like a spring flood that buffets the flanks of the mountains,*
> *The seventh flashed like lightning, none could withstand his power.*
> (*EGHA* 36-44)

The seven leaders of the fifty Anunnakkū bear the form of a lion, eagle, and serpent. They also have control over the elemental powers. More specifically, they are placed in a specific context, *"In heaven they sparkle, on earth they know the path, . . . may they show [Gilgamesh] the way"* (*EGHA* 48-49). These guides also belong to the astral regions, for "in heaven they sparkle." They are the true "knowers of the way" because they know the secrets of the heavenly realm. Their description is remarkably homologous to the sphinx, whose own leonine-eagle-serpent body remains the ultimate symbol of the secret paths that sparkle in heaven. It should not surprise us, therefore, to find that in the *Descent of Inanna* these fifty guides are explicitly identified as the guardians and judges of the underworld.

The fifty helpers of Gilgamesh have corollaries in other myth traditions where similar figures show up in the same context. Perhaps the most obvious comparison is the myth of Jason and his fifty Argonauts.

In the various Greek sources of this myth we encounter stock motifs of kingship. Jason is cast out of his kingdom and is left on a mountain. He is raised by Cheiron. Pelias, the usurper who rules the throne of Iolcus, receives an oracle warning him that a single-shoed man would slay him. Jason arrives in Iolcus wearing a panther skin and one shoe. Pelias recognizes him, and with cunning asks Jason what he would do if he knew a man was fated to kill him. Jason replies he would send that man to fetch the Golden Fleece. Pelias identifies Jason as his bane and demands that Jason obtain the Golden Fleece. The problem is that the Fleece is the solar garment of the underworld, is guarded by a terrible dragon, and is utterly impossible to retrieve. Nevertheless, Jason agrees to the quest.

Of central interest to this Greek myth is that Jason must sail to the land of the Golden Fleece on a boat oared by fifty sailors. At the head of the deck is none other than Orpheus, who leads the sailors along with his music. To accomplish their task, all fifty sailors must be initiated into the mysteries of Persephone at Samothrace (Graves 532). Along their journey Jason and the Argonauts must sail through the clashing stones called the Symplegades (the entrance to the underworld). In both cases Gilgamesh and Jason perform a cosmic quest accompanied by fifty sailors or partners who aid them. Yet these are not the only examples of the famed fifty attendants who help heroes pass between the worlds. In Greek myth the guardian of the underworld is the fifty-headed dog Cerberus, with a serpent for a tail and snakes slithering from its heads. Cerberus is often depicted with only three heads, but this is because there were three specific paths in the underworld. When Aeneas descends in this realm of shades he identifies these three roads: one leads to the underworld proper, another to the deep bowels of Tartarus, and a third to heaven or Elysium (*The Aeneid 6.625-32*). Cerberus's heads guard the three roads. Hesiod provides the earliest description of Cerberus in his *Theogony*, however, where this underworld guardian is described as having fifty heads (310-12).

In the oldest Irish mythology, the primordial Cessair founds Ireland after arriving on a boat oared by fifty female sailors (Rees and Rees 113-14). Their story is not only associated with the founding of the land, but also with a ford where three rivers meet and a tale of a great flood. The holder of the secrets of immortality in the *The Epic of Gilgamesh* is Utnapishtim whose name signifies the "Far Distant One" and who dwells at the "source of the rivers" (11.206-9). This location is also translated as the "mouth of the rivers" or "confluence of the rivers." These are not terrestrial waters but represent the multiple ways of the heavenly underworld. The fact that Utnapishtim also tells a story of a great flood indicates that the underworld, the fifty attendants who help the hero journey through it, and the story of the flood somehow belong together (see next chapter).

Of final interest is the peculiar passage in the Old Testament relating to the celestial ascent of Elijah found in 2 Kings 2.1-11. Elijah travels between two cities, Beth-el and Jericho. Beth-el (the House of God, the place where god dwells) is where Jacob falls asleep on a stone and dreams of a ladder that ascends to heaven. Jacob declares, "This is none other but the house of God, and this is the gate of heaven" (Gen. 28.17). Jericho, on the other hand, is over 800 feet below sea level and is the lowest inhabited city on earth. Topographically, Jericho is an excellent representation of the underworld. Elijah travels to the River Jordan with "fifty men of the sons of the prophets" (2 Kings 2.7). There is no explanation in the text as to who these fifty sons of the prophets are and why they are following the prophet. At the river Elijah "took his mantle, and wrapped it together, and smote the waters, and they were divided hither and thither, so that [Elijah and Elisha] went over on dry ground" (2 Kings 2.8). A chariot with horses of flame appears whence "Elijah went up by a whirlwind into heaven" (2 Kings 2.11). The fifty sons of the prophets witness Elijah's journey across the waters and ascent into heaven, ending in the enthronement of the prophet Elijah on a fiery chariot.

The Anunnakkū, the Argonauts, the heads of Cerberus, the sailors of Cessair, and the sons of the prophets—all are the sacred fifty who aid or witness our hero's journey through the celestial axis or stand guard in the underworld overseeing the celestial axis. Whence do they come? Why are so many companions required to accompany all our heroes between the worlds? What is the significance of the number fifty?

In order to answer these questions we ourselves have to make a cognitive shift in our thinking, remembering that parts of the *Epic of Gilgamesh* were performed and danced. In fact, our most profound clue to the interpretation of the fifty companions of our heroes may be found in the rites of Dionysus, whose Dionysian Chorus generally consisted of fifty members (Brown, *Dionysiak* 113). The rites of Dionysus promised a blessed afterlife to those who knew the way. How was one to learn the way? Euripides tells us in *The Bacchae*, as he has Dionysus declare, "Blessed, blessed are those who know the mysteries of god . . . . Blessed are the dancers and those who are purified, who dance on the hill in the holy dance of god" (72-76). Euripides informs us that this holy dance was central to the mystery tradition: "There I [Dionysus] taught my dances to the feet of living men, establishing my mysteries and rites that I might be revealed on earth for what I am: a god" (17-19).

In the mystery rites of Dionysus the dancing chorus was a central feature, and this chorus was composed of fifty members. Theodore Gaster asserts that the lines just cited by Euripides belonged to the singing, dancing neophytes of the mysteries. Speaking of Euripides' *Bacchae*, Gaster writes:

> the choral odes of [the *Bacchae*] are—as most scholars have recognized—nothing but embellished versions of the traditional chants recited in the Bacchic mysteries. Indeed, if the long and beautiful chorus, *Bacchae* 64-169, be compared carefully with the ritual *Paean to Bacchus* discovered at Delphi, it will be found

that it reproduces not only the general tenor and sentiment of the latter, but also almost all of its standard cliches and technical terms. (101)

Central to every temple cult was a dancing tradition, and at every major festival, coronation, or initiation in the oral world, dancing, singing, and chanting was involved. Hugh Nibley informs us that many cultures reenacted the cosmogony through song and dance and that the modern word *poem* descends from *poema*, a word that means creation hymn, sung by a chorus of priests to music and dance (*TC* 22). Not only was creation reenacted by a chorus of priests, but so apparently was the heavenly journey. We find a description of singing priests reenacting this journey in a liturgy entitled, *Songs of the Sabbath Sacrifice,* found within the Dead Sea Scrolls. Carol Newsom has done a detailed study of this scroll in her work with the same title. In this scroll we learn that there is a heavenly temple with seven celestial sanctuaries attended by seven angelic beings (10). Seven hymns are sung in a choral liturgy associated with the journey through the heavenly temple. The seventh hymn culminates in a description of a celestial holy of holies (15). The angels that attend the heavenly temple are "knowers of the way" (30). Newsome points out that this scroll is mimicked in the Hekalot tradition where the heavenly temple is depicted as a heavenly city, built in a circle, and constructed with seven concentric walls and gates (51).

All this imagery puts new light on the already described Orphic Alabaster Bowl and Pietroasa Bowl. Each of these bowls signify initiates in a round, performing rituals which are in some way associated with a journey through the underworld and the heavens. The circular pose of all the figures is highly suggestive of a choral dance; indeed, within the latter cult object the figures start with Orpheus in the underworld and end with Apollo in the high celestial realm, with a musical lyre connecting both figures. The second-century Greek writer Lucian informs us that dance and initiation were wed in every single mystery religion (Backman 1). The *epiklesis* in the Mysteries of Demeter was a dance (Jost 156). At the center of the Samothrace mystery precinct was a large marble temple called the *Hall of the Choral Dancers.* On the exterior and surrounding the entire building was a frieze of singers and dancers–a mystery chorus–forming in stone a ring dance around the temple in which the mystery initiation took place (Clinton 61).

Remarkably, these initiate dancers are in no small way mimicked by Jesus and his apostles in the gnostic text of *The Acts of St. John*, where Jesus gathers his followers in a circle and performs an initiatory song and dance. Max Pulver observes, "This strange *chorea mystica*, this ecstatic cult dance, . . . is as ancient as the form of the dance mystery itself. In the Mimaut Papyrus we read: 'Come to me, Thou who art greatest in heaven, . . . to whom heaven was given for a dancing round.' Enraptured by hymn and dance, the mystai circle through the gates of initiation" (174-75). This imagery is repeated in *The Acts of St. Thomas*, where Sophia is surrounded by her seven attendants in a choral dance (Backman 16). These attendants represent the heavenly spheres, and in several apocalyptic texts the one journeying through the cosmos must pass through seven gates which are guarded by the singing and dancing *hymnologi*. Pulver's insight is poignant, for the dancing mystery chorus is mimicking the celestial dance of the stars and planets (Backman 15).

This connection is made clear in early Christian ritual. Philo links the mystery dance with the heavenly spheres when he states, "Again, when on soaring wing [the soul] has contemplated the atmosphere and all its phases, it is borne yet higher to the ether and the circuit of heaven, and is whirled round with the dances of the planets and fixed stars, in accordance with the laws of perfect music, following that love of wisdom which guides its steps" (cited in Leisegang 234). According to Philo, the soul that has been initiated ascends into the circuit of heaven where it "whirls" with the planets and fixed stars "in accordance with the laws of perfect music, following that love of wisdom which guides its steps." It is a cryptic phrase having clear allusions to a set dance with ritual steps consonant to both musical and astral symbolism. Saint Gregory also testifies that in early Christian liturgy such ritual dances were enacted, "He who had done everything preserved and prescribed by Providence in its secret mysteries, reposes in Heaven in the bosom of the Father and in the cave in the bosom of the Mother (Christ Jesus). The ring-dance of the angels encircles him, singing his glory in Heaven and proclaiming peace on earth" (Backman 22). The Christian initiate's ascent to heaven is attended by a singing chorus of angels who dance for him.

In the Bacchic mysteries, the choral dance is the ritual gesture of the grand cosmic scheme (Brown, *Dionysiak* 105, 107). The origin of the choral dance rests in ancient cosmology, where both Egyptian and Babylonian priests performed hymns and ring dances around the temple altars modeling the rhythms of the stars and planets (Backman 2, 16). In other traditions there are seven guardians because there are seven planets whereby one ascends up the celestial axis. These seven may also represent the seven bright stars of Ursa Major that circumambulate around the north celestial pole. In many ritual cosmographies this region in the sky is the entrance to the heavenly throne. It does not surprise us, then, that the choral dance is often performed in sevens. The testimony of Epiphanius of Salamis describing the mysteries of Kore is revealing:

> In many places they celebrated a very great festival in the night of Epiphany . . . particularly in the so-called Koreion at Alexandria. There is an immense temple there, the *temenos* of Kore. After watching all night, singing and playing the flute in honor of the sacred image, and celebrating a *pannychis*, they go down after cock crow, bearing torches, into a kind of underground crypt. . . . They carry the [image of the] god seven times around the center of the

temple amid loud playing of flutes and drums and singing hymns, and then carry it to this underground place. When they are asked what mystery this is, they say that at this hour Kore—that is, the virgin—has given birth to the Aeon. (Leisegang 238)

The circumambulating dance and hymning around the temple seven times is a *dromenon* that hails from pre-Greek times. Plutarch informs us that the Egyptians did the very same thing, during the same time of the year, in the mysteries of Isis, where the neophytes would circumambulate around the temple seven times carrying the image of the god in a rite called "Seeking for Osiris" (*On Isis and Osiris* 52.3). An analogous scene is depicted in the twelfth-century BCE Tomb of Tausert, where Egyptian priests circumambulate around a pyramid that has been split in two. The pyramid itself is divided into three sections, indicating the three worlds of the cosmic axis. In between the sections of the pyramid the sun ascends transformed in a new birth. The priests wearing the masks of Horus and Khnum and dancing on the outside of the pyramid are seven in number.

The ring dance and the circumambulating procession were part of a priestly chorus whose dance signaled the ritual theme of rebirth. Theodor Gaster notes that this ritual dance and procession is implicit in other Egyptian texts: "Significant also is the fact that some of the [Egyptian] texts presuppose the presence of a chorus. Thus, the Ramesseum Drama speaks explicitly of a 'group of conductors'—a term which occurs in other Egyptian texts as designating a branch of the clergy. Similarly, the Edfu text implies a choir of temple singers and musicians who enact the part of the friends and supporters of Horus and who shout encouragements to him in the manner of latter-day 'rooters' at a ball game" (Gaster 102). This imagery is very old. It is truly amazing to find in the *Pyramid Texts* that Pharaoh declares he knows the proper dances to the underworld ferryman (§1189). Even more surprising do we find Pharaoh ascending to the throne of heaven accompanied by a group of "Watchers" who dance for him (§1947).

In ancient India we find the same pattern, where Hindu priests performed circumambulations around Hindu temples indicative of movement between the worlds, from the temporal to the eternal (Michell 66-67). Not only would temple priests perform this processional dance, but also the population at large, who, like the hajji of Muslim tradition, would circumambulate around their holy city (itself a model of the temple) during their annual pilgrimage (Worthen 19). The origin of Tibetan and Buddhist praying wheels most likely descends from the choral dance, where the prayer wheel rotates in duplicate motion of the dancing devotee who can now perform complex dance routines symbolically by citing prayers (Worthen 20-23).

The very word *ritual* or *rite* descends from the Sanskrit *rita* and *ritu*, from the root *ri*, which means "to fit, join, fix" and also "to move fitly, to go on the path; the path followed in going" (Worthen 24). This root has cosmological foundations, for *ritu* refers to the circular season and their associated rites, while *rita* refers to ritual correctness, including facing the proper directions of the founded world (Worthen 24). Ritual is to move according to the proper celestial motions along the correct path which mimics those celestial motions. The right path or road is thus journeyed by the correct circular dance; in this sense *ritu* and *rita* are very similar to the Greek *oimos* (road) and *oimê* (song). These words have the same origin and indicate that the correct road is mimicked in song and dance.

The Dionysian chorus gives us the greatest hint as to the origin of the Greek dramatic chorus, whose earliest compositions consisted of fifty members. This feature of Greek drama has never been satisfactorily explained, and scholars have groped in vain over the significance of the chorus of fifty. The Greek chorus descended from very old temple liturgy. While speculative, I think we can posit with confidence that the original Anunnakkū who aided Gilgamesh and who judged Ishtar, while having a celestial archetype in the stars, had a terrestrial counterpart in a chorus of priests or priestesses performing a cult dance within the temple precinct. Jason's fifty Argonauts led by the music of Orpheus is very suggestive in this regard, and the fact that Orpheus can only pass the fifty heads of Cerberus by playing his music and hymns is also intriguing. The indication is that ritual cosmography required a singing, dancing chorus of priests who were mimicking the movement of the celestial vault and who aided the neophyte in his initiation into the next world.

The aforementioned Assyrian hymn declares that there are "seven times seven lions" on the heavenly ship. In the case of the Anunnakkū, the fifty were led by the seven Igigi. This is significant because, if we are dealing with a choral dance and its attendant music, if each of the Igigi were a representation of the seven celestial spheres and each sphere in turn was represented by an octave of seven notes, then the seven Igigi would constitute seven octaves of seven notes, the seventh octave being completed by the termination of the fiftieth note (that is, fifty notes complete seven full octaves). In other words, we are here dealing with the Music of the Spheres, where each celestial heaven may have had a song and dance associated with it, and where the fifty attendants circled through the gates of initiation in a ring dance representing the seven celestial spheres dancing to the music of seven full octaves.

So far our discussion has addressed the dancing chorus in relation to mystery initiations or the celestial journey of the king. A chorus of fifty priests is also an excellent way to maintain a stellar calendar. Giorgio de Santillana, in his work *The Origins of Scientific Thought*, notes that by around 3000 BCE the Babylonians already had a system of measured constellations that were "inherited by unknown predecessors" (12). He also observes that the most ancient star lists in Egypt were also inherited, as they were "no longer grasped in their original significance" (12). Not only were the constellations inherited, but the movement of the planets through those constellations appears to have also been known. De

Santillana writes, "The variety of names given to each planet and the multiplicity of mythical motifs to accompany them were made necessary by the almost incalculable complexity of relations to be expressed. All this had to be set down without coordinates, probably without the aid of writing, in one synoptic vision, and memorized as legends. The colossal intellectual effort, the abstraction, that is entailed are worthy of the greatest modern theorists" (17).

De Santillana believes that every planet had a series of myths associated with it, so that as it moved around the ecliptic it could be tracked. Of course, tracking a planet also means watching it move across a background of stars. As a planet moved into a new constellation a different adventure might be added into a myth. Each planet also moved into conjunction with the other planets, and tales were attuned to the moving pantheon of themes and positions formed in the sky. Richard Heath shows that the origin of the myth about Venus and Mars being caught in their adulterous love affair within the net of Hephaestus is really about planetary motion. Heath notes that the planets Venus and Mars consistently conjoin in the sky, "In four Venus synods, there are three Mars synods. Having made this net, our lovers are naturally and eternally going to be caught in it—they have made their bed and they must lie in it" (Heath 70). An astronomical synod is the period of time it takes an object in the sky to return to the same point in the sky relative to two other objects (also called the synodic period). For every four cycles where Venus returns to the same point in the sky (in a constellation) she meets Mars waiting there for her. These planets make this dance even as the constellations move throughout the year. A net is formed of eternal relationships. According to de Santillana, this game of astronomy was tracked for all the planets in relation to each constellation and in relation to each other. How does an oral society track such complexity? That is a lot of tales to tell!

Under the parameters of oral cognition, concrete analogical performance attuned to everything that must be remembered is a requirement. Somatic gestures aid memory, and singing and chanting are primary forms of mnemonic reinforcement. While fifty members of a chorus seems very crowded, one can almost see and hear every participant in the priestly procession representing a single note in a scale of seven octaves. The chorus leader would represent the fiftieth note. If each set of seven priests represented a planet, then a particular dance set to specific steps and musical beats could reproduce the numeric key to be remembered.

For example, after long observation one can determine the number of days, weeks, or months it takes a planet to move around the ecliptic. If one saw the planet Mars in the stars of Aires, and counted the number of weeks it took the planet to move completely around the zodiac returning to the stars of Aires, one would count 98 seven-day weeks, or 24 lunar cycles. Of course, as the planet Mars moves through this cycle it does so through all the stars along the ecliptic. What if a group of seven priests in our chorus of fifty was "in charge" of knowing where the planet Mars was on any given day of the year. If the leader of the seven represented the planet, and the other six priests assigned to his portion represented certain stars, then this group of seven could sing and dance all the information to be remembered. The requirement of seven priests in a group becomes mandatory for mnemonic purposes alone. If one chants or sings to the notes of the musical scale one can more easily remember what must be chanted. The leader of the seven could sing of how his planet sails down a river and meets a particular god or goddess in such and such a time. The next priest, representing that god or goddess, pipes in and recites what has just been said to a particular note that is played. Then the lead priest continues to another portion of the sky represented by another mythical figure while the next priest pipes in to a new tone on the octave. Soon, everyone in the circle, having heard these repeated chants reinforced by music and even dance, could remember everything this group of seven priests was stating.

If each group of seven priests were "in charge" of a separate planet, then each group could sing in turn identifying, through song, myth, and dance, the position of all the planets against the stars. With more forethought, two separate groups of seven priests could sing in turn, each identifying where their current planet is in the sky and in relation to each other. As each group of seven participates, all the complex movements of all the seven heavenly spheres could be organized in relation to each other.

All of this becomes much easier, of course, if there is a point zero in the sky from which to measure the movement of all the planets. Where is the starting point that the planets are returning to? In different cultures this "point zero" might vary. It is tempting to suggest that the second sun of the "true heaven" may actually be a star visible in the sky—the celestial archetype of the whole system. If this were true, then the oral cosmology of our early Greek masters— where all the heavens are orbiting some fulcrum point of creation—makes perfect sense as a chorus of priests reenacting this cosmology would literally sing and dance around the anchor point of their choral ritual. The cosmology of Philolaus, inherited from much earlier times, may be a natural result of the demands of ritual and orality, where the complex motion of the heavens in oral cultures invents a cosmology of its own.

This "zero point" may not have been a specific star, but the place on the horizon of winter or summer solstice. If the planets were measured in reference to the stars that received the sun on either the solstices or days of equinox, then the entire calendar could be kept in tune with the solar cycle and the seasons. This choral calendar may explain the early cosmogonies where certain deities overthrow their predecessors. Zeus overthrew his father Kronos, who in turn overthrew Uranous. If the chorus of priests represents the heavenly circuit, then as an entire body they would be a form of Uranous (the Heavens). If the first set of seven priests who starts the song and dance represented the "Elder" god and planet that organized the system (i.e., Kronos or Saturn), then the choral liturgy would begin with this planet cutting up the heavens just as described in the myth. At some point the seven priests representing Jupiter may have taken over the role of leading the choral dance. Was this due to the change in the position of the stars from precession, or from altering the "zero point" reckoning from stellar to solar coordinates? In any case, the myths as we have received them are never arbitrary creations forged by primitive minds. They were once attached to a grand network of ritual and cosmology that has been lost. My suggestion that behind these myths may have been a choral liturgy where priests were chanting and moving in repetition of the celestial motion reinforces what we know of the demands of oral cognition and oral cosmology.

Finally, so far as our priestly chorus is concerned, not only would dance and music be necessary accompaniments for the memory, but so also would the actual dancing space itself. If the entire choral dance took place in a temple that had stellar representations built into it, then the ritual and the ritual space could reinforce each other. In fact, if different temples represented different points in the sky, a different choral dance could accompany each temple precinct. This might sound complicated; it is, for this form of cultus presupposes a level of social and scientific organization that is rarely attributed to peoples before the Greeks. The old traditions about Stonehenge, however, remembered that the great stone circle was once named *Choir-guar*, a title signifying "the Giant's Dance or Giant's Carol" (Phillips 13). The astronomically aligned stones resembled choral dancers and was a place where druid priests performed a ring dance (Phillips 13). It is often assumed that these ancient dances were nothing but a series of "Maypole" romps. Perhaps we should consider that a people who constructed a massive gallery of multi-ton stones imported from hundreds of miles away and lined up perfectly with the motions of sun and stars on the horizon had something else in mind.

None of this can be proved. The cult performances have been permanently lost. I have only made suggestions that seek to explain certain features in myth and cult that seem bizarre and fanciful. Removing the Darwinian peg of history and replacing it with the sober considerations of orality begins to put a different light on the subject, and suggests far more sophisticated and elegant explanations than have heretofore been proposed.

My example above is about keeping a calendar in an oral society. It turns out that there was a heavily esoteric meaning behind the entire system of stars and planets that has also been lost. The mysterious paths of the dead associated with certain constellations cannot be explained by calendar making alone. Our celestial "zero point" may have something to do with the Sphinx, whose iconic representations are analogous to certain stars in the sky. These stars seem central in a cultic cosmography dealing with the ascent and descent of the soul in the next world. The singing and dancing chorus of priests or priestesses could not only track certain celestial bodies in their dance but also perform endowments on initiates who were ritually reenacting the celestial journey through the sky. If this is true, then perhaps some surviving myths require reexamination.

CHAPTER 5

MYTH AND COSMOS: A SUMMARY OF PRINCIPLES

In the following chapters I reexamine the *Epic of Gilgamesh*, the Labors of Heracles, and the stories of Abraham, Jacob, and Balaam in the Old Testament. These myths belong to a widely dispersed cultic tradition dealing with the journey of the king or initiate through the cosmos. This tradition was wed to oral thinking and oral cosmology, where one obtained authority to rule by endowment from celestial archetypes. In Egypt and in the Greco-Roman mysteries, this celestial journey also meant acquiring immortality, where one ascended into the heavens with the gods. The Greek Heracles myth is late, and the earliest recorded tradition we have of it resides in the *Epic of Gilgamesh*, who was the restorer of rites and founder of cities after the Flood. All indications, however, point to the fact that this cultic system and cosmographic journey did not originate in Mesopotamia or in Egypt but had been forged behind the curtains of prehistory. Both the Mesopotamians and Egyptians insist that they are restoring or refounding an older order from the days of the mythical patriarchs or the cosmogonic First Time. The fact that the journey of the dead appears already fully formed from before the first dynasty of Egypt shows that this was a central feature of the myth-ritual system in the oral age.

Whence did the origins of the celestial journey derive? Oral cognition, analogical thinking, and oral cosmology produced it. On mnemonic grounds alone, creating a ritual journey through the heavens is a sure way, and perhaps the only way in an oral society, to memorize the entire sky so that it can be incorporated into the calendars and cult activities of a society. Reciting a story and performing a rite linked to this journey ensures that all the proper coordinates are remembered. At least in some cosmographic systems, many of the constellations associated with the underworld are ones that happen to arise on the horizon during winter solstice, and the connection between the dying sun and the underworld can be logically associated between the sky and earth's seasons. The ascent to the North Star, which is a common feature in these cosmic journeys, makes sense because in the northern hemisphere the North Star serves as the throne of heaven. Other journeys seem to allegorically follow the sun or moon around the ecliptic. We cannot, however, attribute the entire cosmological journey to such correspondences. The entire frame of heaven—north, south, east, west, up, and down—was utilized in various cosmographic schemes. The truth is, our knowledge of this celestial journey in different cultural contexts is extremely limited, and the more one digs into them the more complex these cosmographies become.

The journeys as practiced by the cultures in which they originated may have been constantly changing. In fact, over long periods of time the sky is also changing due to precession of the equinoxes. The shift in the polar axis and the equinotical points on the horizon would affect the narratives, motifs, and symbols of a culture. If one group of stars appears on the horizon either at dawn or dusk on a significant day (e.g. winter solstice), then what happens when these stars no longer appear in their appointed hour? The arguments as to when precession was known are exasperated upon modern notions of scientific and literate thinking. Ancient cultures were not thinking in scientific and literate ways as we define them. Their rites and social norms, however, are wedded to the sky, and perhaps we can even say welded to the sky. It is highly unlikely that they would not have noticed the shift in stellar groups on the horizon. Some cultures may have lost the knowledge of precession, most probably never understood it, while others still may have tracked the shifting stars. If the latter is true, then the motifs contained in the mythic complex of the cosmographic journey become obscured because different characters and features show up over time as the sky changes. It is curious that Inanna descends into the underworld on her own cosmographic journey to observe the funeral rites of the Bull of Heaven, only to arise out of the underworld and wed Dumuzi, the heavenly shepherd. Is it coincidence that this text is written at the same time that Taurus the Bull disappeared underneath the horizon at the "right time," as Aires the Ram took its place?

All these notes are still insufficient. The Egyptians crafted an entire drama of the immortality of the soul predicated on this celestial journey. The Mesopotamians, on the other hand, employed a similar cosmography to found their city and cult. The method was the same, but the end was different. Or was it? The motifs of the cubic ark and the search for the immortality of the soul is a central theme in *The Epic of Gilgamesh*. Our knowledge of the view of the afterlife by the common folk in Mesopotamia, or even in Israel—two cultures who are thought to have either a grim view or no view of an afterlife—is deeply muted by scant sources which have long been disconnected from their cultural, cultic, and cosmographic roots. Our modern interpretation of these ancient ideas can only be a caricature of the real thing.

Oral cosmology lies at the root of the myth-ritual structure of the celestial journey. In addition to the examination of death, rebirth, and a royal mandate, this structure was also employed across cultures for numerous uses, including medicinal, agricultural, astrological, political, and weather controlling purposes. The esoterica in many oral cults finds resonance in this complex of motifs, rites, and functions. This is why there are multiple interpretations of the Péretié Plauqe, because in many cultures both funerary and medicinal rites were aligned along a similar cosmovision.

The following chapters explore basic myth structures linked to oral cosmology and the archetypal celestial journey. In each example I show fundamental cosmographic themes and how they are tied to the hero who is establishing his authority to rule the city or to obtain immortality. Many of these myths have various mythic threads that are unexplained, but the overarching narrative is the celestial journey where one obtains knowledge from the "true heaven." *The Epic of Gilgamesh* is one of our earliest examples of the cosmographic journey of the king. The Labors of Heracles reveal a remarkably similar structure. These two myths descend from a similar myth-ritual complex. The myth of Heracles is also about obtaining immortality; unlike Gilgamesh, Heracles is successful in his tasks and appears to be an initiate for apotheosis.

Finally, I present the narratives of Abraham, Jacob, and Balaam found in the Old Testament and show that these stories descend from similar cosmographic and liturgical themes. The context of key plot points within these stories belong to the archetypal celestial journey and the Israelite temple cult. These myths belong to the power and prestige of the oral age, where myth, cult, city, and cosmos were all synonymous expressions of each other.

As a final introduction to the study of these myths, a summary of the major principles discussed in this book is presented in a numbered list. This list is useful when examining any myth construct from the ancient past and frames their interpretations within the structures of oral thinking and oral cosmology.

(1)   There are three overarching prejudices in our modern history books. The first is the ideology of the Howlers who assert that all people in the ancient past were primitives. Second,

the belief of the Romantics who proclaim that people in the ancient past were connected with the earth and the soul in substantively different and better ways and thus were more "in tune" with the environment and the psyche. And third, the belief of the Conspirators who insist that the aliens built the pyramids or various other conspiracy theories that list the Templars, Freemasons, or Hermetic cults as the ultimate source of scientific knowledge.

(2) All these viewpoints are forged from a Darwinian metaphysic underwriting historical evolution. They are inflated views producing historical caricatures and skewing our own understanding about self and society.

(3) History is a reconstruction of the past using present conceptions, often loaded with biases and speculations, as the mortar to affix the "facts" together. When studying the ancient past we must always be aware that "our awesome lack of knowledge about the ancient world imprisons us within a discourse of plausibilities, not probabilities."

(4) The ancient mind was no different than the modern one. It had the same capacity to think, figure, analyze, philosophize, hypothesize, and imagine as do modern humans.

(5) The primary difference between ancient and modern thinking lies in the difference between oral and literate cognition.

(6) Oral thought is permanently wed to the immediate phenomena of nature, and the material world of the above and below is the primary reference "book" for oral thinkers.

(7) Oral thinkers use horizontal memory, mapping essential knowledge onto the visible landscapes of sky and earth. Horizontal memory follows a syntax of its own. Oral mnemonics requires redundancy, formulaic patterns, operational frames of reference, somatic gestures, narratives filled with

monumental or memorable characters, fixed statements, ritual utterance, epic recitals, songs, and performances.

(8) Polytheism is a natural product of orality. Different functions of nature are codified using descriptive dualities (light and dark, life and death, heaven and earth) that are assigned male and female rationales. Nature is a hierophony revealed in the pantheon.

(9) Oral peoples mythologize history. Literate peoples historicize myth.

(10) There is no word for *religion* in the ancient world. Oral peoples seek to reproduce the visible functions of the cosmos in their rites and cultural affairs.

(11) According to oral thought, the visible functions of the cosmos hail from invisible archetypes residing in the heavens. All processes on earth are an outflow from a celestial source. Life, death, and rebirth are the primary cosmic functions, and the secrets to life, death, and rebirth were thought to reside in certain portions of the sky.

(12) Oral cosmology was not mechanistic or spatial; it was synchronistic and ontological. Oral cosmology was a highly developed metaphysic that placed the human soul at the center of the cosmic stage. Man was *anthropocosmos*, and his destiny was not of the earth but was an extension of the heavens.

(13) Various features of oral cosmology have been reduced by modern prejudices into spatial models: a flat and square earth or a solar chariot in the sky are made out to be very primitive approaches to the natural world. Oral minds incorporate the functions of the cosmos into mythic symbols and rituals patterned off of concrete material forms. The flat and square earth was really the extension of the horizon into the sky. Earth had also descended from the heavens and was

framed by cyclical heavenly powers. A solar chariot and its horses was oral mnemonic imagery describing the path of the sun through the seasonal cycle (solstices and equinoxes), or, as in the case of Phaeton, was a rising star that announced that seasonal cycle.

(14) There were celestial archetypes for heaven, earth, and underworld. These archetypes resided in certain stars and constellations that were central to the mysteries of the cult.

(15) In order to imbue the material earth with benevolent powers, a king, priest, shaman, or healer would ritually climb through the sky, analogically ascending through the heavens in a celestial journey where the source of all life processes was engaged and reenacted on earth. The ancient macrocosm was geocentric, but the ancient microcosm was heliocentric, in that a soul could join with the sun and stars and journey to the true heavens. As strange as this is to literate minds, the modern Western tradition begins when Pythagoras and Parmenides started their schools by claiming such heavenly authority.

(16) In the ancient world, proper action in society was a reflection of eternal archetypes. Thus, the ancient city was thought to be the organization of those archetypes on earth. City and cosmos were synonymous.

(17) A city could only be founded through the construction of a sacred center where the land was "cosmicized" through proper ritual. Temple and city were also synonymous.

(18) The cult of the city regulated all its affairs, and temples were often used for multiple purposes including political, economic, cultural, and scientific matters. The line between king and priest is often blurry, and in many societies the king was the officiating priest of the cult. The oral cult was a product of oral cosmology.

(19)   In some myth systems, the object of the cult was to gain immortality in the next world through proper ritual instruction and correct orientation through the sky. This ritual pattern was used for multiple purposes, however, including healing, fertility, weather control, and astrology.

(20)   Oral societies exhausted their most prominent resources to organize this cosmovision. They sought to bring the sky and its archetypal powers down to earth and embed them in the city and society. More than any other interpretation, such structures as the Pyramids or Stonehenge must be seen in this light.

(21)   Not all myths are about a celestial journey. On the other hand, many mythic figures are celestial archetypes that do belong to the liturgical skyscape of oral cosmology. Mythic motifs are pregnant with cosmic themes and one senses that oral cosmology, with its close ties to heavenly archetypes, underwrites many myth cycles in ancient culture.

These points are sufficient to remind us that when dealing with the difficult subject of ancient myth and religion we are not only encountering different cultures, languages, and beliefs, but also an entirely different cosmovision predicated in oral thinking and permanently lost to modern apprehension. This cosmovision was not primitive. It was oral. It had its own high demands and complex philosophies. It strove to resolve the mysteries of nature through number, observation, and calculation. Most of all it sought out a solution for the ultimate heavenly secret: the *mysterium tremendum* that is life, death, and rebirth. Myth was once the guide into this mystery.

With this knowledge before us let us now walk into the ancient forest of myth and examine a few of its trees. The journey is perilous, for the trees are colossal hunks of petrified wood whose tips disappear into an endless reach of sky. Walking beneath their shadows we immediately sense that we are strangers in a strange land. We assuage our anxiety by insisting that our own gilt-dross cities, built upon marble and brass colossi, are the only true receptacles of reality. Then quite by accident we turn a corner in this grand cathedral forest and discover something entirely new and quite unexpected. A lumbering and toppled tree the size of a mountain appears in our view. We see carved in its trunk what must have once been the most grandiose stairway ever conceived ascending beyond broken palace, temple, and tomb.

A decayed, weather-worn inscription lies at its base identifying this vast wreck of ancient ruin as the same city from which we came. How is that possible? Suddenly we recognize that these are the same stairs that lead to our own city gates. A nervous thought passes through our minds, "Could it be that this dark forest, long ignored by almost everyone, is actually the graveyard of our future?"

Another line of inscription is slowly revealed, and we read with some apprehension: "Only the dead may climb these stairs; where they lead is a mystery. Here is the riddle of our civilization: the great mystery stands revealed in the open daylight. It is only made invisible by the lamp and torch blazing alongside the wise and powerful who refuse to see the sun."

CHAPTER 6

THE EPIC OF GILGAMESH

A prime example of the inherent difficulties in understanding ancient myth exists within the Gilgamesh tradition. The famous *Epic of Gilgamesh* is a sacred narrative recorded in cuneiform on clay tablets. As William Moran informs us, most of these ancient texts derive from the seventh century BCE, out of the Nineveh library of the Assyrian king Assurbanipal (175). Other significant portions of the Gilgamesh texts have emerged from many other sites, including Sultantepe, Nimrud, Asshur, Babylon, and Uruk (175). As Thorkild Jacobsen points out, the "Gilgamesh Epic proper, with which we are here concerned, dated from around 1600 B.C., at the end of the Old Babylonian period" (183). Furthermore, the Nineveh collection is a late representation of much earlier materials representing "separate songs of a loosely-connected Gilgamesh cycle" (183). The Gilgamesh cycle itself appears to have taken on a stabilized form as early as 2000 BCE (Moran 175).

Variants of the Gilgamesh cycle exist. In the Hurrian tradition the narrative is known as the *Epic of Huwawa*, named after the giant Gilgamesh defeats (*HM* 314). Further, large lacuna exist within the records, and our modern narrative represents at most only three-fifths of the total story (Moran 175). Additionally, mythic relationships within the text remain unclear. For example, the solar god Shamash is constantly protecting Gilgamesh while at the same time arguing against all the other gods. This adversarial relationship between Shamash and the pantheon reveals "a mythic dimension of the text [that] eludes us" (Moran 179).

Yet these difficulties are only subsets to the problem of understanding mythic texts detached from their cultural source. When Gilgamesh hands the boatman Ur-Shanabi "stone images" as a significant requirement for crossing the Underworld waters, we are left groping after their identity as no scholar has any idea what these "stone images" signify. Associated with these same tokens in some of the cuneiform texts are enigmatic items, including woods and snakes; their presence is confusing and many translators have simply dropped them from the translation (*HM* 410-12). The Benjamin R. Foster translation that I am using hints at these relationships, for Foster states that Ur-Shanabi possesses the Stone Charms "as he trims pine trees in the forest" (10.113). This passing phrase makes no sense and we are missing a significant insight into an ancient tradition. The epic as a whole remains problematic from several points of view, leaving Jacobsen to comment that the narrative's full meaning "may only become clear through future lucky finds" (200).

The epic also contains separate cultural traditions. Jacobsen points out that within the Gilgamesh texts there is a clear demarcation between a hero tradition surrounding a historical warrior king and a cultic system descending from "a vigorous and continuous nonliterary religious tradition." In the latter case Gilgamesh is a reflection of a temple priest, an *en*, whose apparent roles include magic powers over the vegetal cycle, the sacred marriage, and the judge in the underworld (197-200). These two separate traditions show "diametrically opposed attitudes towards death" (201). This situation is very similar to Homer's contradictory attitudes towards death within the *Odyssey*, where the hero Achilles is trapped within the netherworld mud (11.556-58), whereas King Menelaus is promised a celestial ascent to the blessed Elysian garden (4.631-40).

Complicating these parallel thematic motifs is another mythic tradition embedded in the text with apparently little or no roots in the original Gilgamesh cycle. As William Moran notes, most scholars concede that the Flood story told within the epic was a late addition "told for its own sake" (181), and that the Flood pericope "seriously interrupts not only the flow of dialogue between Ut-napishtim and Gilgamesh but the otherwise smooth and natural transition from the end of Tablet 10" (181). However, these conclusions of parallel but opposite traditions regarding death and an extraneous Flood story may actually belong in the Gilgamesh cycle as written. The ancient warrior king was also a temple high priest. The Flood story with its ark and re-juvenating symbols is not really foreign to the complex of underworld myth or temple cult. Scholarly conclusions in these regards may simply result from a lack of understanding of the cultic and cosmographic roots of ancient religion.

The hero Gilgamesh appears to be a historical king as his name is found in a Sumerian king list. He apparently ruled over the city of Uruk around 2700 BCE (Moran 171). His father, Lugalbanda, also appears as a divinized king of Uruk (171). His mother is the cow goddess Ninsun (not unlike Hera, the cow-mother of Herakles). In cuneiform spelling the name *Gilgamesh* wears the divine determinative, indicating that our epic hero is at least a demigod (Puhvel 23), a fact made explicit in the text where he is described as two-thirds divine and one-third human (1.50-51). Already we are in the midst of an apparent contradiction, for Gilgamesh fails to obtain immortality in the epic, despite the fact that he is by nature a divine being destined for a divine end.

Gilgamesh is certainly a titan in stature—a true giant with divine strength whose foot is "a triple cubit" and whose stride is "six times twelve cubits" (1.55-56). He is "towering Gilgamesh [who] is uncannily perfect" (1.38). He traverses the mighty ocean, explores the "furthest reaches of the earth" (1.42), and perceives the "foundations of the land" (1.1-3). Our hero-giant has turned into an explorer, a sort of Christopher Columbus, who has sailed a foreign sea and discovered a new continent. One should be wary of pure, terrestrial interpretations of the imagery. The "foundations of the land" are not geologic strata, but heavenly relationships and cycles. Gilgamesh is one who has measured heaven and earth and thus is "wise in all things" (1.4). "He saw what was secret and revealed what was hidden, he brought back tidings from before the flood" (1.6-7). We are explicitly told that Gilgamesh knows the secrets of the ancient patriarchs (from before the Flood); thus, our hero also establishes the "holy places that the deluge had destroyed," as well as founded the rites of civilization (1.45-46). In a separate poem entitled *The Death of Gilgamesh* we are informed that Gilgamesh is responsible for "establishing the temples of the gods. . . . Resurrecting the forgotten, archaic and ancient rites of Sumer, the ordinances and rituals of the land . . . from before the flood" (39-44). Gilgamesh is a restorer. His greatest accomplishment is establishing the city of Uruk, built within its seven walls laid down by the assistance of seven wise masters (1.21). Gilgamesh restores order in the chaos as he becomes king of city, temple, and cult.

It is clear that we are not dealing with just a warrior king, mighty as he is. Neither are we dealing with an exceptional intellectual, wise as he is. The figure of Gilgamesh represents a vast and complex system of cultic life. This inference is directly made from the text, which tells the reader to inquire after the true story written on a tablet of lapis lazuli and hidden within a copper chest within the temple precinct of Uruk (1.21-22; Moran 176-78). No copper chest or lapis lazuli tablet has ever been found, and it is clear that the prototype of the story does not belong to royal history or ancient literature, but to temple cultus. In my view, it is in a cultic context that the *Epic of Gilgamesh* should be read. Every motif, name, and curious phrase in the epic abounds with meaning and is connected to the ancient storehouse of thought wed to the cosmology of the age. This does not make interpretation easy, as indeed there are too many motifs that remain without explanation or serve only to blur tentative conclusions.

The epic begins with Gilgamesh ruling his city of Uruk as a despot. Men and women cry to the gods because Gilgamesh is bedding the woman and presumably tasking the men beyond their capacities. To answer the people's prayers, the gods make a wild man named Enkidu. He is mortal, covered in hair, and is repeatedly called the "swift wild donkey" (8.49-50). The wild nature of Enkidu is tamed, however, as he learns the arts of civilization. He is taught about relationships and love making by a temple prostitute, learns to eat like a human, and becomes a shepherd and night's watchman. Upon hearing of the despotic behavior of Gilgamesh, Enkidu is incensed and vows to confront the king in combat. The two meet at a wedding and immediately do battle. Gilgamesh is victorious, raising Enkidu over his head while kneeling on one knee and foot. Enkidu confesses the superior strength of his opponent and authentically lavishes compliments upon his victor. Gilgamesh is also awed at the power of Enkidu, and both recognize a sort of kinship with each other. They end up being best friends. Gilgamesh convinces Enkidu to go on various quests to gain glory and reputation.

These two heroes seek out the invincible giant Humbaba (equivalent to the Sumerian Huwawa) who lives in the cedar forest on a great mountain, a "dwelling of the gods, sacred to the goddess [Ishtar]" (5.6-7). They battle the giant and the force and terror of their blows sunders the mountainside. Gilgamesh defeats Humbaba. Afterwards, the goddess Ishtar (the same goddess as the Sumerian Inanna) proposes to Gilgamesh, who refuses her offer. Infuriated, Ishtar unleashes the Bull of Heaven upon the land and it lays waste to the countryside. Gilgamesh and Enkidu face it in battle and after much struggle defeat it. Enkidu tears the haunch of the bull off and throws it at Ishtar. As punishment for these deeds, the gods resolve that one of the heroes must perish, and it is Enkidu who grows sick and dies. Gilgamesh is inconsolable, and seeks out the secrets of immortality to bring his friend back to life. In order to obtain these secrets Gilgamesh descends into the underworld to confront Utnapishtim, the only mortal ever granted immortality. Unfortunately, after several significant trials Gilgamesh fails to obtain the secrets and returns to Uruk facing the reality of mortality.

Like all good mythic narratives this tale is full of curious, oversized, and outrageous characters, monsters, and events. Also like all good mythic narratives, the story is a layered series of allusions. De Santillana and von Dechend insist that these allusions have astronomical referents (*HM* 323). This interpretation is undeniable; although the astronomical allusions themselves belong within a cultic, cosmographic tradition. The text provides many examples.

In a Sumerian variant of the epic entitled *Gilgamesh and Huwawa A* we find Gilgamesh seeking the cedar forest through a path of seven mountains. Only after climbing the seventh mountain peak does our demigod find the true cedar forest. Upon this seventh mountain peak Enkidu and Gilgamesh defeat Huwawa by disrobing him of his seven glories, one at a time (*EG* 5.147; *EGHA* 166-222). Huwawa's glories or radiances are like garments. Contrast this imagery with the Sumerian Inanna texts where this goddess descends into the underworld and delivers her seven tokens or garments to the gatekeepers of the underworld. The seven radiances, garments, or tokens are homologous symbols intimating an initiatory journey through the seven spheres of the cosmos. The giant's glories are also compared to the branches of a tree. This is the cosmic tree that spans the three worlds, for indeed its crown pierces the sky (5.160). The seven branches of this giant tree growing atop the seventh mountain are a representation of the seven planetary spheres that must be trekked through to gain access to the cosmic frame proper. A further hint to this interpretation is the fact that after defeating Humbaba, Enkidu takes the wood from this tree and constructs a massive doorway (72 cubits tall and 24 cubits wide), which no stranger may approach but "only a god [can] go through" (5.164). This image is the gate of heaven, and probably had an earthly parallel in the great gate of the seven-storied ziggurat.

Should anyone doubt the cosmic imagery, there is a more obvious clue in the fact that the name Humbaba or Huwawa is found on a star list as ^{mul}Humba, probably identified as the star Procyon in the modern constellation of Canis Minor (*HM* 289-90, 402-04). In the Elamitic tradition Huma or Humban is related to one of the planets—either Mercury or Jupiter. Although a definitive identification is not forthcoming, and while ancient deities could have simultaneous stellar and planetary correlations, the connection between the giant and a heavenly archetype is certain. The star Procyon presents an interesting possibility as it is one of the three bright stars that form the Winter Triangle, along with Sirius and Betelgeuse. The Greeks identified Procyon with Canis Minor, one of Orion's hunting dogs. However, in ancient times Procyon was probably associated with the constellation of the Crab, or Cancer. This latter constellation is pre-Greek and is often represented on Babylonian entitlement stones as a snapping turtle (White, *Babylonian* 79). Of greater interest in the Babylonian cosmographic scheme is that this constellation lay in the region of the sky where the dead traveled along an astral road. Gavin White, in his book *Babylonian Star-Lore*, asserts: "The path that the ancestors follow to the upper worlds is located in the region of the Crab and is remembered in Greek mythology as the entrance to the underworld situated close to the Hydra's lair. Dionysus used this entrance when he attempted to bring his dead mother back from the realm of shades. And it is also remembered in Roman astrology as the 'Gates of Men,' which is the route taken by the souls of babies destined to be born on earth" (82).

As one gazes at the constellation Cancer one sees the glistening ocean shores of the Milky Way transecting the Winter Triangle and descending to Canopus. At the time and place where these texts were written the stars of the Winter Triangle were the first to appear on the eastern horizon as the sun set at winter solstice, and they were the first to appear on the western horizon as the sun set at spring equinox. In this cosmographic scheme the Milky Way was the place of the dead. The Milky Way circles the entire celestial sphere, crossing the ecliptic at the constellations Scorpio and Taurus. It is not coincidence that when Gilgamesh descends into the underworld to find the secrets of immortality he must go through a great gate at the cosmic mountain guarded by scorpion-men. If Humbaba is associated with Procyon then the suggestion is that the giant is a representation of a heavenly frame connecting the three-tier universe and that by defeating the giant, Gilgamesh and Enkidu have gained access to a passageway through the stellar world.

Juxtaposed along this line of thinking is another curious aspect of the giant Humbaba. In ancient art he is sometimes depicted as a fertility symbol often associated with newborn infants. Humbaba's head is often pictorially placed on an infant's body. In this context, the grotesque and intestinal head of the giant is likened to the wrinkled skin of a newborn child. This strange use of the giant ogre most likely indicates different strands of historical traditions. The hideous war-giant we have discussed above probably belongs to a later Akkadian tradition, whilst the image of the infant Humbaba most likely descends from an earlier Sumerian mythos.

In either case, Humbaba appears to represent a celestial archetype dealing with souls in the celestial world. Gavin White, in his book *Queen of Heaven*, shows several depictions of the infant Humbaba associated with the heavenly seed of the soul that descends to earth at birth. The giant therefore is somehow linked to the communal realm of life. White hypothesizes, "Humbaba must represent something akin to an ancestral collective from which all children are born. And the fertility motifs like the celestial bulls and flowers that are found alongside him indicate that this ancestral collective would have been located in the sunlit heavens, not in any kind of underworld. In fact, as a number of designs show, these lineage figures were portrayed as the abiding life within the waters of heaven in mid 3rd millennium art" (154).

White is conceptualizing the underworld as a dark, subterranean realm. As discussed in Chapter 3, the underworld was in fact a place in the starry sky. Procyon belongs in the celestial underworld. The underworld contained the seeds of rebirth, and in many cosmographic systems there was a ladder set in heaven where souls descended to earth at birth and ascended from earth at death. It is probable that Humbaba represents the archetypal region in space that engenders the soul towards earth. According to White, this giant "is a true denizen of the starry heavens. He is the ancestral potency that resides in the skies; he is the spirit of life that descends on the winds and alights upon the earth in the form of the kneeling child" (*Queen*, 155). The fact that Gilgamesh slays the giant indicates a change in the roles of the pantheon, where Shamash replaces the older Utu as the deity of life and birth. It also shows that Gilgamesh has procured the celestial mandate of birth and fertility for his city. He can rightfully rule because he knows heaven's secrets and has brought them down to earth.

Humbaba is not the only astral motif in the epic. After defeating the great giant, Gilgamesh and Enkidu are faced with a second, equally impossible task—defeating the Celestial Bull. Like Humbaba, this bull's origin is in the sky. According to our text Ishtar is insulted when Gilgamesh refuses her sexual advances. As punishment she demands the Bull of Heaven from her father Anu. Anu concedes and gives Ishtar the lead rope of the Bull of Heaven. She guides the terrifying beast to Earth, where it swallows rivers, opens pits, consumes warriors, and causes cataclysms. Gilgamesh and Enkidu finally face the fierce creature and defeat it in battle. After killing the Bull of Heaven Enkidu removes its hind leg and throws it at Ishtar; that is, he throws the leg of the Bull into the sky (6.153).

The Bull of Heaven is a Babylonian constellation. It is depicted on a clay cylinder seal dating back to about 3000 BCE. It is also associated with the star Venus and with the goddess Ishtar (White, *Babylonian* 65). In other seals the Bull of Heaven is depicted by a winged gate (White, *Babylonian* 68). This Babylonian constellation becomes the Greek Taurus, sitting at the crossroads of the ecliptic and Milky Way. Curiously, the Greek constellation shows only the front half of the bull, the hind quarters are missing. Babylonians knew of this half-bull image as well, at least by the first millennium BCE (White, *Babylonian* 69). Of course, in our epic the hind quarter of the Bull of Heaven is thrown at Ishtar. It is a strange motif by itself, save Enkidu is not the only figure to throw a bull's leg at a celestial being or in a celestial context. The Japanese Susanowo tosses a bull haunch at the sun-goddess Amaterasu, as does Odin at one of his opponents (*HM* 292). Mithras cuts the leg of the bull in the tauroctony scenes of Mithraism. All of these images most likely correlate to the Egyptian *Maskheti*, the thigh of the bull in the sky, or the seven stars of the Big Dipper in Ursa Major (*HM* 405). In Altaic mythology this constellation is the leg of a stag (*HM* 405). This mythic hind leg resolves into the seven stars which dance around the north celestial pole. As such they are a representation, among other things, of the passageway to the northern throne of heaven.

It is intriguing that Gilgamesh and Enkidu must face two great and horrible monsters who are in turn celestial markers of the high heavens. Humbaba (as Procyon) guards the underworld passage, which extends down to the celestial southern pole. The thigh of the Bull of Heaven guards the northern celestial pole. In conquering both, while unwritten, our heroes have gained access to the celestial vault and know its secrets. No wonder Gilgamesh is said to have measured heaven and earth; his adventures seem to prove the case. Meanwhile, after our heroes slay the Bull of Heaven, Ishtar immediately convenes the "cult women" and performs ancient rites over the Bull (6.156-57; *HM* 404). No details are given as to what this cryptic phrase means, but we are again put on notice that what we are dealing with is some form of cultus and not a simple folk or fairytale.

The Underworld: Mountains, Gardens, and Springs

After all these adventures we find our great heroes in a new predicament. Enkidu has perished and Gilgamesh weeps over his friend (8.1-40). Gilgamesh, unable to bear the loss of his companion, resolves to descend into the underworld to retrieve him. He seeks out Utnapishtim, the only mortal who has ever obtained immortality. Here the epic takes another turn, for now we are entering into the underworld proper, and the mythemes we find also have remarkable similarities in other myth-ritual systems. Gilgamesh arrives at a mountain pass guarded by lions. When encountering these lions Gilgamesh says, "I felt afraid" (9.9). After facing the giant Humbaba and the Bull of Heaven, one wonders what Gilgamesh could be afraid of? Surely a few mountain lions are no match for the cosmic creatures Gilgamesh has already defeated. But these lions are no ordinary lions—they exude terror and our demigod trembles. Gilgamesh can only pray to the moon for a blessing, while Shamash the sun comes to his aid (9.10-30). Though we are not told how, Gilgamesh defeats these lions, for when he enters the underworld he wears a lion garment (10.45). It is not coincidental that Jason begins his quest wearing a panther skin. We will explore this motif with the adventures of Herakles in the next chapter.

Surpassing the lions, apparently with the help of the sun and moon, Gilgamesh comes to a pair of peaks called *Mashum*. This word apparently means "twin," and refers to the mirroring peaks which "daily watch over the rising [and setting of the sun], whose flanks thrust upward to the vault of heaven, whose flanks reach downward to hell, where scorpion monsters guard its gateway" (9.32-37). Clearly these are no ordinary mountain peaks, and they certainly do not belong as part of a terrestrial topography. These peaks climb to the apex of the sky and descend to the depths of hell; therefore, we must think of a three-dimensional celestial frame. Our hero has arrived at the Holy Mountain, a cosmographic motif implied in the Babylonian planisphere (White, *Babylonian* 174). "The base of the Mountain is located in the region of the Scorpion," writes Gavin White. "The symbol of the Holy Mountain is best represented in Mesopotamian tradition by the *E-Kur* or 'Temple of the Mountain,' which was Enlil's most holy temple in the city of Nippur" (*Babylonian* 174). Again, the motif in the epic is associated with both an astral analog and a terrestrial sacred temple.

The base of this Holy Mountain is in the sky, at the constellation Scorpio. Not surprisingly, the gate entering the mountain pass leading to the underworld is guarded by scorpion monsters (9.37). Scorpio is another Babylonian constellation inherited by the Greeks. It marks the port that connects the Milky Way and the ecliptic in the south. Unfortunately, there is much lacuna in these lines and it is impossible to resolve the details of the confrontation between Gilgamesh and the scorpion monster. At first it appears that the scorpion monster refuses access, but then the wife of the scorpion monster identifies Gilgamesh as a demigod and access is granted. This marks the first time that a female ward helps our hero. There will be more, for as it turns out, at every critical juncture of Gilgamesh's journey a female figure shows up to offer aid.

As Gilgamesh enters the scorpion gate he descends into a terrifying and unnatural darkness: "Dense was the darkness, no light was there, it would not let him look behind him" (9.84). The darkness was all consuming; Gilgamesh could not even turn around and obtain his bearings from the light entering the gateway. Gilgamesh descends further and further into the tunnel of blackness, racing with superhuman speed to get to the other side, and taking twelve double hours to do so. He is running the race of the midnight sun through the underworld. As Gilgamesh emerges from this terrifying darkness, the first thing he beholds is a garden: "He went forward, seeing . . . the trees of the gods. The carnelian bore its fruit, like bunches of grapes, dangling, lovely to see, the lapis bore foliage, fruit it bore, a delight to behold" (9.115-19). The text breaks up in several spots, and we only get glimpses of this netherworld garden. It is filled with balsam, cedar, green chlorite, sweet dates, coral, rubies, red and green stones, agates, amber, turquoise, and cowrie shells (9.120-31). It is a sort of paradisiacal grove where one may rest and recoup after such a long and arduous journey through the pitch black passageway. We are not sure where the garden is or what Gilgamesh does within it, as the lacuna takes over. We are certain, however, that this paradisiacal garden belongs to a wider cosmographic tradition, for the cosmic garden is the nexus between the worlds.

Departing from this world to the next via a garden grove is the exact imagery we find in the Orphic gold tablets buried with the initiated dead. Walter Burkert explains that the "meadow is a very ancient detail in descriptions of the netherworld," citing one Orphic plate that instructs, "Enter the sacred meadow. The initiate is free from retribution" (*Babylon* 82). The text indicates that one has not only entered a sacred grove, but has past a sort of judgment where he is free from retribution. Other gold tablets described by Susan Cole follow suit: "Take the right hand road to the sacred meadows and grove of [Persephone]," while another states, "Enter the sacred meadow; for the *mystes* is without punishment" (211). Cole comments on this imagery: "The meadow of the tablets is a mythic space. Greek lands were not often blessed with verdant meadows, and real crops were produced only be means of hard work. The Dionysian meadow, in contrast, requires no labor because it is a land lush without cultivation" (212).

The meadow is the supreme juncture between the worlds. As such, it is a place of judgment, where those being born are allotted lives according to their virtue, and those who have just died are judged according to their lives. This is the scene we find in Plato's *Myth of Er,* where we find souls entering a sacred meadow where "those who knew each other exchanged greetings, and those who [came] up from the earth asked those who came down from the heavens about the things there and were in turn questioned by them about the things below," and where each soul coming from earth "paid the penalty ten times over" for every moral wrong (*Republic* 10.614e-615b). This celestial meadow has two gates for the souls traveling back and forth. There is a similar passage in Plato's *Gorgias,* where the dead are said to arrive at a place of judgment "in the Meadow at the Cross Roads, whence the two [paths] lead, one to the Isles of the Blest, the other to Tartarus" (trans. Cope 126).

In both instances in Plato's works, the holy meadow is the temporary way point that allows sustenance and repose before the great dangers of the journey ahead. The journeys include both the trek through the underworld and the birth into mortal flesh. Hugh Nibley makes the same observation, "It would seem that the standard procedure in the mysteries is to enter a new life or a new world through a garden, where one rests for a while and takes nourishment after the exertions and perils of the passage" (*MJSP* 279). It is a tradition that extends into early Christianity, where we find in a late Christian text a vision of Marian (3rd cent. CE) and the journey through the netherworld: "Our road lay through a place with lovely meadows clad with the joyous foliage of flourishing woods, shaded by tall cypresses and pine trees that beat against the heavens, so that you would think that the entire spot all around was crowned with fertile groves. A hollow in the center abounded in fertilizing watercourses and pure water from a clear spring" (Bremmer 164).

It is not by accident that the Bible begins in a garden. In Genesis 2 the world nexus or omphalos is the Garden of Eden, itself the prototype of a celestial archetype. The world has been fashioned from another, heavenly order (Barker, *Gate* 68). The garden is a place of two gates, which are imaged as trees, the one guarded by cherubim and a flaming sword and the other enwrapped by a serpent promising celestial knowledge to all those who partake of the fruit of the Tree of Knowledge of Good and Evil. How very similar this imagery is to Plato's *Gorgias*. Protestant and Catholic interpretation of the Garden of Eden are a misreading of an ancient cosmography. In order to obtain immortality (partake of the Tree of Life), one must first put on the garment of mortality (partake of the Tree of Knowledge). With mortality comes death and a descent into the underworld where one must also pass the guardians inhabiting the celestial regions (Cherubim and a Flaming Sword). If successful, one may ascend to the celestial throne. Adam, the first man, and Eve, the first mother who introduces death just as the Mother Goddess should, must tread the celestial axis on their quest to find the domain of God.

Christian tradition adopts the same imagery. In Revelations the apostle John sees seven spirits of the heavenly regions guarding the celestial throne (1.4). He beholds the Son of Man reborn and bearing the keys of the underworld (1.18). The heavenly throne is guarded by a creature with the heads of a lion, bull, man, and eagle (4.7). A chorus of priests sing and dance around the throne (5.9-12). The soul's journey is perilous. Many are damned never to progress, consumed by formidable monsters, while the successful find themselves at the end of the journey of mortality in a celestial garden with a great tree and eternal spring (Rev. 22.1-2). Here is the throne of God, where the saved shall see the Almighty face to face (22.4) in a moment of transfiguration.

Perhaps of greater interest is the fact that the Temple of Solomon was built as a replica of the primordial garden that stood between the worlds (Barker, *Gate* 27). The "walls of the *hekal,*" writes Margaret Barker, "were decorated with golden palm trees and flowers, set with precious stones;

the bronze pillars were decorated with pomegranate patterns and the great lamp was a stylized almond tree" (57). The temple is more than a representation of the cosmos, but of the *created, ordered* cosmos, which is symbolized by the verdant garden. "In Canaan, the triumph of Baal over the unruly sea was a sign that he had established order in the creation, and this was marked by the erection of his temple. In Genesis, however, when the Lord had finished the work of creation he made for himself not a temple but a garden" (63). Yet the temple with its omphalos and the garden sanctuary are synonymous, "There is, however, a great deal which suggests that the garden of Eden and the temple had at one time been one and the same" (64).

The garden temple belonged to Egyptian cultus and therefore to eschatology. Thus, when the Egyptian dead descend to the underworld they find themselves first in a garden "beside a lake surrounded by trees," where souls are washed, anointed, and given a great meal as they declare, "My garden is in the Field of Rest; my increase is in the Field of Rushes" (*MJSP* 279-80). One word for the Egyptian underworld is *Rostau*, which Thausing describes as a garden or meadow that stands between the worlds of heaven and earth; that is, it is in neither place, but at a crossroads that can only be accessed by the dead (*MJSP* 293-94). Egyptian tombs also contained gardens and were representations of gardens. This tradition existed as early as the Old Kingdom, where "stone basins are found in tombs, representing, according to Hermann Junker, pools, trees, and cooling groves" (*MJSP* 293). The garden that Gilgamesh enters after the long dark passage is this very garden between the worlds, and the Egyptians and Babylonians were employing similar imagery from presumably an *a priori* conception of the heavenly journey.

Emerging from the garden (the lacuna blurs the transition between the garden and the next event), the very first thing Gilgamesh is confronted with is a tavern built at the edge of a great sea. The tavern keeper is a woman named Siduri, and she is hesitant to let Gilgamesh enter her establishment for drinks. She confronts Gilgamesh with a series of questions. Our hero reveals his identity and explains that he has slain the giant Humbaba, has overcome the Bull of Heaven, and has slain wild lions. This last item is a new detail, and we must assume that Gilgamesh has slain the lion guardians who were perched near the mountain passes at the very beginning of his journey. More poignantly, Siduri asks Gilgamesh, "Why are you clad in a lion skin, roaming the steppe?" (10.45). Apparently he has slain the guardian lions at the mountain passes and put on their skins even before he entered the dark passageway of the underworld.

It is the tavern itself, however, that proves the most unique image. It is operated by a divine female. What is its purpose? If no one had ever come this way before, as the text claims, why construct a tavern in the netherworld at all? Where is its location, built at the very edge of an impassable sea, its owner described as one who sits "on the throne of the sea" (*HM* 295). The logic of the motif in the narrative is confusing. Again we are reminded that this epic does not descend from ancient literature, fairytale, or campfire storytelling, but from an ancient cultus rooted in a conception immersed in celestial archetypes. In any case, what we find on the other side of the underworld garden is a place to drink.

Although there does not appear to be any other netherworld taverns in other myth traditions, there are numerous mentions of an underworld "watering hole," a place where one must stop and drink before one can move on. This tavern at the side of the sea must be analogous to the Spring of Lethe and the Spring of Memory. Whatever the tavern's internal logic, it remains a mythic motif parallel to the Orphic gold plates where the traveler must stop and rest by a tree and drink from the correct fount. This image also finds resonance in

Egyptian funerary texts where the Lady of the Sycamore stands in the sacred tree marking the passage between the worlds and distributes drink to the parched dead.

The Underworld: Cubes and Temples

Siduri informs Gilgamesh that in order to cross the great sea and find the shore where Utnapishtim dwells, he must employ the help of a ferryman named Ur-Shanabi. The scene that follows is also confusing. Gilgamesh needs a pair of "Stone Images" as a token to cross the waters of death. Gilgamesh smashes these Stone Images and throws them into the water. We do not know what these things are and why Gilgamesh disposes of them as he does. However, in many myth systems such tokens are required to pass through the underworld. The coins given to the Greek ferryman Charon are such an example. Furthermore, Gilgamesh is made to cut down 120 poles, each 60 cubits in length, and use them to punt the boat across the netherworld waters. These details make little sense, and we are again reminded that much has been lost behind the veil of history.

Gilgamesh lands upon the shore or wharf of Utnapishtim, whose official title is the "Distant One" (10.269). Our hero is joyous that he has made it so far still alive. His happiness turns to surprise, however, as he gazes at Utnapishtim and beholds no dazzling deity, but a being much like himself: "Your limbs are not different, you are just as I am. Indeed, you are not different at all, you are just as I am" (11.2-4). Gilgamesh realizes that no further heroic exploits are required—no great battle with giants or bulls or confrontations with divine beings—he is now with the Distant One on far off shores. The only thing that will aid him is knowledge, which is the very object of his quest. Thus Gilgamesh asks of Utnapishtim, the Distant One, the central question of the entire epic: "How did you join the ranks of the gods and find eternal life?" (11.7).

The answer that Utnapishtim offers is as bewildering as anything one finds in myth. "I will reveal to you, O Gilgamesh, a secret matter, and a mystery of the gods I will tell you" (11.9-10). One expects a description of an ancient rite, or perhaps the disclosing of some magical token—a sort of philosopher's stone or elixir of life. *What we get instead is a myth.* Utnapishtim recites the Flood myth. The introduction of this narrative at this juncture, at the apex of the epic cycle, seems so strange and disjointed that most scholars believe it is an extraneous addition. Perhaps we can learn something by proceeding with the assumption that what Utnapishtim tells Gilgamesh really is the secret to eternal life.

Utnapishtim discloses to Gilgamesh that in ancient times the "great gods resolved to send the deluge," and commanded him to build an ark and place inside it "seed of all living things" (11.24-30). In exchange for building the ark, the gods promised to pour out wealth and abundance upon him, and more important, he was told that he would no longer dwell in the city or on dry land, but would "descend to the watery depths and dwell with my lord Ea" (11.42). Ea, or Enki, is the god of the underworld waters, the *apsu*. Ea had a city and temple built for him called Eridu. This city was always associated with the epithet *pī nārāti* meaning "mouth of the rivers" or "confluence of the rivers" (*HM* 210-11). This city had a celestial archetype in the star Canopus, which is the steering oar in the constellation of the Argo, or the boat that sailed upon the flood waters. This image returns us to our epic, where in order to descend through the underworld waters, Utnapishtim constructs an ark. It is a strange sailing vessel for it dimensions form a cube—it is 120 cubits tall and wide; her deck is an entire square acre. It is built with six decks and seven divides, and covered with immense quantities of tar and pitch, as if the thing were meant to sail under the seas. Meanwhile, the entire construction project takes a massive host of workers, provisions, and sacrifices. Somehow the ark is wed to the image of the sun: "By the setting of Shamash, the ship was completed" (11.77). A curious phrase whose mythic dimension again eludes us. When finished, Utnapishtim boards it with a large crew, including numerous kinds of animals, his entire family and kin, as well as skilled craftsmen of every kind. The ark even has a helmsman named in the text: "To the caulker of the boat, to Puzur-Amurri the boatman, I gave over the edifice, with all it contained" (11.97-98).

These are strange details. If the only people to survive the Flood are Utnapishtim and his wife, as they are the only one's Gilgamesh finds immortalized in the underworld, then what has happened to the rest of the crew? Indeed, the scope of the ark's contents goes well beyond the Noah story, where that Hebrew patriarch brought forth two of every living thing. Utnapishtim adds to this cargo manifest a host of craftsmen and workers as well as his entire family clan. The ark is to be the vessel of civilization containing all the requirements for the growth of the city and the cultivation of the land. It appears that the entire civilization comes together to build the ship in the first place. Of course, this mighty ark that braves the Great Flood is a seven-storied cube, whose unusual dimensions do not lend themselves to floating in terrestrial waters. Clearly more is going on here than we are aware of, and the mythic dimension of the Flood story is rooted in a cultic *mysterium tremendum.*

The ark of Utanapishtim is a seven-storied cube (Saggs 320). It is with great interest that we find the construction of the ziggurat, such as *E-temen-an-ki*, or "House of the Foundation of Heaven and Earth," was built in seven levels and designed so that its foundation's width and length were equal, and that the whole thing could fit within a 300 square-foot-cube (*TC* 162-63; see figure 8). Other ziggurats were built as a series of stacked cubes. Is it possible that the Babylonian pyramid is a representation of the ark of Utnapishtim? Or is the ark of Utnapishtim really a temple-ziggurat?

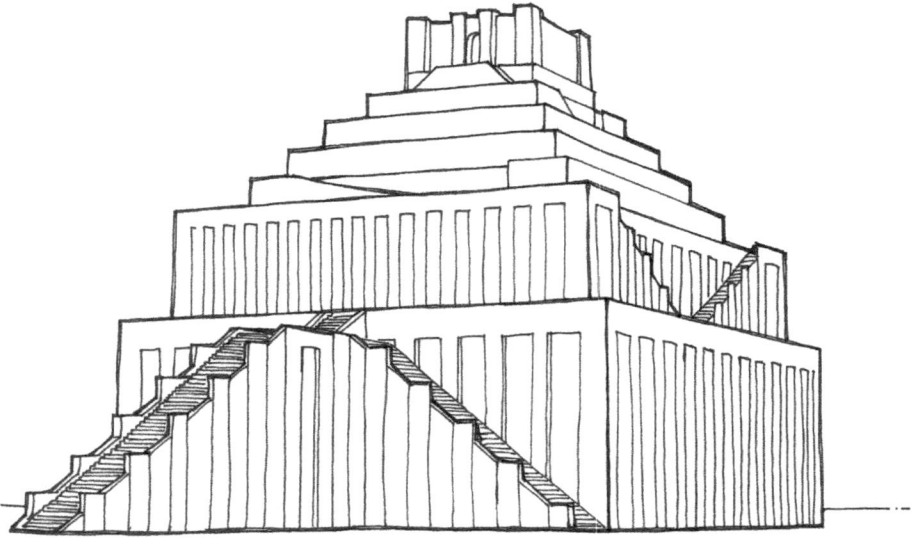

Figure 8. Cubic Ziggarut

Babylonian Ziggurat named *E-temen-anki,* "House of the Foundation of Heaven and Earth." As originally designed the structure would fit within a three hundred foot cube. The pyramid was also built in seven levels. Many ziggurats were built as a series of stacked cubes. It is suggested that this structure had a mythic analog in the ark of Utnapishtim. (Illustration by Lynde Mott, original image in Nibley, *TC* 163)

The answer is a resounding "Yes," for the cube, ark, and temple repeatedly show up associated with each other in the ancient world. When Ani approaches Osiris after the weighing of his heart, he is led by Horus to the cubic shrine of the underworld god who sits upon a cubic throne over the waters of life. The cubic enclosure signifies a temple-ark. This is no idle comparison, as the alabaster canopic chest constructed for King

Tut-ankh-Amun was constructed as a cube (see figure 9). At each of the four corners of the chest stand four goddesses as pillars of the four corners. Each goddess serves as protector and guide for the great cosmic journey of the deceased. In Salt Papyrus 825 we are given a clue that this cubic, canopic chest is the "House of Life," wherein the essence of the deceased is encased as he strides through the cubic heaven (Lamy 95). Like Utnapishtim who sails in a cubic ark by which he gains immortality, Tut-ankh-Amun becomes a "figure in the cube [striding] to the south, on the path of the cyclic return of death and regeneration represented by Osiris-Orion" (Lamy 95).

In 1 Kings in the Old Testament we are given the dimensions of Solomon's temple. At the heart of the temple was the Holy of Holies. Notice how this space was to be constructed and what it contained: "And the oracle he prepared in the house within, to set there the *ark of the covenant* of the Lord. And the oracle in the forepart was twenty cubits in length, and twenty cubits in breadth, and twenty cubits in height thereof; and he overlaid it with pure gold; and so covered the altar which was of cedar" (1 Kings 6.19-20). The Holy of Holies was built as a cube, surrounding an altar made of cedar (see figure 10). In Egyptian, the word for cedar, *seb*, is also the word for star. On top of this "starry" altar was the ark of the covenant, holding the sacred tokens of the Hebrew cultus. Beneath the altar was a sacred cave containing the fount of living waters, or "Well of Souls" (Simpson 102), the Hebrew version of the *apsu*. It is suggested that there were seven chambers constructed above the Holy of Holies (Barker, *Gate* 72). In the *Testament of Levi*, a second century BCE text, we are informed that the high priest who entered the veil of the cubic Holy of Holies obtained seven tokens from seven angelic stewards: including a staff, a robe, a linen vestment, a girdle, a branch, a crown, and a diadem of the priesthood (Barker, *Gate* 162). Like Inanna, the Hebrew high priest must obtain his seven *me* for his heavenly journey, and like Ani and Osiris, or Gilgamesh and Utnapishtim, the Hebrew high priest entered the ark of the gods, which was a cube, holding the mysteries of the cosmos.

Figure 9. Cubic Canopic Chest

Alabaster canopic chest of Tut-ankh-Amun. The canopic chest is a
representation of the cosmos and, according to Salt Papyrus 825, a
representation of the "House of Life." According to the inscriptions
the deceased is represented as inside the cube striding through the
heavens. As the Four Sons of Horus, the canopic jars represent a
quaternary: four directions, four winds, four elements, four stages,
etc. The canopic chest is a temple in miniature and its imagery and
construction indicate the celestial journey the deceased must make in
the afterlife. (Illustration by Lynde Mott, original image in Lamy 95.)

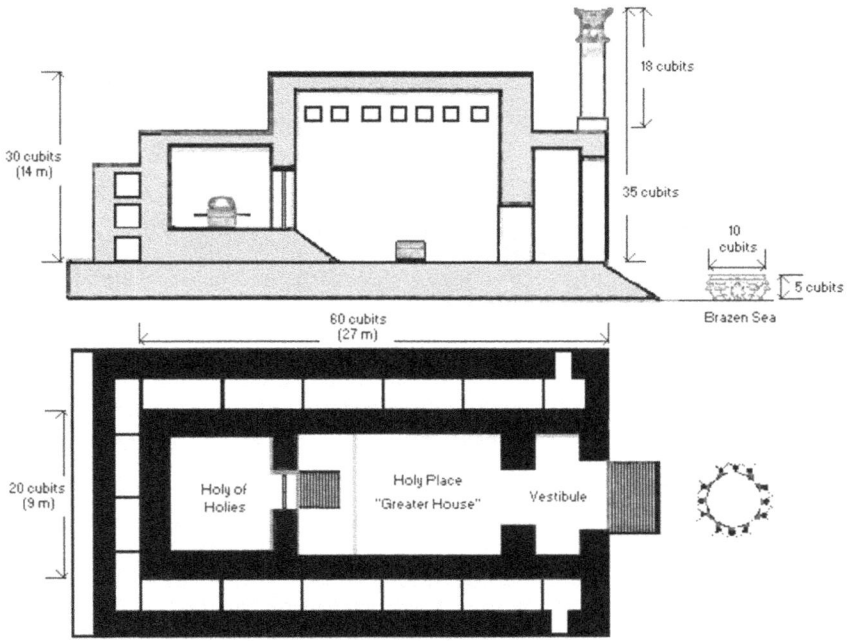

Figure 10. Hebrew Temple

The plan of the Hebrew temple is very similar in its cosmographic aspects to other traditions. One enters at the two pillars representing the twin aspects of nature: life and death, light and dark, heaven and earth. The priest disrobes at the veil signifying a new birth (and thus a death from the old existence). On the other side of the veil were two golden cherubim which guarded the Holy of Holies. These creatures are described in Ezekiel as guarding the four corners of the cosmos with their four faces and wings, analogous with the many sphinx images which guarded the netherworld. The priest would then enter the Oracle proper, where sat the ark of the covenant above a cave of waters (the *apsu*) and where rose the menorah (the Tree of Life) next to the Mercy Seat (the Throne in Heaven). These features follow a general cosmographic scheme as described in this thesis. (Image at wikipedia.com: Solomon's Temple; copyright free.)

This same imagery shows up again in the hieratic vision of John in Revelations. John sees the great city of God descending out of the heavens, much like an ark sailing through the celestial waters. The city is the home of the blessed dead who have achieved immortality. "And the city lieth foursquare, and the length is as large as the breadth; and he measured the city with the reed, twelve thousand furlongs. The length and the breadth and the height of it are equal" (Rev. 21.16). *Cosmos* and *polis* have become one within the image of the cube. There is also the cubic shrine of Islam, the *Kaaba*, whose name signifies the "throne of heaven," much like our ziggurat whose name means "House of the Foundation of Heaven and Earth." The cubic *Kaaba* is not built with seven tiers; however, it is circumambulated by its worshipers seven times once a year in a hieratic choral dance. To all these examples could be added the ancient Chinese notion that the world was constructed as a cube (Menon and Filon 161), and that the Hindu fire altar of Agni was also a cube, itself a representation of the Holy of Holies of the Hindu temple. Temple markers indicating the location of Hindu temples are also constructed as cubes (see Michell, 56-57, 66-67, 86-87 for examples).

We are hitting upon a very archaic tradition that is rooted across cultures in the ancient world. The temple was a model of the cosmos and founded the city. The city was an extension of the temple and was also a model of the cosmos. The rites associated with the temple dealt with journeying through the cosmos. The image or motif of an ark, often represented as a cube on the celestial waters, is repeated for the heavenly boat has to cross the waters to gain immortality. Osiris sits within his cubic shrine on his cubic throne embracing the deceased led to him by Horus. The Hebrew Holy of Holies was a cube with apparently seven chambers above it, it too contained an ark that sat upon the altar over and above the "well of souls." From Hindu temples to the Islamic Kaaba, the cube retains both cosmic form and function. This was especially true in ancient Babylon, where the measure of the floor space of Utnapishtim's ark is an *iku*, translated as a square acre, but the same terminology is employed for the celestial square in the sky (the constellation Pegasus). More important, it is applied to the name of the temple of Marduk in Babylon, where in a New Year's ritual it is named "Iku-star, Esagil, image of heaven and earth" (*HM* 297).

In another Christian tradition the cube motif is surprisingly embedded in a most familiar scene between Jesus and Peter. In ancient scripts words also had numeric values, as every letter in the Hebrew and Greek alphabets, for example, were associated with certain numbers. Reading biblical words through their numeric value is called *gematria*. David Fideler, in his book *Jesus Christ, Sun of God*, shows that when the Lord Jesus tells Peter, "Thou art Simon the son of Jona; thou shalt be called Cephas, which is by interpretation, A stone" (John 1.42), in gematria the word *Cephas* has a value of 729. This number turns out to be a cube (9X9X9), related to the solar year (276-79). The number 729 shows up in Plato's *Republic* and in one of Plutarch's Pythagorean essays in the same context (278-79). In the Clementine Homilies, Simon Peter is shown preaching the doctrine that God is the "center and heart of the cosmos," and His form is that of a "Cube" (276). So when the Lord tells Peter, "And I say also unto thee, That thou art Peter, and upon this rock I will build my church; and the gates of hell shall not prevail against it" (Matt. 16.18), the rock that is the stone upon which the church is built is analogous to the stone that is the leader of the Church—Peter, or Cephas, the cube.

Why does a cube show up across all these traditions? Anu, Osiris, Jehovah, Jesus, Allah, and Agni all provide a cube for their neophytes in some form or another. The answer to this question resides in the backbone of ancient, oral science: geometry, harmony, and astronomy. In the first place, the cube is only the square in three dimensions, and the geometry and mathematics of the square was part of oral philosophy. To understand this, a little geometry must be performed: "By definition the square is four equal straight lines joined at right angles. But a more important definition is that the square *is* the fact that any number, when multiplied by itself, is a square. Multiplication is symbolized by a cross, and this graphic symbol itself is an accurate definition of multiplication" (Lawlor 24). Two intersecting lines crossing at right angles is the first step in forming a square and a cube. This crossing of lines is of course the basis for the Greek word *tem,* which is the root for the word *temple.* Temples were literally a place of crossing inscribed within the square. Both Hindu and Egyptian temple ground-plans utilize the gnomonic expansion of the square (Lawlor 65-73). Squares, cubes, double-squares, golden rectangles, and triangles form the backbone of Egyptian architectural design.

The square appears to be the easiest geometric form for early builders to use. Many people have imposed "simplicity" or "primitive thinking" onto these early square designs. In the ancient world, a square was never just a square. One must understand that mathematics is not the study of number, but the study of relationships. To the ancient mind numeric relationships revealed the hidden laws of nature—their divine origins and manifestations. Numbers were not values, but philosophical relationships identifying macrocosmic fundamentals. The creation of a square was a sacred act and a repetition of the cosmogony. The Earth and Heaven were square (four points of the compass, four winds, four stars on the horizon forming the solstices and days of equinox, etc.). Forming a square meant crossing two parallel lines perpendicularly to two other parallel lines in equal measure creating a pair of opposites. To the oral mind this realization was a grand key—creation comes about through the interaction of opposites: light and dark, dry and wet, warp and weft, male and female, hot and cold, etc. Robert Lawlor explains:

> The principle can be transferred symbolically to the crossing of any contraries such as the crossing of the male and female which

gives birth to an individual being, or the crossing of warp and weft which gives birth to a cloth surface, or the crossing of darkness and light which gives birth to tangible, visible form. . . . So the crossing is an *action-principle* which the square perfectly represents. (Lawlor 24)

The temple, constructed on the square, was the place of creation because it was the place where opposites met. Only where the worlds of the above and below meet can the infinite vibrations of material phenomena emerge from the whole. The cube is the square given volume and to the oral mind represented the first whole from which all opposites emerged forming the infinite variety of creation.

Second, the cube represented the whole tone in the harmonic scale. Not only was every ancient temple built with song and dance, but often the numeric ratios of the song and dance were built within the temple. This harmonic philosophy was another grand key for oral minds interpreting the universe. Gordon Strachan explains, "For the ancient world—not just Pythagoras—all things were numbers and all numbers had correspondences in every area of knowledge. *The cube was symbolic of all the consonances in music because the ratios of all its sides are 1:1.* The ratio of 1:1 in music represents the note of unison or the full string-length and the full string-length contains within itself the vibrations of all the other musical intervals" (Strachan 22-23; italics mine). The cube thus becomes "the architectural equivalent of the full string-length—the fundamental—and was thus held to contain the whole of the overtone series, i.e., all the consonances of the cosmos" (Strachan 23). This relationship between the cube and the harmonic scale is also made known when one considers its structure: the cube has six faces, eight corners, and twelve edges. These numbers provide a simple harmonic correlation, "In other words, if twelve is the fundamental and six the octave, then eight is the dominant fifth" (Strachan 23).

This might seem a little much, but harmonic correspondences were constantly built within sacred structures. The Temple of Solomon was constructed upon the Holy of Holies, which was 20 cubits squared. Before this cubic shrine was a hall called the Holy Place; it was 40 cubits long by 30 cubits high. Resolved to their simplest numerical relationship, 4 X 3 X 2, and divided by each other in sequence, 1 to 2, 2 to 3, 3 to 4, these numbers become "the same as those which mark the musical intervals of the octave, the fifth, and the fourth, or, as the Greeks later called them, the diapason, the diapente, and the diatessaron" (Strachan 23-24). The dimensions of the temple thus contain the musical fundamental (the cube), the octave (the Holy Place of 40 cubits), and the musical fifth and fourth (the relation between the two). As Strachan observes, "These four notes . . . are known as the perfect consonances because they are invariable. They cannot be changed into the major or minor key and are therefore the very basis of harmony" (24). These numeric-harmonic relationships built into the Temple of Solomon are not original to the Hebrews, but borrowed from the cultural milieu of the oral, temple-building age. Egyptian sacred architecture dating centuries before the Hebrew temple resounds in similar harmonic and geometric relationships.

Finally, the cube represented a cosmology. The ark of Utnapishtim is a seven-storied cube. There were seven firmaments or heavens in ancient cosmology. This ark has become the cube of the heavenly squares. Square and cubic shrines were oriented to the four corners, the four winds, the four directions, and to the rising and setting sun on the days of solstice and equinox. In earlier cosmologies it appears the cube was also a symbol for the planet Saturn. This orb governed the firmaments and was the prime steward over the other planets. The cube becomes a profound symbol of the macrocosm manifesting in the microcosm. In geometry it represented creation out of opposition, as well as infinite progression. In harmony it was the whole tone from which all other tones emerge. In astronomy it was the structure aligned to the sacred corners of the world and modeled within the seven heavens. While these things may seem simplistic to us, in an oral age these were the fundamentals in the created order. By aligning square or cubic structures to certain stars on the horizon, and by creating them using song and dance while incorporating harmonic values, these people were encoding everything they knew about the universe in a scale model of the universe.

So what is Utnapishtim doing sailing through the cosmic waters in a great cube? By now we should recognize that Utnapishtim's ark is no simple boat. It has direct correspondences to an ancient cosmology of temple and cult. Nor are the flood waters any kind of terrestrial precipitations. The fact that Utnapishtim specifically states that he and his cubic ark had to "descend to the watery depths [to] dwell with my lord Ea" (11.42) shows us that we are not sailing on the "high seas" of earth. Our sojourners have left the realm of the microcosm and have traveled to the heavenly source of life. In this case, Utnapishtim descends to the bottom of the *apsu*, the underworld waters. This is a cosmic zone, for only in the "true underworld" were the secrets of life and death kept.

The Great Flood

Here is our connecting point between Gilgamesh seeking immortality and Utnapishtim's explanation in the Flood myth. As already stated, because the Flood story seems so out of place in the text, current scholarship believes that it is a late appendage added to the Gilgamesh cycle rather than an essential element in the story. The first indication that the Flood story might actually belong to the question Gilgamesh asks Utnapishtim, "How did you find eternal life?" comes from a remarkable parallel found in *The Egyptian Book of the Dead*. In chapter 175 of the Papyrus of Ani we find a spell entitled "Chapter for not dying again." Thematically, this happens to be the exact information Gilgamesh is looking for on his own journey, and represents the essential theme in the Babylonian epic. The text of this Egyptian funerary scene is unique, and the eminent Raymond O. Falkner provides this translation:

> O Thoth, what is it that has come about through the Children of Nut? They have made war, they have raised up tumult, they have done wrong, they have created rebellion, they have done slaughter, they have created imprisonment, they have reduced what was great to what is little in all that we have made; show greatness, O Thoth!—so says Atum. Shorten their years, cut short their months, because they have done hidden damage to all that you have made. I have your palette, O Thoth, I bring your inkspot to you; I am not among those who have done hidden damage, and none work harm on me.

> *Thus says Ani*: O Atum, how comes it that I travel to a desert which has no water and no air, and which is deep, dark, and unsearchable? . . . [*Atum Replies:*] You shall be for millions on millions of years, a lifetime of millions of years. I will dispatch the Elders and destroy all that I have made; the earth shall return to the Primordial Water, so the surging flood, as in its original state. But I will remain with Osiris, I will transform myself into something else, namely a serpent, without men knowing or the gods seeing. . . . I have made what appertains to his place in the Bark of Millions of Years, and Horus is firm on his throne to found his establishments. (*BD* Chpt 175)

This chapter "for not dying again" opens up to a grim scene. The people of the earth have become corrupt; everywhere they commit rebellion and slaughter. The population of the earth does "secret damage" or evil acts done in darkness and exacted on all living things. This is exactly the same world depicted in the Hebrew account, "And God saw that the wickedness of man was great in the earth, and that every imagination of the thoughts of his heart was only evil continually" (Gen. 6.5). In the biblical tale God vows to wipe the population out with a great flood. The wickedness of the world and God's vow to destroy it survives in Greece, where the same scene is portrayed in Homer's *Illiad*, "when Zeus flings down his pelting, punishing rains—up in arms, furious, storming against those men who brawl in the courts and render crooked judgements, men who throw all rights to the winds with no regard for the vengeful eyes of the gods—so all their rivers crest into flood spate, ravines overflowing cut the hilltops off into lonely islands" (16.457-63).

The world is in chaos. In the Egyptian papyri there is a sudden shift in scenery when the initiate named Ani speaks, declaring that he has descended to "a desert which has no water and no air, and which is deep, dark, and unsearchable." Clearly Ani has entered the underworld. In all myth systems the first encounter in the true underworld was one of disorienting blackness. It was often depicted as a place with no water, food, or air, and where sojourners sought desperately for a drink to parch their thirst (thus the presence of the spring or tavern). The transition between the wicked and tumultuous world and Ani's presence in the underworld is stark, due in part to the fragmentary nature of the original text. Yet the shift in narrative is parallel to the sudden descent into the underworld that Utnapishtim has also made.

Ani begs for assistance from Atum, who responds by declaring he will dispatch a group of beings called "the Elders," who will unleash a great flood upon the earth destroying the wicked. Atum declares that Osiris controls the desert of the underworld, and Horus has achieved victory on his throne established on an ark called the Bark of Millions of Years. From this ark and throne Horus organizes all of his establishments. Ani appears to be saved from his plight by the flood, Osiris, and Horus in his heavenly boat. This parade of images leads Ani into the underworld, where he learns the secrets of immortality and how not to die again.

It should be noted that various translations of chapter 175 obfuscate the flood imagery. In an early translation of the same passage done by E. A. Wallis Budge, the translator has interpreted the dialect of a key passage differently, "Let it be granted to me to pass on to the holy princes, for indeed, I have done away all the evil which I committed, from the time when this earth came into being from Nu, when it sprang from the watery abyss even as it was in the days of old" (Budge, *Book of the Dead* 563-4). Budge makes the waters that inundate the earth the waters of creation. Even though this translation also opens up to a world in chaos, ultimately the evil that is to be cleansed is not a wicked earth but the evil done by Ani himself, who has succeeded in purifying his soul. In this same translation Budge also notes that one of the leading Egyptologists of his day, E. Neville, interprets the same passage as an allusion to a flood story (567). In a more recent translation by Neil Parker, we read, "Truly I will [cast away?] all the harm I have done, when the earth comes from the Celestial Ocean, from the primeval rain as of old. I am time and Osiris; I have made my form as other things and serpents" (Parker, *Papyrus of Ani*, Chpt. 175).

In these latter translations Ani's soul is compared to the earth rising out of the primordial waters and the emphasis is on a new creation from the waters. In each case, however, the wicked world and the ark or boat belonging to Horus is present. The interpretation of this chapter is further complicated by the fact that in flood myths all around the world the flood and creation motifs become almost synonymous. The earth rises from the primordial waters. These cosmic waters are the matrix of creation, and the flood is simply the recreation of the world. These connections are fully present in the biblical text of Genesis, where the parallels between the original creation and Noah's flood are paramount. Earth is created by dividing the waters above from the waters below (1.6-7). The flood occurs when the waters above and the waters below commingle (7.11). Creation begins when the "Spirit of God moved upon the face of the waters" (1.1). Noah sends forth a dove upon the face of the waters (8. 9-11). Creation congeals when the first dry land emerges from the waters (1.9). The dove returns to Noah with an olive leaf, indicating that the first dry land has appeared from the waters (8.11). Vegetation, animals, and man appear on earth (1.11-12, 20-27). Noah lands and releases all manner of life upon the earth (8.16-19). God commands Adam and Eve to multiply and replenish the earth (1.28). God commands Noah to multiply and replenish the earth (9.1).

In this sense, the biblical flood is not a cataclysm story, it is a cosmogonic myth. The flood is a *new creation story*, that is to say, a creation of *a new heaven and a new earth*. The flood by water is to be succeeded by one of fire, which will again produce a new heaven and a new earth (the story of Lot and the destruction of Sodom and Gomorrah fulfill this requirement). The apocalypse aside, our narratives seem to hint at a different interpretation than the traditional and literal one.

Because world flood stories are connected with the creation of new life, it should not surprise us to find that a flood story might be connected with resurrection or immortality. In a Micronesia flood tale of the Pelew Islanders, it is said that a man ascended to the sky and stole a star. The gods were angry at this theft and came to the earth looking for the bandit. They appeared on earth as ordinary men, and went door to door begging for food and observing the virtue of humankind whilst looking for the one who stole their star. Of all the people on earth, only one woman invited them into her dwelling and gave them all that she had. Seeing the selfishness of the inhabitants of the earth, the gods vowed to destroy it by flood, and warned the women who had fed them to build an ark. Soon the flood came and everyone perished save the dame who survived in her boat. The rains lasted a long time, however, and the woman fell asleep in her vessel. When the gods came down to check on her they discovered that she had died. As this woman was under their protection, they summoned a female deity to enter into her corpse and bring her back to life. The woman was resurrected and she begot a new race of human beings.

In another flood story told by the aborigines of Victoria, the creator god Bunjil became angry at the wicked state of the people on the earth and caused a great flood to wipe out the population. All perished except for the worthy ones, who were given immortality by being turned into stars. In a Native American flood story of the Pima tribe, a great eagle descends from heaven and warns a medicine man that a flood is coming. He ignores the warning and all the people of the earth perish except for the son of the Creator God, who saves himself by floating on a ball of tree resin. The waters recede and this sole survivor lands at a mountain by a cave. Thinking the great eagle was at fault for the flood, the son of the Creator God climbed the mountain and killed the eagle in his nest. In this nest were the corpses of numerous people who had died. The son of the Creator God raised all the deceased back to life and repeopled the earth.

In the words of Joseph Campbell, "Only birth can conquer death—the birth, not of the old thing again, but of something new" (*Hero* 16). The world that is destroyed by the flood is born anew. In many instances, the people who are killed by the flood are given new life. Creation and resurrection are key themes in many flood stories. Perhaps the answer given by Utnapishtim to Gilgamesh is not so strange after all! The flood myth provides a paradigm of how the world dies and is created anew. If this can happen to the earth, then why not to the body and soul of man?

In all the myths cited there is another common denominator that is out of place in most scholarly discussions. Behind the terrestrial flood waters are a surge of cosmic motifs. Gilgamesh descends through an astral underworld. So does Ani. In the other stories the gods related to the flood come from the star world, or people are turned into stars. The eagle in the Native American example derives from a similar metaphor. In the Navaho ceremonial *Where the Two Came to Their Father*, there is a great flood during the creation pericope. The Crane People are told by Little Wind to build an ark wherein the progenitors of the race are saved. They sail through the flood waters to the Sky World. Breaching the cosmic veil they find themselves in the midst of a great, heavenly sea occupied by monsters. In this tale the earthly flood is the precipitation of a cosmic region that surrounds the earth. The ark is not only the vessel that braves the flood, but is the instrument that ascends into the heavens.

This last point is key. The ark in many flood myths is a heavenly vessel. The ark of Utnapishtim is a seven-storied cube that descends through the *apsu*. The ark of Osiris also sails through the starry netherworld. In Egyptian cosmography two images stand out: the celestial journey through the sky and the heavenly ship that delivers the dead. In Egyptian funerary texts the coffin of the deceased is treated as a boat, "towed by ropes through the waters of the cosmic sea, which is represented by drenching the coffin with water as it is pulled through narrow passages from one chamber or world to another" (*MJSP* 154). Furthermore, "in the Amduat, the name given throughout to the successive fields of the *duat* (Underworld) is simply *n.t*, meaning 'body of water,'" (*MJSP* 156). These underworld waters are always considered to reside in the heavens (*MJSP* 347), for the crews which tow the boat through the cosmic waters are none other than the Imperishable Stars (circumpolar stars) and the Unwearying Stars (the seven planets) (*MJSP* 154). This funerary ark sails through the star world; such imagery provides an interpretive context for those Caucasian mummies buried within their little boats in the Taklimakan Desert in China.

We find similar imagery employed in a slightly different context in ancient Britain. Many remnants of ancient Celtic lore are preserved in a fourteenth-century Middle Welsh manuscript entitled the *Book of Taliesin*. Edward Davies, in his book *Mythology and Rites of the British*

Druids, provides a myth-ritual interpretation of the text. In one poem we meet a figure identified as Gwyddnaw, the priest or hierophant whose name signifies the leader of the boat, "from *Gwydd*, *presence, attendance,* and *Naw*, an old term for a ship" (Davies 245). This is an appropriate title as Gwyddnaw must survive a raging flood within his ark. Significantly, Gwyddnaw is a Druid high priest who initiates neophytes seeking admittance into the Bardic mysteries. According to another poem, the one seeking the office of a Druid must reenact the journey of Gwyddnaw through the flood. The neophyte must enter a coracle or ark and literally sail across waters to an island where the initiation takes place. Our poem has our high priest declare "To the brave, to the magnanimous, to the amiable, to the generous, who boldly embarks, the ascending stone of the Bards will prove the harbor of life! It has asserted the praise of Heilyn, the mysterious impeller of the sky; and, till the doom shall its symbol be continued" (Davies 250). The initiate responds, "Though I love the strand, I dread the wave: great has been its violence–dismal the overwhelming stroke. Even to him who survives, it will be the subject of lamentation" (Davies 250). To which Gwddnaw assures, "It is a pleasant act, to wash on the bosom of the fair water. Though it fill the receptacle, it will not disturb the heart. . . . As for him who repented of his enterprise, the lofty (wave) has hurried the babbler far away to his death; but the brave, the magnanimous will find his compensation, in arriving safe at the stones. The conduct of the water will declare thy merit" (Davies 250-51).

The ark of the initiate lands upon a mooring place identified as a garden island but also described as "the ascending stone of the Bards." This harbor appears to be some sort of stairway, and the fact that this stairway is overseen by a figure who is "the mysterious impeller of the sky" should place us on notice that we are not talking about a literal staircase. During the crossing of the waters the unworthy perish, but the true initiate finds safety in his boat and is received "at the stones." These special stones are most likely a megalithic ring. The initiate is then embraced by the Druid high priest and conducted to his "father" and acknowledged a "complete Bard of the highest order" (Davies 252). The Bard is given a new name, *Dedwydd*, "one who has recovered intelligence" or one who "has been brought back into the presence" (Davies 252). A curious title as it is synonymous with the Greek Εποπτης, the name that describes the person who has been initiated into the greater mysteries of Eleusis.

The Druid priest Taliesin, who is credited to be the source of these poems, was identified as one who ruled in *Caer Sidi*. The word *Caer* represents a circular sanctuary, while the word *Sidi* signifies a celestial revolution (Davies 292-94). *Caer Sidi* was an earthly temple whose celestial archetype was the zodiac. There are many *Caers* listed in these poems. These circular temples were earthly henges corresponding to the many celestial islands found throughout Celtic mythology. The famous Stonehenge is no doubt a *Caer*, ritually and cosmographically linked to a series of other henges representing both a celestial and terrestrial landscape. Remarkably, these *Caer's* were also identified with "the great deep," not unlike the Mesopotamian *apsu*. In another poem from our Welsh manuscript entitled *The Spoils of the Deep*, the mythical King Arthur must sail to seven Caer's with seven companions to discover the secrets of the deep (Davies 513-26). All who descend into these waters perish save Arthur and his companions.

The initiation of the Druid Bard takes place inside a ship where he is protected against the flood waters. The boat of the dead has turned into the ship of the initiated living. Indeed, after his endowment the Druid is labeled "thrice born," referring to his three births: one from his natural parents; a second from Ceridwen, the goddess of rebirth, obtained in a previous ritual; and the third from his ark. It is not coincidence that the Orphic dead were also labeled "thrice born" relating to a similar ritual cosmography. Even the earliest Christian initiates were also known to be "thrice born," as they had to partake of three sacraments: a cup of water, a cup of milk, and a cup of wine (Eisler 64-66). Like the Druid priest, the Christian neophyte was born again through the waters of birth and baptism, through the milk of the mother goddess (which image was transferred into the bride of Christ or the Church), and through the wine or blood of the Savior. In late Christian liturgy the second sacrament has been eliminated, but the other two remain in the ordinances of baptism and communion. It also appears that the baptismal font is a late and literate mode of initiation. The baptismal font for Utnapishtim, Osiris, Orpheus, and the mystic Druid was an ark sailing through celestial waters.

The initiation of the Druid priest returns us to the themes of flood and rebirth. An initiation is a rebirth. That rebirth need not be from literal death. Clearly the Egyptians sought to overcome death and had to sail in their liturgical arks to do so. Yet rebirth might also be a new existence within a social order as represented by the Druid priests. Or it might be a rebirth into health and well-being as displayed on the Péretié Plaque. Or it might be the acceptance of kingship and power as in the Roman Forum. In all these cases the image of a boat or ark are prominently displayed. This could all be coincidence or we might have to admit that sometime by the mid to late second-millennium BCE (if not sooner) the mythologies of ark and flood had been co-opted into various liturgies of rebirth.

Many mythic figures find themselves in a boat braving the great deep. Dionysus is said to have been placed within an ark (Brown *Dionysiak* 80). In the Homeric hymn dedicated to this god, Dionysus first appears, as if out of nowhere, "by the sand of an empty sea, how it was far out, on a promontory, how he was like a young man, an adolescent" (Boer 9). Like many of our mystery saviors, Dionysus emerges from the sea. Remarkably, in one way or another, so does Gilgamesh, Sargon, Osiris, Noah, Moses, Cyrus, Tammuz, Karna, Oedipus, Adonis, Heracles, Jason, Perseus, Romulus, Siegfried, and Lohengrin, or the Knight of the Swan. All these heroes must board some form of ark and find a new life in a new land. The original primer for this mythic motif is the ritual journey through the celestial axis of the ancient cosmos where the secrets of the true heaven and the true earth were kept.

In the biblical Noah story astral motifs are conspicuously absent. Cosmic themes are always entwined with the temple cult. When the Jews returned from their Babylonian exile their temple tradition was lost. It appears that the Deuteronomists purged many temple themes from the existing Old Testament. There is a hint in the Noah story that suggests they were once there. After the flood, God promises he will never destroy the earth again by water. God seals his promise with a visible sign—he sets a bow in the sky (Gen. 9.13). Jewish and Christian traditions often interpret this bow as a rainbow. The Hebrew word for "bow" is *qesheth*, and while "rainbow" is one possible translation, the preferred meaning remains a "war bow" or "hunting bow."

How does hanging a war bow in the sky make any sense? In the Babylonian creation epic *Enuma Elish*, the thunder god Marduk slays Tiamat and fashions the world from her dead body. Not by coincidence, one of the weapons Marduk uses to slay Tiamat is a tempest and flood waters. These torrents seem to be summoned by Marduk's War Bow, which is also called a Flood Weapon. Marduk organizes the stars and constellations and as a symbol of his victory hangs his War Bow in his temple. This weapon had a stellar archetype and was actually the constellation of the Bow, found in Babylonian, Egyptian, and Chinese sky charts. In the Babylonian sky this constellation was the goddess Ishtar carrying a war bow. This constellation was comprised of the lower stars in Canis Major and the upper stars or the stern of the Argo. It is a remarkable coincidence that the sign of Marduk's victory over the chaos of nature should include the stars of a constellation that would become the celestial ark.

Always associated with the celestial Bow was its Arrow, or the star Sirius. In the Chinese constellations Sirius was the celestial jackal; this dog star was not an arrow but the target of the arrow. At the time these myths were written, this celestial arrow or target heliacally rose at summer solstice and set at winter solstice. This star was used to measure the solar and seasonal cycle. Of profoundest implications, however, is the fact that the Arrow star was given an epithet employed during the New Year's celebrations in Babylon: it was the star "that measures the depths of the sea" (White, *Babylonian* 54). Gavin White interprets this epithet in wholly terrestrial terms, remarking that in Mesopotamia the river levels rose or subsided in accordance to the rising and setting of this star. While true, it appears that it is the cosmic depths of an astral sea that is being measured.

Bow and arrow imagery connected to a flood shows up in other myths. In the Zoroastrian text *Avesta*, the star Sirius is called Tishtriya, which is compared to an arrow shot from an archer. This arrow causes a great body of water to flood, "Lake Vurukasha [surges] up . . ., the whole center surges up" (*HM* 215). The archer in this story predicts that as soon as he shoots his flood-causing arrow that he will perish. He lets the arrow fly halfway around the world while he dies and falls into pieces. The arrow strikes a tree so tall and grandiose that none other like it had been seen in the world. Clearly this is no mortal archer or wooden-stick arrow, nor should we think the great tree is balsam or fir. These motifs point our gaze upward, or perhaps downward, but not earthward.

In Greek myth we have a different scene with the same props. Heracles seeks to steal the cattle of Geryon during his tenth labor. He must sail to the island of Erytheia, which is said to lie near the Ocean stream at the very end of the world. We are no longer on earth, and to prove the point, Heracles must travel to this Ocean stream by sailing on a boat of bronze provided by Helios, the sun god. In some versions of this story Heracles uses his lion garment as a sail. During his journey he sets up his famous Pillars of Heracles traditionally associated with the Strait of Gibraltar. As explained in the next chapter, these famed pillars are also associated with the *axis-mundi* and the gates to the underworld. This is an appropriate image, for as Robert Graves notes, "The bronze urn in which Heracles sailed to Erytheia was an appropriate vessel for a visit to the Island of Death" (459). Graves compares the boat, the garment-sail, and the destination at the end of the world to none other than the underworld journey of Gilgamesh, where much of the same imagery occurs (459). Most important, as Heracles nears his destination he is suddenly beset by flood waters sent by Oceanos. Heracles pulls out his bow, threads his arrow, and threatens the water god until the waters recede.

In the Hindu epic *Ramayana,* the hero Rama must cross an impassable sea, also said to be near the end of the world, in order to save his wife Sita. There is no plausible way to make the crossing, however, and in a strategic move Rama commands his army to throw stones and mountains into the ocean to form a dike. It seems to no avail: no matter how many mountainsides are thrown into the sea, no rock or land ever appears. In anger, Rama pulls his bow and arrow and threatens to shoot the unforgiving sea. Suddenly, a lady appears from the waters and warns Rama that there exists a hole in the ocean leading to the underworld containing the Waters of Life (*HM* 214). Understanding that this hole is swallowing all of his mountains, Rama moves his dike elsewhere and is able to make the passage.

Finally, the Chinese constellation of the bow was represented by the celestial archer Houyi. There were ten sun birds causing havoc on earth, and Houyi shot nine of them out of the sky (Ninurta, a Babylonian deity also associated with the arrow star, shoots the Anzu-bird out of the sky). As punishment for this deed the gods banished the archer and stripped him of his immortality. On earth, Houyi encounters a great flood ushered by the water god. Houyi pulls his bow and shoots his arrow, piercing the god and causing him to flee. Houyi marries the water god's daughter, and together each of them spend their days looking for the elixir of immortality so that together they may re-ascend into the heavens.

It is essential to point out that all these bow and flood myths have one thing in common: the theme of rebirth. In the Zoroastrian example, the bow is fired from a dying archer, but the arrow hits the mythical Tree of Life. In the Greek tale, Heracles is sailing to an island across an impassable sea seeking the secrets of life in order to overcome death. In the Hindu example, the hole in the ocean led to the Waters of Life. In the Chinese myth, only after our hero marries the daughter of the flood is he able to seek out the elixir of immortality.

In the Bible, the bow that is hung in the sky is a promise that the Flood will not happen again. Somehow, this celestial bow is consonant with the rise and fall of waters. Perhaps the biblical account has borrowed the motif without understanding its origin? Further clues in Israelite temple tradition suggest otherwise. In one Jewish legend, the temple altar within the sacred cube was directly linked to the cosmic waters. As L. Ginzberg records in *The Legends of the Jews*, "When David was digging the foundations of the Temple, a shard was found at a depth of 1500 cubits. David was about to lift it when the shard exclaimed: 'Thou canst not do it.' 'Why not?' asked David. 'Because I rest upon the abyss.' 'Since when?' 'Since the hour in which the voice of God was heard to utter the words from Sinai, 'I am the Lord, your God,' causing the world to quake and sink into the Abyss. I lie here to cover the abyss'" (cited in *HM* 220). According to this tradition, when one of David's assistants wrote the name of God on the shard and threw it over the Abyss, the flood waters sank so deeply that David feared the Earth would dry up. To counteract the lowering of the abysmal waters David performed a ritual called the "Songs of Ascents" to bring the waters up again (*HM* 220).

In other traditions of the Hebrew temple, the edifice was built upon a particular rock called the "Foundation Stone." In Hebrew this stone was named *Even ha-Shetiyyah*, a title deriving from a verb meaning "to be settled, satisfied; to drink; to fix the warp, to lay the foundations of" (*HM* 220). The Foundation Stone sat over the Abyss, and the imagery of the cedar altar holding the ark over a deep well or chasm of water within the cubic Holy of Holies draws this entire complex of motifs together. The temple appears not only to be built in accordance with the rising and setting sun and seasons, and marked off by the days of solstice and equinox, but it also seems to be built upon a cosmic plumb line which orders all of creation. The "line" is the celestial axis, while the "plumb" is the Foundation Stone that holds back the flood waters and maintains equilibrium.

The Hebrew temple is not the only structure to be built in this manner. In Lucian's description of the temple in Hierapolis we find very similar imagery. The temple was dedicated to none other than the Greek Deucalion, the survivor of the Great Flood. Lucian reports:

> They say that in their land a great chasm was formed and it took in all the water. When this happened, Deucalion set up altars and built over the chasm a temple sacred to Hera. I myself saw the chasm. It is beneath the temple and quite small. . . . As a symbol of this story they do this: Twice each year water from the sea is carried to the temple. Not only priests, but the whole of Syria and Arabia brings it and from beyond the Euphrates many men come to the sea and all bring water. First they pour it out in the temple. Afterwards it goes down into the chasm, and the chasm, though small, takes in a great deal of water. In doing these things they claim that Deucalion established this custom in the sanctuary as a memorial both of the disaster and of the divine favor. Such is their traditional account about the sanctuary. (Attbridge and Oden trans. 21)

Like the chasm and the shard that David found, the temple of Deucalion also has a crevice that must be fed by liturgical waters. The crevice is specifically under the temple and by the altars. It is directly associated with the Flood, and the ordinances performed there help regulate the waters. Is this a coincidence? Another stark parallel will dispel all notions of chance; in the interior of the cubic Kaaba, in pre-Islamic times, there was a well that was capped by a stone. This stone was a representation of the pre-Islamic god Hubal. This god was said to stop the waters of the abyss from rising. The statue itself was also in the form of a cube (*HM* 221).

We now have a massive web of mythological motifs that are all associated with each other: cubes, arks, temples, foundation stones, cubic stones, wells, chasms, flood waters, stars, measurements, the underworld, resurrection, initiations, immortal beings, bows, arrows, and rivers. These images are bricks of an ancient cultic mosaic whose scattered remnants suggest that all of our scholarly interpretations of the Great Flood in myth have been woefully lacking. If the flood myths around the world originate from a massive geological event in some high off time in history, so be it. The *Epic of Gilgamesh* and chapter 175 of the Egyptian *Book of the Dead* suggest that at some point the flood story had been co-opted into a cultic cosmography well beyond terrestrial affairs. The flood myth had been incorporated into a memory theater associated with initiation into the next world. The underworld becomes an interpretive key. The constellation of the Bow belongs in the astral underworld. Sirius is said to measure "the depths of the sea." This sea is the underworld abyss kept at bay by the Foundation Stone, upon which the temple is constructed. The ark often sails through the astral underworld, and its occupants are often reborn in the star world or by the help of agents from the star world. Throughout multiple traditions the flood myth is clearly connected to the celestial archetype of resurrection.

If the underworld is an interpretive key, the celestial archetype behind the flood myth is the master key. For oral minds certain stars possessed the source and vitality of life processes manifest on earth. From whence did earthly floods come? As already noted, in Egypt, when the star Sirius (the Arrow of the Bow) rose heliacally at summer solstice the Nile began to flood. In Babylon, however, when the Arrow star rose at summer solstice the river waters contracted. On the other hand, when the Arrow star set at winter solstice the river waters rose. This heaven-earth correspondence was duly noted; thus, Sirius really was "the star that measures the sea." As it rose and set with the sun, the earthly waters ebbed and flowed. An arrow only receives its power of flight from a bow. Even as Sirius marked the rising and falling of earthly waters, the power behind it, by analogy, must have been the true Well of Life—the source of all life-giving waters on earth. This became what the Babylonians called the *apsu*—the great cosmic deep that held the seeds of life.

The idea of flood waters being the archetypal signification for life and death is revealed in yet another correspondence that is hard to miss. As a mother gives birth her amniotic sac ruptures and her "water breaks." That is, waters gush from her birth canal signaling that the baby is ready to be born. The creation of new human life follows a remarkable pattern: the infant resides in the darkness of the womb where it grows and comes alive; it develops within an amniotic membrane filled with waters; it is born through a perilous passage from dark to light at the breaking of the waters; many do not survive. In underworld myths around the globe the heroes follow this pattern, often backwards. They do not begin at birth but at death. They leave the world of daylight and enter the dark underworld. The passageway is often narrow and dangerous. The metaphor of sailing across waters, paying a ferryman to cross waters, or meeting an impassable sea is also a universal motif. In other words, the journey of the hero who seeks the secrets of life is the mirror image of a literal human birth.

In both cases the key element to find new life resides at the source—the Waters of Life. Scholars insist that the Flood pericope in the Gilgamesh epic is extraneous. There are enough clues within the text and within other comparative traditions to fully contradict this assessment. The Flood myth was the correct answer after all. The celestial archetype of the flood waters was the *apsu*, regulated by the arrow of the bow, Sirius, that flew over the arch of heaven marking the ebb and flow of both earthly waters and agricultural cycles. The archetype of death was the underworld; only a lucky few appear to be able to descend to its deepest island where the secrets of rebirth are kept. The archetype of the ark is the celestial journey itself, remodeled by temples, ziggurats, and henges and reenacted through sacred rituals and initiations. One obtains immortality by entering the temple precinct and climbing its seven stairways with their attendant gates upon the ziggurat. This cubic-temple space is the cosmic mountain which both reaches the apex of the heavens as well as the very depths of hell, for it is the "House of the Foundation of Heaven and Earth." It is also an ark, constructed as the epic tells us, by the labor and talent of an entire civilization as it founds its cities and its rites. Utnapishtim is the one who leads the construction project, and thus is the one who founds civilization in the golden age. It is no surprise to read that after Gilgamesh's journey through the underworld, he does the very same thing: he re-institutes the age-old rites even as he restores the age-old temples and founds the city of Uruk. Like the neophyte seeking the Bardic mysteries, Gilgamesh has repeated what Utnapishtim has done. He has not obtained immortality, but he has traveled to the heavenly source where life and death are maintained. This journey gave him his celestial mandate to rule. It appears that not only is the ark or flood extraneous, they are central to the cultus from which the epic was written.

Gilgamesh Goes Home

Returning to the narrative of the Babylonian epic, we discover that Utnapishtim and his wife survive the flood; surprisingly, the entire retinue aboard the ark are never mentioned again. The god of heaven, Enlil, descends and blesses the married pair, saying, "Hitherto Utnapishtim has been a human being, now Utnapishtim and his wife shall become like us gods. Utnapishtim shall dwell far distant at the source of the rivers" (11.206-07). In this declaration we learn the source of Utnapishtim's title, the Distant One. Utnapishtim is the one who descends in an ark through the *apsu* at a place called "the source of the rivers" or "confluence of the rivers." We have already mentioned that these epithets are related to Eridu, the city of the underworld god Ea, or Enki. This city had a celestial analog in the southern star Canopus. This star belongs to the Bow constellation, but also is the steering oar of the celestial Argo or heavenly boat. One senses that the true home of Utnapishtim is in the realm of Canopus. This southern star may also turn out to be the stone at the end of the celestial plumb line. Perhaps this star was used to measure the celestial waters? Perhaps it was associated with the "zero point" in a choral dance? Ironically, its true significance lies submerged in the forgotten waters of history.

Utnapishtim finishes his tale and then challenges Gilgamesh with a task: he must stay awake for seven days to see if he is capable of eternal life. Gilgamesh immediately falls asleep and fails the challenge. This failure addresses one of the main themes of the epic; for Gilgamesh, mountainous giants and cosmic bulls are relatively easy obstacles, but the requirements of mortality, sleep and bread (both images used in this scene) are inescapable. Utnapishtim informs Gilgamesh that he has failed his simple challenge and that he must return to Uruk without the essential key to eternal life. For the third time, however, a female intervenes. The wife of Utnapishtim steps forward and gives Gilgamesh another secret associated with eternal life using the same words her husband employed before revealing the Flood story, "I will reveal to you, O Gilgamesh, a secret matter, and a mystery of the gods I will tell you" (11.285-86). She reveals the location of an unusual plant that grows at the bottom of the underworld sea and is capable of restoring one's youth. Immediately Gilgamesh drops his gear, ties stones to his feet, and plunges into the waters, where he obtains this plant of immortality. On his return trip home, however, he lies the plant down near a pond where a serpent steals it, shedding its skin as it escapes. Gilgamesh weeps and is resigned to his own mortality.

The epic has finished. As we look back we find a network of curious details that are of great interest to this thesis. Everywhere celestial imagery abounds. The giant Humbaba or Huwawa, with his seven radiances living atop seven mountains, is synthesized with a great palm tree which "pierces the sky." The fifty companions aid our heroes and sparkle in heaven. The Bull of Heaven descends from the sky and has his rear leg removed. The scorpion gate, the Holy Mountain, and the netherworld garden all have celestial and cultic analogs. There is also a curious bar that serves special drinks, a vast sea requiring a ferryman, and a cubic ark that shares its imagery with worldwide temples. The entire epic takes place within the context of founding the city of Uruk and reestablishing the temples and rites of the city from before the Flood. The flood waters may be terrestrial, perhaps even celestial, but in the context of the epic, it appears that the flood waters resolve into the starry deep, which must be trekked through in order to find whatever secrets the gods have preserved in their true heaven. Whatever the divine end of Gilgamesh, he has become the ideal political leader and culture hero who has measured earth and sky and has brought the celestial order upon the earth.

CHAPTER 7

THE LABORS OF HERACLES

According to traditional accounts, Heracles was the offspring of the immortal Zeus and the mortal Alcmene. Alcmene was the daughter of Electryon, king of Mycenae. She married the mortal Amphitryon and both fled to the Greek Thebes, where they raised an army and defeated the Teleboans and Taphians. While Amphitryon was away at battle, Zeus descended from heaven, took on him the guise of Amphitryon, and, deceiving Alcmene, lay with her. She conceived twins, the demigod Heracles and his mortal brother Iphicles.

In the Theban tradition, when Alcmene realized she had been seduced by Zeus, fearing the wrath of Hera she took Heracles out of the city and laid him bare on a hillside to perish. Zeus, seeing this, took his wife Hera for a stroll, and, walking by the infant, pointed him out. Zeus marveled at how handsome he was and asked Hera if she would nourish him from her breast. Hera agreed, but the moment the infant latched on to Hera he suckled with such great force that Hera flung him away, causing her breast milk to spray across the sky and form the Milky Way. In a variant of the telling, because Heracles had suckled the milk of Hera he became immortal.

Heracles grew in strength and skill. He married Megara, the daughter of the Theban king. He and Megara had several children. Heracles became a ruthless conqueror and defeated all the enemies of Thebes. When the Euboeans attacked Thebes in an act of vengeance, Heracles captured the invading king and tied him to two colts, who pulled his body apart. Heracles then laid the torn body beside a river, leaving the king unburied. This cruel action spread fear throughout Greece. Hera became angry with Heracles as a result and invoked her vengeance upon him (and upon Zeus's dalliance) by filling Heracles with madness. Heracles, under the spell of Hera, slew six of his children and flung their bodies into a fire. He also slew two sons of his mortal brother Iphicles.

Heracles eventually recovered from his insanity and, realizing his horrific deeds, went to Delphi to enquire how he could atone for his sins. The oracle told him that if he went to Tiryns and served King Eurystheus for twelve years he would not only be forgiven but would also obtain immortality. Agreeing, Heracles went to Tiryns and bowed to Eurystheus, who in turn commanded Heracles to perform twelve impossible labors. Heracles accepted the king's command and set out to accomplish his orders. Heracles twelve labors were: (1) defeat the Nemean Lion, (2) defeat the Lernaean Hydra, (3) capture the Ceryneian Hind, (4) defeat the Erymanthian Boar, (5) clean the Augean stables, (6) capture the Stymphalian Birds, (7) conquer the Cretan Bull, (8) harness the Mares of Diomedes, (9) acquire the Belt of Hippolyta, (10) steal the Cattle of Geryon, (11) obtain the Apples of the Hesperides, and (12) bring up Cerberus from the underworld.

Heracles was the greatest of Greek heroes, and depictions of his exploits are repeatedly found on Greek vase paintings and art. He was known from the earliest times in Greece, and the numerous mythic motifs about our hero inform us that there lies a far greater context behind his story. There were also numerous and sometimes competing traditions about this Greek figure. Diodorus Siculus identified three separate heroes named Heracles. Servius claimed that there were four separate Heracles, Cicero counted six, and Varro identified forty-four (Smith 401). Herodotus tells us that the original Heracles hailed from Egypt and says that according to the Egyptian tradition, Heracles was one of twelve deities descended from the original eight gods who created the universe

(2.43-5). Diodorus claimed that when Osiris went to accomplish his labors he left the government of Egypt in the hands of this primordial Heracles (Smith 401). Remarkably, Pausanias, Tacitus, and Macrobius all confirm that Heracles hailed from Egypt (Smith 401).

To say the original Heracles is Egyptian entirely misses the point. Herodotus also travels to Phoenicia, where he discovers a temple dedicated to the Phoenician Heracles and inside which were two curious pillars, one made of gold and the other of emerald (2.44). Herodotus discovered a similar temple in Tyre dedicated to the Thasian Heracles (2.44). Different sources show that there was a Heracles figure hailing from Crete, Carthage, Libya, India, and even from amongst the Germanic Celts (Smith 401). Several Greek myths derive from the famous labors of Heracles. Theseus performs a series of labors in order to inherit kingship and was known as the Athenian Heracles, Bellerophon was the Corinthian Heracles, and Alcathous was the Megarian Heracles (Nilsson 211-3). Even the Israelites had a Heracles figure in the Biblical Samson.

Details within the myth show the Greeks did not create the story of Heracles—they inherited it. Heracles' mortal mother's name is Mycenaean. King Eurystheus is also Mycenaean, and the kingdom to which he belongs is a Mycenaean city. The localized traditions of our hero in Tiryns descend from Mycenaean times, and the first five labors Heracles performs all take place in the northeastern Peloponnese. The seventh labor, capturing the Cretan Bull, originates in either Mycenaean or even Minoan times (Nilsson 217). In other words, the entire cycle attributed to Heracles is not Greek. Martin P. Nilsson writes, "This idea is pre-Greek. The inference to be drawn from this fact is that a cycle of Labors was already formed and provided with its natural and logical end in the Mycenaean age" (214).

If the Egyptian traditions prevail, then the cycle of labors belonging to Heracles is also not of Mycenaean origin. On this point Robert Graves provides a profound insight:

It may be assumed that the central story of Heracles was an early variant of the Babylonian Gilgamesh epic—which reached Greece by way of Phoenicia. Gilgamesh has Enkidu for his beloved comrade, Heracles has Iolaus. Gilgamesh is undone by his love for the goddess Ishtar, Heracles by his love for Deianeira. Both are of divine parentage. Both harrow Hell. Both kill lions and overcome divine bulls; and when sailing to the Western Isle Heracles, like Gilgamesh, uses his garment for a sail. Heracles finds the magic herb of immortality as Gilgamesh does, and is similarly connected with the progress of the sun around the zodiac. (413-4)

Heracles is a Greek Gilgamesh, and the parallels are too numerous to be coincidental. Even the madness of Heracles coincides with the untamed Gilgamesh, who ravishes women and enslaves men. It appears that the temerity of the wild and ferocious hero who must be civilized and endowed with a higher purpose and calling is age old.

Nor should we believe that the origin of the story is Babylonian, as Egypt too had a similar figure from very early times. In fact, we should not believe that the Heracles myth is a story at all, for a story implies a campfire fairytale, and Heracles is not Jack the Giant Slayer. Our hero is towering Gilgamesh, founder of rites and cities, measurer of heaven and earth, king and representative of the celestial realm. Is it coincidental that the mythical Heracles of Egypt was analogized with the first Egyptian king? The fact that we find several of the labors of Heracles engraved on thrones and in royal shrines throughout ancient Greece reveals that these labors were a "ritual marriage-task drama, as a preliminary to coronation, [and were] performed over a wide area" (Graves 473). Heracles is not a figure upon which a story has been attached, rather, the labors of Heracles is a ritual, cosmographic cycle of kingship and initiation from which only narrative fragments remain.

The twelve labors of Heracles were not permanently set. The series of labors as we have them are a late accretion, and a different cycle of tasks were performed and applied to a similar, cultic-ritual cycle in different cities and countries. In all these cases these labors deal with celestial archetypes. Graves mentions that the acts of the Greek hero coincide with the sun moving through the zodiac, and proposes that the Gilgamesh cycle has a similar context within Babylonian astrology. This once popular interpretation has fallen out of favor among scholars as the labors do not line up with the zodiac constellations without a great deal of "fixing." It cannot be denied that the imagery of this myth is astral and follows the themes so far presented. Heracles creates the Milky Way. He is promised immortality through initiation, and in order to acquire it he has to descend into the celestial underworld. The celestial motifs only increase within the details of the story.

When Heracles sets out to perform the first of his tasks, he journeys to Mount Helicon to the city of Thepiae, ruled by King Thespius. Thespius has fifty daughters, and he offers all fifty to Heracles, who sleeps with them and produces fifty sons. It is a strange motif, as Heracles starts his tasks and is given fifty helpers. In this context these helpers are given as wives. The traditional Robert Graves cannot help but connect this motif with ritual imagery, calling this group of fifty a "college of priestesses serving the Moon-goddess, to whom the lion-pelted sacred king had access once a year during their erotic orgies" (420). The modern term *orgy* is highly sexual, but the original meaning of the word signified a ritual dance. The Maenads or Bacchantes were the women priestesses who swirled and swooned in a dancing ecstasy during the rites of Dionysus. As J. E. Harrison writes in her *Epilogemena*, many Mediterranean cults had this dancing band of priests or priestesses: "Greece had not only Satyrs, it had also Kouretes, Korybantes, Titanes, Seilenoi, Bacchoi, Rome had its dancing priests, its Salii, far off India had its dancing Maruts, half daimon half man" (21). In the *Hymn of the Kouretes* it is Zeus that is depicted as the chief dancer, "head of the initiate band" (32). It appears that some of these orgies (ritual dancing) did turn into real orgies (sexual acts).

The origin of this college of priestesses, however, descends from the "knowers of the way" who "sparkle in the sky." The fact that Graves connects the fifty daughters of Thespius with the moon is interesting. A chorus of fifty could perform a ritual dance reenacting the phases and cycles of the moon through the stars. In some myth systems, the moon was the starting point for the soul's celestial journey through the sky. The moon was also associated with the cycles of birth, life, and death. Moon priestesses may be the best companions for a journey through the astral underworld where one is seeking resurrection. The imagery of their mating with Heracles may not be taken literally.

Still, the number and rite belong together, so when Heracles performs his second labor, he must travel to Lerna, where resides a sacred temple built to Demeter and Dionysus. This temple precinct was said to be built and dedicated by the fifty Danaids: "Every year, secret nocturnal rites are held at Lerna in honor of Dionysus, who descended to Tartarus at this point when he went to fetch Semele; and, not far off, the Mysteries of Lernaean Demeter are celebrated in an enclosure which marks the place where Hades and Persephone also descended to Tartarus" (Graves 430). Robert Graves also compares the fifty Danaids to a "college of priestesses" overseeing the temple, and that in one tradition the Hydra itself had fifty heads (Graves 431). The Hydra is also a constellation in the sky belonging to the underworld. The implication is this: the Lernaean Hydra was a dance performed in the temple cult of Demeter and Dionysus where one ritually overcame obstacles or discovered "the way" through the celestial world.

Within the geographic locations of the labors of Heracles there are at least six places where special temples were built with analogical access to the underworld. The Nemean grove with its two-mouthed cave is such a place, and the temple of Demeter and Dionysus in Lerna is another. In the third labor, Heracles travels to Mount Artemisium, where a sacred shrine to Artemis was built. The chase of the Hind takes Heracles to the land of the Hyperboreans, where the mysteries of life and death were ritually enacted: "According to Pollux, Heracles was called Melon ('of apples'), because apples were offered to him, presumably in recognition of his wisdom; but such wisdom came only with death, and his pursuit of the hind, like his visit to the Garden of the Hesperides, was really a journey to the Celtic Paradise" (Graves 433). Heracles journeys to Mount Erymanthus during his fourth labor, where he finds the cave of Pholus. In this cave Heracles discovers a wine jar left by Dionysus, god of the mysteries of the afterlife. The seventh labor has Heracles combating the Cretan Bull, a mytheme shared in the labors of Theseus and Jason. Yet this capturing of the bull was central to the Dionysian mysteries (Graves 442). Heracles' tenth labor takes him to Lusitania, "the most westerly point of the world," where lays a sacred, pillared, temple to Heracles (Graves 454), while his destination in Erytheia appears to be the underworld "by the Ocean stream."

So it is that the famous Pillars of Heracles, thought to be two rock promontories flanking the Straits of Gibraltar, originally belonged to the temple and cult of Heracles. Strabo is instructive on this point, as he delineates a sort of confusion over the exact location of the pillars in question, remarking that Pindar named the Symplegades at the entrance to the underworld as those pillars (Hamilton, trans. 256). Strabo also mentions that Posidonius believed them to be the brass pillars found in the temple of Heracles at Gades (Hamilton, trans. 256). Charles F. Herberger, in his fascinating study entitled *The Thread of Ariadne*, reveals the original context of those pillars: "The earliest version of an iconographic motif which might be called the Pillars of Hercules was probably two sacred trees—the olive and the laurel, each representative of a different aspect of creative fertility—standing before an open-air shrine dedicated to Herakles and his twin, Talos" (111-12).

The pillars are a representation of the mortal and immortal realms, and the fact that many of our celestial heros have a twin companion (Gilgamesh-Enkidu, Heracles-Iphicles, Jacob-Esau, Castor-Pollux, etc.) is a reflection of the duality of existence and the final fate of the soul. The twin pillars in the Israelite temple represented the Tree of Life and the Tree of Knowledge of Good and Evil. One could also imagine them as representations of the top and bottom of the heavenly axis where "Life" and "Knowledge" were found. According to Herberger, the brass pillars in the temple of Heracles are linked to all these associations. These pillars were symbolic of the brazen steps at the threshold of the underworld:

> The true Pillars of Hercules were not the dumb stone columns of a particular local sanctuary dedicated to Hercules any more than they were the heights at the Straits of Gibraltar, although both of these errors are not without a limited truth. As it has been shown, the true Pillars of Hercules are in essence an emblem or artistic image with multiple connotations. But above all—or rather transcending all—they represent the gates of the world which lies beyond death. It is true that the Elysian Fields or Garden of the Hesperides or Island of Ariadne—call it what you will—was, as tradition said, beyond the Pillars of Hercules, but not on a physically existing island beyond the Straits of Gibraltar, which was considered the boundary of the known world in classical times. The Pillars of Hercules marked the gate to the Labyrinth, the gate to death, and the gate to life after death. (114-15)

It is not coincidence that many of the sacred shrines localized in the labors of Heracles dealt with the mysteries of Dionysus. Dionysus is known as the god of wine, but in the Dionysian mysteries he was the god of transformation and transcendence for the dead. The wine of Dionysus was a symbol of the miraculous metamorphoses that occurred in the making of liquid into liquor. The mysteries of Dionysus appear to have promised immortality via a ritual journey through the cosmic axis. An Orphic fragment describes the specialized garment initiates adorned during the rites of the Dionysian mysteries:

> To accomplish all these things, clad in a sacred dress
> The body of God, a representation of the bright-rayed Helios,
> Let the worshiper first throw around him a crimson robe
> Like flowing rays resembling fire.
> Moreover from above the broad all-variegated skin of a wild fawn
> Thickly spotted should hang down from the right shoulder,
> A representation of the wondrously-wrought stars and of the vault of heaven.
> And then over the fawn-skin a golden belt should be thrown,
> All-gleaming, to wear around the breast, a mighty sign
> That immediately from the end of the earth the Beaming-one springing up
> Darts his golden rays on the flowing of ocean,
> The splendor is unspeakable, and mixed with the water
> Revolving it sparkles with whirling motion circularly
> Before God, and then the girdle under the unmeasured breast
> Appears as a circle of ocean, a mighty wonder to behold. (Brown, *Dionysiak* 48)

The initiate is dressed as the god Helios. His deer skin represents the stars and the celestial vault. His golden belt is the ray of sun upon the celestial waters that encircle the cosmic environs of the earth. The initiate whirls and spins in a choral dance mimicking the spinning stars. In fact, it has long been suggested that the procession along the Sacred Way at Eleusis on which the initiates tread towards the mystery temple was itself a representation of the Milky Way, which, in the night sky of autumn was mirrored overhead. The initiates themselves represent the planets moving against the background of stars (Harrison, *Cauldron* 124).

On two cult objects, the Torre Nova Sarcophagus and the Lovatelli Urn, Herakles is shown with his head completely covered and being initiated into the mysteries (Kerényi 38-39). At the end of these mysteries the initiates appear in the dress of a god. It is not coincidental that of all the Greek heroes, Heracles is the only one given immortality on Olympus. Other heroes are blessed with eternal life in the Elysian Fields, but Heracles is given godhood through apotheosis (Nilsson 204).

The Labors of Heracles are narrative allegories to ritual initiations through the heavenly underworld. This conclusion is no idle speculation, and the first labor turns out to be the master key that unties the entire Gordian Knot of this myth complex. Heracles finds himself at the gate of the underworld guarded by the Nemean Lion. Robert Graves recounts one tradition where this fierce, magical creature was born of Selene (a Moon goddess), who bore and dropped it "to earth on Mount Tretus near Nemea, beside a two-mouthed cave" (426). Heracles must find the Nemean Lion, a difficult task as the lion has slain all who have come close to its domain. Our Greek hero is forced to ask Apesantus directions. Ironically, Apesantus is a ghost; he was slain by the Nemean Lion (427).

The connection between the Nemean Lion standing at a two-mouthed cave and the underworld is certain. The cave is the give-away. Just such a cave is described by Homer in the *Odyssey*, where Odysseus lands at Ithaca and finds a curious passageway:

At the harbor's head a branching olive stands with a welcome cave nearby it, dank with sea-mist, sacred to nymphs of the springs we call Naiads. There are mixing-bowls inside and double-handled jars, crafted of stone, and bees store up their honey in the hollows.

There are long stone looms as well, where the nymphs weave out
their webs from clouds of sea-blue wool—a marvelous sight—and
a wellspring flows forever. The cave has two ways in, one facing
the North Wind, a pathway down for mortals; the other facing the
South, belongs to the gods, no man may go that way. . . . It is the
path for all the deathless powers. (13.115-26)

The cave is a passage to the next world with two roads: one for mortals and the other for immortal gods. It is overseen by sea-nymphs called
Naiads or Nereids, who traditionally also number fifty. There are mixing bowls and double-handled jars, stone looms and sea-blue wool, and
two more curious details, a fount of living water and hollows of honey.
These details are unexplained, but they all hail from temple imagery. The
fount of living water is typical in the space of the *temenos*, where a well or
spring is often incorporated into the design signifying the waters of life
or the well waters of the underworld (i.e., the *apsu*).

Hollows of honey may refer to the honey cakes initiates used in the
mysteries. In Aeneas's odyssey through the underworld he is confronted
by the howling canine Cerberus, who bars progression of the netherworld
trek. The guide pulls out "sleeping drugs tucked in a ball of crumbs and
honey" and tosses it to the dog, who consumes it and then falls asleep
(6.420-23). As soon as the dog collapses, our hero hurries "away from
the waters of no return" (6.425). Tertullian, the early Christian father
who derided all pagan practices, informs his readers that just such honey
cakes were employed at the Trophonion, where initiates used them to
appease the guardians in the dark passage (Fellows 152). The same imagery is used by Virgil himself in Book 4 of *The Aeneid*, where he relates
that a priestess at the temple of the Hesperides keeps the guardian snake
drugged with honey and poppy (4.483-86). Honeyed cakes were a common requirement in the underworld journey. Psycho-tropic drugs and
elixirs have long been suspected of being used on the initiates themselves

(Wasson, Hoffman, and Ruck 47-60), which may also explain the mixing bowls inside the cave. The stone looms spun the celestial garment of the initiate who must travel to the stone sky.

The astral imagery cannot be ignored. Specifically, there are two paths of the dead—one to the world below and one to the world above. There are different aspects of this cosmographic system signified in myth. The common plan is this two-road system that sojourns through the celestial axis. Plato has already identified them in his Myth of Er (10.614c) as well as in his *Gorgias*, where lies "the Meadow at the Cross Roads, whence the two [paths] lead, one to the Isles of the Blest, the other to Tartarus" (trans. Cope 126). There are two roads mentioned in the Orphic gold tablets, one that leads to the Spring of Memory and one to the Spring of Forgetfulness. Aeneas comes upon these roads in his own underworld trek in the *Aeneid* (6.535-43).

In the Vedas of India these two roads are called the *devayana* (meaning the higher or northern pass) and the *pitryana* (meaning the right hand or southern pass). These roads are seen on the horizon: the northern path is represented by the passage of the sun journeying north through the constellations of the ecliptic from vernal equinox to autumnal equinox; the southern path is represented by the passage of the sun journeying south through the constellations of the ecliptic from its autumnal to vernal equinox. In other words, the journeys of Heracles and Gilgamesh do follow a sort of zodiac scheme, but the basis of it is not a twelve-constellation solar calendar. It is the secret cosmography through the heavens where one obtains the secrets of life and death, and by so doing, has power and authority to rule as king. In the Vedic system, Yama is the first man to travel this road, and he becomes King of the Dead. A hymn in the Rig Veda describes this astral path:

> The one who has passed beyond along the great, steep straits, spying out the path for many, the sons of Vivasvan, the gatherer of men, King Yama—honor him with oblation. Yama was the first

to find the way for us, this pasture that shall not be taken away. Where our ancient fathers passed beyond, there everyone who is born follows, each on his own path. [To the dead man:] Go forth, go forth on those ancient paths on which our ancient fathers passed beyond. There you shall see the two kings, Yama and Varuna, rejoicing in the sacrificial drink. Unite with the fathers, with Yama, with the rewards of your sacrifices and good deeds, in the highest heaven. Leaving behind all imperfections, go back home again; merge with a glorious body. Run on the right path, past the two brindled, four-eyed dogs, the sons of Sarama, and then approach the fathers, who are easy to reach and who rejoice at the same feast as Yama. Yama, give him over to your guardian dogs, the four-eyed keepers of the path, who watch over men. O king, grant him happiness and health. (10.14.1,2,7,8,10,11; cited in Johnson 53)

In the age these myths were written, four constellations stood on the horizon receiving the sun on the days of equinox and solstice: Taurus, Leo, Scorpio, and Aquarius. These constellations marked the northern and southern path of heaven and were the images of a Bull, Lion, Scorpion, and Man. These images form the iconic representation of the Greek sphinx, keeper of the dead. According to Graves, the Nemean Lion was the offspring of the bull, lion, scorpion, and serpent, and four of Heracle's labors deal with these same four creatures, with the boar replacing the scorpion (428). Dionysus himself was represented in the same manner—as a bull, lion, and snake (*Bacchae* 1016-20).

Due to the precession of the equinoxes, these constellations slowly slipped below the horizon at their appointed hour and were replaced with Aires, Capricorn, Libra, and Cancer. The two constellations that framed the roads of the dead changed from Leo and Aquarius to Cancer and Capricorn. These new constellations are identified by Macrobius as the gates of the dead. Macrobius writes, "Souls are believed to pass through these portals when going from the sky to the earth and returning from the earth to the sky. For this reason one is called the portal of men and the other the portal of gods: Cancer, the portal of men, because through it descent is made to the infernal regions; Capricorn, the portal of gods, because through it souls return to their rightful abode of immortality, to be reckoned among the gods" (*Commentary* 12.2).

Regardless of the change in the celestial scenery, the astral road was always guarded by a ferocious lion. In the ancient world, guardian leonine sphinxes were placed at temples, pyramids, and tombs all across Eurasia. The labor of Heracles facing an impervious lion at a two-mouthed cave is the exact scenario that the deceased in the Egyptian mysteries faced when entering into the realm of the netherworld. At death, the initiate would descend from the horizon protected by none other than the guardian lion. The dead declares, "Get back, O Lion, bright of mouth and shining of head; retreat because of my strength, take care, O you who are invisible, do not await me, for I am Isis" (*BD* 17). In chapter 78 of the *Book of the Dead,* the scenario is repeated, this time the deceased faces the "Double Lion in his cavern" (compare the Nemean Lion in his double cavern), who guards a gateway and asks for the proper passwords and tokens before the deceased may continue. The Double Lion warns, "How can you reach the confines of the sky? Indeed you are equipped with the form of Horus, but you do not possess the Nemes Headdress."

This portion of the funerary text descends from much older material. In a Coffin Text we find the same scene, but this time the dead must pass the "castle of the Leonine One." The fierce guardian lion stands as gatekeeper to this celestial castle in his cavern. The Leonine One queries, "How can you reach the confines of the sky, seeing that you are equipped with the form of Horus, you have not the Nemes Crown in your possession?" (Clark 146). The deceased must defeat the guardian lion, and like Heracles he cannot use any weapon—only the special cultic knowledge of proper initiation. The deceased replies, "I am taking the news of Horus to Osiris in the Underworld. Horus has repeated to me what his father Osiris told him as his [last] wish, on the day of his burial" (Clark 146). It is a cryptic phrase indicative of the secrets possessed by the initiate. The Leonine One asks for these secrets and upon the correct exchange of information the Underworld Lion speaks, "I will give you the Nemes Crown and you may proceed upon the ways of the sky. . . . Let there be song and dancing! He has been initiated into the language of the universal gods; he is a uniquely learned one!" (Clark 146). After a cultic song and dance, the deceased receives the Nemes Crown, passes the Leonine One, and continues his celestial journey through the underworld.

This cultic ensemble is modeled within the already mentioned Temple of Apet in the Egyptian Thebes. As one approaches the main gate to the "secret chamber" within, one finds a unique device—a lion-bolt—which prevents progress from any unworthy person seeking passage (see figure 11). De Lubicz provides a description of this device:

> The working principle of these bolts, whether made of wood, bronze, or stone, is always the same: a small lion slide-bolt partially emerges from the housing encased within the doorpost so that it may be used to block the door proper . . ., pulled by a small chain of seven double links from the last of which hangs a heart. . . . The perfection of the symbolism behind these bolts is astounding. The heart that causes the lion to emerge is therefore the bolts "motor." (*TK* 661-62)

An inscription on the bolt reads, "I am the bolt of the great gate to the dwelling of my lord. I drive off whoever approaches him. I am the great uraeus, the terrifying mistress, who repels the unprovided, who represses the opposition. I attack the vile enemy with my knife. . . . I swallow their blood and I do not let them climb into this temple of eternal life" (*TK* 662).

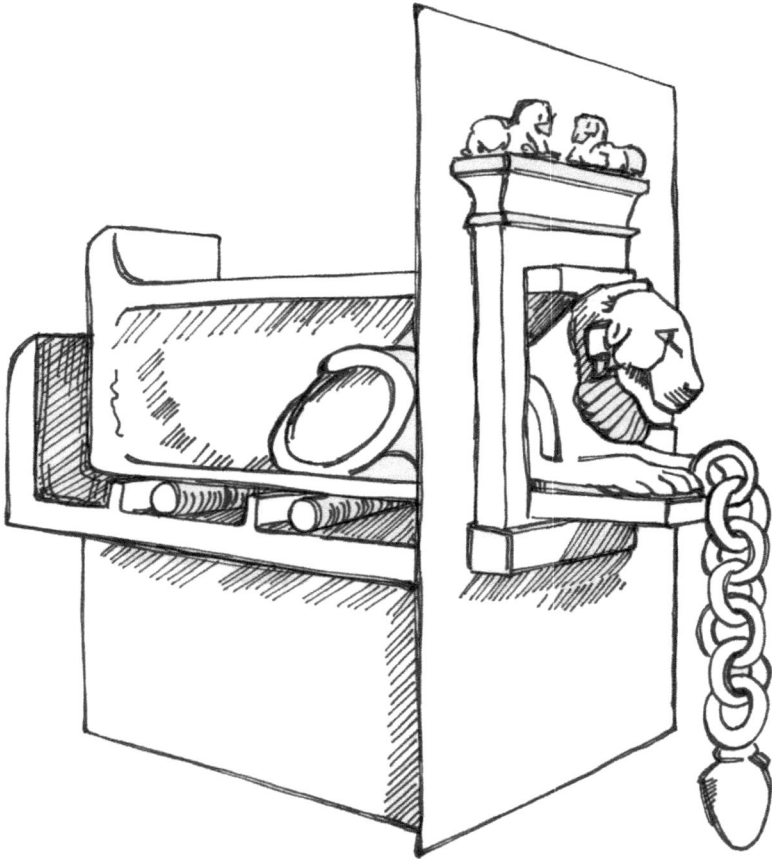

Figure 11. Lion Bolt at the Temple of Apet in Thebes

Within the door lintel of the gate at the Temple of Apet was a Lion Bolt.
Suspended from the lion was a chain upon which hung the heart of the
initiate represented by the vessel ideogram for "heart." In other words,
in order to surpass the lion guardian one's heart had to be purified and
infused with the cultic knowledge necessary for the cosmic journey
beyond. (Illustration by Lynde Mott, original image in *TK* 662.)

This lion guardian is the fierce Sekhmet, who tears all unprepared and counterfeit human beings asunder. Who is a counterfeit? One whose heart is not purified, who cannot pass the forty-two judges of the underworld, who has committed crime against nature and self, and who has not been initiated. A similar scenario is presented in Hindu mythology when a demon named Hiranya-Kaśipu (the name means Golden Garment) challenges the power of Vishnu. The demon, in his counterfeit golden dress, assumes the role and station of one who can tread through the cosmos with power. Vishnu sees through the guise, turns himself into a fierce lion, and tears the deceitful demon into pieces (Zimmer, *Myths* 180).

The counterfeit golden-garment returns us to the Egyptian netherworld, where in order to pass the Leonine One the deceased must have a cult object known as the Nemes Crown. This crown is a striped headdress that covers the entire head and nape of the neck and dates to at least the Third Dynasty (2600 BCE). It is only depicted within a funerary context; the pharaoh is never seen wearing it as part of his daily operations or even as part of his royal status. On the other hand, whenever the pharaoh is depicted as a leonine sphinx he *always* wears the Nemes Crown. This suggests that the crown itself represents the lion's mane and was the royal emblem of the initiated, who was a "uniquely learned one." In other words, only one who can authentically pass the guardian lion takes upon himself the lion garment or crown and therefore may tread through the cosmos. All others, no matter their station or power in life, are counterfeit and therefore resisted and torn asunder.

When the Egyptian deceased passes the lion gate the lion in turn becomes the protector of the deceased. We see this imagery in the tomb of Khaemwaset (1180 BCE), where the deceased is ready to pass the first gate of the netherworld. A leonine figure stands in front of him clearing the way. Above the deceased are the words, "Truth is his defense," while the lion figure is labeled as "Lord of Terror" (*MJSP* 369). The lion retains his horrific aspect, but now is one who guides, aids, and represents the initiate.

The officiating priest in the Egyptian rites always wore a panther skin as part of his cultic repertoire. The lion garment proclaimed his authority to officiate in the arcane secrets. In the *Ramesseum Dramatic Papyrus* Horus acknowledges Osiris and declares, "The panther skin unites thy limbs, . . . the eye [of Horus is] *ssf-cloth*" (*MJSP* 440). The term *ssf-cloth* is symbolized by a panther goddess and represents the mummy wrappings (*MJSP* 440). Every Egyptian mummy symbolically wears a lion garment and is given the lion crown at the gate. These tokens are crucial for the underworld journey.

The cultic complex recounted in the funerary texts and images of Egypt explains the encounter between Heracles and the Nemean Lion. As the myth goes, the great Heracles is unable to slay the lion with any weapon. Alas, he chases it within one of the Nemean caves and wrestles it with his bare hands. In this manner Heracles kills the lion, skinning the beast and wearing his mane as a royal emblem. Wearing the lion garment was the first step Heracles performed in the progression of his twelve labors, for the Nemean skin provided unparalleled protection against the fierce tests that lay ahead.

Heracles is always associated with his lion skin. Either he wears the skin on his back, generally with the lion head forming a sort of "Nemes" crown around his own head, or he is shown holding a lion skin in his arm as if holding a robe (see figure 12). Gilgamesh too wears a lion skin as he treads through the underworld. Both Jason and Theseus don lion skins as they accomplish their own labors. In the mysteries of Attis and Cybele, Attis also overcomes a guardian lion in a mountain cave using only song and dance (Vermaseren 126-7)! The point is that the mystery hero always has a confrontation with a lion-creature whom he must overcome in order to continue along the "sacred way." The lion is a fierce opponent without initiation. With initiation the lion is a fierce protector and ward often represented by the initiate wearing or carrying a lion garment. In all cases in the ancient context the lion must be overcome without a weapon.

Figure 12. Heracles and the Lion Robe

Heracles shown on a red figure vase from Attica, 6th century BCE.
Heracles slays the Nemean Lion with his bare hands, skins the beast,
and wears his garment like a robe and crown. Heracles is most often
recognized in ancient art through the lion garment that he wears or
holds. The lion's head becomes a sort of "Nemes Crown" by which
Heracles is able to complete his labors. Leopard or lion skin was often
worn by officiating priests in multiple traditions, and the spots or
striations on the skin represented the celestial vault. (Illustration by Lynde
Mott, original image on vase in the Museum of Fine Art, Boston.)

It is not surprising, then, to learn that in the mysteries of Mithras the officiating priests were known as "Lions" and their ordinances were called "Leontica" (King 135). The initiates themselves would don lion skins (Willoughby 136). In an inscription written above a depiction of a procession of lions within the mithraeum at S. Prisca we read, "Receive the incense-burners, Father, receive the Lions, Holy One, through whom we offer incense, through whom we are ourselves consumed!" (Clauss 135-36). The initiates, led by the officiating priestly lions, are consumed (transformed) in the element of fire (the sun) as they approach their Lion-God.

In many mithraeum (temples of Mithras) there was a chamber called a *leonteum*, or Lion's Room (Clauss 45, 136). The actual use of this room is unknown. Of greater interest is the fact that in other Mithraic temples there was a gate before the main cult niche, as is depicted in the mithraeum at Nida. On the pedestal post sits a lion, indicative of the lion gate that stands before the celestial journey. Many Mithraic keys have been found that opened the gates and doors of the chambers of the temples. The iron key found at Nida is a "Lion Key." The Lion Key is typical of such implements (Clauss 114). The Mithraic initiate thus had to pass the lion gate with the lion key. If successful, the initiate then became a lion himself, garbed in the lion skin and given a new name—the Lion— whereby he ascended to meet his Father in Heaven.

Whence does the lion imagery come? By Greek times the guardian lion is certainly the constellation Leo, who sits below the seven stars (Ursa Major) dancing around the celestial pole. The Egyptians did not have a lion constellation, at least as far as can be understood. The Egyptian guardian was Aker, the two-headed lion who sits at the entrance to the underworld (compare the Nemean lion at the two-mouthed cave). Still, in New Kingdom tombs the first obstacle the deceased faces, as inscribed on the ceilings, is a guardian lion surrounded by stars. While it is easy to assume that this image relates somehow to the constellation Leo, one is also reminded of the lion-headed dancers on the Péretié Plaque as well as the lion-headed sailors in the Babylonian hymn who number seven times seven and sail across heavenly waters. In these cases the lion imagery may not refer to a specific constellation, but to an entire cultic tradition belonging to the "knowers of the way." The guides to the celestial world are like lions—they rule the plains with speed and intelligence and with their luminescent eyes see through the darkness of night to find their path. What better symbol for the champion of the dark regions of the underworld than the lordly lion?

Heracles' confrontation with the guardian lion at the underworld cave and its parallels with other mythic traditions shows us that the Labors of Heracles originated in the celestial journey. Specifically, Heracles is a *mystes*, one who has been initiated to travel through and past the astral underworld. Heracles' final two labors prove this point, as Heracles descends to the "confluence of rivers" to obtain the golden apples which grant immortality. In his final labor, Heracles drags up the great Cerberus, guardian of the underworld, which is clearly significant of his victory over death (Nilsson 204). The defeat of Death is alluded to in Homer's *Illiad*, where Heracles wounds Hades at Pylos (5.449-53). While traditionally interpreted as the actual Greek city, Nilsson notes that the allusion of the word *pylos* refers to "gate" and that the confrontation between Heracles and Hades occurs at the "Gate of the Underworld" where Hades resides (203). This gate is often reproduced in temple architecture as the pillared entry to the interior Holy of Holies. The true Pillars of Heracles is really this Gate of the Dead which our hero must overcome.

One would like a deconstruction of each Labor of Heracles compared to some aspect of the celestial journey. Such analysis is beyond this work as the myth is a conglomeration of difficult factors. The whole series of twelve labors is a late accretion and certain stellar symbols have changed over time. Changes to the myth are introduced through the process of dispersion from one culture and language to another. Most problematically, the majority of this cultic tradition was kept oral and secret and has been lost. What has been introduced here is not a detailed accounting (which would be impossible), but a general overview of the cosmographic scheme contained in myth and cult. Heracles descends into the underworld at his first labor and ascends out of it with his last. Each of the labors belong to the oral world of celestial archetypes. Heracles journeys to the "true heaven" and "true underworld" in order to inherit Olympus. He is warrior, priest, and king. Above all, he is no longer demi-god, but one who eternally dwells with the gods. He is *anthropocosmos* and is the ultimate, ontological expression of oral cosmology.

CHAPTER 8

OLD TESTAMENT TALES

The Problems with the Old Testament

In many circles it is presumed that Israel had no mythology. Myth is believed to be associated with polytheistic systems, according to some academics, or to the pagans, according to some believers. Yet these assessments essentially miss the mark. Myth is associated with oral cultus. Any oral society built around the sacred-ordered space of a *templum* will have rites and narratives that describe or associate those rites. Israel had a temple tradition for over one thousand years. Myth was part of that tradition.

Innumerable complications impede any attempt to fully understand the Israelite temple cult. One major problem was its constant cross-germination with surrounding cult systems. There were several periods in its history where the Israelites adopted the gods, myths, and cultus of their polytheistic neighbors. Through the discovery and comparison of the *Ras Shamra* texts and the Bible, Geo Widengren demonstrates that ancient Israel was profoundly influenced by the Canaanite-Syrian literature and culture (155). The Biblical text makes this very clear. One example is when Manasseh adopts foreign religious constructs wholesale, "For [Manasseh] built up again the high places . . . and he reared up altars for Baal, and made a grove, as did Ahab king of Israel; and worshiped all the host of heaven, and served them. And he built altars in the house of the Lord. . . . And he built altars for all the host of heaven in the two courts of the house of the Lord" (2 Kings 21.3-5).

He was not the first king to do so. A close reading of the Old Testament text shows that all the way up until the Babylonian exile most of the Hebrew people practiced some form of polytheism. There were numerous cult groves built throughout Israel for worshiping various deities. This all becomes very clear during the reforms of Josiah, Manasseh's grandson. Josiah is said to have found an ancient book in the temple describing the proper rites and laws of the Israelite temple cult. These rites and laws had not been lived for nearly three hundred years. Consequently, Josiah stripped the kingdom of all idolatrous images and creeds, including pagan icons and personnel (2 Kings 22.8-13; 23).

A second major problem exists in the natural erosive forces of textual transmission. Geo Widengren again reminds us that the Old Testament "as it is handed down to us in the Jewish Canon, is only one part—we do not even know if the greater part—of Israel's national literature. And, moreover, this preserved part has in many passages quite obviously been exposed to censorship and correspondingly purged" (158). Emanuel Tov also observes, "Most of the [Old Testament] texts—ancient and modern—which have been transmitted from one generation to the next have been corrupted in one way or another" and that "during the textual transmission many complicated changes occurred, making it now almost impossible for us to reconstruct the original form of the text" (8, 177). According to Tov, these "complicated changes" began in the earliest periods of religious writing, where "massive changes [occurred] in the formative stage of the biblical literature" (266).

While the texts themselves have been modified, the transition from oral cult to written text produces another kind of purging. This transition brings up a third major problem when understanding ancient Israelite religion. The Biblical texts emerge from an oral, cultic, and cosmographic culture. Many of the texts were written by literate scribes numerous centuries after their original creation within the oral cult. Margaret Barker relates that within the non-canonical tradition it is said that an editor named Ezra divided the Jewish scriptures into two parts—the smaller part for public reading and the larger part that was to be kept secret and reserved only for those initiated into the temple cultus (*Hidden* 7-8). Proper understanding of the Hebrew cult came by way of initiatory ritual and not by merely reading words. Like so many other aspects of oral myth and cult, when reading a text that descends from it, we are only getting half of the story and even less of the context.

The transition from oral rites to literate texts brings us to a fork in the road. On the one hand is the realization that the Old Testament is a late production of a localized tradition centering around the national idea of the Exodus and the Mosaic Law. This entire history and tradition is something different than the history and tradition of the ancient Patriarchs: Adam, Noah, Enoch, and Melchizedek. The Torah is rooted in Mosaic history and law. The older Hebrew religion, birthed in the days of Abraham centuries earlier, was rooted in temple cosmography and cult. This realization makes the reforms of Josiah more complex to interpret. Did he only remove foreign elements from their temple? Or did he remove the more ancient elements of Judaism as well? Or did the book discovered in the temple help restore the older religious practices which had already been lost? If so, what was changed when the older order was re-instituted? How could they fully understand what they were reading when the written text itself must have been something different than the much older oral rites?

These questions are only part of another curiosity embedded within the Old Testament text—our other fork in the road. From the time of the Israelite kings onward there is no mention of the Mosaic Law. Isaiah does not mention it. However, there are several allusions within Isaiah that deal with an older tradition rooted in temple cosmography (e.g., chapter 22). Was the Mosaic law itself a product of post-exiled Jews, emerging as an official Israelite code of conduct at the same time of the canonization of the Torah? If this is true, then not only is the Old Testament, as we have it, something entirely different from the earlier forms of worship practiced by Abraham, Isaac, and Jacob, but also it might be an entirely different form of worship than practiced in the days of Moses and Aaron! Of course, there are elements within the law which hail to much older times, but this changes nothing. Martin Luther retained much of the older Christian theology after his schismatic break from Catholicism, but the religion of Luther and Calvin is something entirely different than that of Aquinas and Gregory. This metaphor is apt, as the Mosaic Law and the Old Testament as we have it may represent a sort of "Great Reformation" completely separated from the origins of the religion.

Whatever the answers to these complex questions and issues, one thing is absolutely certain: the entire temple tradition of Israel was eventually extinguished. "Two great events in the history of the temple virtually coincided at the end of the seventh century BC," writes Margaret Barker, "the reform of the Deuteronomists and the destruction of the temple and monarchy by the Babylonians. Between them they destroyed the ancient cult" (*Gate* 134). Margaret Barker relates how a prominent faction in Hebrew society called the Deuteronomists (they wrote the books Deuteronomy as well as 1 and 2 Kings) did not favor the monarchy nor the royal cult attached to the temple. The destruction of the Hebrew temple by Nebuchadnezzar in 587 BCE and the subsequent forced exodus of the Israelites, combined with the reformations of the Deuteronomists, effectively destroyed the old temple order with its rites and myths. As a result, the narratives in the Bible have been de-mythologized and de-cosmologized. They have been reformatted and repackaged as strict historical accounts. Liturgical schemas were forgotten as literate scribes overwrote them using literary technique. The temple, with its myths, rites, and cosmic order, evaporated into a culture of schools and synagogues, trained in letters, books, and doctrinal exegesis. A massive shift in religious practice and understanding occurred in the transition from orality to literacy, and *orthopraxy* to *orthodoxy*.

Despite the cultural erosion of countless centuries, there are several places where the older, oral order peeks through. I assert that where there is a founding story rooted in oral cultures there will be some form of the cosmographic journey connected with it. Oral kings in the hieratic age claimed their authority to rule through celestial mandate. Like Gilgamesh and Heracles, they obtained this mandate by analogically traveling to the stars.

While much of this older order has been stripped from the biblical texts, as Windengren notes, it is fully extant in non-canonical sources. Nowhere is this better illustrated than in the Enoch tradition. According to Genesis, Enoch was born seven generations after Adam. He is mentioned only once, and then only in passing, in the Old Testament (Genesis 5.18-24). Despite the briefest of blurbs, one sentence in the Genesis text stands out, "And Enoch walked with God: and he was not; for God took him" (4.24). It is the slightest of references implying that Enoch saw God face to face and somehow ascended into heaven with the deity. No matter how compelling, this remains the only significant reference to Enoch in all of Old Testament literature.

Something is deeply amiss, however, as the Enoch tradition is found everywhere at Qumran. In the Dead Sea Scrolls, Enoch is mentioned more than any other prophet other than Isaiah (Barker, *Hidden* 10). In the Greek version of the *Jewish Apocrypha*, in a list written by Ben Sira of the greatest men in history, Enoch appears first and last on the list (Barker, *Hidden* 29). It is now recognized that Enoch entered the Christian tradition as the New Testament cites the works of Enoch at least 128 times (Nibley, *Enoch* 10). The entire book of Revelations belongs to the Enoch tradition (Barker, *Hidden* 31). The *Pistia Sophia* also descends from Enoch literature (Nibley, *Enoch* 10). Enoch was remembered as the high priest before the Flood and the founder of the original temple and cult (Barker, *Hidden* 35). Margaret Barker observes, "The new paradigm is that the Enoch tradition is ancient, as it claims, and that it was the original myth of the Jerusalem temple, long before Moses became the key figure and the Exodus the defining history" (Barker, *Hidden* 33).

The name *Enoch* means *the initiated one* (Barker, *On Earth* 22). Enoch is the sole figure initiated into the secrets of the heavenly world. In all existent Enoch texts thus far found, two things stand in common: (1) they all exist within temple and cult imagery as they describe the heavenly Holy of Holies, the throne room, or other sacred sanctuary features; (2) they all represent Enoch as the figure who strides through the heavens, learning its secrets and truths, and bringing them back to earth. In the Enoch text found in Ethiopia we read, "And [the Angels] brought me to the place of darkness, and to a mountain the point of whose summit reached to heaven. And I saw the places of the luminaries and the treasuries of the stars and of the thunder and in the uttermost depths, where were a fiery bow and arrows and their quiver. . . . And they took me to the living waters, and to the fire of the west, which receives every setting sun" (*1 Enoch* 17.2-4).

Like Utnapishtim and Gilgamesh, Enoch descends into the underworld to find the secrets of immortality. During his journey he discovers a heavenly bow and arrows and a place of living waters. This scene is an extraordinary parallel to all the myths employing bow and arrow imagery associated with flood waters and a secret source of life. The parallel is not coincidence, as Enoch is often associated with the story of the Great Flood, "And again I raised mine eyes towards heaven and saw a lofty roof, with seven water torrents thereon, and those torrents flowed with much water into an enclosure. . . . And the water, the darkness, and mist increased upon it; and as I looked at the height of that water, that water had risen above the height of that enclosure, and was streaming over that enclosure, and it stood upon the earth. . . . But [a] vessel floated on the water" (*1 Enoch* 84.2-6). Enoch witnesses the flood, but does so during his celestial sojourn. Again, the flood story is associated with astral themes and transcends interpretations of terrestrial and geological floods.

Does Enoch discover the secrets of immortality? In one of the most controversial verses in *1 Enoch,* our hero enters the Holy of Holies and stands before the throne of heaven: "And I fell on my face, and my whole body became relaxed, and my spirit was transfigured. . . . And [the angel] came to me and greeted me with His voice, and said unto me: '[You] are the Son of Man who is born unto righteousness'" (*1 Enoch* 71.11-4). The title "Son of Man" is euphemistic and does not refer to mortal seed, but rather to an immortal heritage. In the New Testament, only Jesus Christ is ever called the Son of Man. In the Old Testament, the phrase "son of man" is sometimes used to describe natural offspring, but the title reveals its true significance in the book of Ezekiel. This text is the one place in Old Testament literature that clearly depicts a journey through the celestial world. Ezekiel strides through the many heavens learning their powers. During his cosmic tour God calls this prophet "son of man" over ninety times. Only in a heavenly context does man come to understand the source and nature of his origin and divine destiny. Before the throne of heaven, the "initiated one" is changed into a divine being. According to Margaret Barker, at this moment Enoch becomes aware of his own *theosis* (Barker, *Hidden* 41). This is the theme of apocalyptic literature of which Enoch seems to be the source. Such transfiguration is not only reserved for Enoch, but according to the *Apocalypse of Baruch* is given to all who ascend through the heavens:

> For they [the initiated] shall behold the world which is now invisible to them, And they shall behold the time which is now hidden from them: And time shall no longer age them. For in the heights of that world shall they dwell, And they shall be made like unto the angels, and be made equal to the stars. . . . For there shall be spread before them the extent of Paradise, and there shall be shown to them the beauty of the majesty of the living creatures which are beneath the throne. (Barker, *Gate* 130-31)

Abraham

If Enoch represents an earlier form of Israelite worship, are there any clues in the surviving Old Testament text which suggests a similar cosmology? The answer is "yes," but only if one is looking. The principal figure that emerges at the edge of Israelite history is Abraham. His story is found in Genesis, chapters 11 through 25. Over one quarter of the Genesis material focuses on this patriarch, and he remains *the* formative figure in canonized history. In the literary style of the Old Testament text, however, Abraham does not appear to go on any heavenly journey. Like Enoch, there is only one portion in the Genesis text that even hints at the possibility. This part just so happens to be the central tenant of Judaic faith—the covenant God makes with Abraham, "After these things the word of the Lord came unto Abram in a vision, saying, Fear not, Abram: I am thy shield, and thy exceeding great reward. . . . And [God] brought him forth abroad, and said, Look, now toward heaven, and tell the stars, if thou be able to number them: and he said unto him, So shall thy seed be" (15.1,5).

Abraham is childless, and God descends to Abraham and promises offspring as innumerable as the stars. At this point God makes a covenant with Abraham wherein the patriarch performs animal sacrifices and cuts a heifer and a goat into separate pieces. The Hebrew verb for "covenant" is *karath*, which means *to cut*, and refers to the cutting of a token into pieces (in this case two animals). Each piece of the token is given to the parties forming their promise. After this cutting the Lord sends a vision to Abraham, "And when the sun was going down, a deep sleep fell upon Abram; and, lo, an horror of great darkness fell upon him. . . . And it came to pass, that, when the sun went down, and it was dark, behold a smoking furnace, and a burning lamp that passed between those pieces" (15.12, 17). God walks between the pieces of the animals that had been cut by Abraham, sealing His promise. The imagery employed, however, is very suggestive. Abraham only has his vision at the setting of the sun where God appears in the pitch dark as a smoking furnace (a fire pot) and burning lamp (a flaming torch). In other words, God begins his covenant by showing Abraham the stars, and ends it at the setting of the sun and in the dark with a fire and torch that lights the way.

Are these cosmic motifs that have been purged from their original contexts? We may get a glimpse of what those original contexts may have been in extra-canonical sources. For example, the author Pseudo-Philo records in his *Biblical Antiquities* (probably an early first century CE work) the same covenant but in a more elaborated telling, "And [God] said to him, 'Is it not regarding this people [Israel] that I spoke to Abraham in vision, saying, Your seed will be like the stars of heaven, *when I lifted him above the firmament and showed him the arrangements of all the stars?*'" (Tvedtnes, Hauglid, and Gee 24; italics mine). Here, God promises Abraham seed as innumerable as the stars, but set specifically within a stellar context. God has given Abraham a tour of the stars first, and it is while he is in the heavens that the covenant is given. Abraham becomes a "son of man," and like Enoch and Ezekiel comes to understand the destiny of his progeny only in the throne room of heaven. In the *Apocalypse of Abraham* (probably another first century CE text) this same scene is repeated:

And he said [to Abraham], "Look at the expanses which are under the firmament to which you have now been directed and see that on no single expanse is there any other but the one whom you have searched for or who has loved you." And while he was still speaking, behold, the expanses under me, the heavens, opened and I saw on the seventh firmament upon which I stood a fire spread out and a light and dew and a multitude of angels and a host of the invisible glory. . . . And he said, "Look from on high at the stars which are beneath you and count them for me and tell me their number!" . . . And he said to me, "As the number of the stars and their power so shall I place for your seed the nations and men, set apart for me in my lot with Azazel.'" (Tvedtnes, Hauglid, and Gee 57-8)

The Genesis text only mentions the stars as a numeric metaphor—Abraham's seed shall be as innumerable as the stars. The original context seems to have been a heavenly tour of all the stars where Abraham gets his bearings, learns their secrets, and in their midst is given the covenant. It is only within the heavenly realm that the covenant makes any sense. The stars are not a numeric metaphor, but a direct symbol of the destiny of his people. The stars are the repository of all truth and destiny and the only altar upon which an eternal covenant can be made. This leads us to an astonishing insight: the extra canonical texts may be giving us a more accurate look into earlier Israelite religion than the official record.

The Abrahamic covenant has a remarkable analog in the Ethiopian *Book of Enoch*. Enoch is touring the heavens when an Angel speaks, "And he said unto me: 'Observe, Enoch, these heavenly tablets, and read what is written thereon, and mark every individual fact.' And I observed the heavenly tablets, and read everything which was written and understood everything, and read the book of all the deeds of mankind, and of all the children of flesh that shall be upon the earth to the remotest generations" (*1 Enoch* 81.1-2). It is only in the realm of the stars that the innumerable generations of man are perceived and recorded. Abraham is given a covenant whereby his seed shall be numbered as the stars. Enoch is among the stars when he is shown "heavenly tablets" whereon all the covenants of mankind are manifest to the utmost generation. These two episodes between Abraham and Enoch are not antonymous to each other, but appear to belong to the same tradition. The implication is that the covenant, the offspring, and the heavenly tour through the cosmos once belonged together in a unified setting.

Abraham is not only shown journeying through the stars in extra-canonical sources, but he is also associated with the Enoch figure in these same sources. A second century BCE Jew name Eupolemus records that Abraham taught astrology to the Egyptians, but that his knowledge of the stars came from Enoch. In the *Book of Jubilees* (another second century BCE source) Abraham looks into the stars and is given the covenant, but he is also said to have learned from the works of Enoch and Noah. In the *Zohar*, a cabalistic commentary on the *Torah*, it is said that Adam possessed a heavenly book that recorded all the secrets of the cosmos, and that he passed it on to Enoch and to Abraham.

Returning to the Old Testament text, the imagery of God sealing the covenant only at sunset and in the form of a furnace and torch is also suggestive of the underworld. The underworld is the dark abode not only of the dead but also of the secrets of life. In fact, all the generations of humankind are connected through the secrets that are found there. In multiple traditions, those journeying through the underworld carried torches to light their way. God seals his covenant, appearing as a furnace and torch. These images portray both the destruction and glory that comes by breaking or keeping the oath. They also pun on the idea of the oath's loci. The underworld was known as the repository for oaths and covenants. In Greek myth, the River Styx was the medium upon which the most solemn oaths could be made. Whenever a god or goddess took an oath they would dispatch Iris with a golden jug to collect some of the underworld waters. Upon her return, they would swear their promise while pouring a libation using the Stygian waters. Once performed, the oath could not be broken, not even by deity.

Did God take Abraham to the throne of heaven when he showed Abraham his seed? Did God descend with Abraham to the underworld to perform his oath? From the surviving, canonized text, there is no certain answer. A close inspection reveals, however, hints, echoes, and shadows of an older religion. This religion was astral. Its rites and oaths belonged to the realm of the stars, and those participating analogically journeyed through the stars. These muted, cosmographic themes are embedded in scattered puzzle pieces throughout the biblical text. Taken outside of the context of oral cult and cosmology, these broken bricks of history have been assembled using the modern mortar of literary, historical, or devotional criticisms. The cosmology of the oral age would have us look in a different direction. Our heads would have to tilt towards the stars.

Jacob

While Abraham is a patriarch, he is technically not the founder of Israel; that honor goes to his grandson Jacob. Jacob is the one who sees God face to face and is given a new name, *Israel*, a name that means "struggles with God." Jacob is the true founder of the Jewish nation-state. If our thesis is correct—that founders of cities and temples in the ancient Near East and beyond analogically journeyed to the stars to obtain their celestial mandate—then the story of Jacob would perhaps be our best illustrative example. Unlike the muted implications in the cases of Abraham, however, the canonized text of Jacob provides multiple clues that the hieratic journey through the cosmos was central to Israelite worship.

Jacob's tale is retold in Genesis, chapters 25 through 37, and another significant portion of the Genesis text is dedicated to this founding father. Jacob was the son of Isaac and the grandson of Abraham. He would eventually have twelve sons of his own, each becoming the tutelar heads of the twelve tribes of Israel. As the story goes, Jacob's mother conceives with twins, who struggle against each other within her womb (25.21-2). The first child born was covered in red hair and was named Esau, a name signifying "hairy" (25.25). As Esau was birthing from the womb, the twin child grabbed his heel, and he was thus named *Ya 'aqob,* or Jacob, signifying "one who supplants" or "grabs by the heel" (25.26). Esau, as the older brother, held the birthright of Isaac and Abraham. On an unsuccessful hunting trip, Esau returned famished and empty-handed. Jacob offered a bowl of pottage in exchange for the birthright, and Esau gladly agreed to sell (25.29-34). When Isaac lies blind and dying, he seeks to give a blessing to his eldest son. Jacob puts lamb's wool on his arms to trick his father into thinking he is the elder brother, and Isaac blesses Jacob (27.26-30). Esau has thus been "supplanted" from both his birthright and his father's blessing and in rage seeks to slay Jacob.

Fearing for his life, Jacob flees his home and travels to the land of Laban, his father-in-law. During his travels, and at the setting of the sun, Jacob retires and has a dream where he sees "a ladder set up on the earth, and the top of it reached to heaven: and behold the angels of God ascending and descending on it" (28.12). At the top of the ladder is none other than God himself. *It is only during this panoptic vision, set upon the ladder of heaven, that God bestows upon Jacob the covenant of Abraham:* "And thy seed shall be as the dust of the earth, and thou shalt spread abroad to the west, and to the east, and to the north, and to the south, and in thee and in thy seed shall all the families of the earth be blessed" (28.14). Jacob awakes, trembling at the experience, and declares "How dreadful is this place! This is none other but the house of God, and this is the gate of heaven" (28.17). To commemorate the experience, Jacob sets up a stone pillar, signifying a sacred sanctuary, and blesses it. He names the sanctuary Beth-el, "the house of God" (28.19).

Jacob's ladder is none other than the celestial axis. According to tradition, the ladder contained seven steps in concordance with the seven heavenly spheres. In other traditions the ladder contained seventy steps, but the cosmic imagery remains. The souls rising and descending upon it are no different than the souls in the writings of Plato who travel the heavenly circuit in the cycle of life and death. They are also the singing *hymnologi* guarding each gate of heaven. God stands at the very top of the axis, signifying his throne. Jacob is given the same covenant as Abraham, and one can logically connect the dots. At this place called the "house of God" and the "gate of heaven," Jacob has been introduced into the celestial world and has been given the covenant of infinite progeny presumably because he has seen them to the utmost generation. Jacob is the new Enoch, and he builds an altar and temple shrine in Bethel that links heaven and earth. The ark of the covenant is kept there (Judges 20.26-28) and the site becomes an oracle, much like Delphi, where people ask the counsel of God (Judges 20.18,31). As the founding story of Israel, we are already deeply mired in cosmological and trans-historical imagery.

Jacob's heavenly sojourn properly begins at the setting of the sun. This motif is a marker that one has left this world and is heading into the underworld where the secrets of the heavens are kept. Gilgamesh descends into the underworld at the setting of the sun. In chapter 2, the historical vignette of Ramses defeating the Kadesh was shown to be placed within a trans-historical and cosmological setting. He too descends into the underworld at the setting of the sun. Abraham receives a cosmic vision and is given the heavenly covenant at the setting of the sun (Genesis 15.12). Each of these heroes descends into darkness and goes through a series of trials. Gilgamesh finds himself in terrible darkness and must race against the sun to get to the garden at the crossroads. Ramses descends into darkness and must fight the enemy hoard. Abraham descends "and, lo, an horror of great darkness fell upon him" (Genesis 15.12). Abraham beholds the trials of his people as enemies enslave them; he also is promised the blessings of the fathers and this covenant is sealed between a smoking furnace and burning lamp (Genesis 15.13-17).

Jacob's trials fall into the same category but take on a completely different representation. Unlike Gilgamesh, Heracles, or even Ramses, the labors of Jacob do not deal with mighty monsters or supernatural beings. Jacob's trials are firmly set within the imagery of a domesticated, agrarian tribal leader whose power arises from land, marriage, and herds. The cultural theme of the nomadic clan actually argues for its historicity. His trials also have a peculiar structure. Jacob seeks to marry Rachel but is tricked by Laban into working for seven years to wed the hand of Leah. He then indentures himself for another seven years to obtain Rachel. Leah bears children while Rachel is barren; therefore, Jacob takes Rachel's handmaid, Bilhah, to wife so that he might have seed through her. He stays for another seven years. Jacob is exiled from his homeland for three-seven year periods; each period is aligned with a female who aids Jacob during his journey.

Jacob serves Laban for three seven-year periods while his wives bear him twelve children who form the future nation of Israel. Eventually, Laban turns against Jacob and Jacob is forced to return to Canaan. In returning to his homeland, Jacob faces his twin brother, from whom he stole the birthright. "Then Jacob was greatly afraid and distressed" (32.7), for Jacob knows that his brother will more than likely slay him and his people. In these desperate circumstances, Jacob offers a prayer, "Deliver me, I pray thee, from the hand of my brother, from the hand of Esau: for I fear him, lest he will come and smite me, and the mother with the children" (32.11).

Jacob takes his wives and children and passes over the river ford Jabbok. The place-name is a clear pun on the name Jacob. *Ya'aqob*, the one who supplants, flees to *Yabboq*, a place signifying "to make empty or void." As a literary theme, the pun is an elegant play on meanings: the great supplanter must empty himself before the Lord if he is going to be successful. There may have once been a different theme involved, however, for like Ramses, Jacob suddenly finds himself stranded and alone in the middle of the night (32.22-24). Strangely, a man appears and wrestles with Jacob through the night (32.24). More word play seems to be involved. The Hebrew word *'abaq* means "to wrestle," and is similar to *Ya'aqob,* the one who is constantly wrestling. In fact, the wrestle between Jacob and the strange man at the ford mirrors the wrestling with Esau at his birth. At both events Jacob is given a new name. In the latter case, as the day breaks, Jacob's combatant transforms into an angel of

God. At the rising of the sun this angel blesses Jacob and gives him a new name: Israel. The "supplanter" who had wrestled with Esau is now a king "who struggles with God." Like Enoch, a transfiguration has taken place. Like Gilgamesh and Heracles, Jacob has transcended earthly concerns represented by his mortal twin. He has entered the realm of God. In a moment of *epoptes*, "Jacob called the name of the place Peniel; for I have seen God face to face, and my life is preserved" (32.30).

After this divine hierophany, Jacob and Esau are reconciled. Jacob bows before his brother seven times, "And Esau ran to meet him, and embraced him, and fell on his neck and kissed him: and they wept" (Gen 33.4). One last word pun sticks out. The Hebrew word for "embrace" is *chabaq*, and is a paronomasia to the words *'abaq* or "wrestle," and *Ya'aqob*, "the supplanter." There are two unified themes running throughout this text. The first is the one scholars have noted through literary analysis. Jacob wrestles with Esau, then struggles with the angel, then is clasped and given a new name by God, and then is finally embraced and reconciled to his brother Esau. The Hebrew words for "wrestle," "Jacob," and "embrace" all play on each other, just as the story itself is a thematic play between Jacob and his mortal family and Jacob and his divine heritage.

Much of the genius in the Old Testament lies within its elegantly constructed literary puns, parallelisms, and conundrums. What should be obvious, but often goes unnoticed, is the fact that a literary construction, no matter how elegant and profound, is a literate one. All the expert wordplay found throughout the story of Jacob in the Genesis text reveals that official history has been recorded within the container of literary technique. This is all well and good, as long as one remembers that the story of Jacob hails from oral traditions. Oral traditions in the ancient world were not constructed by literary technique; they were patterned after cosmological insights and recorded by cosmogonic myths and rituals.

If we remove all the literary technique from our Genesis text and lay before us the bare-bones plot with its most prominent motifs, we find the second unified theme of the story. Jacob is a founder of rites and civilization and walks a very familiar path. In fact, taking only the plot points, we find that Jacob's history is nearly identical to Ramses at the Battle of Kadesh. Both kings face an enemy that threaten to destroy them. Both kings analogically descend to the underworld at the setting of the sun. They both find themselves in their most perilous circumstances when alone and in the middle of the night. Each offers a prayer to their god, and each finds divine intercession. For Ramses, and after Amun's aid, he begins to re-ascend out of the underworld. At the rising of the sun he is empowered by his god and defeats his enemies in battle. For Jacob, an angel wrestles with him all night. At the rising of the sun he is embraced by God and given a new name. He becomes the founder of a new kingdom.

The parallels to our other kingly narratives are too close for coincidence, and the cosmological motifs are impossible to ignore. Like the Battle of Kadesh engraved upon the temple wall, Jacob's narrative follows a loose but consistent strategy of a cosmic journey—marked, as it is, between the setting and rising sun, and placed within motifs of gates, ladders, pillars, wounds, and covenants. Jacob and Esau also parallel Gilgamesh and Enkidu in intriguing ways. Both meet in combat, the former fighting in the womb, and each resolve the combat by pinning the opponent on knee or foot. Esau and Enkidu are wild, hairy twins and co-companions to those destined to found the city and its cult. Esau loses his birthright, and Enkidu falls sick and dies. Gilgamesh and Jacob must sojourn on a form of cosmographic journey. Gilgamesh treads the heavenly waters, descending into the underworld to obtain heaven's secrets, while Jacob sees the gate of heaven, the face of god, and is given a new name, *Israel*. Both Gilgamesh and Jacob return from their adventures empowered to found their own nation. Gilgamesh builds the city of

Uruk. Jacob creates the nation of Israel. Although the plots of these various narratives are very different, thematically and mythologically they are the same.

There are no direct statements in the text to prove this interpretation; however, there are many markers that suggest the original source hailed from an older temple religion and cosmology. Were this the only tale within the biblical text to echo such motifs, I might be more hesitant with my interpretation. However, when Israel re-founds itself at the exodus from Egypt, we find a remarkably similar and trans-historical narrative. Again we find that behind the founding rites of civilization is the cosmology and cultus of the oral age.

Balaam

In Numbers, chapters 22 through 24, a curious tale is told about a non-Israelite prophet named Balaam and a Moabite king named Balak. According to the story, Balak sees the mighty host of Israel immigrating onto the borders of his land during their exodus from Egypt. Realizing that the Israelites outnumber his own armies, and knowing that Israel has the power to conquer his kingdom, Balak seeks the aid of a famous sorcerer who lives in Pethor. Balak sends messengers to the soothsayer Balaam with the promise of good pay if he will use his powers to curse the Israelites and deliver a military victory to Balak.

Once again myth and history intersect. The name Balaam has been found in Deir 'Alla inscribed on plaster and preserved from the eight century BCE. The inscription speaks of a powerful soothsayer (Alter 797). Balaam is a real, historical person known as a soothsayer, as he appears in the Biblical text. Balaam is a non-Israelite, as his name suggests. As Robert Alter notes, the Hebrew idiom, "And God came unto Balaam," is reserved for God's appearance for non-Israelites (797). Also, God generally appears to non-Israelites in night dreams, just as

Balaam converses with God at night (22.20). The author of our text employs this historical figure in a pro-Israelite way. Despite the fact that the Hebrew God speaks to the foreigner, readers are shown that no power on earth, not even the mightiest sorcerer in the land, can overcome God's chosen people. The way that this moral is taught, however, returns us to our story.

Balaam is visited by God and told not to help the Moabite king; thus, Balaam refuses their offer. Balak is not willing to give up so easily. He sends out his princes with a larger chest of payment to entice the wizard again. In fact, Balak sends forth his most honored and noble princes (presumably his own sons) with an open checkbook in an attempt to acquire the soothsayer's skills. On this last attempt Balaam relents, but tells the princes that he is bound to say and do only what the God of Israel commands him.

The narrative now takes a decisive turn. On the return trip to the king, Balaam is seen riding his donkey unaware that the God of Israel is angry with him for agreeing to go. God sends an angel to bar his way. Balaam, great sorcerer that he is, appears to be entirely clueless that an angel stands before him with a drawn sword ready to strike him down. Balaam's ass, on the other hand, sees the angel and attempts to turn aside from the path they are on. A very humorous scene develops as Balaam ends up cursing his ass and forcing it to return to the path guarded by the angel. The donkey again turns aside, this time crushing Balaam's foot. The soothsayer erupts in anger and smites the donkey. His beast, however, is unwilling to go any further and falls down underneath Balaam, who in turn smites the animal again.

Exasperated, the dumb beast of burden begins speaking, saying, "What have I done unto thee, that thou hast smitten me these three times?" (22.28). In sheer irony the angry sorcerer exclaims, "Because thou hast mocked me: I would there were a sword in mine hand, for now would I kill thee" (22.29). Poignantly, standing in front of Balaam is an angel with a sword in his hand ready to kill him! Only the donkey, the stupidest beast of burden on earth, can see the angel, whilst Balaam, the most powerful sorcerer in the land, is utterly blind. The narrative is elegantly constructed around this theme of vision, and the tale is told in threes: three times God warns Balaam not to go with Balak, the last time with an angel; and three times the donkey sees the angel while the soothsayer remains utterly ignorant and blind. This triune parallelism runs throughout the entire story.

Finally, God opens Balaam's eyes and he sees the angel standing before him. Now it is his turn to fall down, as the donkey had done before, and beg mercy from the guardian standing in the way. The angel commands Balaam to go with the princes of Moab, but again reminds him that he must say and do only what the God in heaven commands him. Balaam promises a third time to obey the Israelite God and continues on his way.

Balaam arrives at the royal court, where Balak immediately takes his prophet-for-hire to the high places overlooking the Israelite hoard. He commands Balaam to build seven altars and offer seven sacrifices and curse Israel. Balaam, atop a mount, builds seven altars and offers seven sacrifices; yet instead of producing a powerful, magical curse against Israel, Balaam offers an oracle to the Moabite king:

> Balak, the king of Moab hath brought me from Aram, out of the mountains of the east, saying, Come curse me Jacob, and come, defy Israel. How shall I curse whom the Lord hath not defied? For from the top of the rocks I see him, and from the hills I behold him: lo, the people shall dwell alone, and shall not be reckoned among the nations. Who can count the dust of Jacob, and the number of the fourth part of Israel? Let me die the death of the righteous, and let my last end be like his! (23.7-10)

Not only does Balaam not curse Israel, but also he identifies Israel with "the dust of Jacob" (that is a great host more numerous than the dust of the earth) and begs that he die the death of Jacob and enter into the afterlife of Jacob. The eminent Hebraist Robert Alter translates part of this verse with a significant change, "Let me die the death of the upright, and may my aftertime be like his." He complains in a footnote that the Israelites at this period had no real notion of an afterlife and therefore the translation of the Hebrew *aharit,* rendered as his *aftertime,* must mean something different than an *afterlife* (Alter 806).

Nevertheless, we shall see the oracle makes sense as it is written. Balak is furious that his soothsayer has failed him, and like Balaam and the donkey before, Balak pleads with Balaam to build another seven altars and offer another seven sacrifices and curse Israel again. Balaam agrees, and offers his second oracle:

Rise up Balak, and hear; hearken unto me, thou son of Zippor: God is not a *man,* that he should lie; neither the son of man, that he should repent: hath he said, and shall he not do it? Or hath he spoken, and shall he not make it good? Behold, I have received commandment to bless: and he hath blessed; and I cannot reverse it.

He hath not beheld iniquity in Jacob, neither hath he seen perverseness in Israel: the Lord his God is with him, and the shout of a king is among them. God brought them out of Egypt; he has as it were the strength of a [*bull*].

Surely there is no enchantment against Jacob, neither is there any divination against Israel: according to this time it shall be said of Jacob and of Israel, What hath God wrought! Behold, the people shall rise up as a great *lion,* and lift up himself as a young lion: he shall not lie down until he eat of the prey, *and drink the blood of the slain.* (23:18-24; italics mine)

Again Balaam rebukes the king of Moab and refuses to curse Israel. Admittedly the language of this second oracle is dense. Alter notes that the last phrase, "and drink the blood of the slain" is the same linguistic idiom employed in Job 39.30, where the *eagle* overcomes her enemies, "Her young ones suck up the blood: and where the slain are, there she is." On the surface, Balaam is identifying the people of Jacob as an impregnable military force which cannot be overcome, but the metaphors used within the parable are poignantly familiar. God and Israel are compared to a man (23.19), a bull (23.22), a lion (23.24), and if the idiomatic language is relevant, an eagle (23.24). These comparisons comprise the image of the cherubim disclosed in Ezekiel 1.10. Were this the sole motif in the Balaam story, than such a comparison might be said to be a stretch. Yet, the story begins with a sword-carrying angel who not only bars Balaam's way but also stands in a garden: "But the angel of the Lord stood in a path of the vineyards, a wall being on this side, and a wall on that side" (22.24). The allusion is clear: the angel with a sword in the vineyard is no ordinary messenger, but the cherubim who guards the way to the tree of life with his radiant sword (Genesis 3.24).

The story continues, Balak is exasperated that his all-powerful sorcerer cannot curse his enemy despite his generous offers, and for a third time pleads with Balaam to build seven altars and offer seven sacrifices and procure a curse. For a third time Balaam relents, then furnishes a third and final oracle:

Balaam the son of Beor hath said, and the man whose eyes are open hath said: He hath said which heard the words of God, which saw the vision of the Almighty, falling into a trance, but having his eyes open:

How goodly are thy tents, O Jacob, and thy tabernacles, O Israel! As the valleys are they spread forth, as gardens by the river's side, as the trees of lign aloes, which the Lord hath planted, and as cedar trees beside the waters. He shall pour the water out of his buckets, and his seed shall be in many waters, and his king shall be higher than Agag, and his kingdom shall be exalted.

God brought him forth out of Egypt; he hath as it were the strength of a [bull]: he shall eat up the nations his enemies, and shall break their bones, and pierce them through with his arrows. He crouched, he lay down as a lion, and as a great lion: who shall stir him up? Blessed is he that blesseth thee, and cursed is he that curseth thee. (24.3-9)

Balaam not only refuses to curse Israel, but also in his third and final parable he blesses Israel with the abundance of a paradisiacal grove. Israel shall find itself within verdant valleys containing gardens, rivers, trees, and abundant waters. She is also as strong as the bull, lion, and eagle, and will forever remain in power.

In the genius structure of the entire narrative, Balak has now taken the place of Balaam as one who is blind, whereas Balaam has become as wise as his donkey, for he receives true vision. In Alter's translation Balaam is now "open-eyed," beholding the vision of God, "prostrate with eyes unveiled" (811). The textual theme has centered on sight and blindness from the beginning, and only after delivering all three prophecies are Balaam's eyes finally unveiled. Like Jacob, he stands beholding God face to face within a vision. The theme of the third parable is that of the celestial garden where God sits on his throne and Israel remains protected forever.

When we look at all three oracles as a united theme we have the following: the first oracle describes the death and "aftertime" of Jacob; the second oracle promises might to Israel, but strictly within the images of man, bull, lion, and eagle; and the third oracle reveals Israel delivered at the celestial garden. The entire story begins in a garden, with an angel barring the way from progress, which apparently is achieved only after the journey through the oracles.

There are several homologous, literary motifs that the stories of Jacob and Balaam share. Each story begins with an important figure seeking a blessing: Jacob seeks the birthright and Balaam seeks the approval of God to grant Balak his wishes. Both protagonists are prone to visions, and their quests begin with a visitation from the Lord. Jacob steals the birthright from his hairy brother by obtaining a blessing from his blind father. Balaam agrees to go to Balak but is blind to the angel standing before him, a figure that his hairy donkey can see. Both figures also have their foot or thigh wounded. Three separate times Jacob works for seven years to obtain the hands of his wives. Three separate times Balaam ascends a mountain to build seven altars in order to curse Israel. Jacob sees God and is renamed Israel. Balaam sees God and blesses Israel.

Aside from these thematic motifs, there is another curious homology in the story of Balaam. The story of Balaam has a cultic background. In order to explicate this cultic background, one must again return to Egypt. The Temple of Apet at Karnak gives us an interpretive key. The cosmographic journey implicit in its three "secret chambers" are remarkably similar to the three oracles Balaam delivers to King Balak. The first chamber shows the end and "aftertime" of Osiris, while Balaam's first oracle deals directly with Jacob's death or "aftertime." The second secret chamber reflects the cosmographic journey the deceased must make to the four corners of the cosmos. Balaam's second oracle is placed specifically within the imagery of the Hebrew cherubim, whose iconic symbolism represented the four corners of the cosmos. The third chamber shows Osiris enthroned in a garden paradise. Balaam's third oracle reveals that Israel has inherited the royal kingship of god within the paradisiacal grove.

As an ensemble, these prophecies from our pagan soothsayer are squarely rooted in temple cult imagery. When one examines the Hebrew temple, one finds an approximate homologous situation. On the day of atonement the high priest would stand before the temple veil, itself an image of the cosmos and a representation of all the elements. He would disrobe and put on a new garment. Like Enoch, the priest standing before the Holy of Holies is transfigured. He enters the throne room in a new body symbolized by the new garment. If we took this imagery as thematic of rebirth, then the action of putting on a new garment at the veil corresponds to Balaam's first oracle where Israel is promised to "die the death of the righteous." Israel's end shall be like Jacob's final state. If our interpretation of the Jacob story is correct, Jacob's end is not existing in endless gloom within the shadows of Sheol, but a celestial ascent to the throne of God. Standing at the veil and putting on a new robe is also similar to the themes found within the first chamber in the Temple of Apet. Osiris and the Hebrew high priest begin their journey to the throne of heaven by rising from the lion couch and passing through the veil.

In the Hebrew temple, after passing the veil the priest would stand facing the golden cherubim who stood guard over the Holy of Holies. These cherubim are described in the book of Ezekiel, "As for the likeness of their faces, they four had the face of a man, and the face of a lion, on the right side: and they four had the face of an ox on the left side; they four also had the face of an eagle" (1.10). Again, these images correspond to constellations in the sky: Aquarius, Leo, Taurus, and Scorpio. These constellations held the four Royal Stars, Fomalhaut, Regulus, Aldebaran, and Antares, respectively. These stars are the "four corners" of the cosmos and were used to regulate calendars and festivals. They also appear to represent key points in the sky for the journey of the dead. It is not without significance that in Balaam's second oracle the God of Israel is compared to these same images. The power of God over Israel is analogized with the power of the cherubim over the cosmos. This second oracle and the

Hebrew cherubim are also analogous to the second chamber of Apet, where Osiris must journey through the four corners of the cosmos to find the secrets of rebirth.

After passing the cherubim, the Hebrew high priest would enter the cubic Holy of Holies. In the center of this sacred chamber was the altar and the ark of the covenant. There was also a seven-tiered menorah representing the Tree of Life. Central to the architectural theme was the Mercy Seat or throne which stood opposite the veil and symbolized the heavenly throne of God. The Tree and Throne, with the waters of life beneath the altar, all combined to represent the heavenly garden in which God dwelt. In putting on a new garment, passing through the veil, sojourning by the cherubim, the high priest had returned to Eden and was prepared to walk with God face to face. This moment was a re-enactment of *theosis*, where the chosen is transformed before the throne of God. This is the same imagery we find when Enoch ascends to the heavenly throne and is given a new name, "Son of Man." It is the same scene when Abram sees the stars and covenants with God whereby he is also given a new name, "Abraham." It is also the same scene where Jacob sees God atop the celestial axis, wrestles and embraces the heavenly messenger, stands before God face to face, and is also given a new name, "Israel." This moment is also analogous to Balaam's third oracle where Israel is delivered to the paradisiacal garden where God shall protect it forever and ever. The third chamber in the Temple of Apet also corresponds to this imagery.

The story of Balaam as presented in the Old Testament is a parable. Balaam is the most powerful diviner in the land, but when it comes to the God of Israel even his donkey is smarter than him. Balaam is blind to the things of the Lord, but eventually gains true vision by passing through the three oracles. Only after seeing the death and aftertime of Jacob; beholding God in the image of a man, bull, lion, and eagle; and seeing Israel delivered in a paradisiacal garden, does Balaam finally comprehend reality. In fact, at the end Balaam is described as having "lifted up his eyes," "whose eyes are open," "having his eyes open," "the man whose eyes are open" and beholding the things of God (Gen. 24.2-4, 15, 17). Balaam has become as wise as his donkey and as insightful as the patriarch Jacob.

The parable is ensconced within cosmographic themes. The story of Balaam begins in a garden. An angel stands in a vineyard holding a weapon. This image is a clear parallel to the cherubim with a flaming sword who guards the Tree of Life. The story ends in a garden. Israel has returned home; it has passed the cherubim and found the paradisiacal grove. Between these two garden loci the soul must journey through death and cosmos. Balaam must even ascend the mountain three times and perform seven sacrifices as part of his spell. Each of these sacrifices were analogical acts in gaining power over each of the seven firmaments which remained the source of reality. Meanwhile, Balaam's three oracles are rooted in the motifs of the cosmographic journey of the ancient temple cult. The temple was the "foundation of heaven and earth," and to enter it was to sojourn the celestial axis and obtain the powers over life and death. Death, celestial journey, and kingship are the fundamental images of Balaam's prophecies, and these remain the significant themes of both the Gilgamesh and Heracles myth complexes, as well as the symbolic architecture of the Temple of Apet and the Hebrew Holy of Holies.

Like the tale of Jacob, direct astral symbols are muted and one senses that both narratives have been purposefully demythologized and decosmologized in an attempt to make the stories sound fully historical. As it is with several Old Testament stories, mythic tropes remain which make a purely historical interpretation absurd. One can hardly believe that Noah placed two of every living thing on an ark slightly larger than a football field, or that Jonah spent three days within the belly of the whale. Such motifs in the Biblical text show an older logic and narrative structure which has been lost. The Bible was written by literate scribes in later centuries. Many of the original tales were oral narratives associated with city, cosmos, and cult.

The stories of Abraham, Jacob, and Balaam descend from the archaic storehouse of thought in the oral age. Each historical narrative was placed in a cultural envelope of myth and cult where the described events follow a peculiar narrative template. As history, each tale accurately describes the establishment of Yahweh's covenant (Abraham), the founding of the nation of Israel (Jacob), and the establishment of Israel in the land of Canaan (Balaam). Oral history is different than modern history, however, for what we get out of an oral culture is *trans-history*, or the homogenizing of history with cultural archetypes. These latter themes are not arbitrary but are always associated with the cult and cosmologies of the tribe or civilization. Thus, these stories have been mythologized with the practices and symbols of the ancient Isrealite temple cult.

One may inquire: "Did Jacob really see a ladder ascending into heaven? Did he really wrestle an angel all night and then see the face of God?" Many believers will insist upon a literal interpretation while many scholars will scoff at such interpretive audacity. Whatever the actual historical occurrences, one thing is certain: when Jacob entered the tent-shrine of his people he entered a sacred space designed as a model of the "true heaven" and the "true earth." This temple was the *axis-mundi* or cosmic center where one could, through ritual, analogically interact with the divine. Here was the true geocentric cosmos where the priest became heliocentric man. In this sense Jacob really did climb the ladder of heaven and see the face of God. He established his nation on an order of cosmic mythologies and rites that haled from high antiquity. These rites were wed to the archetypal realms of heaven, earth, and underworld, where all things came into being in an eternal circuit of life, death, and rebirth. Only upon this cosmic order could one establish a celestial mandate and cosmologize the land into the true Kingdom of God on earth.

Gilgamesh and Heracles also established the Kingdom of God on earth. Their stories, however, were left in an older dress of oral myth. While this conclusion may offend some faithful believers in the Bible, the conclusion also points to a very archaic metaphysics underwriting the creation of civilization and perhaps present at the dawn of conscious time. Darwin's "one grand system" fails to even come close to this celestial cosmovision that stretched its intellect and intuition in an attempt to grasp at the highest heaven and the second sun. The historical belief systems of the Howlers, Romantics, and Conspirators might even be more gullable in their own interpretive audacity! So it is that we are left staring at the shattered shell of ancient history. Anyone with the slightest inclination towards humility might be thinking of a new list of questions. Perhaps the very first question will be, "Have we really understood any of it at all?"

EPILOGUE

At the end of this book one might ask the question, "So what is myth?" I have attempted to show the nature of the human mind, the consequences of oral thinking, and the metaphysics of oral cosmology. In the end, I can only give a strictly functional answer to the question. *Myth is the oral imprinting press of preliterate peoples associated with their cult and cosmology.* I am fully cognizant that my definition employs a literate metaphor to describe an oral category; therefore, my own definition is skewed. To this definition I remind the reader that myth belonged to cultus, and that the memory theater of an oral civilization remains its festivals, rites, myths, and symbols. This cultus is all associated with its own sacred center and cosmologized to celestial archetypes. Whatever myth is, it participates in this cultic complex of oral cognition and social processes wed to the motion and majesty of the stars.

My definition of myth is strictly functional and not interpretive. Some people, once identifying a theory for myth, immediately apply it to all myths. This is misguided. I do not believe that all myths are about the celestial journey. On the contrary, there are all kinds of motifs and themes embedded in myths which relate to history, nature, calendars, social norms, biography, not to mention the technical language of astronomy and harmony. Myth is part of the oral lexicon and may be associated with any important information required for the normal functioning of the society that produced it. Being that the origin of myth is oral, and we have only written remnants, the complete and correct interpretation of all myth is impossible. We can only deal with probabilities, not certainties.

I have attempted to show that at least founding myths participate in an oral cosmos where celestial archetypes lie at the basis of the mythic imagery. The kings and pharaohs of the archaic age obtained their authority by celestial mandate. They re-enacted the cosmogony in rites and symbolically trod the celestial axis bringing down archetypal powers from the "true heaven" and the "true earth" so that the material realm would flourish. This myth-ritual complex, deeply embedded in oral cosmology, pervaded throughout oral cultures for millennia. With the invention of writing, the reductive alphabet, and the printing press, and with literate thinking and vertical memory replacing oral thinking and horizontal memory, the epistemological patterns of the past have been diminished to the point where they are no longer recognizable.

Finally, the processes and patterns of human cognition are never stagnant. For over a century scholars have preached a linear, evolutionary trend to mental capacity and knowledge. Truthfully, our cognitive envelope of knowing has entered a post-literate stage, where texting, tweeting, emailing, and audiovisual discourse have replaced the traditional written word. While there are certain advantages to this shift, such as the immediate transfer of communication, there are also enormous disadvantages to post-literate noetics which have yet to bear their full fruit. Reading and writing skills are on the decline. Critical thinking and historical awareness are also evaporating. Civilization will keep going, of course, but what kind of civilization will it be under these new parameters? Can such things as the Bhagavad Gita, or the Bible, or the Declaration of Independence be produced or understood by a post-literate culture?

Oral cultures exasperated every avenue to retain important knowledge. In the ancient past the archaic mind existed under keen limitations of oral thought which reduced all thinking into the immediate confines of absolute and observable material processes. This form of cognition had an upside—the ubiquitous realization that nature and its constituents everywhere, and at all times ruled the earth and unfolded within determined demands and consequences. It is this kind of concrete thinking, ironically, which the modern mind has abandoned. We think we can ultimately control nature and history. How very bizarre it is to be a sentient moth fluttering towards the light of the fiery furnace.

In short, our oral-literate evolution has not stopped, and whatever its end, some thousand years from now scholars will be debating what we believed. Perhaps they will write in awe at our capacities? Perhaps they will be highly incredulous at our incapacities? Perhaps our age shall be called an age of reason? Perhaps, with no small irony, and a touch of humor, scholars of the future will describe us as quite primitive. Such is the nature of history.

In the end we are all a product of historical thinking. What we think about the past is in large part how we frame ourselves in the present. Our cosmology is our ultimate framework of imagination, and it also determines how we organize history. With so much assuredness in some quarters of scholarship, we sometimes forget that modern cosmology and history are sheer metaphysical products of the psyche. We are at all times and in all places philosophical beings eternally conjecturing about our place in the universe.

The celestial axis continually recycles the infinite patterns of being. At the top is the ideal. At the bottom is real. In the middle is the sticking point where every potential can be realized. In this Earth at the center, every kingdom has its untamed Gilgamesh, and every soul, no matter how small, contains the seed of the immortal Heracles. On this point, the wisdom of ancient myth is eternal. Let us always remember that our most ancient past still remains undiscovered. The earliest echoes of the human soul whisper to us from primeval cave paintings and astronomically aligned mounds, indicating that what was once considered so primitive is actually what is most essential—the will to understand the true nature of things, above and below. In our post-modern, post-literate, secular age, our own comprehension of our place in the cosmos has not been alleviated by greater scientific advances. On the contrary, these advances have only opened up new doors into which one must look and journey, ever finding new possibilities, new questions, and new discoveries. We are never done with our cosmic journey, just as we are never done searching out our own humanity. Our cosmological imagination must roam to hitherto unknown heights. It must explore the source of heavenly realities in ways which embrace all the tiers of the heavenly axis, above and below, inside and out, conscious and unconscious, beyond, beneath, and between the stars.

WORKS CITED

Abt, Theodor and Erik Hornung. *Knowledge for the Afterlife, The Egyptian Amduat–A Quest for Immortality*. Zurich: Living Human Heritage, 2003.

Abram, David. *The Spell of the Sensuous*. New York: Vintage, 1997.

Adams, Walter Marsham. *Book of the Master of the Hidden Places*. London: The Search, 1933.

Alighieri, Dante. *The Divine Comedy*. *Paradiso*. Trans. John Ciardi. Franklin Center, PA: Franklin Library, 1983. 373-552.

Alter, Robert, trans. *The Five Books of Moses*. New York: Norton, 2004.

Anderson, Rasmus B. *Norse Mythology: Myths of the Eddas*. Honolulu, HI: UP of the Pacific, 2003.

Appleman, Philip, ed. *Darwin. A Norton Critical Edition*. New York: Norton, 2001.

Apuleius. *The Golden Ass*. Trans. by E. J. Kenney. New York: Penguin, 1998.

Assmann, Jan. *The Search for God in Ancient Egypt.* Trans. David Lorton. Ithaca: Cornell UP, 2001.

Attridge, Harold W. And Robert A. Oden, trans. *The Syrian Goddess (De Dea Syria) Attributed to Lucian.* Missoula, MT: Scholars Press, 1976.

Aveni, Anthony. *Stairways to the Stars, Skywatching in Three Great Ancient Cultures.* New York: John Wiley & Sons, 1997.

Backman, E. Louis. *Religious Dances in the Christian Church and in Popular Medicine.* London: George Allen & Unwin, 1952.

Balabanova, Svetlana. "Detection of nicotine and cocain in ancient human remains from different locations out of America and an archeological period spans a range from 9000 BC to 700 AD." *Migration and Diffusion: An International Journal.* Vol 1.1 (2000): 1-6

Barber, Elizabeth Wayland. *The Mummies of Ürümchi.* New York: Norton, 1999.

Barber, Elizabeth Wayland and Paul T. Barber. *When They Severed Earth From Sky: How the Human Mind Shapes Myth.* Princeton: Princeton UP, 2004.

Barker, Margaret. *The Gate of Heaven, The History and Symbolism of the Temple in Jerusalem.* Sheffield: Sheffield Phoenix, 2008.

—. *The Hidden Tradition of the Kingdom of God.* London: SPCK, 2007.

—. *On Earth as it is in Heaven, Temple Symbolism in the New Testament.* Sheffield: Sheffield Phoenix, 2009.

Bernal, Marin. *Black Athena: The Afroasiatic Roots of Classical Civilization, Vol. 3, The Linguistic Evidence.* Newark, NJ: Rutgers UP, 2006.

Betegh, Gábor. *The Derveni Papyrus, Cosmology, Theology, and Interpretation.* Cambridge UP, 2004.

Betz, Hans Dieter. *The "Mithras Liturgy." Text, Translation, and Commentary.* Tübingen, Germany: Mohr Siebgeck, 2003.

Bloom, Harold. "Preface." *Alone with the Alone: Creative Imagination in the Sūfism of Ibn'Arabī.* Princeton: Princeton UP, 1969, ix-xx.

Bonnechere, Pierre. "Trophonius of Lebadea. Mystery aspects of an oracular cult in Boeotia." Cosmopoulos 169-192.

Boser, Ulrich. "Solar Circle." *Archaeology.* July/Aug. (2006): 30-35.

Bottéro, Jean. *Mesopotamia: Writing, Reasoning, and the Gods.* Trans. Zainab Bahrani and Marc Van de Mieroop. Chicago: U of Chicago P, 1992.

Boustan, Ra'anan S. and Annette Yoshiko Reed, eds. *Heavenly Realms and Earthly Realities in Late Antique Religions.* Cambridge: Cambridge UP, 2004.

Boyce, Mary. *Textual Sources for the Study of Zoroastrianism.* Chicago: U of Chicago P, 1984.

Bremmer, Jan N. "Contextualizing Heaven in Third Century North Africa." Boustan and Reed 159-173.

Brown, Robert. *The Great Dionysiak Myth, Part 1.* London: Longmans, Green, & Co., 1877.

—. *Semitic Influence in Hellenic Mythology.* Clifton, NJ: Reference Book, 1966.

Brundage, Burr Cartwright. *The Phoenix of the Western World: Quetzalcoatl and the Sky Religion.* Norman: U of Oklahoma P, 1982.

Buckley, Jorunn Jacobsen. "A Cult-Mystery in The Gospel of Philip." *Journal of Biblical Literature* 99/4 (1980): 569-581.

Budge, E. A. Wallis. *Egyptian Religion, Ideas of the Afterlife in Ancient Egypt.* New York: Gramercy, 1959.

—. *The Gods of the Egyptians.* 2 vols. New York: Dover, 1969.

Burkert, Walter. *Ancient Mystery Cults.* Cambridge: Harvard UP, 1987.

—. *Babylon Memphis Persepolis, Eastern Contexts of Greek Culture.* Cambridge: Harvard UP, 2004.

—. *Greek Religion.* Malden, MA: Blackwell, 1985.

Campbell, Joseph. *The Flight of the Wild Gander.* Chicago, IL: Regnery Gateway, 1969.

—. *The Hero with a Thousand Faces.* Princeton: Princeton UP, 1949.

—. ed. *The Mysteries. Papers from the Eranos Yearbooks.* Princeton: Princeton UP, 1990.

—. *Occidental Mythology*. New York: Penguin Compass, 1976.

—. *Primitive Mythology*. New York: Penguin Compass, 1976.

Campion, Nicholas. *A History of Western Astrology. Vol. 1: The Ancient World*. New York: Continuum International, 2008.

—. *Astrology and Cosmology in the World's Religions*. New York: New York UP, 2012.

Casson, Lionel. *Libraries in the Ancient World*. New Haven: Yale UP, 2001.

Chapman, Allan. *Gods in the Sky: Astronomy from the Ancients to the Renaissance*. London: Channel 4, 2001.

Charles, R. H. *The Book of Enoch or 1 Enoch*. Oxford: Claredon, 1912.

Chevalier, Jean and Alain Gheerbrant. *The Penguin Dictionary of Symbols*. Trans. John Buchanan-Brown. New York: Penguin Putnam, 1996.

Clagett, Marshall. *Greek Science in Antiquity: How human reason and ingenuity first ordered and mastered the experience of natural phenomena*. New York: Collier, 1963.

Clark, R. T. Rundle. *Myth and Symbol in Ancient Egypt*. London: Thames and Hudson, 1978.

Clauss, Manfred. *The Roman Cult of Mithras, The God and His Mysteries*. Trans. Richard Gordon. New York: Routledge, 2001.

Clinton, Kevin. "Stages of Initiation in the Eleusinian and Samothracian Mysteries." Cosmopoulos 50-78.

Cole, Susan. "Landscapes of Dionysus and Elysian Fields." Cosmopoulos 193-217.

Condos, Theony. *Star Myths of the Greeks and Romans: A Sourcebook.* Grand Rapids, MI: Phanes, 1997.

Cook, Albert. *Zeus: A Study in Ancient Religion.* New York: Bilbo and Tannen, 1964.

Cope, Edward Meredith, trans. *Gorgias.* Cambridge: Deighton, Bell, & Co., 1864.

Copeland, Kirsti B. "The Earthly Monastery and the Transformation of the Heavenly City." Boustan and Reed 142-158.

Corbin, Henry. *Alone with the Alone: Creative Imagination in the Sūfism of Ibn'Arabī.* Princeton: Princeton UP, 1969.

Cornford, F. M. *From Religion to Philosophy. A Study in the Origins of Western Speculation.* New York: Dover Publications, 1912.

Cosmopoulos, Michael B, ed. *Greek Mysteries: The Archaeology and Ritual of Ancient Greek Secret Cults.* New York: Routledge, 2003.

Darwin, Charles. "The Descent of Man." *Darwin, A Norton Critical Edition.* Ed. Philip Appleman. New York: Norton, 2001. 175-254.

—. "The Origin of Species." *Darwin, A Norton Critical Edition.* Appleman 175-254.

De Lubicz, R. A. Schwaller. *Sacred Science: The King of Pharaonic Theocracy.* Rochester, VT: Inner Traditions, 1988.

—. *The Temples of Karnak.* Rochester, VT: Inner Traditions, 1982.

De Santillana, Giorgio. *The Origins of Scientific Thought: From Anaximander to Proclus, 600 B.C. to A.D. 500.* New York: Mentor, 1961.

—. *Reflections on Men and Ideas.* Cambridge: M.I.T. Press, 1968.

De Santillana, Giorgio and Hertha Von Dechend. *Hamlet's Mill: An Essay Investigating the Origins of Human Knowledge and its Transmission through Myth.* Boston: David R. Godine, 1977.

Doria, Charles and Harris Lenowitz. *Origins: Creation Texts from the Ancient Mediterranean.* New York: Anchor, 1976.

Dubuisson, Daniel. *The Western Construction of Religion. Myths, Knowledge, and Ideology.* Trans. by William Sayers. Baltimore: John Hopkins UP, 2003.

Eisenstein, Elizabeth L. *The Printing Revolution in Early Modern Europe.* Cambridge: Cabridge UP, 1983.

Eliade, Mircea. *Cosmos and History: The Myth of the Eternal Return.* New York: Harper Torchbooks, 1959.

—. *The Sacred and the Profane: The Nature of Religion.* New York: Harcourt, Brace & World, 1959.

Euripides. "The Bacchae." *Euripides V.* Trans. by William Arrowsmith. Chicago: U of Chicago P, 1959.

—. "The Phoenician Women." Euripides V. Trans. by Elizabeth Wyckoff. Chicago: U of Chicaco P, 1959.

Faulkner, Raymond, trans. *The Ancient Egyptian Pyramid Texts.* Oxford: Clarendon, 1910.

—. trans. *The Egyptian Book of the Dead, The Book of Going Forth by Day.* San Francisco: Chronicle, 1994.

Fellows, John. *Mysteries of Freemasonry or An Exposition of the Religious Dogmas and Customs of the Ancient Egyptians.* 1877. Whitefish, MT: Kessinger 2006.

Fernández, Adela. *Pre-hispanic Gods of Mexico: Myths and Deities from Nahuatl Mythology.* México, D.F: Panorama Editorial, 1984.

Ferriera, Pedro G. *The State of the Universe: A Primer in Modern Cosmology.* London: Orion, 2007.

Gaster, Theodor H. *Thespis: Ritual, Myth, and Drama in the Ancient Near East.* New York: Harper Torchbooks, 1961.

Gimbel, Steven. *Exploring the Scientific Method: Cases and Questions.* Chicago: U of Chicago P, 2011.

Gimbutas, Marija. *The Civilization of the Goddess*. San Francisco, CA: Harper San Francisco, 1991.

Görlitz, Dominique. "The Reed Boat ABORA on the Mediterranean Sea." *Migration and Diffusion: an International Journal*. Vol 1.2 (2000): 90-109.

Gottschalk, H. B. *Heraclides of Pontus*. Oxford: Clarendon, 1980.

Graf, Fritz. "The Bridge and the Ladder: Narrow Passages in Late Antique Visions." Boustan and Reed 19-33.

Graves, Robert. *The Greek Myths*. 2 vols. London: The Folio Society, 1955.

Gregory, Andrew. *Eureka: Birth of Science*. Cambridge: Totem, 2003.

Griaule, Marcel. *Conversations with Ogotemmêli: An Introduction to Dogon Religious Ideas*. New York: Oxford UP, 1970.

Griffith, R. Drew. *Mummy Wheat: Egyptian Influence on the Homeric View of the Afterlife and the Eleusinian Mysteries*. New York: UP of America, 2008.

Hadingham, Evan. *Early Man and the Cosmos*. New York: Walker & Company, 1984.

Hamilton, H. C., trans. *The Geography of Strabo*. London: George Bell & Sons, 1892.

Hare, Tom. *Remembering Osiris: Number, Gender, and the Word in Ancient Egyptian Representational Systems*. Stanford, CA: Stanford UP, 1999.

Harrison, Jane Ellen. *Ancient Art and Ritual.* Oxford: Dodo Press, 1913.

—. *Epilogemena: A Brief Summary of the Origins of Greek Religion.* Sequim, WA: The Alexandrian Press, 1992.

Harrison, Hank. *The Cauldron and the Grail, Ritual Astronomy and the Stones of Ancient Europe.* San Francisco: The Archives Press, 1970.

Havelock, Eric. *The Muse Learns to Write: Reflections on Orality and Literacy from Antiquity to the Present.* New Haven: Yale UP, 1986.

Heath, Sir Thomas. *A History of Greek Mathematics, Vol. I.* New York: Dover, 1981.

Herberger, Charles F. *The Thread of Ariadne: The Labyrinth of the Calendar of Minos.* New York: Philosophical Library, 1972.

Herodotus. *The Histories.* Trans. by Aubrey de Sélincourt. New York: Penguin, 2003.

Holy Bible, KJV. Salt Lake City, UT: Deseret, 2002.

Homer. *The Illiad.* Trans. by Robert Fagles. New York: Penguin, 1990.

—. *The Odyssey.* Trans. by Robert Fagles. New York: Penguin, 1996.

Hooke, S. H., ed. *Myth, ritual, and Kingship: Essays on the Theory and Practice of Kingship in the Ancient Near East and in Israel.* Oxford: Clarendon, 1958.

Jacobsen, Thorkild. "'And Death the Journey's End': The Gilgamesh Epic." *The Epic of Gilgamesh, Norton Critical Edition*. Benjamin R. Foster trans. New York: Norton, 2001, pp 183-207.

Jenkins, John Major. *Maya Cosmogenesis 2012*. Santa Fe, NM: Bear & Co.,1998.

Johnson, Laurin R. *Shining in the Ancient Sea: The Astronomical Ancestry in Homer's Odyssey*. Portland, OR: Multnomah House Press, 1999.

Jost, Madeleine. "Mystery Cults in Arcadia." Cosmopoulos 143-168.

Kahn, Charles H. *Pythagoras and the Pythagoreans: A Brief History*. Indianapolis: Hackett Publishing, 2001.

Kehoe, Alice Beck. "Phobias in Archaeology." *Migration and Diffusion: An International Journal*. Vol. 1.4 (2000): 42-57.

Kerényi, Carl. "The Mysteries of the Kabeiroi." Campbell *The Mysteries* 32-63.

King, C. W. *The Gnostics and Their Remains: Ancient and Medieval*. London: D. Nutt, 1887.

Kingsley, Peter. *In the Dark Places of Wisdom*. Inverness, CA: Golden Sufi Center, 1999.

Koestler, Arthur. *The Sleepwalkers: A History of Man's Changing Vision of the Universe*. London: Penguin, 1959.

Krupp, E. C. *Beyond the Blue Horizon: Myths and Legends of the Sun, Moon, Stars and Planets*. New York: Harper Collins, 1991.

— *Echoes of the Ancient Skies: The Astronomy of Lost Civilizations*. New York: Oxford UP, 1983.

—. "Negotiating the Highwire of Heaven." *Alexandria 5*. Grand Rapids, MI: Phanes Press, 2000.

Kuhn, Thomas S. *The Structure of Scientific Revolutions*. Chicago: U of Chicago P, 1996.

Lamy, Lucie. *Egyptian Mysteries, New Light on Ancient Knowledge. Art and Imagination*. New York: Thames and Hudson, 1989.

Leisegang, Hans. "The Mystery of the Serpent." Campbell *The Mysteries* 194-260.

Lettvin, Jerome Y. "The Gorgon's Eye." *Astronomy of the Ancients*. Ed. Kenneth Brecher and Michael Feirtag. Cambridge: MIT Press, 1980, 133-52.

Lévi-Strauss, Claude. *Myth and Meaning, Cracking the Code of Culture*. New York: Schoken, 1978.

Lundquist, John. "The Legitimizing Role of the Temple." Parry 179-235.

—. "What is a Temple? A Preliminary Typology." Parry 83-117.

Macrobius. *Commentary on the Dream of Scipio*. Trans. William Harris Stahl. New York: Columbia UP, 1990.

Magee, Bryan. *Philosophy and the Real World: An Introduction to Karl Popper*. La Salle, IL: Open Court, 1985.

Magli, Giulio. *Mysteries and Discoveries of Archaeoastronomy*. New York: Copernicus, 2005.

Major, John S. "The Five Phases, Magic Squares, and Schematic Cosmology." *Explorations in Early Chinese Cosmology*. Chico, CA: Scholar Press, 2006.

Mathews, Thomas F. *The Clash of Gods: A Reinterpretation of Early Christian Art*. Princeton: Princeton UP, 1995.

Maurice, Thomas. *Observations Connected with Astronomy and Ancient History, Sacred and Profane, on the Ruins of Babylon, as Recently Visited and Described by Claudius James Rich, Esq., Resident for the East India Company at Bagdad*. London: John Murray, 1816.

Melville, Herman. *Moby Dick*. New York: Norton, 1967. 7- 492.

McClain, Ernest G. "Musical Theory and Ancient Cosmology." *The World and I* (1994): 371-391.

— *The Myth of Invariance: The Origin of the Gods, Mathematics and Music from the Ṛg Veda to Plato*. York Beach, MI: Nicolas-Hays, 1976.

McEvilley, Thomas. *The Shape of Ancient Thought: Comparative Studies in Greek and Indian Philosophies*. New York: Allworth, 2002.

McLuhan, Marshall. *The Gutenberg Galaxy*. Toronto: U of Toronto P, 1962.

Menon, C. P. S., and L. N. G. Filon. *Early Astronomy and Cosmology*. London: George Allen & Unwin, 1932.

Mercatante, Antony S. *Who's Who in Egyptian Mythology*. New York: Clarkson N. Potter, 1978.

Meyer, Marvin W., ed. *The Ancient Mysteries: A Sourcebook of Sacred Texts*. Philadelphia: U of Pennsylvania P, 1987.

Michell, George. *The Hindu Temple*. Chicago: U of Chicago P, 1988.

Moran, William. "The Gilgamesh Epic: A Masterpiece from Ancient Mesopotamia." *The Epic of Gilgamesh, Norton Critical Edition*. Benjamin R. Foster trans. New York: Norton, 2001, 171-83.

Naydler, Jeremy. *Temple of the Cosmos: The Ancient Egyptian Experience of the Sacred*. Rochester, VT: Inner Traditions, 1996.

Needleman, Jacob. *A Sense of the Cosmos, Scientific Knowledge and Spiritual Truth*. Rhinebeck, NY: Monkfish, 1975.

Neugebauer, O. *The Exact Sciences in Antiquity*. New York: Dover Publications, 1969.

Newsom, Carol. *Songs of the Sabbath Sacrifice, A Critical Edition*. Atlanta: Scholars, 1985.

Nibley, Hugh. *An Approach to the Book of Abraham*. Salt Lake City, UT: Deseret, 2009.

—. *The Ancient State*. Salt Lake City, UT: Deseret, 1981.

—. *Enoch the Prophet.* Salt Lake City, UT: Deseret, 1986.

—. *The Message of the Joseph Smith Papyri, an Egyptian Endowment.* Salt Lake City, UT: Deseret, 2005.

—. *Old Testament and Related Studies.* Salt Lake City, UT: Deseret, 1986.

—. *Temple and Cosmos.* Salt Lake City, UT: Deseret, 1992.

Nilsson, Martin P. *The Mycenaean Origin of Greek Mythology.* Berkeley: U of California P, 1972.

Oakes, Maud and Joseph Campbell. *Where The Two Came To Their Father: A Navaho War Ceremonial Given By Jeff King.* Princeton: Princeton UP, 1943.

Olcott, William Tyler. *Star Lore of All Ages.* New York: Putnam, 1911.

Oldmeadow, Harry. *Journeys East: 20ᵗʰ Century Western Encounters with Eastern Religious Traditions.* Bloomington IN: World Wisdom Inc., 2004.

Ong, Walter J. *Orality and Literacy.* New York: Routledge, 2000.

Otto, Walter F. *Dionysus, Myth and Cult.* Trans. Robert B. Palmer. Bloomington, IN: Indiana UP, 1965.

Palmer, Enrest G. *The Secret of Ancient Egypt.* London: William Rider and Son, 1924.

Parry, Donald W., ed. *Temples of the Ancient World.* Salt Lake City, UT: Deseret, 1994.

Penprase, Bryan E. *The Power of the Stars: How Celestial Observations Have Shaped Civilization*. New York: Springer, 2011.

Pernet, Henry. *Ritual Masks, Deceptions and Revelations*. Columbia, SC: U of South Carolina P, 1992.

Perrot, Georges and Charles Chipiez. *A History of Art in Chaldea and Assyria*. London: Chapman and Hall, 1884.

Phillips, William J. *Carols Their Origin, Music and Connection with Mystery Plays*. London: Geo. Routledge & Sons, 1921.

Piankoff, Alexandre, Trans. *Egyptian Religious Texts and Representations, Vol. 3*. New York: Pantheon, 1957.

—. *The Wandering of the Soul*. Princeton: Princeton UP, 1974.

Plato. *Complete Works*. Ed. by John M. Cooper. Indianapolis, IN: Hackett Publishing, 1997.

Plutarch. *On Isis and Osiris*. Trans. G. R. S. Mead. Whitefish, MT: Kessinger 2007.

Popper, Karl. *The Logic of Scientific Discovery*. New York: Routledge, 1992.

Puhvel, Jaan. *Comparative Mythology*. Baltimore, MD: John Hopkins UP, 1987.

Pulver, Max. "Jesus' Round Dance and Crucifixion According to the Acts of St. John." Campbell *The Mysteries* 169-193.

Quirke, Stephen and Werner Forman. *Hieroglyphs and the Afterlife in Ancient Egypt*. Norman: U of Oklahoma P, 1996.

Raglan, "The Hero; A Study in Tradition, Myth, and Drama." *In Quest of the Hero*. Ed. Robert A. Segal. New York: Vintage, 1956. 58-165.

Rees, Alwyn and Brinley Rees. *Celtic Heritage, Ancient Tradition in Ireland and Wales*. New York: Thames and Hudson, 1978.

Reiche, Harald A. "The Language of Archaic Astronomy: A Clue to the Atlantis Myth?" *Astronomy of the Ancients*. Eds. Kenneth Brecher and Michael Feirtag. Cambridge: MIT, 1980. 153-189.

Rose, Mark. "Top 10 Discoveries of 2009: World's First Zoo— Hierakonopolis, Egypt." *Archaeology*. Vol 63.1 (2010): 1-24.

Rubalcaba, Jill and Eric H. Cline. *The Ancient Egyptian World*. New York: Oxford UP, 2005.

Russell, Bertrand. *A History of Western Philosophy, and Its Connection with Political and Social Circumstances from the Earliest Times to the Present Day*. New York: Book of the Month Club, 1995.

Ruck, Carl A. P., Blaise D. Staples, and Clark Heinrich. *The Apples of Apollo: Pagan and Christian Mysteries of the Eucharist*. Durham, N.C.: Carolina Academic Press, 2001.

Ryan, William and Walter Pitman. *Noah's Flood: The New Scientific Discoveries about the Event that Changed History*. New York: Simon & Schuster, 1998.

Sadakata, Akira. *Buddhist Cosmology: Philosophy and Origins*. Tokyo: Kōsei Publishing, 1999.

Saggs, H. W. F. *The Babylonians, A Survey of the Ancient Civilization of the Tigris-Euphrates Valley*. London: Folio Society, 1988.

Sandys, John. *The Odes of Pindar*. New York: Macmillan Co., 1915.

Schäfer, Peter. "In Heaven as It Is in Hell: The Cosmology of *Seder Rabbah di-Bereshit*." Boustan and Reed 233-274.

Séjourné, Laurette, and Irene Nicholson. *Burning Water: Thought and Religion in Ancient Mexico*. New York: Vanguard Press, 1956.

Shaw, Ian. *The Oxford History of Ancient Egypt*. Oxford: Oxford UP, 2000.

Simpson, William. *The Jonah Legend, A Suggestion of Interpretation*. London: Grant Richards, 1899.

Smith, William. *Dictionary of Greek and Roman Biography and Mythology*. Boston: C. C. Little and J. Brown, 1849.

Sophocles. *Oedipus at Colonus*. Trans. Robert Fagles. New York: Penguin, 1984. 279-419.

—. *Oedipus the King*. Trans. Robert Fagles. New York: Penguin, 1984. 155-277.

Temple, Robert. *The Crystal Sun*. London: Century, 2000.

—. *Oracles of the Dead, Ancient Techniques for Predicting the Future.* Rochester, VT: Destiny, 2002.

Teresi, Dick. *Lost Discoveries: The Ancient Roots of Modern Science–from the Babylonians to the Maya.* New York: Simon & Schuster, 2002.

Toulmin, Stephen. *Cosmopolis: The Hidden Agenda of Modernity.* Chicago: U of Chicago P, 1990.

Tov, Emanuel. *Textual Criticism of the Hebrew Bible.* Minneapolis: MN, Fortress, 1992.

Tvedtnes, John A., Brian M. Hauglid, and John Gee. *Traditions About the Early Life of Abraham.* Provo, UT: BYU, 2001.

Tylor, Edward B. *Primitive Culture: Researches into the Development of Mythology, Philosophy, Religion, Language, Art, and Custom. Vol. I.* London: John Murray, 1891.

Ulansey, David. "Mithras, the Hypercosmic Sun, and the Rockbirth." *Alexandria 5.* Ed. David Fideler. Grand Rapids, MI: Phanes, 2000. 161-174.

—. *The Origins of the Mithraic Mysteries, Cosmology and Salvation in the Ancient World.* New York: Oxford UP, 1989.

Vermaseren, Maarten J. *Cybele and Attis, the Myth and the Cult.* London: Thames and Hudson, 1977.

Virgil. *The Aeneid.* Trans. by Robert Fagles. New York: Penguin, 2006.

Von Franz, Marie-Louise. *Creation Myths.* Boston: Shambala, 1995.

Wade, Nicholas. "A Hose of Mummies, a Forest of Secrets." *The New York Times,* March 15, 2010. <http://www.nytimes.com/2010/03/16/science/16archeo.html>.

Walton, John H. *Ancient Near Eastern Thought and the Old Testament, Introducing the Conceptual World of the Hebrew Bible.* Grand Rapids, MI: Baker Academic, 2006.

Wasson, R. G., Albert Hofmann and Carl A. P. Ruck. *The Road to Eleusis: Unveiling the Secret of the Mysteries.* Berkeley, CA: North Atlantic, 2008.

Weston, Jessie L. *From Ritual to Romance.* Mineola, NY: Dover, 1920.

White, Gavin. *Babylonian Star-Lore, An Illustrated Guide to the Star-lore and Constellations of Ancient Babylon.* London: Solaria, 2007.

—. *The Queen of Heaven: A New Interpretation of the Goddess in Ancient Near Eastern Art.* London: Solaria, 2013.

Widengren, G. "Early Hebrew Myths and Their Interpretation." Hooke 149-203.

Wilford, John Noble. "Who Began Writing? Many Theories, Few Answers." *The New York Times,* April 6, 1999. <http://www.nytimes.com/library/national/science/040699sci-early-writing.html>.

Wili, Walter. "The Orphic Mysteries and the Greek Spirit." Campbell *The Mysteries* 64-92.

Wilkinson, Richard H. *The Complete Gods and Goddesses of Ancient Egypt.* New York: Thames and Hudson, 2003.

Willoughby, Harold R. *Pagan Regeneration: A Study of Mystery Initiations in the Graeco-Roman World.* Chicago: U of Chicago P, 1960.

Wolkstein, Diane and Samuel Noah Kramer. *Inanna, Queen of Heaven and Earth.* New York: Harper & Row, 1983.

Worthen, Thomas D. *The Myth of Replacement, Stars, Gods, and Order in the Universe.* Tucson, AZ: The U of Arizona P, 1991.

Yeats, Frances A. *The Art of Memory.* Chicago: U of Chicago P, 1966.

Yoshida, Nobuhiro. "The Considerable Connection Between Europe and Asia Seen from Epigraphic Viewpoint." *Migration and Diffusion: An International Journal.* Vol 1.2 (2000): 29-43.

Zimmer, Heinrich. *Myths and Symbols in Indian Art and Civilization.* Ed. Joseph Campbell. Princeton: Princeton UP, 1974.

www.ingramcontent.com/pod-product-compliance
Lightning Source LLC
Chambersburg PA
CBHW020147090426
42734CB00008B/727